RESPONSIBILITY ON TRIAL

Establishing individual criminal responsibility for mass atrocities is the foundational principle of international criminal justice, but this process is highly complex, and is accompanied by political and legal dilemmas about its operation. The book examines the drafting, interpretation, and application of the rules for assessing individual criminal responsibility as those rules emerge from the intense contestations among judges, lawyers, and academics within the legal field. Focusing on the International Criminal Court (ICC), the book provides a rich analysis of the international debates around questions of criminal responsibility by interrogating formal legal documents and legal scholarship alongside more candid accounts (interviews, memoirs, minutes). These debates are of key importance for international criminal law and global justice because how criminal responsibility laws are construed in practice determines which conduct merits punishment and, ultimately, demarcates the boundaries of what are considered the 'gravest' acts that 'shock' humanity.

LIANA GEORGIEVA MINKOVA is a junior research fellow at Newnham College, University of Cambridge, and a fellow at the Lauterpacht Centre for International Law, Cambridge. Her work has appeared in *International Criminal Law Review, Journal of Genocide Research, Leiden Journal of International Law*, and *Politics & Gender*.

RESPONSIBILITY ON TRIAL

Liability Standards in International Criminal Law

LIANA GEORGIEVA MINKOVA

University of Cambridge

CAMBRIDGE UNIVERSITY PRESS

CAMBRIDGE
UNIVERSITY PRESS

Shaftesbury Road, Cambridge CB2 8EA, United Kingdom

One Liberty Plaza, 20th Floor, New York, NY 10006, USA

477 Williamstown Road, Port Melbourne, VIC 3207, Australia

314–321, 3rd Floor, Plot 3, Splendor Forum, Jasola District Centre, New Delhi – 110025, India

103 Penang Road, #05–06/07, Visioncrest Commercial, Singapore 238467

Cambridge University Press is part of Cambridge University Press & Assessment, a department of the University of Cambridge.

We share the University's mission to contribute to society through the pursuit of education, learning and research at the highest international levels of excellence.

www.cambridge.org
Information on this title: www.cambridge.org/9781009320177

DOI: 10.1017/9781009320191

First published 2023

A catalogue record for this publication is available from the British Library.

A Cataloging-in-Publication data record for this book is available from the Library of Congress

ISBN 978-1-009-32017-7 Hardback

To my mother and father

CONTENTS

ACKNOWLEDGEMENTS

I would like to thank my PhD supervisor Professor Adam Branch – for believing in me and my project, for dedicating so much of his time to read and comment on my work, and for encouraging me to write this book. I would not have been able to complete this project without his constant help and support.

I would also like to thank my PhD examiners Professor Sarah Nouwen and Professor Phil Clark and my adviser Professor Jason Sharman who helped me clarify the scope of my research and highlight the novelty of my approach to the subject. I am grateful to Dr Anna Gwiazda who has always supported and encouraged my research. I would like to thank Georgi Minkov, H. E. Rumen Alexandrov, Nadia Zhivkova-Vaneva, Melinda Reed, Professor Elies van Sliedregt, Professor Kai Ambos, Professor Kevin Jon Heller, Professor Darryl Robinson, Professor Douglas Guilfoyle, and Sir Howard Morrison KCMG CBE QC for discussing this project with me and offering invaluable insights.

I am grateful to my amazing family for always believing in me.

This book builds upon my PhD research conducted at the University of Cambridge and funded by the Arts and Humanities Research Council Doctoral Training Partnership (2017–2020).

ABBREVIATIONS

AC	Appeals Chamber
ASP	Assembly of State Parties
CAR	Central African Republic
CICC	Coalition for the International Criminal Court
CLS	critical legal studies
DCC	Document Containing the Charges
DRC	Democratic Republic of the Congo
FDLR	Forces démocratiques pour la libération du Rwanda (Democratic Forces for the Liberation of Rwanda)
FDS	Defence and Security Forces
FPI	Front populaire ivoirien (Ivorian Popular Front)
FPLC	Forces patriotiques pour la libération du Congo (Patriotic Forces for the Liberation of Congo)
ICC	International Criminal Court
ICL	international criminal law
ICTR	International Criminal Tribunal for Rwanda
ICTY	International Criminal Tribunal for the former Yugoslavia
IDP	internally displaced persons
IMT	International Military Tribunal
IMTFE	International Military Tribunal for the Far East
JCE	joint criminal enterprise
LRA	Lord's Resistance Army
MLC	Mouvement de Libération du Congo (Movement for the Liberation of the Congo)
NGO	non-governmental organization
ODM	Orange Democratic Movement
OTP	Office of the Prosecutor
PrepCom	Preparatory Committee
PNU	Party of National Unity
PTC	Pre-Trial Chamber

RS	Rome Statute
RTI	Radiodiffusion Télevision Ivoirienne
TC	Trial Chamber
UN	United Nations
UPC	Union des Patriotes Congolais (Union of Congolese Patriots)
UPDF	Ugandan People's Defense Force
WIGJ	Women's Initiatives for Gender Justice

1

Introduction

International Criminal Law between Legalism and Critique

In 1998, the year in which the Rome Statute (RS) of the permanent International Criminal Court (ICC, the Court) was adopted, the former Nuremberg prosecutor Benjamin Ferencz expressed his belief that the 'force of law' could 'replace the law of force'.[1] The introduction of the legal norm of holding individuals criminally responsible for international crimes, many human rights advocates hoped, would put an end to the rule of power politics that had historically dominated the international arena. Yet, when the Court began operation, those lofty expectations were soon toned down.[2] As of February 2022, only five persons, all nationals of African countries, have been convicted for core international crimes at the ICC, states continue to cooperate only with those investigations that seemingly do not infringe upon their political interests, and the prosecutor still faces significant pressure from global powers with respect to the opening of investigations. Non-governmental organizations (NGOs), some of the key supporters of international criminal law (ICL), described the situation as a 'crisis point in international justice'.[3] The clash between expectations and reality has prompted debate on the question of whether ICL can function successfully as a legal regime or whether it merely reintroduces the traditional modes of state power politics under the guise of legal reasoning.[4]

Much of the critical interdisciplinary scholarship, which examines the ICC as a legal institution functioning within the realm of international

[1] B. Ferencz, 'International Criminal Courts: The Legacy of Nuremberg' (1998) 10(1) *Pace International Law Review* 203, 225.

[2] N. Roht-Arriaza, 'Just a Bubble? Perspectives on the Enforcement of International Criminal Law by National Courts' (2013) 11(3) *Journal of International Criminal Justice* 537, 542.

[3] Amnesty International, 'The ICC Must Become a Champion of Justice over Abuse of Power', 23 February 2018, www.amnesty.org/en/latest/news/2018/02/the-icc-must-become-a-champion-of-justice-over-abuse-of-power/.

[4] B. Sander, 'International Criminal Justice as Progress: From Faith to Critique', in M. Bergsmo, C. W. Ling, S. Tianying, and Y. Ping (eds.) *Historical Origins of International Criminal Law*, Vol. 4 (Brussels: Torkel Opsahl Academic EPublisher, 2015) 749, 752–755.

politics, has focused on the process of opening investigations, selecting individual suspects at the ICC and cooperating with governments to collect evidence and have those suspects transferred to the Court for trial.[5] From this perspective, ICL can be enforced only against developing nations and vanquished countries after a war,[6] or when the ICC aligns with governments by prosecuting members of insurgent organizations while tacitly offering de facto immunity to supporters of the regime.[7] Consequently, the operation of the international criminal justice field is understood as a function of international power politics: ICL provides a seemingly depoliticized tool for the most powerful actor in a given situation, whether Western states, the United Nations (UN) Security Council, or the ruling elite in a particular country, to pursue its political ends.

But the core aspect of the ICC's operation has remained neglected in the critical scholarship: namely the assessment of criminal responsibility, that is, the process of determining whether the person on trial is guilty or not guilty. This is a crucial element of the international criminal justice field, not only because it bears implications for trial outcomes but also because the interpretation and application of individual criminal responsibility rules are far from a straightforward and uncontested process. From Nuremberg to the ICC judgments, lawyers, scholars, and human rights organizations have debated the scope, structure, and purpose of those rules. By demarcating the boundaries of 'guilt' and 'innocence' against the messy reality of mass atrocities, the debates over assessing criminal responsibility bear implications not only for the future of the individuals at trial but also for the future of international criminal justice more generally.

The interpretation and application of the RS provisions that concern criminal responsibility, namely Articles 25, 28, and 30,[8] have triggered

[5] D. Bosco, *Rough Justice: The International Criminal Court in a World of Power Politics* (New York: Oxford University Press, 2014). A. Branch, *Displacing Human Rights: War and Intervention in Northern Uganda* (New York: Oxford University Press, 2011). P. Clark, *Distant Justice: The Impact of the International Criminal Court on African Politics* (Cambridge: Cambridge University Press, 2018). S. Nouwen, *Complementarity in the Line of Fire* (Cambridge: Cambridge University Press, 2013). W. Schabas, *Unimaginable Atrocities: Justice, Politics, and Rights at the War Crimes Tribunals* (Oxford: Oxford University Press, 2012).

[6] D. Zolo, *Victors' Justice: From Nuremberg to Baghdad*, translated by M. W. Weir (London and New York: Verso, 2009).

[7] A. Branch, 'Dominic Ongwen on Trial: The ICC's African Dilemmas' (2017) 11(1) *International Journal of Transitional Justice* 30, 35.

[8] Rome Statute of the International Criminal Court, done at Rome on 17 July 1998, in force on 1 July 2002, United Nations, Treaty Series, vol. 2187, No. 38544, Depositary: Secretary-General of the United Nations, http://treaties.un.org.

significant interest in legal academia.[9] The legal literature generally presents the principled beliefs of different scholars concerning what the assessment of criminal responsibility in ICL *should be* like. Because those debates take place inside the legal field, the arguments are often framed along the legal/non-legal spectrum: different interpretations of the rules on criminal responsibility are assessed as more or less legal, depending on how close they come to the abstract ideal of objective legal rules.

While the discussions in the legal literature are crucial for the operationalization of ICL rules in practice and for developing the international criminal justice field, their internal perspective on ICL practice precludes an enquiry into some key questions: What differentiates legal norms from other forms of social control?[10] What is the meaning of the term 'legal' in the ICL field? Are there alternative visions of legality? If so, what makes one vision more authoritative than another inside the ICL field? How is a particular vision of legality constructed, promoted, and contested? What types of actors participate in those processes? The critical scholarship on international criminal justice has raised similar questions with respect to the ICL system in general,[11] as well as more specific aspects of its operation, such as the ICC complementarity regime.[12] But the interpretation and application of the RS provisions that concern criminal responsibility,

[9] Chapter 6 presents a detailed discussion of the legal scholarship on Articles 25, 28, and 30. See E. Van Sliedregt, *Individual Criminal Responsibility in International Law* (Oxford: Oxford University Press, 2012). K. Ambos, 'Article 25: Individual Criminal Responsibility', in K. Ambos and O. Triffterer (eds.) *Rome Statute of the International Criminal Court: A Commentary*, 3rd ed. (London: Bloomsbury T&T Clark, 2016) 979. N. Jain, *Perpetrators and Accessories in International Criminal Law: Individual Modes of Responsibility for Collective Crimes* (London: Hart Publishing, 2014). L. Sadat and J. Jolly, 'Seven Canons of ICC Treaty Interpretation: Making Sense of Article 25's Rorschach Blot' (2014) 27(3) *Leiden Journal of International Law* 755. G. Werle, 'Individual Criminal Responsibility in Article 25 ICC Statute' (2007) 5(4) *Journal of International Criminal Justice* 953.

[10] M. Finnemore, 'Are Legal Norms Distinctive?' (2000) 32(3) *New York University Journal of International Law & Politics* 699.

[11] A. Branch, 'What the ICC Review Conference Can't Fix', in *Oxford Transitional Justice Research: Debating International Justice in Africa* (The Foundation for Law, Justice and Society; The Centre for Socio-Legal Studies, University of Oxford, 2010). K. Engle, 'A Genealogy of the Criminal Turn in Human Rights', in K. Engle, Z. Miller, and D. Davis (eds.) *Anti-Impunity and the Human Rights Agenda* (Cambridge: Cambridge University Press, 2016) 15. K. Clarke, *Fictions of Justice: The International Criminal Court and the Challenge of Legal Pluralism in Sub-Saharan Africa* (New York: Cambridge University Press, 2009).

[12] Nouwen, *Complementarity in the Line of Fire*. C. De Vos, *Complementarity, Catalysts, Compliance: The International Criminal Court in Uganda, Kenya, and the Democratic Republic of Congo* (Cambridge: Cambridge University Press, 2020).

namely Articles 25, 28, and 30, have remained neglected by that critical interrogation, despite their crucial role for the outcome of ICC trials and, more generally, for the functioning of the Court.

Responsibility on Trial explores the political and legal dilemmas arising from the principle of individual criminal responsibility in ICL. Specifically, the book focuses on the drafting, interpretation, and application of the rules for assessing criminal responsibility – known technically as 'modes of liability' – at the ICC as those rules emerge from the intense contestations among judges, lawyers, academics, NGOs, and diplomats within the legal field. Furthermore, the book seeks to understand where the interpretative preferences of different actors within that field, including legal academics, come from and to trace their influence on the development of criminal responsibility laws. The book draws attention to the internal politics of the ICL field – the continuous battles over the meaning of the legal rules concerning criminal responsibility – and to the influence of those battles on the construction of legal norms and, ultimately, on trial outcomes at the ICC.

Before engaging further with the interdisciplinary literature on international criminal justice and the place of this book in those debates, a few caveats should be mentioned. The book does not argue that the normative battles inside the ICL field are the only factors influencing trial outcomes at the ICC. Other factors, such as the limited opportunities for collecting evidence, especially when crimes have taken place years before the investigation, could significantly obstruct the prosecutor's ability to link the accused to the crimes. Scholars have pointed out the pervasive problems with the early ICC investigations, such as the use of intermediaries to collect evidence and the lack of local knowledge of the situation.[13] As Chapter 7 demonstrates, different factors, such as the problems of collecting evidence, the interests of governments, and the politics of the legal field, can together significantly influence trial outcomes. For example, depending on the understandings shared among the judges about the requirements of the legal rules concerning criminal responsibility, they may be more or less lenient towards the prosecutor's investigation hurdles.

The main contribution of this book is, thus, to examine an important factor influencing trial outcomes at the ICC, which has remained overlooked in the critical interdisciplinary literature on the Court, without denying the importance of the other factors. *Responsibility on Trial* also

[13] C. De Vos, 'Investigating from Afar: The ICC's Evidence Problem' (2013) 26(4) *Leiden Journal of International Law* 1009.

examines a particular stage of ICC proceedings, namely the confirmation of charges proceedings and the trials, a stage that has triggered little interest in the critical scholarship as compared to the process of opening investigations. The focus of this book is on the reasoning of judges with respect to the assessment of criminal responsibility and not on the selection of suspects by the ICC prosecutor. Although the Office of the Prosecutor (OTP) is part of the ICC, the politics of the legal field may play out differently in the practice of selecting sites for investigations and individual suspects, with the possibility for more direct and consistent state involvement given the high importance of those decisions to governments. The interaction between law and politics in the prosecutor's strategy falls outside the scope of this book, but as will be discussed later in this chapter, indeed, it has often been examined in ICL scholarship. Instead, this book examines what happens *after* the suspects enter the courtroom.

Another important caveat is that this book problematizes the juxtaposition between ideologically driven lawyers/NGOs and power-seeking states. It borrows insights from Abbott and Snidal's analysis of international legalization that recognizes that values and interests are often intertwined in practice in international law.[14] International lawyers can act strategically to promote their vision of the best formulation of a particular legal norm, just as states can defend principled positions influenced by their domestic norms during international negotiations. Consequently, when discussing states, the book does not explore whether they act only out of self-interest or only out of principled beliefs (because actions are often a combination of both). Rather, this book differentiates between the actions of states as members of the ICL community, which requires states to comply with the rules of legal reasoning, and the actions of states' external actors on which the ICC depends on for enforcing ICL, which affords states a broad range of strategic actions.

Furthermore, while this book is in dialogue with the legal scholarship on modes of liability, including the work of Jain,[15] Van Sliedregt,[16]

[14] K. Abbott and D. Snidal, 'Law, Legalization and Politics: An Agenda for the Next Generation of IR Scholars', in J. Dunoff and M. Pollack (eds.) *Interdisciplinary Perspectives on International Law and International Relations: The State of the Art* (Cambridge: Cambridge University Press, 2013) 33.

[15] Jain, Perpetrators and Accessories. N. Jain, 'The Control Theory of Perpetration in International Criminal Law' (2011) 12(1) *Chicago Journal of International Law* 159.

[16] Van Sliedregt, *Individual Criminal Responsibility*. See also E. Van Sliedregt, J. D. Ohlin, and T. Weigend, 'Assessing the Control Theory' (2013) 26(3) *Leiden Journal of International Law* 725.

Ambos,[17] and Robinson,[18] it also differs from those works in an important manner. *Responsibility on Trial* presents a perspective that is in part 'external' to the international criminal justice field by assessing the role of those and other scholarly works in (re)producing specific norms and ideas about criminal responsibility. As the book demonstrates, the influence of legal academia on ICL jurisprudence is particularly significant with respect to the questions that are perceived to be of a highly technical legal nature, as is the case with the rules regulating the assessment of criminal responsibility.

Finally, while this book comprises an interdisciplinary research project that examines legal documents and legal scholarly analysis, its findings will also be of interest to the international relations academic audience. The fact that the battles over the interpretation of legal norms are central for understanding the outcomes of international trials, and thus the political impact of international courts, has largely been neglected as a topic of analysis in the international relations literature. Interdisciplinary studies that borrow insights from both legal studies and political science have explored other aspects of ICL, such as the ICC's 'complementarity' mechanism,[19] but no study has been conducted on the laws of criminal responsibility. A contributing factor to this is the fact that the legal scholarship on criminal responsibility issues is largely written in a highly technical manner and aimed at legal scholars and lawyers. By providing a detailed analysis of the main debates within legal scholarship and international legal practice concerning criminal responsibility, this book aims to present an important aspect of international criminal justice to the international relations audience in a comprehensive manner. The rest of this chapter situates *Responsibility on Trial* within the existing interdisciplinary literature on international criminal justice and presents the research aims of the book.

[17] K. Ambos, *Treatise on International Criminal Law: Foundations and General Part*, Vol. 1 (Oxford: Oxford University Press, 2013). K. Ambos, 'Command Responsibility and *Organisationsherrschaft*: Ways of Attributing International Crimes to the 'Most Responsible', in A. Nollkaemper and H. van der Wilt (eds.) *System Criminality in International Law* (Cambridge: Cambridge University Press, 2009) 127. Ambos, 'Article 25'.

[18] D. Robinson, 'The Identity Crisis of International Criminal Law' (2008) 21(4) *Leiden Journal of International Law* 925. D. Robinson, *Justice in Extreme Cases: Criminal Law Theory Meets International Criminal Law* (Cambridge: Cambridge University Press, 2020).

[19] See Nouwen, *Complementarity in the Line of Fire*. De Vos, *Complementarity, Catalysts, Compliance*.

1.1 Research Scope

The scope and subject matter of international criminal justice have been subject to significant dispute.[20] Here, international criminal justice is defined as the legal norms that formulate ICL, the jurisprudence of the ICC, and tribunals and their policies.[21] ICL covers crimes that are said to be of concern to *humanity* as such.[22] While it is still debatable precisely which conducts fit into this definition, the RS of the ICC lists four specific types of international crimes: genocide, crimes against humanity, war crimes, and the crime of aggression,[23] all of which have been referred to as 'atrocity' crimes.[24] This definition of international criminal justice, while open to dispute, reflects what is generally understood by this term within the ICL field.[25]

Unlike other branches of international law, ICL imposes *individual* responsibility rather than state responsibility for international crimes.[26] Another distinguishing characteristic of ICL is that it provides for *criminal* responsibility rather than civil responsibility. Given the nature of mass atrocities, the individuals prosecuted through ICL would often be high-ranking state or military officials, especially with respect to the crime of aggression.[27] Nevertheless, under ICL, the accused are being prosecuted in their capacity as rational individuals bearing criminal responsibility for their personal conducts and not as state representatives.[28]

20 For a historical overview of the debates, see F. Mégret, 'International Criminal Justice History Writing as Anachronism: The Past That Did Not Lead to the Present', in I. Tallgren and T. Skouteris (eds.) *The New Histories of International Criminal Law* (Oxford: Oxford University Press, 2019) 72.

21 C. Stahn, 'Between "Faith" and "Facts": By What Standards Should We Assess International Criminal Justice?' (2012) 25(2) *Leiden Journal of International Law* 251, 252.

22 E. Van Sliedregt, 'International Criminal Law', in M. D. Dubber and T. Hörnle (eds.) *The Oxford Handbook of Criminal Law* (Oxford: Oxford University Press, 2014) 1139, 1140.

23 Rome Statute, Article 5.

24 D. Scheffer, 'The Future of Atrocity Law' (2002) 25(3) *Suffolk Transnational Law Review* 389, 400.

25 Chapter 3, Section 3.1.2.

26 M. Drumbl, *Atrocity, Punishment, and International Law* (Cambridge: Cambridge University Press, 2007) 5–6. Van Sliedregt, *Individual Criminal Responsibility*, 61–65.

27 R. Bellelli, 'The Establishment of the System of International Criminal Justice', in R. Bellelli (ed.) *International Criminal Justice: Law and Practice from the Rome Statute to Its Review* (London and New York: Routledge, 2016) 5, 33.

28 R. Cryer, Friman, H., Robinson, D., and E. Wilmhurst, *An Introduction to International Criminal Law and Procedure*, 3rd ed. (Cambridge: Cambridge University Press, 2014) 7.

Although the notion of individual criminal responsibility for mass atrocities constitutes the 'underlying logic' of ICL,[29] it presents a relatively recent phenomenon in international law. International treaties from the early twentieth century, such as the Hague Conventions on the Laws and Customs of War, concerned states' obligations to punish the perpetrators of war crimes.[30] In 1945, the International Military Tribunal (IMT) in Nuremberg, established to prosecute the defeated Nazi major generals, instituted the norm of individual criminal responsibility in international law by proclaiming that international crimes were committed by 'men, not abstract entities'.[31] The individual criminal responsibility norm was then applied at the International Military Tribunal for the Far East (IMTFE) in Tokyo, which prosecuted former Japanese officials in the aftermath of the Second World War.[32] But even after the Nuremberg and Tokyo judgments, discussions about the establishment of a permanent ICC continued to contemplate the possibility of imposing state responsibility for international crimes.[33] The norm of individual criminal responsibility finally re-emerged in international law in the 1990s with the UN Security Council's establishment of the International Criminal Tribunal for the former Yugoslavia (ICTY) and for the International Criminal Tribunal for Rwanda (ICTR),[34] and was permanently institutionalized in the RS of the ICC in 1998.[35]

The early 2000s have seen the rise of 'hybrid' courts, including the Special Court for Sierra Leone (2002), the Special Panels for the Serious Crimes in East Timor (2000), the Extraordinary Chambers in the Courts of Cambodia (2006), and the Special Tribunal for Lebanon, in an attempt to 'blend

[29] M. Baaz, 'Dissident Voices in International Criminal Law' (2015) 28(3) *Leiden Journal of International Law* 673, 674.

[30] I. Bantekas, 'Reflections on Some Sources and Methods of International Criminal and Humanitarian Law' (2006) 6(1) *International Criminal Law Review* 121, 122.

[31] Trial of the Major War Criminals before the International Military Tribunal, *Trial of the Major War Criminals before the International Military Tribunal, Nuremberg*, 14 November 1945–1 October 1946, Vol. 22 (Germany: Nuremberg, 1947–1949), 466, www.loc.gov/rr/frd/Military_Law/pdf/NT_Vol-XXII.pdf.

[32] For an overview of the similarities and differences between the IMT and IMTFE, see Z. Kaufman, 'The Nuremberg Tribunal v. the Tokyo Tribunal: Designs, Staffs, and Operations' (2010) 43(3) *John Marshall Law Review* 753.

[33] Mégret, 'International Criminal Justice History', 83. See, e.g., V. Pella, 'Towards an International Criminal Court' (1950) 44(1) *The American Journal of International Law* 37, 51–52.

[34] P. Gaeta, 'The History and the Evolution of the Notion of International Crimes', in R. Bellelli (ed.) *International Criminal Justice: Law and Practice from the RS to Its Review* (London and New York: Routledge, 2016) 169, 169.

[35] See W. Schabas, *An Introduction to the International Criminal Court*, 3rd ed. (Cambridge: Cambridge University Press, 2007).

international supervision with local ownership'.[36] In addition, nation-states play an important role in the enforcement of individual criminal responsibility for atrocities, although the relationship between national and international courts varies.[37] The UN tribunals enjoyed 'primacy' over national courts, which allowed the tribunals to request the deferral of cases by national courts to the competence of the international tribunals, but the ICC operates under a 'complementarity' regime, which renders the ICC a court of last resort.[38] The RS gives priority to national proceedings: a case would be inadmissible at the Court unless the state that has jurisdiction is 'unwilling or unable genuinely to carry out the investigation or prosecution'.[39]

While domestic proceedings and hybrid courts demonstrate the spread of international criminal justice globally, the scope of this book is limited to an analysis of *international* courts by view of examining the particular challenges that the realm of international power politics poses to the assessment of individual criminal responsibility, with the main focus on the permanent ICC. Other international tribunals – the IMT, IMTFE, and the UN tribunals – will be examined to provide a contextual understanding of the historical development of individual criminal responsibility norms in ICL. Because they were set up by the victorious Allies, the IMT and IMTFE have sometimes been described as 'multinational' rather than truly 'international',[40] but they are also included in the analysis because of their significant role in ICL scholarship and practice.

1.2 Theories of International Criminal Justice

The interdisciplinary literature on international criminal justice could be grouped into two branches: liberal-legalist scholarship and critical

36 Bellelli, 'Establishment of the System', 14–15.

37 E. Lutz and K. Sikkink, 'The Justice Cascade: The Evolution and Impact of Foreign Human Rights Trials in Latin America' (2001) 2(1) *Chicago Journal of International Law* 1.

38 For a discussion of the two types of jurisdiction, see F. Lattanzi, 'Concurrent Jurisdictions between Primacy and Complementarity', in R. Bellelli (ed.) *International Criminal Justice: Law and Practice from the RS to Its Review* (London and New York: Routledge, 2016) 186 et seq.

39 Rome Statute, Article 17(1)(a). ICC case law has further established that the Court can take on a case in the situations where the state with jurisdiction has remained 'inactive', i.e. has not initiated proceedings. Situation in the Democratic Republic of Congo, Decision on the Prosecutor's Application for Warrants of Arrest, Article 58, ICC-01/04-02/06-20-Anx2, Pre-Trial Chamber I, 10 February 2006 (hereinafter *DRC* First Arrest Warrants Decision), § 29.

40 Bellelli, 'Establishment of the System', 11–12. Nevertheless, most commentators describe the IMT as an international tribunal. See K. J. Heller, *The Nuremberg Military Tribunals and the Origins of International Criminal Law* (Oxford: Oxford University Press, 2011) 110–111.

scholarship. These generic notions do not suggest that there are no differences between the works discussed within each branch. Rather, the aim is to examine the main arguments made by, on the one hand, those scholars who have been generally sympathetic to the promotion of international criminal justice, and, on the other hand, those more critical scholars. Liberal scholars often criticize various aspects of ICL, but their arguments usually constitute an 'internal' critique aimed at *improving* the performance of international courts rather than contesting the existence of ICL.[41] Similarly, not every critical scholar has rejected the idea of international criminal justice, but those authors have generally sought to problematize 'underlying assumptions' on which the system is based by foregrounding the systemic inequality in international politics.[42]

The critical approach appears better at explaining *which cases enter the ICC*, but not the judicial reasoning behind the assessment of the defendant's guilt or innocence. The liberal-legalist approach provides insights into this latter question, by suggesting that certain aspects of the ICC's operation, such as the assessment of the accused's guilt or innocence, are determined by legal norms. But the liberal-legalist scholarship neglects the question on how those legal norms are constructed in practice and through what processes they play out in judicial reasoning. To address the lack of detailed analysis of the manner in which legal norms matter with respect to the assessment of individual criminal responsibility at the ICC and the politics of the legal field, this book proposes building an 'intersubjective' framework of analysis – one that recognizes the law's inherent normativity not as an objective fact but as a form of social practice.

1.2.1 Liberal-Legalist Scholarship: An Internal View of the ICL Field

From a liberal perspective, the rule of law constitutes a mechanism for ordering social relations that constrains the arbitrary use of power.[43] The legal realm is associated with 'harmony' and the provision of *objective* means to resolve disputes and is distinguished from the political realm, associated with 'competition, conflict and supremacy'.[44] The liberal

[41] F. Mégret, 'International Criminal Justice: A Critical Research Agenda', in C. Schwöbel (ed.) *Critical Approaches to International Criminal Law: An Introduction* (Abingdon and New York: Routledge, 2014) 17, 18.

[42] Sander, 'International Criminal Justice', 753.

[43] K. S. Gallant, *The Principle of Legality in International and Comparative Criminal Law* (Cambridge: Cambridge University Press, 2008) 21.

[44] M. Shaw, *International Law*, 5th ed. (Cambridge: Cambridge University Press, 2003) 12.

scholarship perceives the legal approach to addressing mass atrocities as more balanced and objective compared to the alternative of political action. International trials are considered to end the cycle of 'private uncontrolled vengeance' in the aftermath of mass atrocities by substituting for it a 'measured process of fixing guilt' to individual perpetrators.[45] Furthermore, scholars have increasingly argued that international trials have an important socio-pedagogical effect.[46] By stigmatizing atrocious acts as socially unacceptable, international trials are said to promote the internalization of norms of lawful behaviour within the international community, and thus prevent future atrocities.[47]

The liberal understanding of ICL is grounded in a vision of the world as composed of equal rational individuals, responsible for their personal conducts.[48] Contrary to the 'simplistic myths of primordial hatred', mass atrocities are often considered to be deliberately incited by power-thirsty rational elites.[49] Consequently, the notion of individual criminal responsibility is considered particularly appropriate for addressing mass atrocities, compared to the 'primitive and archaic' forms of collective accountability, such as state responsibility, which harbour the danger of rekindling inter-group violence.[50] Unlike forms of collective accountability, the liberal

[45] J. Shklar, *Legalism* (Cambridge, Mass. and London, England: Harvard University Press, 1964) 158. See also G. Bass, *Stay the Hand of Vengeance: The Politics of War Crimes Tribunals* (Princeton and Oxford: Princeton University Press, 2000) 7. M. Minow, *Between Vengeance and Forgiveness: Facing History after Genocide and Mass Violence* (Boston: Beacon Press, 1998) 26.

[46] For a commentary on that branch of ICL scholarship see B. Sander, 'The Expressive Turn of International Criminal Justice: A Field in Search of Meaning' (2019) 32(4) *Leiden Journal of International Law* 851.

[47] P. Akhavan, 'Beyond Impunity: Can International Criminal Justice Prevent Future Atrocities?' (2001) 95(1) *The American Journal of International Law* 1, 12–13. M. Damaška, 'What Is the Point of International Criminal Justice' (2008) 83(1) *Chicago-Kent Law Review* 329, 345.

[48] G. Fletcher, 'The Storrs Lectures: Liberals and Romantics at War: The Problem of Collective Guilt' (2002) 111(7) *The Yale Law Journal* 1499, 1507–1508.

[49] Akhavan, 'Beyond Impunity', 7. See also P. Akhavan, 'Are International Criminal Tribunals a Disincentive to Peace?: Reconciling Judicial Romanticism with Political Realism' (2009) 31(3) *Human Rights Quarterly* 624, 629–630. F. Bensouda, 'Keynote speech, OpenForum 2012: Money, Power and Sex: The Paradox of Unequal Growth', 23 May 2012, www.icc-cpi.int/NR/rdonlyres/A73A2D85-37C4-40C0-8CB2-0577D90436B7/284578/23052012DPSpeechOpenForumPowerDay.pdf, 6.

[50] United Nations, 'Annual Report of the International Tribunal for the Prosecution of Persons Responsible for Serious Violations of International Humanitarian Law Committed in the Territory of the former Yugoslavia since 1991,' A/49/342, 29 August 1994, § 16.

individualized notion of criminal responsibility is said to ensure that 'the guilt of the few would not be shifted to the innocent'.[51]

Legal scholars and practitioners have recognized that the use of individual criminal responsibility also poses challenges. The term 'system criminality' has often been used to denote the scale and the peculiar normative context of mass atrocities.[52] International crimes generally involve mass participation[53] and appear to be facilitated by a social climate of fear and hatred that 'authorize[s]' conducts that would be considered criminal behaviour under normal circumstances.[54] Such considerations have raised suspicion whether individual criminal responsibility, a legal tool used in Western countries to address 'ordinary' domestic criminality, can provide an adequate accountability mechanism for the 'extraordinary evil' of atrocity crimes.[55] Nevertheless, such observations generally constitute an 'internal' critique because they do not completely reject the use of individual criminal responsibility as a response to mass atrocities. Rather, those scholars suggest that ICL presents only part of the solution to the problem of mass atrocities and needs to be *complemented* by mechanisms, such as truth and reconciliation commissions, that address the systemic dimensions of international crimes.[56] Even ardent critics of the direct replication of individual criminal responsibility from domestic to international law, Mark Drumbl, have proposed that a reformed model of international criminal trials could be useful in addressing mass atrocities.[57] Consequently,

[51] ICTY, *Nikolić*, Sentencing Judgment, IT-02-60/1-S, Trial Chamber, 2 December 2003, § 60. See also M. Sassòli and L. Olson, 'The Judgment of the ICTY Appeals Chamber on the Merits in the Tadic Case' (2000) 82(839) *International Review of the Red Cross* 733, 756.

[52] A. Nollkaemper, 'Introduction', in A. Nollkaemper and H. van der Wilt (eds.) *System Criminality in International Law* (Cambridge: Cambridge University Press, 2009) 1, 16. Van Sliedregt, *Individual Criminal Responsibility*, 20–21.

[53] D. Nersessian, 'Whoops, I Committed Genocide – The Anomaly of Constructive Liability for Serious International Crimes' (2006) 30(1) *The Fletcher Forum of World Affairs* 81.

[54] H. Kelman, 'The Policy Context of International Crimes', in A. Nollkaemper and H. van der Wilt (eds.) *System Criminality in International Law* (Cambridge: Cambridge University Press, 2009) 26, 36, emphasis omitted.

[55] Drumbl, *Atrocity, Punishment, and International Law*, 6. M. J. Aukerman, 'Extraordinary Evil, Ordinary Crime: A Framework for Understanding Transitional Justice' (2002) 15 *Harvard Human Rights Journal* 39, 41.

[56] Nollkaemper, 'Introduction', 4. L. Fletcher and H. Weinstein, 'Violence and Social Repair: Rethinking the Contribution of Justice to Reconciliation' (2002) 24(3) *Human Rights Quarterly* 573, 625. L. May and S. Fyfe, *International Criminal Tribunals: A Normative Defense* (Cambridge: Cambridge University Press, 2017) 95.

[57] Drumbl, *Atrocity, Punishment, and International Law*, 207–208. See also L. Fletcher, 'From Indifference to Engagement: Bystanders and International Criminal Justice' (2005) 26(4) *Michigan Journal of International Law* 1013, 1018.

despite the conceptual differences between domestic crimes and atrocity crimes, the punishment of *individual persons* through criminal trials has become an integral part of the transitional justice toolbox.[58]

The liberal-legalist scholarship has portrayed the development of ICL as a continuous struggle between, on the one hand, human rights advocates promoting legal norms and, on the other, self-interested states seeking to protect their sovereignty and the immunity of government officials from international prosecution.[59] The promotion of ICL has been rooted in the liberal idea that the sovereignty claims of a state that jeopardizes the physical security of its citizens should lose ground to the ability of international tribunals to prosecute the responsible individuals.[60] The liberal-legalist account recognizes the role of some 'good-will' states in the promotion of international criminal justice but mostly in terms of 'canalizing the inputs' of global civil society, with the latter acting as the main drivers of the ICL movement.[61]

The promotion of ICL over traditional power politics has generally been presented as a 'journey' marked by several stepping stones.[62] The Nuremberg trial of the Nazi major generals has largely been considered the foundation on which the system of individual criminal responsibility for mass atrocities was built.[63] Many liberal-legalist scholars do not deny that political considerations played a crucial role at Nuremberg, most notably in relation to the discriminatory selection of the accused[64] and to the retroactive nature of some of the laws applied by the tribunal.[65] But

[58] R. G. Teitel, *Globalizing Transitional Justice* (New York: Oxford University Press, 2014) xviii.

[59] See K. Sikkink, *The Justice Cascade: How Human Rights Prosecutions Are Changing World Politics* (New York and London: W. W. Norton & Company, 2011) 17. Lutz and Sikkink, *The Justice Cascade*. A. Cassese, 'Reflections on International Criminal Justice' (2011) 9(1) *Journal of International Criminal Justice* 271, 272. C. Safferling, 'Can Criminal Prosecution Be the Answer to Massive Human Rights Violations' (2004) 5(12) *German Law Journal* 1469, 1472.

[60] L. May, *Crimes against Humanity* (Cambridge: Cambridge University Press, 2004) 32.

[61] I. Tallgren, 'The Voice of the International: Who Is Speaking?' (2015) 13(1) *Journal of International Criminal Justice* 135, 147.

[62] Sander, 'International Criminal Justice', 751.

[63] See Bass, *Stay the Hand of Vengeance*, 204–205. A. Eser, 'Towards an International Criminal Court: Genesis and Main Features of the Rome Statute' (2001) 20(1) *University of Tasmania Law Review* 1, 4–5. Ferencz, 'International Criminal Courts'. G. Robertson, 'General Editor's Introduction to Essays on Fairness and Evidence in War Crimes Trials' (2006) 4(1) *International Commentary on Evidence* 1.

[64] C. Tomuschat, 'The Legacy of Nuremberg' (2006) 4(4) *Journal of International Criminal Justice* 830, 834.

[65] Minow, *Between Vengeance and Forgiveness*, 32–33.

the advocates of international criminal justice have generally perceived the Nuremberg trial to be a success of the legalist movement against state power politics, even if a limited one.[66] This victory of law over politics at Nuremberg is considered significant because it 'launched a remarkable international movement for human rights founded in the rule of law'.[67] Hence, while the liberal scholarship has recognized that the complete success of law over politics was not accomplished at Nuremberg, the tribunal is seen as the first step towards a *better* system of legal accountability for mass atrocities. The proponents of international criminal justice then often point to the political stalemate during the Cold War that reportedly prevented the institutionalization of the Nuremberg legal principles into a permanent ICC.[68] The establishment of the UN tribunals in the 1990s, hence, is viewed as an important accomplishment for the rule of law.[69] However, the ICTY and ICTR remained 'no more than ad hoc tribunals' that were created by a political institution – the UN Security Council.[70] For ICL advocates, the next step in the promotion of international criminal justice was the development of a permanent and independent ICC.[71]

The creation of the ICC was perceived as a testament of the efforts of human rights advocates and 'like-minded' states to defeat the 'power-preserving politics-dominated frame' of international negotiations and to build an institution that would be guided by 'the fundamental principles of law'.[72] Nevertheless, scholars and practitioners sympathetic to the court's establishment recognized that ICL continued to face significant political challenges even after the permanent court began operation.[73] Those

[66] See A. Cassese, 'From Nuremberg to Rome: International Military Tribunals to the International Criminal Court', in A. Cassese, P. Gaeta, and J. R. W. D. Jones (eds.) *The Rome Statute of the International Criminal Court* Vol. I (Oxford: Oxford University Press, 2002) 3, 8. Tomuschat, 'Legacy of Nuremberg', 837.

[67] Minow, *Between Vengeance and Forgiveness*, 47. See also Sikkink, *Justice Cascade*, 5.

[68] Ferencz, 'International Criminal Courts', 218–219. V. Nanda, 'The Establishment of a Permanent International Criminal Court: Challenges Ahead' (1998) 20(2) *Human Rights Quarterly* 413, 414.

[69] Lutz and Sikkink, *Justice Cascade*, 17.

[70] Eser, 'Towards an International Criminal Court', 6.

[71] Ferencz, 'International Criminal Courts', 225.

[72] N. Deitelhoff, 'The Discursive Process of Legalization: Charting Islands of Persuasion in the ICC *Case*' (2009) 63(1) *International Organization* 33, 60. See also C. Welch and A. Watkins, 'Extending Enforcement: The Coalition for the International Criminal Court' (2011) 33(4) *Human Rights Quarterly* 927, 960.

[73] Cassese, 'Reflections on International Criminal Justice', 273. M. Ignatieff, 'International Justice Possible Only When in the Interest of Powerful States', *International Center for Transitional Justice*, 9 February 2015, www.ictj.org/debate/article/justice-interests-of-powerful-states.

hurdles were attributed to the fact that great powers were 'not yet ready' to surrender some of their sovereign rights to the ICC.[74] Nevertheless, in the liberal-legalist literature, this has not been perceived as an evidence of the failure of international criminal justice as a tool for addressing mass atrocities. Rather, it is commonly considered that the 'progressive internalization' of ICL norms in the world of power politics[75] would take a 'fairly long period of time'.[76] In the meantime, the sympathetic scholarship has called for managing expectations with respect to the ICC's capacity to conduct successful prosecutions and for seeking an incremental rather than immediate change of state attitudes towards ICL.[77] Hence, while the liberal scholarship acknowledges that the *complete* triumph of law over politics may never take place in the state-dominated international realm, ICL is said to have come a long way since its early days.[78] The proponents of international criminal justice appear to aim at gradually achieving an ever-greater role for the rule of law in addressing mass atrocities.

The liberal-legalist account recognizes that power politics and legal norms have often interacted during the development and enforcement of international criminal justice. But the literature treats law and politics as distinct phenomena: the 'political' is associated with the efforts of states to protect their sovereignty from the reach of international criminal justice, and the 'legal' is perceived as a set of objective norms constraining the arbitrary use of power. While the legalistic position recognizes that the manner in which the rule of law is institutionalized and enforced has historically been compromised, and may never be completely separated from political interests, the very existence of objective legal norms that are distinct from state interests is not questioned.

[74] Interview with Benjamin Ferencz in N. Khomami, '"It Was as If I Had Peered into Hell": The Man Who Brought the Nazi Death Squads to Justice', *Guardian*, 7 February 2017, www.theguardian.com/law/2017/feb/07/nazi-death-squads-nuremberg-trials-benjamin-ferencz.

[75] Akhavan, 'Beyond Impunity', 30.

[76] A. Cassese, 'The Statute of the International Criminal Court: Some Preliminary Reflections' in A. Cassese, P. Gaeta, and S. Zappalà (eds.) *The Human Dimension of International Law: Selected Papers of Antonio Cassese* (Oxford: Oxford University Press, 2008) 499, 499. See also Van Sliedregt, International Criminal Law, 1146. C. Stephen, 'International Criminal Law: Wielding the Sword of Universal Criminal Justice?' (2012) 61(1) *International and Comparative Law Quarterly* 55, 84.

[77] M. Kersten, 'Whither the Aspirational ICC, Welcome the 'Practical' Court?', EJIL: Talk!, 22 May 2019, www.ejiltalk.org/whither-the-aspirational-icc-welcome-the-practical-court/. J. Harrington, 'An End to War through a Court of Law? Perhaps – and in Time', EJIL: Talk!, 14 June 2010, www.ejiltalk.org/an-end-to-war-through-a-court-of-law-perhaps-and-in-time/.

[78] D. Luban, 'Fairness to Rightness: Jurisdiction, Legality, and the Legitimacy of International Criminal Law', in S. Besson and J. Tasioulas (eds.) *The Philosophy of International Law* (Oxford: Oxford University Press, 2010) 569.

1.2.2 Critical Scholarship: An External View of the ICL Field

But other scholars, drawing on insights from critical legal studies (CLS) and Marxist legal studies, have provided an 'external', or a 'meta-' critique of ICL that questions the fundamental liberal logic of the field and the objectivity and distinctiveness of international law from power politics.[79] CLS perceives international legal norms as ultimately *indeterminate* due to the ambiguity of the legal language, which, on that account, can be invoked to 'justify *any* behaviour' and, therefore, can be instrumentalized by politically powerful actors.[80] Marxist studies problematize the liberal account of international law further by observing that, historically, the indeterminacy of international legal norms has been employed in a very *specific* manner, namely by interpreting international law in favour of the materially powerful classes and nations.[81] By creating the perception of sovereign equality between nations, it is suggested, international law has in reality 'facilitated' the material inequality between states.[82] Hence, international law is considered not as normatively superior to power politics, but, on the contrary, as a tool of global imperialism.[83] Therefore, from a critical perspective, the purported separation of law from politics masks social reality by concealing the driving role of power politics and global capitalism in international relations.[84]

Building upon the insights of CLS and Marxist studies on international law, some ICL scholars have problematized the liberal-legalist narrative and argued that the legal norm of individual criminal responsibility has in practice served to decontextualize and depoliticize international crimes.[85]

[79] Baaz, 'Dissident Voices', 676.

[80] M. Koskenniemi, *From Apology to Utopia: The Structure of International Legal Argument* (Cambridge: Cambridge University Press, 2006) 67, emphasis added. See also A. Sinclair, *International Relations Theory and International Law: A Critical Approach* (Cambridge: Cambridge University Press, 2010) 79–80.

[81] B. Chimni, *International Law and World Order: A Critique of Contemporary Approaches*, 2nd ed. (Cambridge: Cambridge University Press, 2017) 356. C. Miéville, *Between Equal Rights: A Marxist Theory of International Law* (London: Pluto, 2006) 54–60.

[82] R. Knox, 'Marxist Approaches to International Law', in A. Orford and F. Hoffmann (eds.) *The Oxford Handbook of the Theory of International Law* (Oxford: Oxford University Press, 2016) 306, 323, emphasis omitted.

[83] Chimni, International Law and World Order, 264. Miéville, *Between Equal Rights*, 225–226.

[84] Knox, 'Marxist Approaches', 319–320.

[85] M. Koskenniemi, 'Between Impunity and Show Trials' (2002) 6(1) *Max Planck Yearbook of United Nations Law* 1, 13–14. Engle, 'Genealogy of the Criminal Turn', 45. K. Ainley, 'Excesses of Responsibility: The Limits of Law and the Possibilities of Politics' (2011) 25(4) *Ethics & International Affairs* 407. K. Clarke, 'Refiguring the Perpetrator: Culpability, History and International Criminal Law's Impunity Gap' (2015) 19(5) *International Journal of Human Rights* 592.

Critical scholars have suggested that the individualization of criminal responsibility obfuscates the role of *structural* factors such as colonialism and global capitalism in facilitating the conditions that enable mass atrocities.[86] The fight against impunity for mass atrocities through the rule of law is argued to have historically legitimized other forms of physical and economic violence that were 'routinized' by the neoliberal international order, such as land grabs, humanitarian intervention, and the imposition of structural adjustment programmes on developing countries.[87]

Furthermore, the enforcement of ICL is said to produce a particular image of the perpetrator of mass atrocities as non-white, male, and particularly barbaric.[88] From a critical perspective, the nationals of the Global South have become the 'scapegoats' for the international community that has itself been involved in producing the socio-economic conditions enabling mass atrocities.[89] In other worlds, rather than challenging political power, ICL and the individual criminal responsibility norm are said to reaffirm the existing power inequalities, or the 'double standards', between the Global North and the Global South.[90]

The critical scholarship also approaches the historical development of ICL from a different perspective compared to the liberal-legalist scholarship by reframing the role of key actors and events. Human rights activists and NGOs have been presented in less benign terms in critical scholarship, namely as actors who have become complicit in the process of maintaining the dominance of Western ideas in international criminal justice.[91]

[86] K. Clarke, 'The Rule of Law through Its Economies of Appearances: The Making of the African Warlord' (2011) 18(1) *Indiana Journal of Global Legal Studies* 7. C. Schwöbel-Patel, 'Spectacle in International Criminal Law: The Fundraising Image of Victimhood' (2016) 4(2) *London Review of International Law* 247, 268–269. T. Krever, 'International Criminal Law: An Ideology Critique' (2013) 26(3) *Leiden Journal of International Law* 701, 703–704. S. Marks, 'Human Rights and Root Causes' (2011) 74(1) *The Modern Law Review* 57, 71. I. Tallgren, 'The Sensibility and Sense of International Criminal Law' (2002) 13(3) *European Journal of International Law* 561, 594–595.

[87] V. Nesiah, 'Doing History with Impunity', in K. Engle, Z. Miller, and D. Davis (eds.) *Anti-Impunity and the Human Rights Agenda* (Cambridge: Cambridge University Press, 2016) 95, 112–113.

[88] Schwöbel-Patel, 'Spectacle in International Criminal Law', 256–257. M. Mutua, 'Savages, Victims and Saviors: The Metaphor of Human Rights' (2001) 42(1) *Harvard International Law Journal* 201, 202.

[89] E. Bikundo, 'The International Criminal Court and Africa: Exemplary Justice' (2012) 23(1) *Law and Critique* 21, 27. Clarke, 'Rule of Law', 11–12.

[90] Schabas, Unimaginable Atrocities, 85. H. Tosa, 'Global Constitutional Order and the Deviant Other: Reflections on the Dualistic Nature of the ICC Process' (2018) 18(1) *International Relations of the Asia-Pacific* 45, 57.

[91] Zolo, *Victors' Justice*, xii. K. Lohne, 'Global Civil Society, the ICC, and Legitimacy in International Criminal Justice', in N. Hayashi and C. Bailliet (eds.) *The Legitimacy of*

Contrary to the liberal narrative, Danilo Zolo, for instance, has described the creation of ad hoc international tribunals not as steps of the gradual journey of promoting law within the realm of power politics, but as manifestations of 'victors' justice' against the 'vanquished, weak, and oppressed peoples'.[92] The permanent ICC has not escaped criticism of perpetuating the double standards among states either.[93] The selection of defendants at the Court – as of February 2022, all nationals of African countries – has led some scholars to describe the ICC as: 'a Western court to try African crimes against humanity'.[94] Notably, scholars have observed that ICL can be instrumentalized to serve the interests not only of great powers but also of the governments of less powerful states when enforced against rebels or opposition members by undermining international support for such groups and legitimizing oppressive governmental policies.[95]

Therefore, on this account, the practice of international criminal justice cannot be insulated from political interests.[96] Nouwen and Werner propose that with each investigation, the ICC inevitably becomes implicated in the realm of the political by implicitly stigmatizing the suspects as 'enemies of mankind' and praising the cooperating parties as 'friends of humanity'.[97] Scholars have argued that the difficulties of enforcing ICL further subordinate the Court to power politics because sovereign states would cooperate with international courts only to the extent that the latter prosecute their opposition, but not if government officials are subject to proceedings themselves.[98] Acting heads of states have been charged at

International Criminal Tribunals (Cambridge: Cambridge University Press, 2017) 449, 465–468. M. Mutua, 'Politics and Human Rights: An Essential Symbyosis' in Byers, M. (ed.) *The Role of Law in International Politics* (Oxford: Oxford University Press, 2001) 49. F. Mégret, 'Where Does the Critique of International Human Rights Stand? An Exploration in 18 Vignettes', in J. M. Beneyto, D. Kennedy, J. C. Varela, and J. Haskell (eds.) *New Approaches to International Law: The European and the American Experiences* (The Hague: Springer, 2012) 3, 14.

92 Zolo, Victors' Justice, xii.

93 Bikundo, 'International Criminal Court', 28.

94 M. Mamdani, 'The New Humanitarian Order' (2009) 36(122) *Review of African Political Economy* 621, 627.

95 P. Clark, 'Law, Politics and Pragmatism: The ICC and Case Selection in the Democratic Republic of Congo and Uganda', in N. Waddell and P. Clark (eds.) *Courting Conflict? Justice, Peace at the ICC in Africa* (London: Royal African Society, 2008) 37, 43. W. Schabas, 'Complementarity in Practice': Some Uncomplimentary Thoughts' (2008) 19(1) *Criminal Law Forum* 5, 16. Branch, Displacing Human Rights, 186.

96 P. Clark, *Distant Justice*, 80.

97 S. Nouwen and W. Werner, 'Doing Justice to the Political: The International Criminal Court in Uganda and Sudan' (2011) 21(4) *European Journal of International Law* 941.

98 Schabas, Complementarity in Practice, 19. V. Peskin, 'Things Fall Apart: Battles of Legitimation and the Politics of Noncompliance and African Sovereignty from the Rwanda

the ICC only when the situation was referred by the UN Security Council, which some interpreted as a confirmation of the further politicization of international criminal justice.[99] Overall, it has been suggested, only those individuals with 'no powerful friends left' become subjects to international trials.[100] Consequently, critical scholars remain unconvinced by the suggested objectivity of the legal approach to addressing mass atrocities because the selective application of ICL has enabled '*any* politicization of justice, *any* instrumentalization of legal institutions to political interests'.[101]

Crucially, the critical scholarship problematizes the attempt by liberal legalists to present the law as separate from and superior to politics.[102] Phil Clark's analysis of ICC interventions demonstrates that the failure to acknowledge that the practice of ICL cannot be 'distanced' from local politics has affected adversely both the Court and the afflicted communities.[103] Scholars have also expressed concerns that the emphasis on the necessity of ICL for 'ending impunity' for mass atrocities has obscured the need to justify such practices and precluded constructive criticism thereof.[104] From this perspective, to question the fundamental premises of international criminal justice is not equivalent to justifying impunity for mass atrocities. As Moyn observes, the alternative to liberal legalism 'is not doing nothing; it is doing something else'.[105] By subsuming 'all issues of liability within a criminal and individual frame', ICL is said to divert attention away from other forms of accountability, which may be particularly relevant in the context of mass violence, such as civil or

Tribunal to the ICC', in N. Hayashi and C. Bailliet (eds.) *The Legitimacy of International Criminal Tribunals* (Cambridge: Cambridge University Press, 2017) 401, 405. T. Krever, 'Dispensing Global Justice' (2014) 85(1) *New Left Review* 67.

99 M. Kersten, *Justice in Conflict: The Effects of the International Criminal Court's Interventions on Ending Wars and Building Peace* (Oxford: Oxford University Press, 2016) 163. A. Kiyani, 'Legitimacy, Legality, and the Possibility of a Pluralist International Criminal Law', in N. Hayashi and C. Bailliet (eds.) *The Legitimacy of International Criminal Tribunals* (Cambridge: Cambridge University Press, 2017) 92, 96–97.

100 P. McManus, 'Enemy of Mankind or Just No Powerful Friends Left? Insights from International Relations about the Efficacy of the ICC' (2017) 17(2) *International Criminal Law Review* 302, 318, emphasis omitted.

101 Branch, 'ICC Review Conference', 34, emphasis in the original

102 Nouwen and Werner, 'Doing Justice to the Political', 961–964.

103 P. Clark, *Distant Justice*, 17.

104 S. Moyn, 'Anti-Impunity as Deflection of Argument', in K. Engle, Z. Miller, and D. Davis (eds.) *Anti-Impunity and the Human Rights Agenda* (Cambridge: Cambridge University Press, 2016) 68, 68–69. See also Krever, 'International Criminal Law', 710.

105 Moyn, 'Anti-Impunity', 69. See also Clarke, Fictions of Justice, 237.

corporate liability.[106] By 'monopolizing' the discourse of global justice, ICL has left 'fundamental issues outside the scope of what can be defined as unjust'.[107]

1.3 Internal v. External Positions: Strengths and Weaknesses

By focusing on the ICC's embeddedness within domestic and international politics, the critical scholarship provides key insights into the determination of the Court's jurisdiction, including the question of which cases enter the ICC and which proceedings have the potential to be successful. The liberal-legalist scholarship has justified the prosecutor's geographical focus on developing countries on legal or pragmatic grounds,[108] but more critical analyses have revealed the influence of the Court's institutional interests in those decisions, namely to achieve effectiveness of prosecutions, when the proceedings align with the interests of the political actors upon which the Court depends for obtaining cooperation.[109]

For instance, scholars have suggested that political considerations influenced the OTP's decision to refrain from prosecuting acting government officials from cooperating states.[110] The practice of 'self-referrals', where a state voluntarily refers a conflict situation taking place on its territory to the ICC for investigation, has been perceived as another illustration of the way in which ICL favours rather than challenges political power.[111] Self-referrals have been made by several states, including

[106] K. Anderson, 'The Rise of International Criminal Law: Intended and Unintended Consequences' (2009) 20(2) *European Journal of International Law* 331, 347.

[107] Branch, 'ICC Review Conference', 34.

[108] K. Ambos, 'Expanding the Focus of the "African Criminal Court"', in W. Schabas, Y. McDermott and N. Hayes (eds.) *Ashgate Research Companion to International Criminal Law: Critical Perspectives* (Farnham: Ashgate, 2012) 499, 510–514. C. Bassiouni and D. Hansen, 'The Inevitable Practice of the Office of the Prosecutor', in R. Steinberg (ed.) *Contemporary Issues Facing the International Criminal Court* (Leiden: Brill Nijhoff, 2016) 309, 316–317. M. DeGuzman, 'Is the ICC Targeting Africa Inappropriately? A Moral, Legal, and Sociological Assessment', in R. Steinberg (ed.) *Contemporary Issues Facing the International Criminal Court* (Leiden: Brill Nijhoff, 2016) 333, 333–334.

[109] Kersten, *Justice in Conflict*, 17.

[110] A. Branch, 'Uganda's Civil War and the Politics of ICC Intervention' (2007) 21(2) *Ethics & International Affairs* 179, 188. K. Rodman and P. Booth, 'Manipulated Commitments: The International Criminal Court in Uganda' (2013) 35(2) *Human Rights Quarterly* 271, 286. Kersten, *Justice in Conflict*, 162.

[111] Nouwen, *Complementarity in the Line of Fire*, 116–120. P. Clark, *Distant Justice*, 55. W. Schabas, 'Prosecutorial Discretion v. Judicial Activism at the International Criminal Court' (2008) 6(4) *Journal of International Criminal Justice* 731, 751–753.

Uganda, the Democratic Republic of Congo (DRC), the Central African Republic (CAR), and Mali.[112] While the investigation in Côte d'Ivoire was initiated *proprio motu* by the ICC prosecutor pursuant to their power under Article 15(1) RS, because the ICC was previously invited to intervene by the Ivoirian government, that investigation also resembled the self-referral dynamics.[113] It has been suggested that self-referrals 'signa[l]' to the OTP which actors to cooperate with and which actors to target as suspects.[114] In all of the self-referred investigations, the ICC has charged only members of rebel movements or the political opposition, but not acting state officials, essentially enabling governments to dispose of dangerous rebels.[115] Liberal scholars have responded that states are not able to easily instrumentalize legal rules as a tool because the RS requires the referral of 'situations' rather than specific cases to the ICC, which leaves the government officials just as vulnerable to potential prosecution as the rebel leaders.[116] However, more critical analyses have suggested that while in principle the ICC's law should operate in that manner, in practice the governments making referrals have often been able to exert enough political pressure on the court to protect their officials from prosecution.[117] Consequently, in international criminal justice, power politics often plays out with respect to the decisions of where not to open investigations and whom not to prosecute.[118]

More recently, some ICC decisions regarding the opening of investigations have challenged the view of the inevitable politicization of ICL. Since

112 ICC, Situations under Investigations, www.icc-cpi.int/pages/situation.aspx.

113 P. Clark, *Distant Justice*, 288.

114 Kersten, *Justice in Conflict*, 163.

115 F Jessberger and J. Geneuss, 'The Many Faces of the International Criminal Court. Journal of International Criminal Justice' (2012) 10(5) *Journal of International Criminal Justice* 1081, 1089. Schabas, *Prosecutorial Discretion*, 757. See also A. Cassese, 'Is the ICC Still Having Teething Problems?' (2006) 4(3) *Journal of International Criminal Justice* 434, 436.

116 B. Simmons and A. Danner, 'Credible Commitments and the International Criminal Court' (2010) 64(2) *International Organization* 225, 230–231.

117 See Rodman and Booth, 'Manipulated Commitments'. L. Vinjamuri, 'The International Criminal Court the Paradox of Its Authority', in K. Alter, L. Helfer, and M. Madsen (eds.) *International Court Authority* (Oxford: Oxford University Press, 2018) 337. T. Chapman and S. Chaudoin, 'Ratification Patterns and the International Criminal Court' (2013) 57(2) *International Studies Quarterly* 400, 404–405.

118 M. Mutua, 'Closing the "Impunity Gap" and the Role of State Support in the ICC' in R. Steinberg (ed.) *Contemporary Issues Facing the International Criminal Court* (Leiden: Brill Nijhoff, 2016) 99, 103. F. Mégret, 'What Sort of Global Justice Is "International Criminal Justice"?' (2015) 13(1) *Journal of International Criminal Justice* 77, 81–82.

2016, the OTP has started to open investigations outside Africa.[119] Notably, despite the announcement by the United States that visas would be denied to any ICC staff members involved in the investigations of American forces operating in Afghanistan,[120] the OTP requested the judges to open a *proprio motu* investigation in Afghanistan. The Pre-Trial Chamber (PTC) judges considered that without state cooperation, the Afghanistan investigation would be 'doomed to failure' and declined the prosecutor's request.[121] However, the AC judges subsequently unanimously decided to authorize the OTP's investigation, thus demonstrating that the court would not so easily give up on politically challenging cases.[122] Such developments might suggest that the influence of power politics in international criminal justice cannot completely explain the selection of sites for investigation and specific cases.

The critical scholarship has, nevertheless, provided important insights into the overall picture of the cases that actually proceed from investigation to the ICC courtroom. Bosco's detailed analysis of the ICC's investigations record proposes that in practice the ICC has 'accommodated' itself to the state-dominated international reality, rather than challenging that reality.[123] For example, in September 2021, the ICC OTP decided to focus the Afghanistan investigation only on 'crimes allegedly committed by the Taliban and the Islamic State – Khorasan Province ("IS-K") and to *deprioritise* other aspects of this investigation' on the grounds of limited resources.[124] While the ICC OTP's announcement does not name those

[119] The first investigation outside Africa was opened in Georgia in 2016, followed by investigations in Afghanistan, Bangladesh/Myanmar, Palestine, The Philippines, and Venezuela, www.icc-cpi.int/pages/situation.aspx.

[120] *The Guardian*, 'US to Deny Visas for ICC Members Investigating Alleged War Crimes', 15 March 2019, www.theguardian.com/us-news/2019/mar/15/mike-pompeo-us-war-crimes-investigation-international-criminal-court.

[121] Situation in the Islamic Republic of Afghanistan, Decision Pursuant to Article 15 of the Rome Statute on the Authorization of an Investigation into the Situation in the Islamic Republic of Afghanistan, ICC-02/17-33, Pre-Trial Chamber II, 12 April 2019, § 90, §§ 94–95.

[122] J. Trahan, 'The Significance of the ICC Appeals Chamber's Ruling in the Afghanistan Situation', OpinioJuris, 10 March 2020, opiniojuris.org/2020/03/10/the-significance-of-the-icc-appeals-chambers-ruling-in-the-afghanistan-situation/.

[123] Bosco, Rough Justice, 20. On that point see also Vinjamuri, 'International Criminal Court', 340.

[124] ICC, Statement of the Prosecutor of the International Criminal Court, Karim A. A. Khan QC, following the application for an expedited order under Article 18(2) seeking authorization to resume investigations in the Situation in Afghanistan, 27 September 2021, www.icc-cpi.int/Pages/item.aspx?name=2021-09-27-otp-statement-afghanistan, emphasis added.

'other aspects', the statement has been perceived as an indication that the OTP would deprioritize investigations into the conducts of the Afghan National Security Forces and the US armed forces.[125] Human rights organizations criticized this decision, which was seen as an affirmation of the 'double standards' of justice applied at the ICC.[126] Furthermore, as of February 2022, the only suspects that have stood (pre-)trial proceedings at the ICC have been either members of insurgent organizations, deposed state officials, or persons who appeared voluntarily after being summoned by the Court, as was the case with the six Kenyan suspects and the rebel leaders from Darfur.[127] Those cases in which states have refused to comply with their obligations and arrest the accused, such as the case against the former Sudanese president Al-Bashir, have not yet reached the courtroom.[128] In other cases, this time against Kenyan nationals, the suspects appeared voluntarily at the court but the proceedings were terminated due to the prosecutor's inability to collect evidence as a result of the Kenyan government's obstruction of ICC proceedings.[129] Hence, in those ICC cases that have failed to obtain the cooperation of at least some states, the court has not had the opportunity to enter judgments on the accused's alleged criminal responsibility.

Important as those observations are for understanding the field of international criminal justice, the critical scholarship often stops short of examining what happens in those ICC cases in which the court has obtained sufficient government cooperation to have the accused apprehended and to conduct investigations – that is, what happens once in the courtroom. Yet, the trial record of the ICC is a key aspect of the Court's operation for understanding the way in which ICL functions in the international realm. The outcomes of international trials are not preordained to end up in conviction, and the ICC is a stark example of this. As of

125 Amnesty International, 'Afghanistan: ICC Prosecutor's Statement on Afghanistan Jeopardises His Office's Legitimacy and Future,' 5 October 2021, www.amnesty.org/en/documents/ior53/4842/2021/en/

126 Ibid.

127 Women's Initiatives for Gender Justice, 'Gender Report Card on the International Criminal Court 2011' (2011) https://4genderjustice.org/ftp-files/publications/Gender-Report-Card-on-the-International-Criminal-Court-2011.pdf, 120.

128 For a discussion of the reaction of African states to the Al-Bashir case see K. Mills, '"Bashir Is Dividing Us": Africa and the International Criminal Court' (2012) 34(2) *Human Rights Quarterly* 404. R. Cole, 'Africa's Relationship with the International Criminal Court: More Political than Legal' (2013) 14(2) *Melbourne Journal of International Law* 670, 685–689.

129 For an insightful analysis of the attempts of the Kenyan government to challenge the ICC investigation see Peskin, 'Things Fall Apart', 413–422.

February 2022, the court has served only five convictions, in the *Lubanga*, *Katanga*, *Al-Mahdi*, *Ntaganda*, and *Ongwen* cases, and four acquittals, in the *Ngudjolo*, *Bemba* and *Gbagbo and Blé Goudé* cases. Moreover, the ICC has dismissed some or all charges in several cases, such as *Mbarushimana* and *Abu Garda*.

The Court's trial record is not without consequences for its institutional standing. Even though in principle liberal legalists are interested in holding international trials rather than obtaining a certain number of convictions, in practice commentators have suggested that a significant rate of acquittals risks undermining the project of international criminal justice as an apparent 'enormous waste of time and money'.[130] The performance of international criminal tribunals has increasingly been assessed in terms of the costs spent on investigations and proceedings.[131] Consequently, a high rate of acquittals could 'impair the reputation' of the Court by dissuading the global public of its ability to fight impunity.[132] The ICC has already been criticized for turning into a 'very expensive "acquittal machine"'.[133] At the 2018 Assembly of State Parties (ASP) the United Kingdom expressed serious concern about the fact, 'After 20 years, and 1.5 billion Euros spent we have only three core crime convictions'.[134] Trial outcomes have implications for the image that the Court projects to the actors on which it depends for material and moral support, including the ICC's ASP, which determines the Court's budget,[135] and human rights advocates.

From a liberal-legalist perspective, the failure of critical studies to explain the outcomes of ICC trials can be attributed to the lack of appreciation of the normative distinctiveness of legal reasoning. For liberal scholars, international criminal justice institutions constitute '*more* than just vehicles for the crude application of power'.[136] The ICC is differentiated

[130] M. Osiel, *Making Sense of Mass Atrocity* (New York: Cambridge University Press, 2009) 22. See also N. Combs, *Fact-Finding without Facts: The Uncertain Evidentiary Foundations of International Criminal Convictions* (Cambridge: Cambridge University Press, 2010) 228–233.

[131] Stahn, 'Between "Faith" and "Facts"', 256.

[132] Combs, *Fact-Finding without Facts*, 358.

[133] D. Robinson, 'International Criminal Law as Justice' (2013) 11(3) *Journal of International Criminal Justice* 699, 700.

[134] Foreign & Commonwealth Office, 'UK statement to ICC Assembly of States Parties 17th session', 5 December 2018 www.gov.uk/government/speeches/uk-statement-to-icc-assembly-of-states-parties-17th-session.

[135] H. Woolaver and E. Palmer, 'Challenges to the Independence of the International Criminal Court from the Assembly of States Parties' (2017) 15 *Journal of International Criminal Justice* 641, 656–659.

[136] Bass, *Stay the Hand of Vengeance*, 12, emphasis added.

from political organizations precisely by its obligation to make determinations on the basis of the law.[137] Thus, the overall consensus that 'law matters' unites the liberal-legalist view of ICL, although there is some variation of opinion among liberal legalists with respect to the *extent* to which law matters in international criminal justice. ICC officials have generally maintained that all aspects of the interpretation and enforcement of ICL should remain separated from political considerations.[138] The ICC's prosecutor Fatou Bensouda argued that politics had '*no* place' in the execution of her mandate.[139] Sympathetic scholarship, however, has generally warned against such manifestations of 'judicial romantic[ism]' that may lead to misguided expectations about the possibility of completely separating international criminal justice from political considerations.[140] Many supporters of international criminal justice acknowledge that, due to the ICC's incapacity to prosecute all persons responsible for international crimes, a certain degree of selectivity with respect to the choice of suspects is inevitable.[141] On that account, the prosecutor may, for example, 'sequence' investigations by starting with those actors who lack state support before moving on to more significant political figures in order to increase the ICC's chances of apprehending suspects.[142] But it is still deemed unacceptable if the prosecutor targets individuals without sufficient evidence, or if the judges assess the defendant's guilt or innocence without following the criminal responsibility laws.[143]

137 Cassese, 'ICC Still Having Teething Problems', 441. Sikkink, *Justice Cascade*, 13.

138 As observed by Sander, 'International Criminal Justice', 784. See, e.g., *Gbagbo and Blé Goudé*, 'Reasons of Judge Geoffrey Henderson', ICC-02/11-01/15-1263-AnxB-Red, Trial Chamber I, 16 July 2019, www.icc-cpi.int/RelatedRecords/CR2019_07450.PDF, § 10.

139 F. Bensouda, 'Address to the Assembly of State Parties, 12th Session of the Assembly of State Parties', 20 November 2013, asp.icc-cpi.int/iccdocs/asp_docs/ASP12/ASP12-OP-Statement-PROS-ENG-FRA.pdf, § 14, emphasis in the original.

140 Akhavan, 'International Criminal Tribunals', 629. See also J. Goldston, 'More Candour about Criteria: The Exercise of Discretion by the Prosecutor of the International Criminal Court' (2010) 8(2) *Journal of International Criminal Justice* 383, 386–387.

141 Akhavan, 'Beyond Impunity', 30. D. Luban, 'After the Honeymoon: Reflections on the Current State of International Criminal Justice' (2013) 11(3) *Journal of International Criminal Justice* 505, 508–509.

142 S. Rosenberg, 'The International Criminal Court in Côte d'Ivoire: Impartiality at Stake?' (2017) 15(3) *Journal of International Criminal Justice* 471. A. S. Weiner, 'Prudent Politics: The International Criminal Court, International Relations, and Prosecutorial Independence' (2013) 12(3) *Washington University Global Studies Law Review* 545, 556–560. Goldston, 'More Candour', 393–402.

143 Luban, 'After the Honeymoon', 508. Weiner, 'Prudent Politics', 548–549. A. Danner, 'Enhancing the Legitimacy and Accountability of Prosecutorial Discretion at the International Criminal Court' (2003) 97(3) *American Journal of International Law* 510, 536–537.

Yet, the liberal-legalist approach also falls short of examining how the laws of individual criminal responsibility operate and influence trial outcomes. It is simply remarked that *some* acquittals constitute the inevitable price of relying on a criminal justice system that respects the rule of law.[144] The most obvious explanation for the potentially embarrassing ratio of acquittals and dismissals of charges at the ICC on this account is the inability of the ICC prosecutor to collect sufficient evidence for obtaining a conviction,[145] often attributed to the refusal of individual states to cooperate with the collection of evidence[146] or the ASP's reluctance to grant the OTP additional funding.[147] Because international judges are presumed to refrain from entering a conviction unless the defendant's guilt has been clearly established, despite potential political benefits of such decisions, the liberal-legalist perspective locates the reason behind the failure of ICC prosecutions in the desire of states to protect their sovereignty and financial interests and the resulting inability of the OTP to collect sufficient incriminatory evidence.

While all the above affect trial outcomes, this book argues that the liberal-legalist perspective presents an incomplete picture of the assessment of criminal responsibility because it falls short of enquiring into the manner in which legal norms are enacted in practice in the trial. The problem with the liberal-legalist literature is that by spending so much effort on explaining the distinctiveness of law from state power politics, it effectively projects legal norms as objective standards having a universally uniform influence on judicial reasoning with respect to the assessment of criminal responsibility across all institutional settings regardless of the socio-political context. However, important differences have been observed between the ICC and the UN tribunals in terms of the judges' response to the prosecutors' investigatory hurdles, which indicates that the availability of evidence, while an important factor, is not the only one that influences trial outcomes.

[144] Women's Initiatives for Gender Justice, Gender Report Card on the International Criminal Court 2018 (2018) https://4genderjustice.org/ftp-files/publications/Gender-Report_design-full-WEB.pdf, 57. M. Jackson, 'Commander's Motivations in Bemba', EJIL: Talk!, 15 June 2018, www.ejiltalk.org/commanders-motivations-in-bemba/.

[145] See De Vos, 'Investigating from Afar'. D. Guilfoyle, 'This Is Not Fine: The International Criminal Court in Trouble Part II', 22 March 2019, www.ejiltalk.org/part-ii-this-is-not-fine-the-international-criminal-court-in-trouble/.

[146] Amnesty International, 'Kenya: Ruto and Sang Decision Must Not Derail Efforts to Ensure Justice for Victims', 5 April 2016, www.amnesty.org/en/latest/news/2016/04/kenya-ruto-and-sang-decision-must-not-derail-efforts-to-ensure-justice-for-victims/.

[147] E. Evenson and J. O'Donohue, 'States Shouldn't Use ICC Budget to Interfere with Its Work', Amnesty International, 23 November 2016, www.amnesty.org/en/latest/news/2016/11/states-shouldnt-use-icc-budget-to-interfere-with-its-work/.

Because liberal-legalist approaches perceive legal norms as objective, they fail to convincingly explain why ICC judges and those at the UN tribunals have treated differently the prosecutors' arguments and evidence. Empirical studies have called attention to the UN tribunals' general willingness to admit evidence that would otherwise not meet the standards of domestic criminal proceedings, essentially lowering the burden of proof on the prosecutor,[148] especially in cases concerning leadership figures.[149] In effect, commentators have noted that rather than the prosecutor seeking to prove the defendants' guilt, the latter have had to prove their innocence at the UN tribunals.[150] By contrast, the ICC has shown 'unparalleled willingness to reject the prosecution's evidentiary offerings'.[151] In decisions like the *Bemba* appeal judgment or the *Gbagbo and Blé Goudé* trial decision, the ICC judges have demonstrated 'zeal for impeccable standards' and a 'hypersceptical' attitude towards incriminating evidence, which has resulted in the prosecutor's failure to prove the defendant's guilt.[152] Even though the small number of verdicts at the ICC – nine, as of February 2022 – precludes a conclusive comparison, the record of acquittals at the Court is telling of the implications of the restrained evidentiary assessment. The acquittal rate at the ICTY was about 17 percent[153] and about 18 percent at the ICTR,[154] compared to 44 percent at the ICC. The permanent court has served only five convictions and four acquittals for international crimes as defined under Article 5 RS.[155] Unlike the UN tribunals, which displayed a 'proconviction bias',[156] the ICC has looked at the prosecutor's incriminating evidence with a 'jaundiced eye'.[157] As this

[148] Combs, *Fact-Finding without Facts.*

[149] A. Zahar, 'Pluralism and the Rights of the Accused in International Criminal Proceedings', in E. van Sliedregt and S. Vasiliev (eds.) *Pluralism in International Criminal Law* (Oxford: Oxford University Press, 2014) 225, 242–244.

[150] S. Bertodano, 'Judicial Independence in the International Criminal Court' (2002) 15(2) *Leiden Journal of International Law* 409, 410. Robinson, 'Identity Crisis', 934.

[151] N. Combs, 'Grave Crimes and Weak Evidence: A Fact-Finding Evolution in International Criminal Law' (2017) 58(1) *Harvard International Law Journal* 47, 124.

[152] D. Robinson, 'The Other Poisoned Chalice: Unprecedented Evidentiary Standards in the Gbagbo Case? (Part 1)', EJIL: Talk!, 5 November 2019, www.ejiltalk.org/the-other-poisoned-chalice-unprecedented-evidentiary-standards-in-the-gbagbo-case-part-1/.

[153] Based on data from 'Key Figures of the Cases', www.icty.org/en/cases/key-figures-cases.

[154] Based on data from 'The ICTR in Brief', at unictr.irmct.org/en/tribunal.

[155] Excluding the cases for offences against the administration of justice. See ICC's 'Defendants' database at www.icc-cpi.int/defendants.

[156] Combs, *Fact-Finding without Facts*, 222.

[157] J. O'Sullivan, 'The Relationship between the Office of the Prosecutor and the Judicial Organ', in M. Minow, C. True-Frost, and A. Whiting (eds.) *The First Global Prosecutor: Promise and Constraints* (Ann Arbor: University of Michigan Press, 2015) 156.

book will show, by looking into the normative dynamics of the ICL field, namely the ideas about the scope and purpose of ICL norms that have been promoted and contested within that field, one gets a deeper understanding of the different practices of the ICC and its predecessors.

Some legal scholars have attributed the difference of approaches between the ICC and the UN tribunals to ICL's 'matur[ation]' into a more sophisticated legal system over time that has allegedly led the permanent court to exhibit greater respect for legal norms than its predecessors.[158] The notion of 'progress' is rooted in the Enlightenment tradition and serves as a powerful rhetorical tool in international law.[159] The optimistic discourse of progress and renewal implies that international law can *improve* and that the historical pitfalls of its creation and enforcement can be avoided. This discourse perceives the existence of a single telos of perfect legal order, legalism, that can be reached. From a critical perspective, however, this liberal narrative of progress is deemed 'dangerous' because it obfuscates the repetition and continuity of the power inequalities that have historically underpinned the development of international law.[160] On the critical account, every supposed step towards the expansion and consolidation of the 'international legal community' has been supplemented by 'a gesture of exclusion' of certain peoples and classes.[161]

The issue with the 'maturation' thesis is that it depicts ICL's development as a natural progression towards an idealized objective system of criminal law 'that cannot be located anywhere' in the real world.[162] Even liberal-legalist scholars have warned that no criminal law system is immune to 'illiberal' excess in criminalization.[163] By presenting criminal

[158] Combs, 'Grave Crimes', 124. See also V. Spiga, 'Non-retroactivity of Criminal Law' (2011) 9(1) *Journal of International Criminal Justice* 5, 11–12. D. Robinson, 'A Justification of Command Responsibility' (2017) 28(4) *Criminal Law Forum* 633, 635. B. Van Schaack, 'Legality & International Criminal Law', in S. Sivakumaran, B. Van Schaack, D. Robinson. T. Meron, and B. Roth (eds.) *The Principle of Legality in International Criminal Law* (American Society of International Law, 2009) 103.

[159] For an analysis of the 'progress' discourse in international law see T. Altwicker and O. Diggelmann, 'How Is Progress Constructed in International Legal Scholarship?' (2014) 25(2), *European Journal of International Law* 425.

[160] Mégret, 'Critique of International Human Rights', 12.

[161] N. Berman, 'In the Wake of Empire' (1999) 14(6) *American University of International Law Review* 1521, 1523.

[162] Tallgren, 'Sensibility and Sense', 567.

[163] K. Ambos, 'The Overall Function of International Criminal Law: Striking the Right Balance between the Rechtsgut and the Harm Principles' (2015) 9(1) *Criminal Law and Philosophy* 301, 317. M. Dubber, 'Common Civility: The Culture of Alegality in International Criminal Law' (2011) 24(4) *Leiden Journal of International Law* 923, 925–926. See also J. Stewart,

law in idealized and abstract terms, the 'maturation' thesis thus obfuscates the role of the social context in shaping legal rules and places the latter outside the realm of critical analysis and contestation. The 'maturation' thesis ultimately fails to recognize that there are different interpretations of what legalism means in practice instead of a single, necessary telos of the development of international law. This book aims to provide a pluralist, instead of progressivist, understanding of the changes within international law.

1.4 Between the Two Approaches: An Intersubjective Perspective on ICL

This book seeks to address two gaps in the literature on international criminal justice – one theoretical and one empirical. Both the external critique of ICL and the liberal-legalists accounts have made important insights into the field of international criminal justice. The liberal scholarship suggests that, despite the influence of state politics, ICL exhibits a distinctive form of objective legal reasoning. The external critique of the field has responded by problematizing the notion of legal norms and pointing out that law and politics do not simply interact as distinctive logics of reasoning – rather, power relations *permeate* the process of developing and enforcing the law. However, by focusing on the subjectivity of the law and its potential use by the global elite as a tool to pursue their political goals, the critical scholarship risks simplifying the complex modes of operation of legal norms.[164] Both approaches have a very specific and limited idea of what 'politics' entails – the self-interest of states, or classes in the Marxist critique. The difference is that the liberal-legalist accounts see law and politics as able to be progressively divorced in practice, while critical scholarship perceives law and politics as impossible to separate.

By contrast, this book develops an integrated 'intersubjective' approach that is sensitive to both the distinctiveness of legal reasoning and the role of power in shaping the law. The work of scholars such as Judith Shklar and Otto Kirchheimer, written following the aftermath of the Nuremberg

'The End of 'Modes of Liability' for International Crimes' (2012) 25(1) *Leiden Journal of International Law* 165.

164 P. Rock, 'The Sociology of Deviancy and Conceptions of Moral Order' (1974) 14(2) *British Journal of Criminology* 139, 144. P. Bourdieu, 'The Force of Law: Toward a Sociology of the Juridical Field', translated by R. Terdiman (1978) 38(5) *Hastings Law Journal* 805, 815.

and Tokyo trials, provides important insights in that regard. Those scholars have suggested that the use of legal norms to address social issues does not constitute an antithesis to politics, but rather: 'one form of political action among others'.[165] Trials on mass atrocities are considered political trials, not because they lack legal foundation, but because they demarcate the fields of politically and legally acceptable decisions.[166] Yet, that form of political action, namely the decision to resolve social issues through legal procedure, is considered distinct because it is guided by the norms that are specific to the legal field.[167] Consequently, there is a difference between a legalist political trial guided by the liberal-legalist norm of following the rule of law, and one that is not: specifically, the practice of legal rule-following is said to introduce within the political trial 'an element of irreducible risk for those involved', because of the judges' relative independence to apply legal norms.[168] The uncertain outcome of legalist trials, as opposed to purely political show trials, and the ability of the defendant to present a persuasive counternarrative to the prosecutor's case, are said to bestow on such proceedings normative legitimacy.[169] Hence, it is argued that the legalistic political trial can be persuasively distinguished from 'an action which for propaganda purposes is called a trial but partakes more of the nature of a spectacle with prearranged results'.[170] Those political trials that have been 'unconstrained' by legal norms, such as the Moscow show trials following the Second World War, essentially become a matter of 'just politics'.[171] Hence, from this perspective, legal rules matter in international criminal justice because they demarcate the boundaries of legally permissible decisions and differentiate legalized politics under the form of trials guided by the concept of individual criminal responsibility from other types of political responses to mass atrocities.

More specifically, this book aims to analyse the assessment of individual criminal responsibility at the ICC from the perspective of what I would call 'intersubjective legalism'. Intersubjective legalism differs from the

[165] Shklar, *Legalism*, 143. See also O. Kirchheimer, *Political Justice: The Use of Legal Procedure for Political Ends* (Princeton: Princeton University Press, 2015[1961]) 6.

[166] G. Simpson, *Law, War and Crime: War Crime Trials and the Reinvention of International Law* (Cambridge: Polity Press, 2007), 11.

[167] Abbott and Snidal, 'Law, Legalization and Politics', 35.

[168] Kirchheimer, Political Justice, 339. See also Bass, *Stay the Hand of Vengeance*, 7.

[169] M. Osiel, 'Making Public Memory, Publicly', in C. Hesse and R. Post (eds.) *Human Rights in Political Transitions: Gettysburg to Bosnia* (New York: Zone Books, 1999) 217, 249.

[170] Kirchheimer, Political Justice, 339. See also Bass, *Stay the Hand of Vengeance*, 16.

[171] Simpson, *Law, War and Crime*, 12.

'internal' liberal-legalist view because the former recognizes that legalism is not a purely objective system of rules but merely one among competing 'ideologies'.[172] As such, legalism cannot be understood separately from the social context that (re)produces it. Indeed, to take the superiority of an idealized version of the law for granted, as the 'maturation' thesis does, is problematic from an intersubjective perspective because it creates the flawed perception that all international problems can be resolved through an international court and that no other action is needed.[173] The intersubjective perspective also differs from critical studies because it recognizes law's normativity, even if that normativity is equated with legalism among competing ideologies, rather than *the most* morally worthy ideology. Critical scholars, such as Martti Koskenniemi, consider the practice of rule-following a professional habit of lawyers, deprived of any normative value.[174] But an intersubjective perspective recognizes the inherent normativity of that practice. Although she objects to the attempts to distinguish law as a distinct entity from politics, Shklar nevertheless perceives legal formalism, exemplified in the constant search for rules, as a value-oriented order.[175] Within the legal field, the ability to follow rules impartially is considered a 'virtue' and not just empty formalism.[176] The normativity of the law is, hence, neither purely objective, nor purely subjective – instead, it is based on social recognition and practice.

Consequently, intersubjective legalism provides a perspective on the ICC that is both internal and external – internal, because it aims to understand the perceptions of the actors within the ICL field regarding the meaning of the law and the constraints it imposes upon judicial reasoning; external, because it recognizes the subjectivity of those understandings and the extent to which they reflect and reproduce the dominance of Western-influenced ideas of law and legal process. Chapter 2 builds the intersubjective theoretical framework of this book by, firstly, examining rationalist international relations approaches and normative legal approaches to the study of judicial independence and the interpretation of international law within the realm of power politics. Chapter 2 then builds an intersubjective legalist framework that borrows insights from the 'practice' approach to studying international relations and 'field' studies and presents the

172 Shklar, *Legalism*, 2.
173 Shklar, *Legalism*, 134.
174 Koskenniemi, *From Apology to Utopia*, 67–68.
175 Shklar, *Legalism*, 15–16.
176 Shklar, *Legalism*, 113.

methods for interdisciplinary analysis that will be used in this book. Chapter 3 applies the intersubjective framework specifically to the ICL field by discussing the main set of norms, or 'shared understandings', that bind the ICL field together, and the *internal* debates about the meaning of the laws regulating individual criminal responsibility within the field.

Chapters 4–9 seek to address an empirical gap in the interdisciplinary literature on international criminal justice. Most interdisciplinary ICL studies have focused on the selection of situations for investigation and individual suspects[177] or the judicial decisions that concern the jurisdictional reach of the court, especially with respect to the RS's complementarity provisions.[178] Yet, the analysis of the ICC's judicial pronouncements in relation to individual criminal responsibility laws has been largely confined to internal discussions among legal scholars and practitioners. To address this gap, Chapters 4 to 9 examine the assessment of the guilt or innocence of the accused at international courts and tribunals with reference to the influence of both the politics of state interests that surrounded their establishment and operation and the internal debates about the meaning of the law that were taking place within the ICL legal field at the time. Chapter 4 provides a historical perspective by looking to the IMTs at Nuremberg and Tokyo and the UN tribunals and the arguments that have been forwarded to contest and justify the legal reasoning of the judges at those tribunals. Chapter 5 examines the process of drafting the RS, focusing on the provisions that codify the modes of attribution of criminal responsibility, and Chapter 6 analyses the interpretation of those provisions by the ICC judges. Chapter 7 examines the judicial reasoning behind the application of the relevant provisions in relation to the assessment of the criminal responsibility of the accused in specific cases, by providing an overview of ICC jurisprudence. Chapter 8 presents a detailed analysis of the assessment of criminal responsibility in cases that ended up in acquittals – *Bemba* and *Gbagbo and Blé Goudé*. Chapter 9 embarks upon the same task, but with respect to cases that ended up in convictions – *Ongwen* and *Ntaganda*. The analysis takes into consideration the legal reasoning of the judges, the political context surrounding the proceedings, and the reactions to the judgments by legal scholars, practitioners, and NGOs.

177 S. Vasiliev, 'Between International Criminal Justice and Injustice: Theorising Legitimacy', in N. Hayashi and C. Bailliet (eds.) *The Legitimacy of International Criminal Tribunals* (Cambridge: Cambridge University Press, 2017) 66, 68.

178 Nouwen, *Complementarity in the Line of Fire*. Schabas, 'Complementarity in Practice'.

2

The International Legal Field

A Practice-Based Perspective

This chapter positions my argument within the interdisciplinary literature on international law and develops the book's theoretical framework and the concept of intersubjective legalism, borrowing insights from 'practice' studies. The research framework builds upon the work of Kratochwil, Brunnée and Toope, and Johnstone, situating the meaning of legal rules within the 'community of practice' of international law, which enforces a set of shared understandings about what constitutes sound *legal* reasoning.[1] Next, this chapter integrates insights from CLS and sociological studies of the juridical field to elucidate the power inequalities shaping interactions within the community of legal practice. The centrality of expert knowledge as a source of power inside the juridical field suggests a reordering of the traditional perception of international politics as, within the community of international legal practice, states lose their central position and actors such as judges, legal scholars, and NGOs gain leverage. Furthermore, this framework enables the investigation of the politics peculiar to the legal field – an internal politics that takes the form of competition over the authority to determine the meaning of the law and involves a variety of forms of action. Finally, this chapter discusses the methods of analysis.

2.1 International Law and Politics: A Rationalist Approach

Much of the interdisciplinary international relations and international law research from the 1990s to the early 2000s adopted a rationalist

[1] J. Brunnée and S. Toope, 'Interactional International Law and the Practice of Legality', in E. Adler and V. Pouliot (eds.) *International Practices* (Cambridge: Cambridge University Press, 2011) 108. F. Kratochwil, *Rules, Norms, and Decisions: On the Conditions of Practical and Legal Reasoning in International Relations and Domestic Affairs* (Cambridge: Cambridge University Press, 1989). I. Johnstone, *The Power of Deliberation: International Law, Politics and Organizations* (New York: Oxford University Press, 2011).

perspective.[2] Examples include the work of Kenneth Abbott,[3] Anne-Marie Slaughter Burley,[4] and the special *International Organization* volume on 'Legalization and World Politics', which famously defined the legalization of international affairs in relation to three procedural dimensions, namely the degrees of 'obligation' and 'precision' of international legal regimes and the level of 'delegated' authority by states to international courts.[5] Those rationalist studies recognize the distinctiveness of the logic of law from the logic of politics and even suggest that legal rules can influence international relations,[6] but nevertheless usually perceive international adjudication as deeply embedded in state politics.[7] The relationship between law and state politics is presented as reciprocal, mediated by international *institutions*.[8] By shaping a court's mandate and choosing whether or not to comply with judicial decisions, states can exert influence on international law.[9] But, in turn, judicial institutions can induce states into compliance with international law by providing certain benefits such as information and reputational benefits to compliant states.[10]

While rationalist accounts provide different answers to the question of the relative balance of forces – that is, the ability of states to pressure international courts or the latter's ability to secure their autonomy from political interests – as observed by Pollack, most rationalist studies support some version of the argument that international courts operate under a mode of 'constrained

2 For an analysis of the literature see J. Dunoff and M. Pollack, 'International Law and International Relations: Introducing an Interdisciplinary Dialogue', in J. Dunoff and M. Pollack (eds.) *Interdisciplinary Perspectives on International Law and International Relations: The State of the Art* (Cambridge: Cambridge University Press, 2013) 3, 8–9.

3 K. Abbott, 'Modern International Relations Theory: A Prospectus for International Lawyers' (1989) 14 (2) *The Yale Journal of International Law* 335–411.

4 A. M. Slaughter Burley, 'International Law and International Relations Theory: A Dual Agenda' (1993) 87(2) *The American Journal of International Law* 205.

5 K. Abbott, R. Keohane, A. Moravcsik, A. M. Slaughter, and D. Snidal, 'The Concept of Legalization' (2000) 54(3) *International Organization* 401, 401–402.

6 Slaughter Burley, 'International Law', 221.

7 J. Goldstein, Kahler, M., Keohane R., and A. M. Slaughter, 'Introduction: Legalization and World Politics' (2000) 54(3) *International Organization* 385, 387. Abbott et al., 'Concept of Legalization', 404.

8 R. Keohane, 'International Relations and International Law: Two Optics' (1997) 38(2) *Harvard International Law Journal* 502, 499–501.

9 L. Helfer and A. Slaughter, 'Why States Create International Tribunals: A Response to Professors Posner and Yoo' (2005) 93 *California Law Review* 899, 949–953.

10 Keohane, 'International Relations and International Law', 500. A. Guzman, *How International Law Works: A Rational Choice Theory* (New York: Oxford University Press, 2008).

independence'.[11] A subset of rationalist scholars, pertaining to the realist tradition of international relations, diverge from this common argument and have dismissed the existence of international law as independent from the realm of power politics. International law is seen as epiphenomenal, a reflection of the interests of great powers without any independent force of its own.[12] Building upon the realist premise of the dominance of state power within international relations, 'economic' approaches to international law argue that international legal norms could, nevertheless, serve a limited function, to the extent that they help states to obtain the benefits of international cooperation.[13] According to Posner and Yoo, international courts can provide relatively neutral information about the facts and the law when disputes between otherwise cooperating states arise.[14] Notably, on this account, nothing prevents states from ignoring the rulings of international courts if they do not believe that submitting the matter to those courts would be in their interest.[15] Consequently, only those international courts that are completely dependent on state control are considered to be able to survive in the international arena. If international judges interpret the law in a manner that does not conform with states' interests and forward decisions based on 'moral' ideals, those rulings would likely be ignored.[16]

By contrast, those rationalist approaches that have been animated by liberal institutionalism consider that international law serves a more fundamental role in international relations. From this perspective, international courts not only provide information to the disputing parties but also serve as trustees that secure states' credible commitments.[17]

[11] M. Pollack, 'Political Science and International Adjudication', in C. Romano, K. Alter, and Y. Shany (eds) *The Oxford Handbook of International Adjudication*, 1st ed. (Oxford: Oxford University Press, 2013) 373. The term 'constrained independence' was coined by Helfer and Slaughter, 'Why States Create International Tribunals'.

[12] J. J. Mearsheimer, 'The False Promise of International Institutions' (1994) 19 *International Security* 5. H. Morgenthau, *Politics among Nations: The Struggle for Power and Peace* (New York: Knopf, 1948).

[13] E. Posner and A. Sykes, *Economic Foundations of International Law* (Cumberland: Harvard University Press, 2013). E. Posner and J. Yoo, 'A Theory of International Adjudication' (2004) University of Chicago Law & Economics, Olin Working Paper No. 206; UC Berkeley Public Law Research Paper No. 146, https://ssrn.com/abstract=507003.

[14] Posner and Yoo, 'Theory of International Adjudication', 12.

[15] Ibid., 10.

[16] Ibid., 5.

[17] K. Alter, 'Agents or Trustees? International Courts in Their Political Context' (2008) 14 *European Journal of International Relations* 33. G. Majone, 'Two Logics of Delegation: Agency and Fiduciary Relations in EU Governance' (2001) 2 *European Union Politics* 103, 105–107. See also Helfer and Slaughter, 'Why States Create International Tribunals', 904.

According to Guzman, if a state wants to reap the gains of future cooperation with other states, then compliance with international law is in their interests because it enables that state to build a good reputation of a reliable partner.[18] Notably, preserving the law's autonomy from state interests is deemed necessary if international courts are to fulfil their function as trustees.[19] Judicial independence is said to contribute to the image of international courts as trustworthy institutions that oversee states' compliance with international law.[20]

But even if international judges manage to obtain some independence from state interference in their decision-making as liberal institutionalists suggest, this factor in itself is insufficient to protect the integrity of legal decisions. As Voeten puts it, an independent judge is 'not by a definition a good judge'.[21] Judicial independence has thus long been recognized to be separate from judicial impartiality:[22] the former concerns the set of institutional and other factors ensuring that judges make decisions free from external influence, while the latter constitutes 'the lack of interest or bias' in relation to the parties of the case.[23] Consequently, according to liberal institutionalists, the practice of legal reasoning needs to be autonomous not only from state power but also from the idiosyncratic personal ideologies of individual judges.

Several interdisciplinary studies, evoking the concept of 'constrained independence', have provided insights into the mechanisms for protecting judicial impartiality at the international arena. Those studies suggest that the integrity of international law requires courts to balance the competing claims made by a variety of international actors over the correct interpretation of the law.[24] Alter and Helfer have observed that the 'substate and

[18] Guzman, How International Law Works, 33. See also Helfer and Slaughter, 'Why States Create International Tribunals', 904. S. Voigt, 'The Independence of International Courts – Making Reputation Work?' (2017) 24 *Maastricht Journal of European and Comparative Law* 511, 512.

[19] R. Grant and R. Keohane, 'Accountability and Abuses of Power in World Politics' (2005) 99 *American Political Science Review* 29, 32.

[20] Voigt, 'Independence of International Courts', 512.

[21] E. Voeten, 'International Judicial Independence', in J. Dunoff and M. Pollack (eds.) *Interdisciplinary Perspectives on International Law and International Relations: The State of the Art* (Cambridge: Cambridge University Press, 2013) 421, 424.

[22] D. Guilfoyle, 'Lacking Conviction: Is the International Criminal Court Broken? An Organisational Failure Analysis' (2019) 20(2) *Melbourne Journal of International Law* 1–52.

[23] A. Pérez, 'From Judicial Independence to Interdependence in the International Sphere' (2017) 24 *Maastricht Journal of European and Comparative Law* 462, 467.

[24] Helfer and Slaughter, 'Why States Create International Tribunals'. See also R. Steinberg, 'Judicial Lawmaking at the WTO: Discursive, Constitutional, and Political Constraints'

societal interlocutors' of international courts, such as domestic judiciaries, advocacy networks, and the general public play an important role in safeguarding the legality of judicial decisions from political and idiosyncratic influences.[25] Firstly, those 'interlocutors' can empower international courts to render legally independent decisions by creating social pressure on states to comply with the decisions of international courts.[26] Consequently, international courts are considered to lose their power not when their judgments oppose existing governmental policies, but when they fail to obtain the support of legal experts and civil society – the actors that can pressure governments into compliance.[27] Secondly, non-state actors, and in particular the epistemic community of international lawyers, are said to protect the integrity of international adjudication from the personal biases of individual judges.[28] The 'peer pressure and professional norms emanating from an increasingly global community' of legal institutions induces international courts to follow the rule of law in their decisions.[29] In other words, non-state actors protect the integrity of the law from the political preferences of both states and individual judges.

Nevertheless, the 'constrained independence' literature recognizes that states retain a key role in international law. States can constrain courts not only by renegotiating the court's mandate or withdrawing from its jurisdiction but also by questioning the court's reasoning, delegitimizing its authority, and even 'starving' the court by reducing its diet of cases.[30] Hence, from this perspective, two types of 'constraints' simultaneously influence the interpretation and application of international law – those imposed by self-interested states and those imposed by non-state actors that support the rule of law. Consequently, Helfer and Slaughter make a

(2004) 98(2) *American Journal of International Law* 247, 249. T. Ginsburg, 'Political Constraints on International Courts', in C. Romano, K. Alter, and Y. Shany (eds) *The Oxford Handbook of International Adjudication*, 1st ed. (Oxford: Oxford University Press, 2013) 484. P. Mahoney, 'The International Judiciary – Independence and Accountability' (2008) 7(3) *Law & Practice of International Courts and Tribunals* 313, 320. Pérez, 'From Judicial Independence', 471–472.

25 K. Alter and L. Helfer, 'Nature or Nurture? Judicial Lawmaking in the European Court of Justice and the Andean Tribunal of Justice' (2010) 64 *International Organization* 563, 565.

26 K. Alter, *The New Terrain of International Law: Courts, Politics, Rights* (Princeton and Oxford: Princeton University Press, 2014) 20.

27 Ibid., 24.

28 Helfer and Slaughter, 'Why States Create International Tribunals', 953.

29 Ibid., 905. See also Voeten, 'International Judicial Independence', 427. Pérez, 'From Judicial Independence', 469.

30 Helfer and Slaughter, 'Why States Create International Tribunals', 949–952. See also Steinberg, 'Judicial Lawmaking', 263–267.

convincing argument that the 'strategic space' within which international courts operate ensures that international judges produce decisions that are both 'politically tolerable' *and* 'legally plausible'.[31]

The rationalist scholarship, and especially the theory of 'constrained independence', provides important insights into the interaction between politics and law, which this book seeks to develop by addressing the gaps in the rationalist framework. Specifically, 'constrained independence' studies, which focus on the instrumental significance of international law, have failed to account for the internal logic of international law and what distinguishes legal norms from other international norms. Goldsmith and Posner hold that states' occasional compliance with international law stems not from any 'sense of legal obligation' but merely 'results from states pursuing their interests'.[32] Similarly, Guzman notes that states do not inherently seek to obtain reputational benefits as law abiding, but they do so only when the perceived future gains from international cooperation outweigh the costs of complying with international law.[33] This rationalist approach precludes further inquiries into the qualities of international legal norms because the latter are perceived merely as coordination devices enabling states to fulfil their interests in a world of imperfect information.[34] Indeed, even those studies that, inspired by liberal institutionalist theories, challenge the dominant state-centric analyses of international law perceive law in instrumentalist terms. The crucial difference is that, from the perspective of the latter, international law '*empowers*' a broader set of actors by giving them 'symbolic, legal, and political resources' to voice their claims, whereas the former branch of studies focuses mainly on the instrumental value of international law for states.[35]

Helfer and Slaughter's account provides some insights as to how the legal integrity of international adjudication could be preserved, but the authors do not examine in detail the process through which the 'peer pressure' of the epistemic community of international lawyers ensures such outcomes. Indeed, the authors acknowledge that '[m]any' of the possible interpretations of the law would be legally convincing and, consequently, acceptable to the epistemic community of international lawyers.[36] It is

[31] Helfer and Slaughter, 'Why States Create International Tribunals', 942–943.
[32] J. Goldsmith and E. Posner, *The Limits of International Law* (Cary: Oxford University Press, 2006) 39.
[33] Guzman, 'How International Law Works', 35.
[34] Keohane, 'International Relations and International Law', 488–489.
[35] Alter, *New Terrain*, 19, emphasis added.
[36] Helfer and Slaughter, 'Why States Create International Tribunals', 942.

suggested that '[l]aw matters' but also that '*within the constraints of law*, flexibility exists' with regard to the remedies that the court orders.[37] The observation that the pressure from the international legal epistemic community ensures that judgments are delivered in a legally convincing manner and are not reducible to state interests itself provides little insights into the nature of the legal arguments that would be produced. The flexibility of the law suggests that international judges could render decisions as varied as deferring to state sovereignty or, conversely, entering novel interpretations of the law that impose stricter restrictions on states, where types of remedy may be considered legally convincing.[38] But if law is so flexible, it becomes susceptible to the critique that there is in fact nothing to distinguish international law from international politics apart from the professionalization of the juridical field – the fact that only lawyers have the authority to determine whether a solution is congruent with the law.[39] This descriptive view on legalism also precludes further inquiries into the normative dynamics taking place *within* the international legal field.

Dunoff and Pollack attribute the failure of rationalist studies to examine the internal logic of international law to the unequal 'terms of trade' between the international relations and international law disciplines. They observe that international relations theory has provided much of the theoretical and methodological content of the studies on international courts, while the role of international law studies has been limited to providing deep knowledge about legal doctrine, process, and institutional design.[40] This has resulted in presenting law as 'a set of rules used to alter behaviour by modifying the costs and benefits associated with different actions'.[41] By reducing international law to a sanctioning mechanism, these rationalist studies have failed to differentiate international legal norms from other forms of political and social control, thus denying law's normative distinctiveness.

This book aims to contribute to the 'constrained independence' literature by arguing that international law constitutes more than just state politics advanced through a seemingly apolitical mechanism, exploring instead the norms and practices, which differentiate legal reasoning from

[37] Alter, *New Terrain*, 60, emphasis added.

[38] J. Wessel, 'Judicial Policy-Making at the International Criminal Court: An Institutional Guide to Analyzing International Adjudication' (2006) 44(1) *Columbia Journal of Transnational Law* 377, 420–421. Steinberg, 'Judicial Lawmaking', 258.

[39] Koskenniemi, *From Apology to Utopia*, 56.

[40] Dunoff and Pollack, 'International Law and International Relations', 4.

[41] Ibid., 18.

cultural, economic, or religious norms. Specifically, following Kratochwil, this book approaches the constrained independence of international judges as an arena for 'rule-guided' decisions and not as 'merely instrumentally rational actions'.[42] Section 2.2 turns to the normative legal scholarship on international law in order to show that states may also comply with legal rules out of a principled belief in the legitimacy of those rules.

2.2 International Law and Politics: A Normative Approach

Unlike rationalist approaches, normative studies[43] suggest that there is more to law than its coercive power or the ability to appeal to the self-interest of international actors.[44] Chayes and Chayes identify a central problem inherent to relying on a purely rationalist logic: in international law, sanctioning authority is 'rarely granted by treaty, rarely used when granted, and likely to be ineffective when used'.[45] Normative studies have proposed that international law is not epiphenomenal but rather possesses specific qualities that generate 'perceived obligation' to comply with international rules, despite the lack of traditional enforcement or sanctioning mechanisms at the international arena.[46] The distinctiveness of international law is considered to hide in its ability to generate a duty to comply that goes 'beyond the fear of penalties' for violations.[47] Because legal norms are perceived as 'prescriptions' for appropriate conduct, rather than as an enforcement mechanism with causal power, on this account examples of states' non-compliance with a legal rule do not invalidate the existence of that legal rule.[48] The factors that (in)validate a legal norm are instead rooted in the *internal* characteristics of that norm.

Thomas Franck's influential work has identified four distinctive traits that legitimize international legal norms: the 'determinacy' of the content of the norm in terms of either its textual clarity ('substantive determinacy') or a 'legitimate clarifying process' (procedural determinacy);[49] the

[42] Kratochwil, *Rules, Norms, and Decisions*, 18.

[43] The term refers also to 'constructivist' studies. See Dunoff and Pollack, 'International Law and International Relations'.

[44] T. M. Franck, *Power of Legitimacy among Nations* (Cary: Oxford University Press, 1990) 20–21.

[45] A. Chayes and A. Chayes, *The New Sovereignty: Compliance with International Regulatory Agreements* (Cambridge: Harvard University Press, 1995) 32–33.

[46] Franck, *Power of Legitimacy*, 40–41.

[47] Chayes and Chayes, *New Sovereignty*, 116.

[48] Ibid., 113–114.

[49] Franck, *Power of Legitimacy*, 66–67, emphasis omitted.

symbolic validation of legal rules, referring to law's ability to communicate its authority through 'cues', such as specific rituals, or with reference to the rule's pedigree;[50] the coherence of legal rules – constructing rules that are generally applicable, as opposed to '[i]diosyncratic' and 'aberrational';[51] and the 'adherence' to legal rules, understood as the vertical nexus between a 'primary rule of obligation' and a hierarchy of secondary rules that regulate the application of the primary rule.[52] These internal qualities are considered to generate international law's 'compliance pull' upon states without resorting to sanctioning mechanisms of self-interested gratification.[53] For Franck, though, the determinacy, symbolic validation, coherence, and adherence of international law cannot be determined in the abstract. Rather, the international 'community', understood generally as a 'community of nations',[54] is said to validate these qualities of the law and, consequently, the overall legitimacy of international legal norms.[55]

Franck significantly advances the discussion of the distinctive qualities of international legal norms, but his account has been criticized for displaying a 'positivists' focus on state recognition as a requisite for maintaining the legitimacy of international law.[56] In effect, as Keohane observes, Franck's argument resembles circular reasoning. On the one hand, the legitimacy of legal rules, rather than any sanctioning mechanism, is said to trigger state compliance. But on the other hand, state recognition is requisite for establishing that legitimacy.[57]

The challenges of situating the inherent normativity of international law have been famously identified by Koskenniemi: if international law is justified merely as a reflection of state practice, the law risks being transformed into a mere 'apology' for politics. Yet, if international law is understood as a set of abstract normative standards, akin to natural law, that commands states, it turns into a speculative 'utopia'.[58] Koskenniemi's verdict is that nothing can simultaneously distinguish international law

[50] Ibid., 92.

[51] Ibid., 152.

[52] Ibid., 184, emphasis omitted.

[53] Ibid., 26, 193.

[54] Ibid., 181.

[55] Franck, *Power of Legitimacy*, 51–52. See also T. M. Franck, *Fairness in International Law and Institutions* (Oxford: Oxford University Press, 1998) 10.

[56] J. Brunnée and S. Toope, 'Constructivism and International Law' in J. Dunoff and M. Pollack (eds.) *Interdisciplinary Perspectives on International Law and International Relations: The State of the Art* (Cambridge: Cambridge University Press, 2013) 120, 131.

[57] Keohane, 'International Relations and International Law', 493.

[58] Koskenniemi, *From Apology to Utopia*, 17–18.

from politics and from idiosyncratic visions of morality.[59] In this view, there is nothing inherently distinctive about the characteristics that, according to Frack, generate compliance with international law – the qualities of determinacy, symbolic validation, coherence, and adherence could also be observed in relation to other social norms in international relations.[60]

While Koskenniemi's critical reflections highlight the problems with normative accounts of international law, this book argues that reducing international law to either 'apology' or 'utopia' is not the only possible outcome. Building on the work of Kratochwil, Section 2.3 argues that international law could be distinguished from other social control mechanisms by examining it not as a combination of static characteristics, but as an intersubjective 'practice' – a specific mode of reasoning assessed by an epistemic community. Section 2.3 integrates propositions by the studies of international law as a specific form of 'practice' in international relations[61] and in field studies, borrowing from Bourdieu's work on the 'juridical field'.[62] This approach enables both an 'internal' perspective on the field of legal practice and an 'external' view on the power relations that shape that field.

2.3 The 'Practice' of International Law

2.3.1 The Distinctiveness of Legal Reasoning

A group of interdisciplinary studies have examined law as a dynamic phenomenon that is generated and maintained 'through continuing struggles of social practice'.[63] Practices comprise 'socially meaningful patterns of action'[64] that are (re)produced by epistemic communities, or communities of practice, centred around a specific knowledge domain that 'endows practitioners with a sense of joint enterprise'.[65] Kratochwil argues that the

[59] Ibid., 23.

[60] Finnemore, 'Are legal norms distinctive?', 703.

[61] E. Adler and V. Pouliot, 'International Practices: Introduction and Framework', in E. Adler and V. Pouliot (eds.) *International Practices* (Cambridge: Cambridge University Press, 2011) 3.

[62] Bourdieu, 'Force of Law'.

[63] J. Brunnée and S. Toope, *Legitimacy and Legality in International Law: An Interactional Account* (Cambridge: Cambridge University Press, 2010) 22. See also Brunnée and Toope, 'Constructivism and International Law', 135–136. Kratochwil, *Rules, Norms, and Decisions*. Johnstone, *Power of Deliberation*.

[64] Adler and Pouliot, 'International Practices', 6.

[65] Ibid., 17.

practice of law constitutes the application of legal rules to a given controversy and the process of appraising the reasons given for that decision before a particular community. Consequently, law is understood as a form of *principled reasoning*, distinct from politics or morality.[66] Kratochwil rejects the proposition that the logical consistency of legal reasoning requires all legal experts to converge on one 'correct' interpretation of a legal rule. To recognize that a plurality of possible legal interpretations exists is not to say 'that anything goes and/or because there is no single right answer, any answer is as good as another'.[67] From this perspective, the uniqueness of the legal practice is not the existence of one objective answer or solution but the specificity of the legal reasoning behind *an* answer or *a* solution. Consequently, from the practice perspective of law, the indeterminacy of the legal outcome neither invalidates the distinctiveness of legal reasoning nor reduces law to state politics under a different name.

The distinctiveness of legal reasoning is safeguarded by the communities of practice, which are said to ensure 'competent performances' of the practice of law and to protect legal reasoning from idiosyncratic interpretations of the legal text.[68] Brunnée and Toope suggest that the competent practice of law is assessed against the background of 'shared understandings' held by the participants of the community of legal practice regarding the meaning and application of the law.[69] Whenever an individual member of that community breaches a norm, it triggers criticism by the rest of the members.[70] In effect, as observed by Johnstone, legal norms should be understood neither as objective rules codified in a legal text nor as the subjective reflection of state interests or judicial biases; instead, legal norms constitute intersubjective standards, the meaning of which resides within the argumentative process taking place in the community of practice.[71]

[66] Kratochwil, *Rules, Norms, and Decisions*, 18. See also R. Higgins, *Problems and Process: International Law and How We Use It* (Oxford: Clarendon Press, 1995), 2–3. A. Von Bogdandy and J. Habermas, 'Discourse Theory and International Law: An Interview with Jürgen Habermas', *Verfassungsblog*, 12 May 2013, https://verfassungsblog.de/discourse-theory-and-international-law-an-interview-with-jurgen-habermas/.

[67] F. Kratochwil, 'How Do Norms Matter?' in Byers, M. (ed.) *The Role of Law in International Politics* (Oxford: Oxford University Press, 2001) 35, 46.

[68] Brunnée and Toope, 'Interactional International Law', 108. Kratochwil, 'How Do Norms Matter', 51–52. J. Habermas, *Between Facts and Norms: Contributions to a Discourse Theory of Law and Democracy* (Cambridge: Polity Press, 1996) 224.

[69] Brunnée and Toope, *Legitimacy and Legality*, 24.

[70] S. Lechner and M. Frost, *Practice Theory and International Relations* (Cambridge: Cambridge University Press, 2018) 14.

[71] Johnstone, *Power of Deliberation*, 35.

The practice perspective, hence, provides a bridge between the role of agency and structure in the study of international law.

Koskenniemi's concern about Kratochwil's approach, which allows for relative indeterminacy and room for contestation in judicial pronouncements, is that 'there is no consensus on the extent of permissible discretion'.[72] From this perspective, Kratochwil's approach merely displaces the problem of the lack of objectivity in international law: The question now becomes 'how to count for the objectivity of the second-order solution', i.e. how to set up an objective limit to judicial discretion.[73] Koskenniemi's point is valid to the extent that the practice perspective of law cannot be used to prove the absolute objectivity of a legal rule or a judicial pronouncement. But this is also not the goal of the practice perspective framework.

To perceive legal practice as intersubjective is not to suggest that the subjectivity of judicial interpretations is constrained by the objectivity of shared understandings about the meaning of the law. Rather, the very notion of shared understandings is intersubjective because those understandings constitute 'standards of competence that are socially recognized'.[74] This bears important implications for the study of international law because it reveals the dynamic nature of shared understandings as vehicles for both continuity and change. The content of the shared understandings is constantly being 'renegotiated' by the members of the epistemic community.[75] While the results of their efforts remain bound by the broader normative environment of pre-existing shared understandings, individuals or groups with common vision could work to promote specific interpretations of the law.[76] Consequently, the structural constraints on international legal reasoning are simultaneously objective, in the sense that they shape legal reasoning in a particular point in space in time, and subjective, since they are themselves the product of the dominant social consensus at that place and time. The 'duality' of structure, i.e. its quality to constantly (re)produce itself through continuous practices, simultaneously constraining and enabling agents' actions, has for long been examined in the humanities and social sciences.[77] The implication

[72] Koskenniemi, *From Apology to Utopia*, 35.

[73] Ibid., 57.

[74] See Adler and Pouliot, 'International Practices', 15.

[75] Adler and Pouliot, 'International Practices', 17.

[76] Brunnée and Toope, 'Interactional International Law', 111. Bourdieu, 'Force of Law', 839.

[77] See, e.g., Anthony Gidden's 'structuration theory'. A. Giddens, *The Constitution of Society: Outline of the Theory of Structuration* (Cambridge: Polity Press, 1984) 25–27.

of that 'duality' is that any changes in social perceptions are not random, but 'orderly and, to some extent, predictable', because those changes constitute revisions of pre-existing shared understandings, rather than completely novel phenomena.[78]

One important caveat should be mentioned here: while practice studies of international law can be used to make normative judgments about the desirability or appropriateness of particular legal interpretations and solutions, this is not the purpose of this book. The philosophical underpinnings of the 'practice'-oriented legal scholarship are reminiscent of Habermas's well-known theory of law as an 'argumentative process'.[79] According to Habermas, the individual validity claims in relation to the meaning of the law are subjected to an 'ongoing critique' by the participants in the legal discourse. Hence, 'the cooperative search for *truth*' is considered to render legally convincing decisions.[80] This line of reasoning creates the perception that the practice through which law is enacted makes it not only distinctive from other forms of social control, but also normatively legitimate – able to produce desirable outcomes. Brunnée and Toope's 'interactional theory' of international law, which borrows from Lon Fuller's influential theory of the 'internal morality' of law, could similarly be used to make normative arguments.[81] Brunnée and Toope distinguish between the 'social legitimacy' of legal rules and their 'legal legitimacy'. While the former (people's perception of legal rules as legitimate) is a component of the latter, for a legal rule to obtain 'legal legitimacy' it needs to be 'created and maintained' through interaction.[82] The distinction between social and legal legitimacy can be taken to suggest that the practice of legality, sustained through continuous interaction within society, *adds value* to legal rules.

This book does not make normative statements about the practice of international law. The intersubjective legalism framework of this book concurs with the proposition made by critical legal scholars that to claim that certain understandings about the meaning of the law are socially shared is not to suggest that those understandings are also 'just or fair'.[83] Habermas's argumentative reasoning theory implies the existence of a

[78] S. Fish, *Is There a Text in This Class?: The Authority of Interpretive Communities.* (Cambridge, Mass.: Harvard University Press, 1980) 349.

[79] Habermas, *Between Facts and Norms*, 227, emphasis omitted.

[80] Ibid., 226–227, emphasis added.

[81] L. Fuller, *The Morality of Law*, Revised ed. (Delhi: Universal Law Publishing, 2004 [1963]) 39.

[82] Brunnée and Toope, *Legitimacy and Legality*, 54.

[83] Sinclair, *International Relations Theory*, 32.

consensual society of equally situated interlocutors, but in reality, some actors within the community of legal practice might possess stronger influence over the discourse than others.[84] Social practice can easily reproduce various forms of discrimination.[85] The existence of society-wide prejudices and inequalities suggests that social injustice is often rooted not in the poor quality of the law but within society itself.[86] For instance, feminist studies have deeply problematized the argumentative rationality model by pointing out the unequal 'dialogical capacities' of men and women in relation to the formation of 'public opinion'.[87] Similarly, as Brunnée and Toope acknowledge, some actors have been 'disproportionately influential' in shaping international legal regimes.[88]

Consequently, whether the argumentative rationality of legal practice produces a distinctive normative order and whether that normative order is 'good' or 'just' are two separate questions. If legal rules reflect the power inequalities between states or social classes, as argued by CLS and Marxist legal scholars such as Miéville,[89] one may well argue that those rules are 'unjust', but that does not make international law less 'legal' or less distinctive. Nevertheless, it is worth emphasizing that, while this book separates the *distinctiveness* of legal reasoning from the *normative value* of legal reasoning, this need not be (and most of the time it is not) the perspective of the actors participating in the international legal community of practice. Many participants in the international legal field consider that the distinctiveness of legal reasoning from state politics vests the law with normative legitimacy, and not merely with social legitimacy. As observed by Shklar, inside the legal field, the ability to follow the rules of legal reasoning is considered a 'virtue',[90] in other words it is normatively assessed as something good and desirable. Consequently, the debates that this book explores involve normative arguments – judges, lawyers, and academics arguing whether an interpretation of a legal rule was the 'correct' one, or whether a trial outcome was the 'just' one. But this book approaches those debates from

[84] M. Zehfuss, *Constructivism in International Relations: The Politics of Reality* (Cambridge: Cambridge University Press, 2002) 148.

[85] Brunnée and Toope, 'Interactional International Law', 112.

[86] Sinclair, *International Relations Theory*, 174.

[87] N. Fraser, 'What's Critical about Critical Theory? The Case of Habermas and Gender' (1985) 35(1) *New German Critique* 97, 116. See also J. Cohen, 'Critical Social Theory and Feminist Critiques', in J. Meehan (ed.) *Feminists Read Habermas* (London: Taylor and Francis, 2013).

[88] Brunnée and Toope, 'Interactional International Law', 119.

[89] Chapter 1, Section 1.2.2.

[90] Shklar, *Legalism*, 113.

an external perspective. It explores the distinctiveness of legal reasoning in ICL and the different forms it takes without evaluating the rightness (or wrongness) of specific lines of legal reasoning.

2.3.2 *The Internal Politics of the International Legal Field*

Accepting legal rules as socially embedded and rejecting the idea of purely objective legal reasoning means that the practice of law is, as observed by Shklar and Kirchheimer, inherently political. However, the form of politics that enters the international legal field is 'constrained and shaped' by the mode of reasoning governing that field.[91] Johnstone notes that, because the evolution of shared understandings takes time, even the most powerful actors cannot directly replace a legal regime with a new one in accordance with their preferences.[92] Thus, the practice framework, focusing on reasoning, interaction, and social validation, is a particularly apt approach for exploring Kirchheimer's distinction between legal proceedings and mere propaganda, based on the former's 'element of irreducible risk' resulting from the judges' relative autonomy to evaluate the facts and deliver a verdict.[93] It elucidates the politics that animate legal decision-making – ideologies, beliefs about morality, the ordering of society, and the rule of law within it – as well as the distinctiveness of that form of politics from interstate politics.

The international legal field is home to a unique type of politics – Bourdieu's 'competition for monopoly of the right to determine the law'.[94] Consequently, *expert* knowledge, or 'knowledge of the rules' of practice,[95] becomes a crucial source of power within the legal field because it vests with authority those members of the epistemic community that are able to claim it.[96] Even though the practice framework of international law requires that all interpretations of legal rules demonstrate certain congruence with the pre-existing normative environment, the more authoritative the opinion of an actor within the epistemic community is, the more powerful influence that actor can project during the continuous process of renegotiating the rules and boundaries of what can be legitimately argued.

91 Abbott and Snidal, 'Law, Legalization and Politics', 35.
92 Johnstone, *Power of Deliberation*, 52.
93 Kirchheimer, *Political Justice*, 339.
94 Bourdieu, 'Force of Law', 817.
95 Fish, *Is There a Text*, 343.
96 Bourdieu, 'Force of Law', 816.

2.3.2.1 Types of Actors

International courts, as the bureaucratic embodiment of legal expertise, are likely to be particularly influential members of the legal community of practice. Barnett and Finnemore's work reveals that the bureaucratic nature of international organizations bestows upon them the image of depoliticized, impartial, and technocratic actors, which boosts their 'rational-legal' and 'expert' authority as providers of specialized knowledge.[97] As observed by Kirchheimer, modern society has been marked by 'the omnipresence of the professional, the learned judge, who brings special education and experience to his job'.[98] In effect, international organizations derive the power to construct social reality by 'naming' what constitutes a problem in global politics and establishing the boundaries of acceptable action in addressing those issues.[99] The expert authority of international courts is further enhanced by the increasing specialization of the legal field into separate regimes of knowledge, such as 'trade law', 'international criminal law', or 'human rights law'.[100]

Even though courts are generally considered to assist in the interpretation of the law, rather than create new law, scholarly analysis has challenged this view.[101] Judicial decisions are binding only to the parties to a given case, but their reasoning is often later evoked in other cases. Judicial practice can lead to the adoption of 'soft law' norms – nonbinding rules that are habitually obeyed and that eventually 'harden' into formal law, in a process Johnstone called 'law-making through the back door'.[102] Another avenue for judges to develop the law is by enacting secondary legal norms that regulate the relationship between the primary legal norms when primary norms rise together as competing approaches to a particular factual situation.[103] Moreover, because of the expert knowledge required for

[97] M. Barnett and M. Finnemore, *Rules for the World: International Organizations in Global Politics* (Cornell University Press, 2004) 20–24.

[98] Kirchheimer, Political Justice, 13.

[99] Ibid., 30–33.

[100] M. Koskenniemi, 'The Politics of International Law – 20 Years Later' (2009) 20(1) *European Journal of International Law* 7, 9.

[101] See A. Boyle and C. Chinkin, *The Making of International Law* (New York: Oxford University Press, 2007), Chapter 6.

[102] I. Johnstone, 'Law-Making by International Organizations: Perspectives from IL/IR Theory', in J. Dunoff and M. Pollack (eds.) *Interdisciplinary Perspectives on International Law and International Relations: The State of the Art* (Cambridge: Cambridge University Press, 2013) 266, 274–276.

[103] V. Lowe, 'The Politics of Law-Making: Are the Method and Character of Norm Creation Changing?', in Byers, M. (ed.) *The Role of Law in International Politics* (Oxford: Oxford University Press, 2001) 207.

developing international law, states may implicitly encourage judicial activism. Data from the European Court of Human Rights revealed that governments may intentionally select more activist judges.[104] While law-making could not be explicitly delegated to international judges, in practice it may constitute a form of 'implied delegation' by states.[105]

Nevertheless, following Brunnée and Toope's observations about legal practice, the interpretations of international judges need to resonate with the shared understandings about the meaning of the law held by the broader legal epistemic community. The community of legal practice extends beyond the 'narrow' circle of court bureaucrats and includes legal scholars and practitioners, international civil society, government officials, and even members of the general public of international trials.[106] As a form of international organization, international courts rely on their external environment not only for material resources – technologies, facilities, staff – but also for symbolic resources, namely obtaining social legitimacy for their decisions.[107] The authority of an international court needs to be both 'asserted' by the court and 'recognized' by its various audiences.[108] Yet, not all of those audiences possess the same power to influence the development of shared understandings about the meaning of the law.

Because of the importance of expertise, legal practitioners and academics enjoy significant authority within the epistemic community, essentially instituting a 'professional monopoly' over the provision of juridical interpretations.[109] Law journals have been argued to 'structure and demarcate' the ICL field by offering venues for presenting and contesting new understandings of legal norms.[110] Schachter famously called this the 'invisible college' of international lawyers – a transnational community of

104 E. Voeten, 'The Politics of International Judicial Appointments: Evidence from the European Court of Human Rights' (2007) 61(4) *International Organization* 669, 669–701.

105 Johnstone, 'Law-Making', 268. See also A. Danner, 'When Courts Make Law: How the International Criminal Tribunals Recast the Laws of War' (2006) 59(1) *Vanderbilt Law Review* 1.

106 Johnstone, *Power of Deliberation*, 41–42.

107 M. Barnett and L. Coleman, 'Designing Police: Interpol and the Study of Change in International Organizations' (2005) 49(4) *International Studies Quarterly* 593, 597–598.

108 See K. Alter, L. Helfer, and M. Madsen, 'International Court Authority in a Complex World', in K. Alter, L. Helfer, and M. Madsen (eds). *International Court Authority* (Oxford: Oxford University Press, 2018) 3, 13.

109 Bourdieu, 'Force of Law', 834–835. See also Kirchheimer, Political Justice, 13.

110 S. Vasiliev, 'On Trajectories and Destinations of International Criminal Law Scholarship' (2015) 28(4) *Leiden Journal of International Law* 701, 703.

legal experts who sustain cooperation through academic publishing and attending conferences.[111] The more technical the question under judicial review, the more authoritative legal experts are likely to be. The perceived professional nature of an enquiry could shield legal experts and practitioners from state interference in their deliberations on the law.[112]

The reputation of trustworthy information providers has similarly elevated the authority of NGOs within the international law field. While NGOs are not delegated any law-making power, commentators have observed that they have often become involved the development of international law in an attenuated manner.[113] NGOs have participated during treaty negotiations and consulted state delegations.[114] Furthermore, NGO members have increasingly staffed international courts.[115] Nevertheless, as with legal experts, the power of NGOs to influence legal norms is not unlimited. Consistent with the 'law as practice' framework, those organizations can frame problems and norms in novel ways but not introduce ones that are utterly disconnected from the pre-existing normative environment.[116]

Precisely the emphasis on expert power, however, has rendered the actors on which international relations theory has traditionally focused – states – in a relatively disadvantaged position in the legal field. The practice framework does not deny the ability of states to exert significant pressure on international courts by constraining their budgets or attempting to influence judicial appointments, discussed by the rationalist international relations literature. As discussed in Chapters 7–9, states can also indirectly affect trial outcomes by offering or refusing to cooperate with the prosecutor to collect evidence. However, these types of state power politics take place *outside* the legal field. By contrast, the political battles taking place

[111] O. Schachter, 'The Invisible College of International Lawyers' (1977–1978) 72(2) *Northwestern University Law Review* 217.

[112] K. Alter, Helfer, L., and M. Madsen, 'How Context Shapes the Authority of International Courts', in K. Alter, L. Helfer, and M. Madsen (eds). *International Court Authority* (Oxford: Oxford University Press, 2018) 24, 44.

[113] Johnstone, 'Law-Making', 269.

[114] Boyle and Chinkin, *Making of International Law*, 64–65. Z. Pearson, 'Non-Governmental Organizations and the International Criminal Court: Changing Landscapes of International Law' (2006) 39(2) *Cornell International Law Journal* 243, 273.

[115] Boyle and Chinkin, *Making of International Law*, 92.

[116] P. Spiro, 'Nongovernmental Organizations in International Relations (Theory)', in J. Dunoff and M. Pollack (eds.) *Interdisciplinary Perspectives on International Law and International Relations: The State of the Art* (Cambridge: Cambridge University Press, 2013) 223, 233.

within the legal field[117] require states to present arguments with reference to the pre-existing shared understandings accepted by the international law community of practice. Consequently, when acting within the legal field, states could exert power by questioning the court's legal reasoning or by trying to delegitimize its expert authority.[118] For example, states can allege that a court exhibits an in-built bias against certain states that affects the judges' legal reasoning.[119] Furthermore, states could exert indirect power, for example, by coopting NGOs or legal experts to advocate for particular understandings of the law.[120] But on this account, state interests do not directly influence legal outcomes because once states enter the legalized political arena, they could no longer claim to be the sole, or indeed, the most authoritative type of actors.[121]

2.3.2.2 Competition of Ideas

The plurality of actors within the international legal field suggests a plurality of ideas in relation to the meaning of the law premised on different visions of justice. Brunnée and Toope have observed that international law communities of practice need not hold 'deep' shared understandings of the right ordering of society. They could coalesce around 'thin' moral commitments, such as 'a basic acceptance of the need for law to shape certain social interactions'.[122] Hence, the minimum set of shared understandings that binds the community of practice by providing a background for assessing 'competent performances' does not necessarily create 'uniformity' of thought on more substantive questions.[123] An overall consensus exists within the legal communities of practice, regardless of their issue area, that some form of a 'general rule' is to be 'applied to an individual instance'. As noted by Shklar, while 'the duty of following rules' is not a

117 Abbott and Snidal, 'Law, Legalization and Politics', 36.

118 Helfer and Slaughter, 'Why States Create International Tribunals', 949–952. K. Alter, 'Delegation to International Courts and the Limits of Re-contracting Political power', in D. Hawkins, D. Lake, D. Nielson, and M. Tierney (eds). *Delegation and Agency in International Organizations* (Cambridge: Cambridge University Press, 2006) 312, 315–316.

119 J. Pauwelyn and M. Elsig, 'The Politics of Treaty Interpretation: Variations and Explanations across International Tribunals', in J. Dunoff and M. Pollack (eds.) *Interdisciplinary Perspectives on International Law and International Relations: The State of the Art* (Cambridge: Cambridge University Press, 2013) 445, 467.

120 Spiro, 'Nongovernmental Organizations', 229. Zolo, *Victor's Justice*, xii.

121 Alter, 'Delegation to International Courts', 337.

122 Brunnée and Toope, 'Interactional International Law', 113. Brunnée and Toope, *Legitimacy and Legality*, 32–33.

123 Adler and Pouliot, 'International Practices', 16.

source of disagreement, 'the *content* of the rules' is.[124] At the most general level, opinions could diverge whether to prioritize 'procedural' justice in the form of fair process or 'substantive' justice in the form of fair outcome.[125] In international law the differences of opinion are likely to be exacerbated by the variety of domestic legal backgrounds of the participants in the community of practice. Consequently, the 'law as practice' approach provides a particularly useful tool for understanding the interplay between different visions of justice in international law.

The divergence in the sets of shared understandings on substantial issues among subgroups of the legal epistemic community bears implications for the authority that international courts could claim in determining the law. On the one hand, international courts could hardly ever achieve legitimacy in relation to all the actors in their environment.[126] If an international court's legal determinations resonate particularly strongly with the understandings of one subgroup, they will probably be contested by other subgroups. On the other hand, the existence of multiple audiences with different expectations makes it hard to determine certain behaviour exhibited by international organizations as 'bad' because that behaviour will likely concur with at least *some* ideas.[127] Consequently, the divergent understandings within the community of legal practice provide international courts with 'multiple pathways' to gain authority.[128] This is not to suggest that any interpretation of the law would be accepted. The court's decisions still have to correspond with the overall set of minimal shared understandings around which the community of practice has coalesced, and the interpretations advanced by international courts would be subject to constant contestation and justification within the broader community of legal practice.

Similar 'battles' over the interpretation of the law could also take place within international courts. Studies of organizational culture have shown that international civil servants, such as judges, can internalize the norms of the organizations in which they work.[129] In effect, a set of

124 Shklar, *Legalism*, 114, emphasis added.

125 Franck, Fairness in International Law, 7. See also Kirchheimer, Political Justice, 11.

126 J. Black, 'Constructing and Contesting Legitimacy and Accountability in Polycentric Regulatory Regimes' (2008) 2(1) *Regulation & Governance* 137, 153.

127 Barnett and Finnemore, *Rules for the World*, 35–36.

128 Alter, Helfer and Madsen, 'How Context Shapes', 49.

129 J. Trondal, M. Marcussen, T. Larsson, and F. Veggeland. *Unpacking International Organizations: The Dynamics of Compound Bureaucracies* (Manchester: Manchester University Press, 2010) 12–13.

internal shared understandings, or a 'bureaucratic culture', can formulate within courts.[130] The existence of a strong internal culture of collegiality among judges could enhance the perception of the court's legal decisions as authoritative and sound.[131] But the establishment of internal consensus at a court is not preordained. When judges are selected at international courts, they already have a wealth of experience as practitioners, academics, or diplomats.[132] Previous research has found that judges consider their professional backgrounds almost more important than national backgrounds in their job.[133] The influence of the personal professional experience on the decisions of some international officials may prove stronger than the court's internal shared understandings.[134] Internal court disagreements about the meaning of the law can be manifested by issuing 'dissenting' or 'separate' opinions to a particular judgment.[135] While the decision of an international court to form accountability relationships with a specific subgroup of the community of practice could influence that court's approach to the interpretation and application of the law, the within-court battles over the interpretation of the law would determine whether that court could formulate a uniform line of legal reasoning in the first place.

2.4 Concluding Remarks on the Theoretical Framework

The 'practice' approach to international law revealed the intersubjective nature of legalism. On the one hand, legal norms constrain and enable the behaviour of actors within the community of legal practice. On the other hand, legal norms are continuously (re)produced by the routine practices of those same actors. However, beyond the set of minimum shared understandings that mark the outer boundaries of the community of legal practice, namely the importance of rule-guided decision-making, significant divergence exists within that community with respect to more substantial

130 M. Barnett and M. Finnemore, 'The Politics, Power, and Pathologies of International Organizations' (1999) 53(4) *International Organization* 699, 718.

131 H. Mistry, 'The Significance of Institutional Culture in Enhancing the Validity of International Criminal Tribunals' (2017) 17(4) *International Criminal Law Review* 703, 706.

132 R. Mackenzie and P. Sands, 'International Courts and Tribunals and the Independence of the International Judge' (2003) 44 *Harvard International Law Journal* 271, 280.

133 E, Voeten, 'International Judicial Behaviour', in C. Romano, K. Alter, and Y. Shany (eds.) *The Oxford Handbook of International Adjudication*, 1st ed. (Oxford: Oxford University Press, 2013) 550, 566.

134 Trondal et al., *Unpacking International Organizations*, 14.

135 Mistry, 'Significance of Institutional Culture', 712.

issues of legal practice. Hence, the international legal field is constantly witnessing battles of contestation over the interpretation and application of the law.

The theoretical framework of this book seeks to combine the 'internal' understanding of the background rules shaping the field of international law with the 'external' sensitivity to the powerful forces that influence those understandings. Even though the background understandings that bind the community of legal practice are shared, this does not imply that the law presents a better solution to problems in international relations compared to policy approaches, nor that the practice of law is impermeable to politics. Rather, this book aims to show the distinctiveness of legal reasoning and its key role in the operation of international criminal justice. While legal reasoning is always underpinned by specific morals and beliefs, the practice of international law is guided by a distinct ideology shared by legal practitioners – Shklar's 'legalism', or the continuous search for rules to follow.[136] Consequently, legal practice is political, but the politics of the legal field, premised on the competition for claiming expert authority, are inherently different from the politics of international relations. In this respect, the framework of this book departs from those of Kratochwil and Brunnée and Toope. Both their models search for particular characteristics of legal reasoning that do not merely differentiate law from politics, but that also render normatively legitimate outcomes. This book separates the question whether the interpretation and application of ICL rules is underpinned by legal reasoning from the question on whether such interpretations and applications are 'right' or 'wrong'. Decisions that are considered right or convincing *within* the community of ICL practice may well be viewed as deeply problematic *outside* the legal field.

2.5 Methodology

2.5.1 Concepts

Before proceeding with the analysis of the ICL field of practice, several points concerning methodology and concepts should be mentioned. The practice of criminal law involves a set of related but distinctive terms, such as responsibility and liability. A person could be responsible for a conduct and yet avoid liability by offering a justification or an excuse, such

[136] Shklar, *Legalism*, 15.

as duress, for her actions.[137] Hence, the terms responsibility and liability bear different consequences for the individual. Responsibility calls for accounting, but not necessarily for punishment because the person could offer a convincing defence for her actions, whereas liability implies a punitive response.[138]

This book also refers to 'individual criminal responsibility' and 'the individual criminal responsibility legal rules', which are related but distinct concepts. Individual criminal responsibility is understood in this book not as a legal norm per se, but as the expectation held by a variety of international actors that the perpetrators of mass atrocities need to be *personally* held accountable and that their conduct triggers *criminal* responsibility, as opposed to different forms of responsibility, such as civil liability. The norm of individual criminal responsibility is given effect in practice through specific legal norms, which are here referred to as the 'individual criminal responsibility legal rules'. While the 'individual criminal responsibility legal rules' comprise a broad range, in this book the term will be used specifically in relation to the legal rules developed in ICL for the purpose of attributing criminal responsibility to the accused, also known as 'modes of liability' or 'liability standards'.[139] Consequently, the analysis will focus on the ICC judges' findings in relation to the most relevant RS provisions in that regard, namely Article 25(3)(a)–(d), which defines the modes of participation in the commission of a crime, Article 28 on the command responsibility principle, and Article 30 that sets the mental element requirements of liability. Future research can focus on other intriguing aspects of criminal responsibility, such as the liability for inchoate crimes, including the attempt to commit a crime under Article 25(3)(f) and incitement to commit genocide under Article 25(3)(e),[140] and the grounds for excluding criminal responsibility under Article 31 RS.[141]

137 R. A. Duff, 'Responsibility and Liability in Criminal Law', in M. H. Kramer, C. Grant, B. Colburn, and A. Hatzistavrou (eds.) *The Legacy of H.L.A. Hart: Legal, Political, and Moral Philosophy* (Oxford: Oxford University Press, 2008) 101, 103.

138 May and Fyfe, *International Criminal Tribunals*, 55.

139 D. Scheffer, 'The International Criminal Court', in W. Schabas and N. Bernaz (eds.) *Routledge Handbook of International Criminal Law* (London: Routledge, 2010) 67, 76. M. Jackson, *Complicity in International Law* (Oxford: Oxford University Press, 2015) 87–88.

140 K. J. Heller, 'The Rome Statute of the International Criminal Court', in K. J. Heller and M. Dubber (eds.) *The Handbook of Comparative Criminal Law* (Stanford: Stanford University Press, 2010) 593, 609. Werle, 'Individual Criminal Responsibility', 956.

141 A. Eser, 'Mental Elements – Mistake of Fact and Mistake of Law', in A. Cassese, P. Gaeta and J. Jones (eds.) *The Rome Statute of the International Criminal Court*, Vol. 1 (Oxford: Oxford University Press, 2002) 889.

2.5.2 Primary Methods of Analysis

Practices, including the practice of law, are often embedded in discourses that enable the signification of particular meanings.[142] Consequently, the primary method that this book employs to collect evidence[143] is discourse analysis, or the study of the meanings that actors assign to concepts when they use language in specific contexts.[144] This book analyses a wide variety of forms of written discourse in order to examine the understandings of different actors about the meaning of the legal rules concerning criminal responsibility.

Firstly, this book examines over 200 legal documents, including the decisions on issuing arrest warrants or summons to appear, decisions on the confirmation of charges against the accused, trial judgments, appeal judgments, dissenting opinions of judges, and other relevant decisions that were issued by the pre-trial, trial, and appeals chamber with respect to every ICC case from July 2002 to February 2022. Even though judicial decisions are presumed to embody measured reasoning, in reality, the judges often use expressive language that conveys their attitudes towards the question at hand.[145] The analysis focuses on two types of written legal discourse, namely the judges' findings on the meaning of criminal responsibility provisions in all ICC cases, and the judges' factual findings on the alleged criminal responsibility of the defendant in every ICC case in which the confirmation of charges proceedings was completed (Table 2.1). The analysis of the factual findings is limited to cases concerning core international crimes, as defined by Article 5 RS. Nevertheless, material from the cases for offences against the administration of justice under Article 70 is also analysed, specifically with respect to the judges' findings on the general meaning of criminal responsibility norms.

Secondly, to place in context the judges' factual findings on the defendant's guilt or innocence, this book further analyses submissions by the prosecutor, including applications for arrest warrant and documents containing the charges (DCC). The goal is not to determine whether the ICC judges have correctly assessed the defendant's criminal responsibility

[142] F. Kratochwil, 'Making Sense of "International Practices"', in E. Adler, and V. Pouliot (eds.) *International Practices* (Cambridge: Cambridge University Press, 2011) 36, 56.

[143] M. Lange, *Comparative-Historical Methods* (London: Sage Publications, 2013), 42.

[144] J. P. Gee and M. Handford, 'Introduction', in J. P. Gee and M. Handford (eds.) *The Routledge Handbook of Discourse Analysis* (London: Routledge, 2012) 1.

[145] E. Finegan, 'Legal Writing: Attitude and Emphasis', in M. Coulthard and A. Johnston (eds.) *The Routledge Handbook of Forensic Linguistics* (London: Routledge, 2010) 65, 68.

Table 2.1 *List of ICC cases involving international crimes according to Articles 5 RS with completed confirmation of charges proceedings*

Situation under investigation	Case	Defendant	Confirmation of charges decision	Current status
Kenya	Kenyatta, Muthaura & Ali	Uhuru Muigai Kenyatta	Charges confirmed*	Charges withdrawn by the prosecutor
Kenya	Kenyatta, Muthaura & Ali	Francis Kirimi Muthaura	Charges confirmed*	Charges withdrawn by the prosecutor
Kenya	Kenyatta, Muthaura & Ali	Mohamed Hussein Ali	Charges dismissed	–
Kenya	Ruto, Kosgey & Sang	William Samoei Ruto	Charges confirmed	Charges vacated at trial
Kenya	Ruto, Kosgey & Sang	Henry Kiprono Kosgey	Charges dismissed	–
Kenya	Ruto, Kosgey & Sang	Joshua Apar Sang	Charges confirmed	Charges vacated at trial
Uganda	Ongwen	Dominic Ongwen	Charges confirmed	Convicted*, pending appeal decision
Côte d'Ivoire	Gbagbo & Blé Goudé	Laurent Gbagbo	Charges confirmed	Acquitted, pending appeal decision
Côte d'Ivoire	Gbagbo & Blé Goudé	Charles Blé Goudé	Charges confirmed	Acquitted, pending appeal decision
DRC	Katanga & Ngudjolo	Germain Katanga	Charges confirmed*	Convicted*
DRC	Katanga & Ngudjolo	Mathieu Ngudjolo Chui	Charges confirmed*	Acquitted
DRC	Mbarushimana	Callixte Mbarushimana	Charges dismissed	–
DRC	Lubanga	Thomas Lubanga Dyilo	Charges confirmed	Convicted

Table 2.1. (*cont.*)

Situation under investigation	Case	Defendant	Confirmation of charges decision	Current status
DRC	Ntaganda	Bosco Ntaganda	Charges confirmed	Convicted
CAR I	Bemba	Jean-Pierre Bemba Gombo	Charges confirmed*	Acquitted
CAR II	Yekatom & Ngaïssona	Alfred Yekatom	Charges confirmed	Trial commenced
CAR II	Yekatom & Ngaïssona	Partice-Edouard Ngaïssona	Charges confirmed*	Trial commenced
CAR II	Said	Mahamat Said Abdel Kani	Charges confirmed*	Awaiting trial
Mali	Al-Mahdi	Ahmad Al Faqi Al Mahdi	Charges confirmed	Convicted
Mali	Al-Hassan	Al Hassan Ag Abdoul Aziz Ag Mohamed Ag Mahmoud	Charges confirmed	Trial commenced
Darfur, Sudan	Banda & Jerbo	Abdallah Banda Abakaer Nourain	Charges confirmed	Awaiting the suspect's appearance for trial
Darfur, Sudan	Banda & Jerbo	Saleh Mohammed Jerbo Jamus	Charges confirmed	Suspect declared deceased
Darfur, Sudan	Abu Garda	Bahar Idriss Abu Garda	Charges dismissed	–
Darfur, Sudan	Abd-Al-Rahman	Ali Muhammad Ali Abd-Al-Rahman	Charges confirmed	Awaiting trial

*The judges declined to confirm some of the charges/the defendant was acquitted on some of the charges.

Data: ICC Defendants Database, available at: www.icc-cpi.int/Pages/defendants-wip.aspx, accessed on 22 February 2020.

but to examine what general types of facts and evidence the judges find convincing with respect to the assessment of criminal responsibility and whether a stable line of judicial reasoning could be identified across different cases. Even though sensitive information, including names of persons and places, was redacted in some legal documents, overall there was sufficient publicly available information to gain insights into those questions.

Two main databases were used to access legal documents: the ICC's Court Records and Transcripts portal[146] and the Legal Tools Database, which provides a digitalized archive of the case law of the ICC, ICTY, ICTR, IMT, and the IMTFE.[147] Most of the documents were available in English, with few exceptions that were published only in French.

Thirdly, to examine the understandings of legal academics with respect to criminal responsibility in ICL, the book employs discourse analysis of more than 330 publications that address the question. The analysis examines scientific discourse from a critical perspective that recognizes the embeddedness of scholarly publications into the social world[148] and the way they can reproduce, but also gradually reform the structure of the respective field of practice. The sources of data include books, chapters, and articles in leading international law and criminal law journals in English, including *Journal of International Criminal Justice*, *European Journal of International Law*, *Leiden Journal of International Law*, *International Criminal Law Review*, and *Criminal Law Forum*, to name a few. In addition, the analysis examines publications by legal academics in well-established online blogs, such as EJIL: *Talk!*, OpinioJuris, Justice in Conflict, and International Justice Monitor. The discourse analysis of academic publications also provides insight into the understandings about the laws on criminal responsibility of several RS drafters, including Mahmoud Cherif Bassiouni, Roger Clark, Kai Ambos, and Per Saland, and former judges at the UN tribunals, including Antonio Cassese, Theodor Meron, David Hunt, and Mohamed Shahabuddeen, who have extensively published extensively on matters of ICL.

Fourthly, regarding NGOs' understandings on criminal responsibility matters, the analysis relies on articles, statements, reports, and *amicus curiae* submissions by human rights organizations, such as Coalition for the International Criminal Court (CICC), Human Rights Watch, Amnesty International, Women's Initiatives for Gender Justice (WIGJ), REDRESS, and the International Federation for Human Rights (FIDH). Those organizations generally support online archives dating back to the 1990s.[149]

146 www.icc-cpi.int/court-records.

147 www.legal-tools.org.

148 T. Van Dijk, 'Critical Discourse Analysis', in D. Schiffrin, D. Tannen, and H. E. Hamilton (eds.) *The Handbook of Discourse Analysis*, 1st ed. (John Wiley & Sons, Incorporated, 2001) 352.

149 See Coalition for the ICC archive, http://archive.iccnow.org/?mod=documents, WIGJ's database at: https://4genderjustice.org/#, Human Rights Watch: www.hrw.org/sitesearch?search=international+criminal+court, Amnesty International: www.amnesty.org/en/search/?q=international+criminal+law&sort=date.

Finally, in relation to the views expressed by states and government officials, the book looks to the official records of the Preparatory Commission for the establishment of the ICC and those of the Rome Conference, available through the Legal Tools Database and the official UN records.[150] The analysis also included records from the annual ICC ASP sessions[151] and news reports for the purpose of examining state reactions to ongoing trials and the overall functioning of the Court. In addition to discourse analysis, this book relies on secondary sources of data, including historical academic analysis, to provide insights into the political dynamics that surrounded the establishment of the IMT, IMTFE, and the UN tribunals.

2.5.2.1 Interviews

The textual discourse analysis is supplemented by interviews, which provide further insights into the variety of understandings about criminal responsibility within the ICL field. The interviewees included one sitting ICC judge, legal academics who had written extensively on questions of criminal responsibility in ICL, former participants in the Rome Conference, NGO officials, and diplomats from state parties to the RS. Some of the interviews were conducted during a field trip to The Hague in May 2019 that included meetings with state diplomats and NGO officials. The aim was to gain better understanding of the socio-political environment of the Court, namely its relationship with state representatives and civil society. Other interviews were conducted in 2019 during a visit to the Ministry of Foreign Affairs in Bulgaria, a State Party to the RS since 2002. The discussions with Ministry officials who worked on ICC-related matters provided important insights into the relationship between a State Party and the Court and the domestic reactions to the ICC's interpretation of criminal responsibility provisions. Some of the works of the legal scholars who were interviewed have been referenced in ICC decisions with respect to interpretation of the RS's criminal responsibility provisions. The interview with the WIGJ Executive Director further revealed insights into the work of an NGO that specifically monitors the work of the ICC and that has often submitted *amicus curiae* observations at the Court, including in the *Lubanga* and the *Bemba* cases. In this book, the interviews comprise a supplementary method for collecting data, the main method being discourse analysis. References to interview statements will be used in the following chapters mainly to provide additional illustration of trends or ideas that have been observed in the legal literature, in judgments or in NGO commentaries.

150 https://legal.un.org/icc/rome/proceedings/contents.htm.

151 https://asp.icc-cpi.int/en_menus/asp/sessions/documentation/19th%20session/Pages/default.aspx.

2.5.3 Secondary Method of Analysis

This study comprises an interpretative research that follows abductive reasoning – 'a continuous movement' between observations from the empirical world and theoretical insights.[152] The processes of collecting data and analysing it were ongoing and interlinked throughout this research project. The goal was to build an understanding of how the ICL field functions before making more specific observations on the influence of the politics of legal interpretation on the assessment of criminal responsibility.

In addition, this book conducts an 'internal comparison', i.e. a comparison of different spatial and temporal manifestations of the phenomenon under investigation, in order to illustrate any changes into the nature of that phenomenon.[153] Specifically, the assessment of criminal responsibility at the ICC is compared with the judicial reasoning at earlier international tribunals – the IMT, IMTFE, and the UN tribunals – for the purpose of identifying shifts in the dominant sets of shared understandings in the ICL community of practice. With respect to the UN tribunals, the analysis generally focuses on the ICTY, because many of the landmark decisions on modes of liability in ICL were delivered in ICTY cases, including *Tadić*, *Čelebići*, *Stakić*, and *Brđanin*. Nevertheless, the analysis is supported with reference to the findings of relevant ICTR decisions. Furthermore, all questions on appeal at the ICTY and ICTR were addressed by the same set of judges.[154]

2.5.4 Explanatory Goals and Limitations

This book does not aim to present the politics of the legal field as the only explanation for the ICC's trial outcomes. Legal norms, understood as intersubjective beliefs shared by a group of members of the ICL field, cannot be considered the 'causes' of a specific line of judicial reasoning in the classic positivist sense. Norms often do not prescribe a particular behaviour but 'serve only as determinants of a zone of permissibility'.[155] Furthermore, legal norms are not static but are constantly reproduced and reformed in the practice of law. Consequently, this book does not treat legal norms as either the direct or the only cause of the ICC approach to the assessment

152 A. Dubois and L. Gadde, 'Systematic Combining: An Abductive Approach to Case Research' (2002) 55(7) *Journal of Business Research* 553, 554.

153 Lange, 'Comparative-Historical Methods', 58.

154 M. Drumbl and K. Gallant, 'Appeals in the Ad Hoc International Criminal Tribunals: Structure, Procedure, and Recent Cases' (2001) 3(2) *Journal of Appellate Practice and Process* 589, 595.

155 Kratochwil, 'How Do Norms Matter', 63.

of criminal responsibility. Instead, it seeks to contribute to the interdisciplinary literature on the Court by tracing the simultaneously constraining and enabling influence of legal norms on judicial reasoning. Thus, the book explores one contributing factor to trial outcomes, that has so far remained underexplored in the literature on the Court, while recognizing that there may be alternative explanations, such as the ICC's complex relationship with states and the challenges of obtaining high-quality evidence of mass atrocities. In fact, those alternative explanations may work in conjunction with the politics of legal interpretation. As observed in Chapters 7–9, the prosecutor's problems of the unavailability of state support for investigations and the difficulties of collecting evidence could be exacerbated when she faces a bench that interprets the law in a narrow fashion and is particularly unwilling to tolerate the prosecutor's investigatory hurdles.

Another reason for refraining to make bolder claims regarding the role of legal norms is the limited set of cases available for observation. Even though the Court began operation in 2002, as of February 2022 it has completed confirmation of charges proceedings in relation to 24 suspects and only nine verdicts for core international crimes (Table 2.1).[156] Nevertheless, while this number of cases at the ICC may be relatively small compared to that at the ICTY and ICTR, it provides sufficient evidence to gain insights into the role of judicial reasoning in relation to the assessment of criminal responsibility, which could in the future be supplemented by further empirical research. Therefore, the goal in this book is not only to examine the operation of legal norms within the ICL field, but also to set a research agenda for future interdisciplinary research on international criminal justice.

With these caveats in mind, even if one cannot speak of causality in the positivist sense with respect to legal norms, the findings of this book can be used to make inferences about a broader range of case studies. For instance, the insights gained from this book in relation to the constraining and enabling impact of the legal norms on the assessment of criminal responsibility can be used in future research for examining other types of ICL norms, apart from criminal responsibility.[157] This book contributes to the emerging scholarship on the intersubjective 'practice' of ICL and aims to provide insights that facilitate further research in that direction.

[156] Excluding offences against the administration of justice under Article 70 Rome Statute.

[157] De Vos has already employed similar analytical approach to examine the construction of meanings of the legal norms of 'complementarity' in ICL. De Vos, Complementarity, Catalysts, Compliance.

3

The International Criminal Justice Field from Within

Demarcating the Debates on Criminal Responsibility

This chapter explores the field of international criminal law practice, which is bound by two core understandings shared among its participants: that the perpetrators of mass atrocities deserve to be punished, and that punishment should follow a fair criminal process. Next, the chapter turns to the internal debates taking place within the ICL field concerning questions of individual criminal responsibility. The analysis reveals a variety of competing views on the meaning of criminal responsibility rules, resulting not only from the different professional background of the persons engaging in ICL practice, but also from the lack of agreement on the function of criminal law in society.

3.1 The ICL Community of Practice

Sarah Nouwen suggests that ICL has developed 'mostly out of practice rather than theory', as a form of 'ad hoc creation and application' of legal norms in response to specific atrocities.[1] Several sociological studies have explored the institutionalization and operationalization of the ICL field resulting from the creation and application of legal rules.[2] Hagan and Levi, for instance, observe that, at the ICTY, specific practices, such as collecting onsite forensic evidence, issuing secret indictments, and inducing arrests, have over time become socially validated elements of the ICL field, which enabled the tribunal to conduct those practices relatively autonomously from politically

[1] S. Nouwen, 'International Criminal Law: Theory All over the Place', in A. Orford and F. Hoffmann (eds.) *The Oxford Handbook of the Theory of International Law* (Oxford: Oxford University Press, 2016) 738, 751.

[2] J. Hagan, *Justice in the Balkans: Prosecuting War Crimes in the Hague Tribunal*, (Chicago: University of Chicago Press, 2003). J. Hagan and R. Levi, 'Crimes of War and the Force of Law' (2005) 83(4) *Social Forces*, 1499. P. Dixon and C. Tenove 'International Criminal Justice as a Transnational Field: Rules, Authority and Victims' (2013) 7(3) *International Journal of Transitional Justice* 393.

powerful actors.[3] The sociological scholarship provides important insights into the practices enabling the administration *of* international criminal justice in the context of state politics. However, it largely overlooks the practices of interpretation and application of the legal norms regulating the core ICL function – the assessment of individual criminal responsibility. This chapter aims to contribute to the sociological scholarship on the ICL field of practice by providing a systematic analysis of the variety of understandings shared among its members situated within and outside the tribunal regarding the meaning of criminal responsibility laws and the power of those understandings to influence the (re)production of legal rules.

3.1.1 Actors inside the ICL Field

Sociological studies observe that the field of international criminal justice brings together 'a diverse set of actors with diverse aims and forms of authority'.[4] States remain key players in the ICL field, especially at the ICC ASP, which constitutes the 'management oversight and the legislative body' of the Court.[5] But states are not involved in all aspects of ICL practice equally. The nature of the legal norms under consideration appears to be of particular importance for the level of state involvement within the ICL field. Whether states would seek to protect their nationals from international prosecution[6] or, conversely, to dispose of troublesome rebel leaders by transferring those persons to international tribunals,[7] the most important ICL norms for states are those regulating the jurisdictional reach of the court and the powers of the prosecutor. Danner's study of the ICTY reveals that when states have appeared confident in the unlikeliness of having their own nationals prosecuted, they have tolerated bold judicial interpretations of the criminal responsibility rules.[8] The laws concerning the assessment of guilt or innocence exhibit particular 'flexibility' in ICL, especially in comparison with domestic penal systems.[9] With states

3 Hagan and Levi, 'Crimes of War', 1527.
4 Dixon and Tenove, 'Crimes of War', 411.
5 ICC, 'Assembly of State Parties', https://asp.icc-cpi.int/en_menus/asp/assembly/Pages/assembly.aspx.
6 J. Charney, 'Progress in International Criminal Law?' (1999) 93(2) *American Journal of International Law* 452, 460. S. Ratner, 'The International Criminal Court and the Limits of Global Judicialization' (2003) 38(3) *Texas International Law Journal* 445, 452.
7 Schabas, 'Complementarity in Practice', 757.
8 Danner, 'When Courts Make Law', 19–29.
9 Van Sliedregt, 'International Criminal Law', 1147.

focusing generally on jurisdiction-related legal norms and given the malleable nature of individual criminal responsibility norms, the interpretative authority of judges increases in relation to the latter.

Furthermore, while states seek to protect their sovereignty, interdisciplinary studies of international law have disputed the assumption that states are driven only out of rational self-interest. As suggested by Abbott and Snidal, international law 'simultaneously' engages states' self-interest and normative preferences.[10] Consequently, as participants inside the ICL field, states display not only sovereignty concerns but also normative preferences about the construction of legal rules depending on the specificities of their domestic legal traditions. Chapter 5 discusses the lack of uniformity in states' preferences concerning the scope of several modes of liability, with some states preferring lower liability standards than others.

Judges have also become key actors in the construction of international legal norms,[11] especially in ICL, which is a 'relatively new body' of international law.[12] Judicial decisions have often been treated in ICL almost like an independent source of law.[13] Given the importance of expert knowledge in claiming authority inside the legal field, judicial lawmaking in ICL has sometimes been perceived as a legal corrective to the 'flawed process' of politically motivated state lawmaking.[14] Danner called 'judicial lawmaking' the 'truth of international politics that cannot be named'.[15] In an interview, a Bulgarian diplomat working on ICL observed that 'judges, more or less, develop further some legal provisions' in their interpretations of the legal text.[16]

Nevertheless, the practice framework of ICL suggests that judicial determinations must display congruence with the understandings of at least some participants in the broader ICL community outside the court. Of particular importance is international legal scholarship. Christensen's

[10] K. Abbott and D. Snidal, 'Hard and Soft Law in International Governance' (2000) 54(3) *International Organization* 421, 422.

[11] J. Powderly, 'Judicial Interpretation at the Ad Hoc Tribunals: Method from Chaos?', in S. Darcy and J. Powderly (eds.) *Judicial Creativity at the International Criminal Tribunals* (Oxford: Oxford University Press, 2010) 17, 18.

[12] Cryer et al., *Introduction to International Criminal Law*, 3.

[13] S. Darcy, 'Bridging the Gaps in the Laws of Armed Conflict? International Criminal Tribunals and the Development of Humanitarian Law', in N. Quenivet and S. Shah-Davis (eds.) *International Law and Armed Conflict: Challenges in the 21st Century* (The Hague: T.M.C. Asser Press, 2010) 334.

[14] Van Sliedregt, 'International Criminal Law', 1147.

[15] Danner, 'When Courts Make Law', 47.

[16] Interview with Georgi Minkov, Ministry of Foreign Affairs, Bulgaria, April 2019.

comprehensive empirical study reveals that academia has played a crucial role in the development of legal norms. Scholarship has served as a 'testing ground' for innovative interpretations of ICL.[17] Judges have often relied on academic research to validate their interpretations of the law, essentially rendering ICL scholarship a 'tool' for fighting legal battles in court.[18] Academic international law blogs have recently become a particularly popular forum for discussion within the ICL field. Blogs such as *OpinioJuris* and EJIL: *Talk*! publish short commentaries by legal experts on a daily basis. In an interview, one influential ICL scholar observed that ICC judges seemed to follow academic publications and take into consideration the ideas expressed outside the Court.[19]

NGOs constitute another important set of actors within the ICL field that were particularly influential during the ICC's establishment.[20] Ever since, NGOs have retained a complex relationship with the court, serving simultaneously as 'its most vigorous champions and its most demanding taskmakers'.[21] The involvement of NGOs in the ICL field is often examined in relation to their efforts to improve the administration of international criminal justice by mobilizing states to provide financial and logistical support to international courts.[22] However, NGOs are also able to claim expert authority with respect to determining the scope and meaning of ICL norms, as demonstrated by their important contribution to the drafting of the RS.[23] Some NGOs dedicated to monitoring the work of the court have produced expert legal analyses of ICC decisions, including on issues of individual criminal responsibility.[24] Furthermore, NGOs often provide the link between ICL practitioners and the victims of atrocities and seek to integrate insights from their work into the development of ICL norms and thus to reconcile abstract legal rules

[17] M. Christensen, 'Preaching, Practicing and Publishing International Criminal Justice: Academic Expertise and the Development of an International Field of Law' (2017) 17(2) *International Criminal Law Review* 239, 246.

[18] Ibid., 248.

[19] Interview with Douglas Guilfoyle, 12 August 2020.

[20] M. Glasius, *The International Criminal Court: A Global Civil Society Achievement* (London: Routledge, 2006). Welch and Watkins, 'Extending Enforcement,' 987–989. Deitelhoff, 'Discursive Process of Legalization'.

[21] B. Schiff, *Building the International Criminal Court* (New York: Cambridge University Press, 2008), 144.

[22] Lohne, 'Global Civil Society', 450. Schiff, *Building the International Criminal Court*, 152.

[23] Pearson, 'Non-Governmental Organizations', 272

[24] See the expert papers published by the Women's Initiatives for Gender Justice, https://4genderjustice.org/home/publications/gender-report-cards/ and https://4genderjustice.org/home/publications/expert-papers-and-reports/.

with reality. The executive director of WIGJ described their mission as one of 'translating lived experience into law'.[25]

Overall, within the ICL field of practice, the determinations of legal experts – judges, academics, practitioners, and activists – appear to be particularly influential in relation to the interpretation of highly technical rules, such as the criminal responsibility laws.[26] States play a role in the drafting of the text of those laws, but they may also grant significant autonomy to judges and other experts to develop the law on individual criminal responsibility. As discussed in Chapter 5, the preoccupation of states with matters of jurisdiction and the prosecutor's powers rendered legal experts highly influential during the drafting of the RS criminal responsibility provisions.

3.1.2 Outer Boundaries of the ICL Field

The current constitution of the ICL field is the product of decades of contestation and justification of ideas about international criminal justice.[27] Eventually, the ideas that gained dominance included narrowing the scope of ICL to violations of the 'physical integrity rights' of persons, rather than their political or socio-economic rights,[28] and relying on individual criminal responsibility, rather than state responsibility, as an enforcement mechanism.[29] The success of this particular vision of international criminal justice appears to be the combined outcome of ideology and interests – the institutionalization of ICL resonated with the evolving international human rights movement during the immediate post–Cold War period, but it was also argued to have coincided with the 'territorial, economic, and governance agendas' of the Global North during that period.[30]

Thus, a community of practice coalesced around two central shared understandings. Firstly, that the perpetrators of mass atrocities bear criminal responsibility and should be punished, also referred to as the

[25] Interview with Melinda Reed, Women's Initiatives for Gender Justice, The Hague, 15 May 2019.
[26] Christensen, 'Preaching, Practicing and Publishing,' 247. C. Steer, 'Legal Transplants or Legal Patchworking? The Creation of International Criminal Law as a Pluralistic Body of Law', in E. van Sliedregt and S. Vasiliev (eds.) *Pluralism in International Criminal Law* (Oxford: Oxford University Press, 2014) 39, 40–41.
[27] Mégret, 'International Criminal Justice History', 77–84.
[28] Sikkink, *The Justice Cascade*, 16, emphasis omitted.
[29] Mégret, 'International Criminal Justice History', 81–84.
[30] Nesiah, 'Doing History with Impunity', 98.

'anti-impunity' norm.[31] As observed by Engle, in the twenty-first century the human rights movement has become 'almost synonymous' with the idea of attributing criminal responsibility for human rights violations, whilst the reliance on amnesties has been met with increasing criticism.[32] Yet, not any form of punishment would be compatible with the promotion of human rights. Consequently, the second shared understanding binding the ICL field is that punishment should be determined through a fair trial, or the norm of liberal 'legalism'.[33] The rationale is that 'the accused are also bearers of rights' and deserve a 'fair trial'.[34] As a core ICL norm, legalism refers to the 'essential modalities' of the criminal process: 'the possibility of acquittal, standards of evidence, and proportionate punishment'.[35] Within the ICL community of practice, it is considered that, despite the Western outlook of this trial model, it provides a minimum common denominator of fairness that unites criminal justice systems worldwide.[36] Together, the anti-impunity norm and the legalism norm constitute the outer boundaries of the field of international criminal justice and provide the background framework against which members of the ICL community of practice present, contest, and justify different understandings of the law. However, the precise meaning and requirements of specific criminal responsibility norms remain subject to contestation within the ICL field.

3.2 Inside the ICL Field

The broad shared understandings that mark the outer boundaries of the ICL field have enabled a variety of actors with different professional backgrounds and views about the law to engage in ICL practice. This section traces three internal debates of importance for examining the competition over determining the meaning of criminal responsibility laws in ICL: the debates between practitioners from criminal law and public international law backgrounds; between representatives of the common and the civil law domestic legal traditions; and between those who prioritize morality

[31] For a critical analysis of the 'anti-impunity' movement see K. Engle, Z., Miller, and D. Davis (eds.) 2016. *Anti-Impunity and the Human Rights Agenda* (Cambridge: Cambridge University Press).

[32] Engle, 'Genealogy of the Criminal Turn', 15. See also N. Roht-Arriaza, 'Combating Impunity: Some Thoughts on the Way Forward' (1996) 59(4) *Law and Contemporary Problems* 93.

[33] The term is borrowed from Bass, *Stay the Hand of Vengeance*.

[34] Sikkink, *Justice Cascade*, 13.

[35] Bass, *Stay the Hand of Vengeance*, 24.

[36] D. Robinson, 'A Cosmopolitan Liberal Account of International Criminal Law' (2013) 26(1) *Leiden Journal of International Law* 127, 142–143.

and those who prioritize dispassionate rationalism as a guiding principle in ICL. Even though the last debate has triggered relatively less attention in ICL literature, it is of utmost importance for understanding the dynamics surrounding the assessment of individual criminal responsibility at international courts and tribunals.

3.2.1 Criminal Law v. Public International Law

The variety of branches of law involved in ICL's development has long been recognized as a source of controversy within the field.[37] Van Sliedregt describes ICL as an 'uncomfortable combination' between two bodies of law based on inherently different foundational principles and enforcement mechanisms, namely domestic criminal law and public international law.[38] Darryl Robinson famously called this clash of ideas the 'identity crisis' of ICL.[39]

3.2.1.1 Defendant-Oriented v. Victim-Oriented Approaches

Of utmost importance for actors with a core commitment to criminal law participating in the ICL field is the principle of legality, generally understood as the maxim *nullum crimen sine lege* ('no crime without law'), which requires that the law is sufficiently clear to provide 'fair notice' about the criminality of the conduct.[40] Important corollaries of that principle are the requirement that criminal statutes are drafted with precision, the prohibition of extending criminal law provisions by analogy, and the requirement to resolve ambiguities in favour of the defendant (the rule of lenity).[41] While the indeterminacy of the legal language precludes the achievement of absolute certainty about the meaning of legal prohibitions, the legality principle is generally viewed as constraining judicial interpretation and protecting the law from purely idiosyncratic determinations on the criminality of a given conduct.[42]

[37] See A. Danner and J. Martinez, 'Guilty Associations: Joint Criminal Enterprise, Command Responsibility, and the Development of International Criminal Law' (2005) 93(1) *California Law Review* 75. B. Van Schaack, 'Crimen Sine Lege: Judicial Lawmaking at the Intersection of Law and Morals' (2008) 97(1) *Georgetown Law Journal* 119. G. Fletcher and J. D. Ohlin, 'Reclaiming Fundamental Principles of Criminal Law in the Darfur Case' (2005) 3(3) *Journal of International Criminal Justice* 539.

[38] Van Sliedregt, *Individual Criminal Responsibility*, 8. Osiel, Making Sense.

[39] Robinson, 'The Identity Crisis'.

[40] Gallant, *Principle of Legality*, 13.

[41] Van Schaack, 'Crimen Sine Lege,' 121.

[42] Gallant, *Principle of Legality*, 31–33.

Another key rule for those members of the ICL community with criminal law background is that of personal culpability or guilt, which requires that a person is liable only for her own conducts.[43] Those members of the ICL community emphasize that punishment based on mere association with the wrongdoer or imposed collectively on the family, ethnic, or religious group of the wrongdoer is precluded by the principle of personal culpability.[44] Of particular importance from a criminal law perspective are the rules concerning the assessment of the mental element of liability, or *mens rea* (guilty mind). From a criminal law perspective the mental element, the requisite intent to commit the crime, 'is at the heart of the culpability principle' because it denotes the blameworthiness of the individual.[45] Most domestic systems accept that *mens rea* below intention can attract liability, including the concepts of recklessness in common law systems and *dolus eventualis*, found in some Continental systems, which denote conscious risk-taking that one's conduct could result in a crime.[46] Liability could also be imposed for negligent behaviour,[47] but, in light of the culpability principle, the less guilty the mind of the accused is, the less justified the imposition of liability appears. Consequently, negligence liability has proven a controversial concept among criminal law experts.[48]

Increasingly, criminal law scholars participating in the ICL field have emphasized that the culpability principle requires not only evidence of personal guilt but also proportionality between the accused's guilt and the harshness of the punishment.[49] 'Proportionality' refers not only to the

[43] Danner and Martinez, 'Guilty Associations', 83–84.

[44] Gallant, *Principle of Legality*, 17.

[45] T. Weigend, 'Subjective Elements of Criminal Liability', in M. Dubber and T. Hörnle (eds.) *The Oxford Handbook of Criminal Law* (Oxford: Oxford University Press, 2014) 490, 491.

[46] G. Werle and F. Jessberger, 'Unless Otherwise Provided: Article 30 of the ICC Statute and the Mental Element of Crimes under International Criminal Law' (2005) 3(1) *Journal of International Criminal Justice* 35, 51–52.

[47] Van Sliedregt, *Individual Criminal Responsibility*, 44.

[48] See L. Alexander, K. K., Ferzan, and S. Morse, *Crime and Culpability: A Theory of Criminal Law* (Cambridge: Cambridge University Press, 2009) 79. G. Williams, *Criminal Law: The General Part*, 2nd ed. (London: Stevens & Sons Ltd, 1964) 122–123. In support of negligence liability see H. L. A. Hart, *Punishment and Responsibility: Essays in the Philosophy of Law*, 2nd edition (Oxford: Oxford University Press, 2008) 147–148. K. Huigens, 'Virtue and Inculpation' (1995) 108(7) *Harvard Law Review* 1423, 1474–1476. J. Montmarquet, 'Zimmerman on Culpable Ignorance' (1999) 109(4) *Ethics* 842, 845.

[49] G. Werle and B. Burghardt, 'Establishing Degrees of Responsibility: Modes of Participation in Article 25 of the ICC Statute', in E. van Sliedregt and S. Vasiliev (eds.) *Pluralism in International Criminal Law* (Oxford: Oxford University Press, 2014) 301, 304. Robinson, 'The Identity Crisis', 927.

length of the sentence but also to 'fair labelling' – the idea that the label of the offence ought to fairly express the offender's wrongdoing.[50] 'Labels' include the name of the offence or the type of criminal liability that the accused bears, for example principal liability, aiding a crime, and negligent commission. Those labels 'reveal the story of an offender's criminality'.[51]

However, as Robinson has observed, in addition to criminal law scholars and practitioners, the ICL field has also integrated experts from the fields of human rights and international humanitarian law who have brought their own background understandings about legal sources and procedure.[52] Important differences exist, however, between coercive penal norms and what Danner and Martinez call 'gentle' human rights norms, which do not have the authority to incarcerate individuals, but rely instead on mechanisms such as public shaming, forward-looking capacity building, and symbolic findings of state wrongdoing.[53] Because of the different forms of punishment, criminal law places the burden of proof on the prosecution and protects the defendant's rights, while human rights law focuses on the victims' suffering and allows broader interpretations of legal norms to ensure that harm is addressed.[54] While defendant-oriented criminal law norms favour a restrained approach to the rules of assessing criminal responsibility, human rights and humanitarian norms favour more expansive interpretations of the culpability principle by view of preventing the perpetrators of mass atrocities from escaping punishment and enabling the victims to see justice being served.[55]

Due to their different rationales, the communities of practice of the defendant-oriented criminal law and the victim-oriented human rights and humanitarian law differ in their understandings in relation to the sources of law. For example, public international law, including human rights and humanitarian law, often rely on customary international law and the general principles of law recognized by nations around the world. But some members of the ICL community of practice have expressed concerns that customary international law threatens the principle of legality because customs rarely establish clear rules and often exist alongside counter-customs.[56] The 'malleability' of the general principles of law has raised similar

[50] G. Williams, 'Convictions and Fair Labelling' (1983) 42(1) *Cambridge Law Journal* 85.
[51] Nersessian, 'Whoops, I Committed Genocide', 96.
[52] Robinson, 'Identity Crisis', 928.
[53] Danner and Martinez, 'Guilty Associations,' 86.
[54] Ibid., 86–89.
[55] Robinson, 'Identity Crisis'.
[56] L. May, *Aggression and Crimes against Peace* (New York: Cambridge University Press, 2008) 161. Van Schaack, 'Crimen sine Lege', 138.

concerns among those with criminal law backgrounds.[57] International law and criminal law practice also diverge regarding the methods of interpreting legal rules. Because of the fair notice requirement, some scholars have suggested that the textual approach appears more appropriate than teleological approaches from a criminal law perspective.[58] By contrast, because human rights and humanitarian law aim at maximizing protection to the vulnerable, 'little legitimacy is gained by unquestioning reliance on text' in those fields.[59] For instance, the Martens Clause allows for *moral* considerations, such as 'the laws of humanity, and the dictates of the public conscious', to be evoked to determine humanitarian obligations.[60] Similarly, human rights institutions often interpret treaties and conventions as 'living instruments' that must be adapted to the needs of modern society.[61]

3.2.1.2 A Clash of Ideas

This book takes a different approach to that of the criminal law scholars commenting on the clash between criminal law norms and public international law norms in ICL. Criminal law scholars usually take a critical stance on the influence of human rights/humanitarian norms on ICL. Participants in the ICL community of practice with criminal law backgrounds tend to justify the prioritization of criminal law principles on the grounds that international trials affect foremost the liberty of individual persons.[62] Robinson has expressed concern that human rights norms have resulted in an ICL system that is 'increasingly authoritarian in its disregard for constraining principles'.[63] Criminal law practitioners and academics advocate for compliance with the principles of legality and culpability on the grounds that criminal liability constitutes the 'ultimate infliction of moral blame'[64] and imposes 'the highest legal sanctions available to

[57] F. Raimondo, 'General Principles of Law, Judicial Creativity, and the Development of International Criminal Law', in S. Darcy and J. Powderly (eds.) *Judicial Creativity at the International Criminal Tribunals* (Oxford: Oxford University Press, 2010) 45, 46.

[58] L. Grover, 'A Call to Arms: Fundamental Dilemmas Confronting the Interpretation of Crimes in the Rome Statute of the International Criminal Court' (2010) 21(3) *European Journal of International Law* 543, 557.

[59] Wessel, 'Judicial Policy-Making', 440. See also Danner and Martinez, 'Guilty Associations', 89.

[60] Fourth Hague Convention, Laws and Customs of War on Land, The Hague, 1907, 633.

[61] Van Schaack, 'Crimen Sine Lege', 146–147.

[62] B. Sander, 'Unravelling the Confusion Concerning Successor Superior Responsibility in the ICTY Jurisprudence' (2010) 23(1) *Leiden Journal of International Law* 105, 127.

[63] Robinson, 'Identity Crisis', 931.

[64] Safferling, 'Can Criminal Prosecution', 1473.

society', namely deprivation of freedom.[65] Because international crimes bear even stronger stigma than domestic offences,[66] many legal scholars called for bringing ICL closer to domestic criminal law by exhibiting stricter compliance with the principles of legality,[67] culpability,[68] and fair labelling[69] when assessing criminal responsibility. From this perspective, since the accused are the ones whose liberty is at risk, their rights must be shielded to preserve the integrity of liberal trials.[70]

Consequently, criminal law scholarship often frames the influence of human rights and humanitarian norms on the practice of ICL as a problematic intrusion of alien norms in what should be foremost a system of *criminal* justice. The criminal law scholarship takes a normative stance on the clash between criminal law and public international law in ICL by advocating for placing greater emphasis on the former. If one focuses only on the criminal law scholarship commenting on this clash of ideas, it is very easy to conclude that reliance on human rights and humanitarian norms falls outside the scope of one of the core shared understandings that bind the ICL field – legalism. From this perspective, the human rights and humanitarian logics constitute unsound legal reasoning in ICL.

This book takes an external sociological view of the ICL field, with its goal being to analyse the actors and ideas that construct the field, without making normative arguments about the field should look like. Consequently, this book treats this clash of ideas as an internal dispute taking place within the ICL field – a clash between different visions of legalism, rather than a clash between legalism and unsound legal reasoning. Both the criminal experts and the human rights advocates share the core understanding that international trials should follow the principles of the liberal legal process. The difference is in the interpretation of those principles, animated by different visions of the purpose and significance of international criminal justice.

[65] Gallant, *Principle of Legality*, 17.

[66] Mégret, 'What Sort of Global Justice'.

[67] See, e.g., K. Ambos, 'Remarks on the General Part of International Criminal Law' (2006) 4(4) *Journal of International Criminal Justice* 660. Sander, 'Unravelling the Confusion'. Robinson, 'Identity Crisis'. Fletcher and Ohlin, 'Reclaiming Fundamental Principles'.

[68] K. Ambos, 'Joint Criminal Enterprise and Command Responsibility. Journal of International Criminal Justice' (2007) 5(1) *Journal of International Criminal Justice* 159, 173–173. Van Sliedregt, *Individual Criminal Responsibility*, 85.

[69] Robinson, 'Identity Crisis'. Nersessian, 'Whoops, I Committed Genocide'.

[70] Ambos, *Treatise on International Criminal Law*, 87.

From a human rights and humanitarian perspective, ICL's ability to punish individuals has been perceived as an 'enforcement revolution'.[71] International prosecutions have been described as a 'sword' for protecting the victims of human rights abuses.[72] Speaking on behalf of the 800 member organizations of CICC, William Pace remarked that the ICC's creation 'would save millions of humans from suffering unspeakably horrible and inhumane death'.[73] Some scholars have also suggested that the punishment of the perpetrator could offer some remedy for the emotional and psychical injuries afflicted to the victims.[74]

The fact that human rights scholars and advocates seek to protect the rights of the victims has produced a somewhat distorted image of their role inside the ICL field – as actors who seek to obtain convictions and are willing to compromise the quality of the legal process. But a closer look at the arguments made by human rights actors often suggests otherwise. According to WIGJ's executive director:

> What the victims want is not always what the law allows. However, the assumption that only a conviction is considered justice by the victims could be misguided. Many nuances of victims' experiences are lost by using the notion 'victims rights' … Accountability is especially important for victims. Accountability does not necessarily imply a conviction – bringing up charges against an accused and conducting fair proceedings also accomplishes the goal of providing accountability.[75]

As will be discussed in Chapters 7 and 8, while human rights and humanitarian experts might question the reasoning behind certain interpretations of the legal rules, they often tend to be committed to the

[71] M. Ignatieff, 'Human Rights as Politics. Human Rights as Idolatry' (2000), *The Tanner Lectures on Human Values*, Princeton University, April 4–7, 294. J. Heath, 'Human Dignity at Trial: Hard Cases and Broad Concepts in International Criminal Law' (2012) 44(2) *George Washington International Law Review* 317, 321. M. Bassiouni, 'International Recognition of Victims' Rights' (2006) 6(2) *Human Rights Law Review* 203, 264–265.

[72] Stahn, 'Between "Faith" and "Facts"', 255. Gallant, *Principle of Legality*, 90.

[73] United Nations Diplomatic Conference of Plenipotentiaries on the Establishment of an International Criminal Court Rome, 15 June–17 July 1998, Vol. II: Summary records of the plenary meetings and of the meetings of the Committee of the Whole, https://legal.un.org/icc/rome/proceedings/E/Rome%20Proceedings_v2_e.pdf, (hereinafter *Rome Conference Official Records*) 129.

[74] A. Sepinwall, 'Failures to Punish: Command Responsibility in Domestic and International Law' (2009) 30(2) *Michigan Journal of International Law* 251, 293.

[75] Interview with Melinda Reed, Women's Initiatives for Gender Justice, The Hague, 15 May 2019.

core principle of liberal legalism. In fact, their disappointment regarding unsuccessful trials has often been directed towards governments for failing to cooperate with investigations or the ICC prosecution for failing to collect sufficient evidence and, thus, to meet the requirements of the liberal trial. This book identifies those human rights advocates who display such commitment to the principles of the fair criminal trials as members of the ICL community who can validify or contest specific lines of judicial reasoning concerning the assessment of criminal responsibility.

3.2.2 Common Law v. Civil Law

Even though the clash between criminal law experts and human rights experts is a source of normative tension inside the ICL field, it is not the only one. Significant differences of opinion can also be observed within the criminal law community of practice, often mirroring variations between the common law and the civil law traditions. The text of many ICL provisions may appear neutral in terms of domestic pedigree, but the pre-existing professional experience of international judges, which often involves serving at domestic courts, can influence the interpretation of those provisions in practice.[76]

Both common and civil law penal codes respect the foundational norms of criminal law – but with some variations. Some commentators have observed that the legality principle is well established in civil law but does not have the same legal authority in all common law systems.[77] Furthermore, common law systems have applied less strictly the principle of personal culpability in some instances of group criminality.[78] Examples of such practices include the US *Pinkerton* conspiracy doctrine,[79] the felony murder rule,[80] and the English common purpose

[76] Van Sliedregt, *Individual Criminal Responsibility*, 8. S. Merope, 'Recharacterizing the Lubanga Case: Regulation 55 and the Consequences for Gender Justice at the ICC' (2011) 22(3) *Criminal Law Forum* 311, 331.

[77] S. Lamb, 'Nullum Crimen, Nulla Poena Sine Lege in International Criminal Law', in A. Cassese, P. Gaeta, and J. R. W. D. Jones (eds.) *The Rome Statute of the International Criminal Court* Vol. I (Oxford: Oxford University Press, 2002) 733, 740.

[78] J. Van der Vyver, 'The International Criminal Court and the Concept of Mens Rea in International Criminal Law' (2005) 12(1) *University of Miami International and Comparative Law Review* 57, 58.

[79] M. Noferi, 'Towards Attenuation: A New Due Process Limit on Pinkerton Conspiracy Liability' (2006) 33(2) *American Journal of Criminal Law* 91, 94.

[80] S. Kadish, 'Complicity, Cause and Blame: A Study in the Interpretation of Doctrine' (1985) 73(2) *California Law Review* 323, 352. N. Roth and S. Sundby, 'The Felony-Murder Rule a Doctrine at Constitutional Crossroads' (1985) 70(3) *Cornell Law Review* 446.

doctrine.[81] Further differences exist in relation to the process of determining and applying legal rules. Common law generally relies on pragmatism or 'common sense',[82] while civil law systems adopt a highly systematized and theoretically developed approach to criminal law.[83] This principled approach, known as *Dogmatik* in Germany, has been increasingly discussed in the context of ICL.[84] Civil law countries often codify a set of fundamental legal norms valid for all crimes into the 'general part' of their penal statutes.[85] The codification of the general part is considered to provide better 'fair warning' about the applicable law, in accordance with the legality principle.[86] The difference between the pragmatic and the theoretical approaches to criminal law practice is also reflected in the authority of legal academia in both systems. While the official sources of law in common law are often limited to statutes and juridical precedents, civil law systems have historically relied on scholarly teachings.[87] It has been observed that some German judges have changed long-standing jurisprudence on a certain topic when convinced by renowned academics that their previous views had been wrong.[88]

Nevertheless, a look at the ICL field of practice renders support for Dubber's argument that the common law versus civil law division should not be exaggerated.[89] Firstly, there are important divergences within those systems themselves, including on questions of criminal responsibility.[90]

[81] B. Krebs, 'Joint Criminal Enterprise' (2010) 73(4) *Modern Law Review* 578, 590. See also S. Kadish, 'Reckless Complicity' (1997) 87(2) *Criminal Law & Criminology* 369, 375–378.

[82] M. Bohlander, 'Radbruch Redux: The Need for Revisiting the Conversation between Common and Civil Law at Root Level at the Example of International Criminal Justice' (2011) 24(2) *Leiden Journal of International Law* 393, 400.

[83] S. Trechsel, 'Command Responsibility as a Separate Offense' (2009) 3(1) *Berkley Journal of International Law Publicist* 26, 26–27. Ambos, 'Remarks on the General Part,' 665. Van der Vyver, 'International Criminal Court', 58.

[84] G. Fletcher, 'New Court, Old Dogmatik' (2011) 9(1) *Journal of International Criminal Justice* 179.

[85] F. Mantovani, 'The General Principles of International Criminal Law: The Viewpoint of a National Criminal Lawyer' (2003) 1(1) *Journal of International Criminal Justice* 26, 26–27. A. Simester and S. Shute, 'On the General Part in Criminal Law', in A. Simester and S. Shute (eds.) *Criminal Law Theory: Doctrines of the General Part* (Oxford: Oxford University Press, 2002) 1, 3.

[86] Simester and Shute, 'On the General Part', 4.

[87] G. Fletcher, 'Truth in Codification' (1998) 31(3) *U.C. Davis Law Review* 745, 754.

[88] Bohlander, 'Radbruch Redux', 401–402.

[89] Dubber, 'Common Civility', 925.

[90] R. Clark, 'The Mental Element in International Criminal Law: The Rome Statute of the International Criminal Court and the Elements of Offences' (2001) 12(3) *Criminal Law Forum* 291, 295.

Van Sliedregt's comparative analysis provides a useful illustration: most countries, including Germany, Spain, and England employ the 'differentiative' model of perpetration, which distinguishes between those actors who *commit* the crime, that is the 'principal' perpetrator/s, and those who merely *assist* its commission, that is the 'accessory/accessories' to the crime.[91] But the differences between differentiative models cut across the civil-common law division. Anglo-American common law and French civil law both follow the 'naturalistic' approach, which considers a principal only the physical perpetrator of the crime, while the co-perpetrators and indirect perpetrators (those who have used someone else to commit the crime) are considered mere accessories to that crime. From a naturalistic perspective, the terms 'principal' and 'accessory' do not carry any normative significance. By contrast, Germany's 'normative' approach treats the co-perpetrators and indirect perpetrators as principals to the crime to emphasize the degree of their culpability.[92] As the following chapters discuss, the different approaches to perpetratorship are of utmost importance for understanding the development of theories, or modes, of liability in ICL.

Another reason why the common-civil law distinction should be treated with caution is the trend towards convergence between the two traditions. Academic works have played an important role in bridging the two traditions,[93] as has the creation of the United States' Model Penal Code, which constituted the 'first systematic approach' to developing a general part of criminal law in the Anglo-American world.[94] Nevertheless, the practice of codification has not enjoyed uniform popularity across common law countries. The urge to categorize the law has triggered criticism among some common law scholars[95] who associate that practice with 'the inflexibility of top-down … anti-democratic, civil dogmaticism'.[96]

This debate has played out in the context of the development of a general set of principles in ICL. Some legal experts have described the search for uniformity in all aspects of ICL's doctrine and practice as 'misguided'.[97]

[91] Van Sliedregt, *Individual Criminal Responsibility*, 66.

[92] Ibid., 71–73. See also Jain, *Perpetrators and Accessories*.

[93] Ambos, 'Remarks on the General Part'. Trechsel, 'Command Responsibility'.

[94] Ambos, 'Remarks on the General Part', 661. See also Dubber, 'Common Civility', 928.

[95] See J. Gardner, 'Criminal Law and the Uses of Theory: A Reply to Laing' (1994) 14(2) *Oxford Journal of Legal Studies* 217. K. Simmons, 'Rethinking Mental States' (1992) 72 *Boston University Law Review* 463.

[96] Dubber, 'Common Civility', 928.

[97] A. K. A. Greenawalt, 'The Pluralism of International Criminal Law' (2011) 86(3) *Indiana Law Journal* 1063, 1067–1068.

But many other legal scholars and practitioners have actively called for the development of a general part in ICL for the purpose of ensuring a more coherent legal system.[98] It has been considered that the development of a general part would mark 'the formal coming of age' of ICL and 'emancipate' the discipline from the 'rudimentary' nature of public international law.[99] Some scholars suggest that ICL should adopt something akin to the German *Dogmatik*,[100] while others, that ICL should 'walk its own path' taking into account 'the peculiarities of *international* criminal liability'.[101] Chapter 5 illustrates the significance of this debate with regard to the drafting of the rules for assessing criminal responsibility in the RS.

3.2.3 *Interpreting Legality: Morality v. Rational Logic*

The ultimate source of normative tension inside the ICL field is rooted deep into the essence of criminal law: the question 'what is the rationale behind punishing individuals?'. As discussed, broad interpretations of the principles of legality and personal culpability in ICL have generally been explained with the influence of human rights and humanitarian law norms. This section discusses another set of competing understandings, one that originates from within the criminal law community. Criminal law practice follows the shared understanding that a person is punished for her wrongful conduct. However, it has been debated whether such conduct represents a wrongful choice or a manifestation of an immoral character. In essence, this is a debate between those who consider the *immorality* of certain conducts to be sufficient to merit punishment and those who perceive immorality as a nebulous source of guidance for social behaviour and insist that only the violation of clearly established legal rules should trigger punishment. Exploring this internal debate helps understand why not only human rights activists but also some criminal law scholars and judges adopt a more flexible approach to legality. It also illuminates why other members of the ICL community perceive this practice as a threat to the integrity of the discipline.

[98] E. Van Sliedregt, 'Pluralism in International Criminal Law' (2012) 25(4) *Leiden Journal of International Law* 847, 852. See Eser, 'Towards an International Criminal Court'. Ambos, 'Remarks on the General Part'. Mantovani, 'General Principles', 26.

[99] V. Militello, 'The Personal Nature of Individual Criminal Responsibility and the ICC Statute' (2007) 5(4) *Journal of International Criminal Justice* 941, 943.

[100] G. Fletcher, 'New Court, Old Dogmatik', 179. Jain, *Perpetrators and Accessories*, 97–98.

[101] G. Vanacore, 'Legal Culpability and Dogmatik: A Dialogue between the EctHR, Comparative and International Criminal Law' (2015) 15(5) *International Criminal Law Review* 823, 859, emphasis in the original.

3.2.3.1 Choice v. Character

The Anglo-American legal literature has debated the appropriate basis of attributing criminal responsibility – a wrongful choice or an immoral character. According to the 'choice' model, criminal responsibility should be imposed only when a person has had 'the normal capacities, physical and mental', to act in accordance with the law and 'a fair opportunity' to exercise those capacities, but for whatever reason has failed to do so.[102] It is considered that, while people rightly pass moral judgments on other persons' characters in non-legal contexts, criminal law should refrain from punishing bad characters.[103] The emphasis on rational choice implies that individuals determine the wrongfulness of their actions guided by the law, rather than by their moral consciousness. The law becomes a 'choosing system' that allows individuals to find out the costs of their actions.[104] By contrast, some criminal law scholars consider that the characters of individual persons – their values, motives, and emotions – matter for the attribution of criminal responsibility.[105] On this account, the wrongful choice might constitute an occasion for punishment, but not the reason behind it. Blame and punishment are perceived as negative responses for the socially undesirable character dispositions of a person, which have resulted in criminal behaviour.[106]

This debate marks a clear division between those who consider morality and law as separate realms and those who perceive them as inevitably interlinked. According to the choice-based model, one need not be a good man to identify what is unlawful.[107] By contrast, the character-based model stresses that the ability of individuals to reason with the law is premised on their capacity to correct their characters and make morally right choices.[108]

The two sides hold different understandings of the legality principle. Because the choice-based model does not rely on other sources of guidance, such as moral consciousness, a narrow interpretation of the legality principle

[102] Hart, *Punishment and Responsibility*, 152. See also M. Moore, 'Choice, Character, and Excuse' (1990) 7(1) *Social Philosophy & Policy* 29.

[103] M. Moore, *Act and Crime: The Philosophy of Action and Its Implications for Criminal Law* (Oxford: Oxford University Press, 2010 [1993]), 54.

[104] Hart, *Punishment and Responsibility*, 44.

[105] D. Kahan, 'Ignorance of Law Is an Excuse: But Only for the Virtuous' (1997) 96(1) *Michigan Law Review* 127, 128–129.

[106] M. Bayles, 'Character, Purpose, and Criminal Responsibility' (1982) 1(1) *Law and Philosophy* 5, 7–8.

[107] O. W. Holmes, 'The Path of Law' (1997 [1897]) 110(5) *Harvard Law Review* 991, 993.

[108] P. Arenella, 'Character, Choice and Moral Agency: The Relevance of Character to Our Moral Culpability Judgments' (1990) 7(1) *Social Philosophy & Policy* 59, 73.

is important since it ensures that the law provides fair notice regarding prohibited conducts.[109] By contrast, according to the character-based model, strict adherence to the letter of the law enables individuals to exploit the 'grey zone' between what is merely immoral and what is officially illegal. On this account, 'a good person' would avoid criminal punishment without looking to the law for excuses.[110] According to the character-based model, strict legality is important in relation to conducts sitting on the border between socially desirable and socially undesirable behaviour, such as financial violations. But in relation to conducts such as murder, the role of legal provisions is not to provide notice, but to punish behaviour that is already understood as socially and morally forbidden.[111]

Duff makes a compelling argument that the controversy between the 'choice' and the 'character' model of criminal responsibility ultimately reflects 'a real tension between two different political conceptions of law and the state'.[112] The 'choice' model fits the ideology of liberal individualism and a contractual model of law and society. From this perspective, law imposes 'fairly modest constraints', whose observance would enable individuals to pursue their own goods. The public/private sphere distinction of liberal contractualism suggests that a person's feelings and character traits may be relevant in their personal relationships, but not for criminal law as a system of rules that regulates our public lives.[113] Consequently, the legality principle is considered to protect the individual's personal matters 'from the arbitrary power of the political, the prosecutorial, or the judicial departments'.[114] By contrast, the 'character' perspective favours a communitarian vision of society, where fellow members of a community are interested in each other 'as friends', collectively building strong communal relationships, rather than 'as strangers', observing the limited terms of a social contract.[115] Notably, in ICL the character-based model of

[109] See H. L. A. Hart, 'Problems of the Philosophy of Law' in H. L. A. Hart (ed.) *Essays in Jurisprudence and Philosophy* (Oxford: Oxford University Press, 1983) 88, 114. M. Moore, 'A Tale of Two Theories' (2009) 28(1) *Criminal Justice Ethics* 27, 31.

[110] Kahan, 'Ignorance of Law', 129.

[111] D. Kahan, 'Lenity and Federal Common Law Crimes' (1994) *Supreme Court Review* 345, 400.

[112] R. A. Duff, 'Choice, Character, and Criminal Liability' (1993) 12(4) *Law and Philosophy* 345–383, 346.

[113] Ibid., 381.

[114] Gallant, *Principle of Legality*, 21. See also G. P. Fletcher, *Rethinking Criminal Law* (Boston: Little, Brown, 1978) 800–801. D. Husak, *The Philosophy of Criminal Law: Selected Essays* (Oxford and New York: Oxford University Press, 2010) 203.

[115] Duff, 'Choice, Character', 382–383.

criminal responsibility and the communitarian vision of an international community of mankind have gained traction.

3.2.3.2 Morality v. Rational Logic in ICL

In addition to the impact of human rights and humanitarian norms, the character-based model of punishment, i.e. the idea of punishing the lack of moral consciousness rather than the violation of codified legal rules, has influenced some members of the ICL community of practice to suggest that the principles of criminal law must be interpreted in broad and flexible manner for the purpose of ending impunity. Osiel transfers to the international level the argument concerning the redundancy of fair notice in criminal law concerning serious crimes. According to Osiel, an individual of 'good character' would instinctively stay away from the borderline demarcating merely immoral from officially illegal conducts concerning atrocities. From this perspective, ICL merely 'tracks the core of "common morality"',[116] any person who chooses to enter the 'grey zone' of internationally prohibited conduct deserves harsh treatment by the law,[117] and any legal ambiguities that could enable the defendant to avoid responsibility should be resolved against her.[118] International criminal law is different from domestic criminal law: while the latter stands on the presumption of the accused's innocence, ICL, because of the grave nature of the crimes at stake, is considered to proceed from a moral 'presumption of guilt'.[119] Even proponents of the choice-based model in domestic law have acknowledged that the legality principle cannot be interpreted in the same manner in proceeding against international criminals.[120]

Osiel's arguments constitute a rare explicit reference to the character-based model of punishment discussed in the Anglo-American literature. But the assumption that a person of high morality would have abstained from such conducts has been implicit in many of the arguments for relaxing the principle of legality in ICL. As observed by Van Schaack, there is a general tendency in ICL to conflate what is morally wrong with what is legally criminal, reminiscent of the natural law tradition.[121] The more heinous the conduct, the more permissive the assumption that it violates not

[116] Osiel, Making Sense, 139.
[117] Osiel, Making Sense, 140. Luban, 'Fairness to Rightness', 586.
[118] Osiel, Making Sense, 142.
[119] Dubber, 'Common Civility', 936.
[120] Moore, 'Tale of Two Theories', 45.
[121] Van Schaack, 'Crimen Sine Lege', 157.

only moral norms but also positive law.[122] In much of ICL practice, even when the conduct's criminalization has not been clearly established by the law, the decisive question has been whether the accused '*should have foreseen* it, since the conduct, in any case, violated natural law and morality'.[123] Hence, the separation of 'intuitive' morals from 'rational' criminal law in ICL has been particularly challenging.[124] Some authoritative legal scholars even suggest that ICL concerns 'not criminal guilt' but 'moral guilt' for violating the norms of the human community.[125]

This understanding has invited many members of the ICL community of practice to introduce qualification to the principle of legality.[126] It has been argued that because the wrongfulness of mass atrocities has established 'deep roots' in the mind of every person,[127] the defendants cannot simply evoke the legality principle, understood as the requirement of pre-existing codified law, and claim that they did not know that their conduct was wrong.[128] From this perspective, a broad range of rules and soft norms, such as human rights treaties or the general principles of law, can provide fair notice of the conduct's criminality and, thus, satisfy the legality principle even though such instruments address mostly state parties rather than individuals.[129]

NGOs, too, have displayed a preference for the character-based model of criminal responsibility in ICL. Those organizations often engage in moral-based judgments by directly 'naming' alleged perpetrators in their reports.[130] Osiel makes an interesting observation: the same human rights advocates who generally favour the rehabilitative ideals of punishment at the domestic level have often pressed for retributive responses

[122] T. Meron, 'The Geneva Conventions as Customary Law' (1987) 81(2) *American Journal of International Law* 348, 361.

[123] K. Ambos, 'Current Issues in International Criminal Law' (2003) 14(3) *Criminal Law Forum* 225, 231, emphasis in the original.

[124] Tallgren, 'Sensibility and Sense', 591.

[125] Dubber, 'Common Civility', 933.

[126] A. Cassese, *International Criminal Law*, 2nd ed. (Oxford: Oxford University Press, 2008), 38–41.

[127] Tomuschat, 'Legacy of Nuremberg', 835.

[128] Schabas, W. 2003b. 'Interpreting the Statutes of the Ad Hoc Tribunals', in L. C. Vohrah et al. (eds.) *Man's Inhumanity to Man: Essays on International Law in Honour of Antonio Cassese* (The Hague: Kluwer Law International) 887. Luban, 'Fairness to Rightness', 584–585.

[129] Van Schaack, 'Crimen Sine Lege'. Tomuschat, 'Legacy of Nuremberg', 835.

[130] M. Bergsmo and W. Wiley, 'Human Rights Professionals and the Criminal Investigation and Prosecution of Core International Crimes', in I. Hurley and H. Mark (eds.) *Manual on Human Rights Monitoring: An Introduction for Human Rights Field Officers*, (Oslo: Norwegian Centre for Human Rights, 2008), 23.

at international tribunals, where harsh legal measures against 'repressive rulers' are seen as empowering the victims of human rights abuses.[131] Understanding the different views of the basis of criminal responsibility explains why acquittals at international trials have sometimes been perceived as a failure to punish.[132] Even though the influence of human rights norms for protecting the victims might play a role in such reactions, those reactions also tend to display a moral judgment on the guilt of the defendant long before the trial verdict is delivered.

The willingness of some members of the ICL community to integrate morality with legality should not be interpreted as a rejection of legalism or as an attempt to compromise the quality of legalism by imposing more lenient standards of criminal responsibility. Indeed, to argue so would be to embrace the 'maturation' thesis discussed in Chapter 1,[133] which perceived the criminal responsibility laws as objective standards against which the performance of international courts can be measured. Instead, the idea of integrating morality with legality presents a different vision of legalism. It is still a 'legalist' ideology because it conforms to the understanding that the perpetrators of mass atrocities must be punished in accordance with criminal law procedure, which makes the outcome of international trials uncertain. But the precise requirements of those criminal law rules, including the ones regulating the assessment of criminal responsibility, are subject to contestation. From the perspective of many human rights advocates, criminal law principles, including those of legality and personal culpability, do not require blind application, regardless of their broader social implications, but a 'balance' between the interests of the victims and the rights of the accused.[134] This account takes into consideration both fair process and fair outcome in international trials.

Nevertheless, this view, which balances process with outcome, has been increasingly contested by other members of the ICL community of practice. It has often been suggested that, because strict compliance with the principles of criminal law should limit judicial discretion, states would be particularly keen to emphasize the importance of the legality and

[131] M. Osiel, 'Modes of Participation in Mass Atrocity' (2005) 38(3) *Cornell International Law Journal* 793, 803–804.

[132] Bertodano, 'Judicial Independence', 410.

[133] Chapter 1, Section 1.3.

[134] L. Moffett, 'Meaningful and Effective? Considering Victims' Interests through Participation at the International Criminal Court' (2015) 26(2) *Criminal Law Forum* 255, 262. Women's Initiatives for Gender Justice, 'Gender Report Card 2018', 147.

culpability principles in ICL.[135] However, once the political dynamics of the legal field, that is, the competing claims over the meaning of the law, are taken into consideration, the relationship between the protection of state interests and strict compliance with the principles of criminal law becomes less straightforward. As discussed, states act out of a combination of self-interest and normative beliefs, and domestic systems display some variations regarding the interpretation of the legality principle. Furthermore, a look at state interests also precludes definitive conclusions on their attitude towards legality and culpability. If governments seek to dispose of rebel or opposition leaders, it appears unlikely that they would insist on a narrow interpretation of the principles of criminal law that increases the chances of acquittal. If states seek to protect certain individuals, such as government officials, from prosecution, they are likely to challenge the reasoning of international judges concerning questions of the ICC's jurisdictional reach, rather than criminal responsibility rules. For instance, some states disputed their legal obligation to arrest and surrender the accused in the *Al-Bashir* case.[136] Other states contested the Court's jurisdiction over a specific case, like Côte d'Ivoire did with respect to the case against Simone Gbagbo.[137] Contestation of expansive interpretations of the criminal responsibility rules is likely to arise only if, despite state opposition, the Court somehow manages to apprehend the suspects and proceed with a confirmation of the charges against them. Although such a scenario is by no means precluded, due to the lack of police force at international tribunals and their dependency on state cooperation for completing arrests, it is likely to occur less often.[138]

Crucially, an analysis that focuses on the direct state influence on the ICL field obscures the fact that other members of the ICL community of practice may favour strict and technical application of the principles of criminal law for reasons different from state interests. The so-called 'liberal critique of ICL' has sought to sustain the presumption of the defendant's innocence and

[135] B. Broomhall, 'Article 22: *Nullum Crimen Sine Lege*', in K. Ambos and O. Triffterer (eds.) *Rome Statute of the International Criminal Court: A Commentary*, 3rd ed. (London: Bloomsbury T&T Clark, 2016) 949. Grover, 'Call to Arms', 553. Schabas, *Introduction to the International Criminal Court*, 202.

[136] For an analysis of the possible motivations of states to refuse to arrest Al-Bashir see Cole, 'Africa's Relationship'. Mills, 'Bashir Is Dividing Us'.

[137] For an analysis of the admissibility challenge in the *Simone Gbagbo* case see K. J. Heller, 'Radical Complementarity' (2016) 14(3) *Journal of International Criminal Justice* 637.

[138] Bosco, Rough Justice, 4. D. Rieff, 'The End of Human Rights?', *Foreign Policy*, 9 April 2018, https://foreignpolicy.com/2018/04/09/the-end-of-human-rights-genocide-united-nations-r2p-terrorism/.

insisted on restricting the scope of personal culpability.[139] Contrary to arguments prioritizing substantive over procedural justice, from the perspective of a liberal fair trial, one cannot 'work backwards from the proposition that the defendant must be punished' to interpret the existing law in such manner that it will enable conviction.[140] From this perspective, the fact that the defendant may bear moral responsibility for being implicated in the collective violent conduct does not imply that she bears criminal responsibility for specific crimes. Like the choice-based model of punishment, the advocates of legality in ICL have rejected the conflation of illegality with immorality. While mass atrocities seem horrendous, it is considered that moral outrage alone could not constitute the basis for criminal prosecutions.[141] There are various forms of reprisal for moral wrongs, such as public shaming or compulsory contributions to victim compensation funds. But because of the severity of criminal punishment, the imposition of criminal responsibility, even when the morality is clear-cut, is said to require a clear legal rule.[142]

Legal scholars have also noted that the social climate of normative permissiveness that accompanies mass atrocities makes it 'extremely hard to assess the character of the individual'.[143] Criminological research has revealed that it does not take 'intrinsically evil people' to commit atrocious crimes,[144] supporting Hannah Arendt's famous observations of the 'banality of evil'.[145] This makes judgments of the accused's moral worth in ICL particularly perplexing. As one commentator observes:

> Of course, banal evil is still evil. But are we prepared to blame a character which we evaluate as banal rather than full of burning hatred, sadistic inclinations, and cruelty?[146]

Even proponents of the morality approach in ICL have acknowledged the difficulties of making moral judgments in relation to some war crimes, because when war is waged for self-defence lethal violence is said to serve 'the publicly prized end of collective self-preservation'.[147]

139 Robinson, 'Cosmopolitan Liberal Account', 128.

140 J. D. Ohlin, 'Three Conceptual Problems with the Doctrine of Joint Criminal Enterprise' (2007) 5(1) *Journal of International Criminal Justice*, 69–90, 72.

141 May, Crimes against Humanity, 3–4.

142 May, *Aggression*, 154–155.

143 Aukerman, 'Extraordinary Evil', 58.

144 A. Smeulers, 'Historical Overview of Perpetrator Studies', in A. Smeulers, M. Weerdesteijn, and B. Holá (eds.) *Perpetrators of International Crimes: Theories, Methods, and Evidence* (Oxford: Oxford University Press, 2019) 11, 18.

145 H. Arendt, *Eichmann in Jerusalem: A Report on the Banality of Evil* (New York: Viking Press, 1964).

146 C. S. Nino, *Radical Evil on Trial* (New Heaven, CT: Yale University Press, 1996) 142.

147 Osiel, *Making Sense*, 139.

From the perspective of the liberal critique then, strict legality protects not the interests of ingenious criminals trying to exploit gaps in the law, but the normative worth of the legal system – it is said to differentiate criminal law from both 'a purely administrative system of sanctions'[148] and from moral-based judgment.[149] Arguments for compromising the principle of personal culpability in order to avoid embarrassing acquittals have been rejected[150] and the fairness of the trial, regardless of the trial outcome, is presented as necessary for preserving ICL's integrity.[151] While delivering substantive justice appears to legitimize legal proceedings for those members of the ICL community of practice who allow for balancing morality with legal formalism, the same reasoning could delegitimize international tribunals in the eyes of those who cherish the narrow and predictable application of legal rules.[152]

These are two different understandings of what the norm of legality requires in practice. Both perspectives share an agreement that the criminal law norm of 'legality', broadly understood as the predictable interpretation of laws that make it clear to the lay person what conduct is proscribed, has to be complied with in order to punish a person for international crimes, but disagree as to what 'legality' requires. For some members of the ICL field, moral norms can serve as indicia of what the law requires, while others favour the technical and dispassionate application of legal rules, regardless of the broader consequences of the judgment for the afflicted communities.

It should not be assumed that the advocates of the separation of morality from legality disregard the 'anti-impunity' norm and do not express interest in whether the perpetrators of mass atrocities are punished. But again, the meaning of 'ending impunity' is contested. The term 'ending impunity' implies a quest for accountability, but accountability does not necessarily mean punishment. It could also mean holding a fair trial. Furthermore, for those members of the ICL field who separate morality from legality, the strict compliance with legal rules would contribute to ending impunity in the long term, even if in the short term some ingenious criminals take advantage of the gaps in the law and escape punishment, because it would institute a stable and legitimate international legal order.

148 Weigend, 'Subjective Elements', 492.

149 D. Robinson, 'Legality and Our Contradictory Commitments', in S. Sivakumaran, B. Van Schaack, D. Robinson. T. Meron, and B. Roth (eds.) *The Principle of Legality in International Criminal Law* (American Society of International Law, 2009) 104.

150 Damaška, 'What Is the Point', 355.

151 Minow, *Between Vengeance and Forgiveness*, 37.

152 May and Fyfe, *International Criminal Tribunals*, 20.

Just as some members of the community of practice have maintained that the special context of mass atrocities requires the relaxation of the principles of criminal law, according to others that same reason means that the principles of criminal law should be upheld even more stringently in ICL. Scholars have suggested that due to the 'highly discretionary' nature of ICL judgments, the legitimacy of international trials is particularly dependent on anchoring the infliction of punishment to the principles of criminal law.[153] Furthermore, legal scholars have suggested that judgments based on modes of liability that expand the scope of personal culpability could leave room for doubt about the defendant's responsibility and obstruct social reconciliation within the afflicted communities.[154] In the context of ICL, strict compliance with criminal law principles has been perceived as a safeguard against the excessive politicization of international criminal justice. Strict legality is said to 'restrain tyranny that arises from the arbitrary application of coercive force'.[155] Consequently, the power inequalities among states that result in the uneven enforcement of ICL, on this account, increase the importance of legality.[156] Furthermore, compliance with the culpability principle is considered to counter the perception of undue harshness against the individuals from vanquished nations.[157] Given the political selectivity of international prosecutions that could result in the prosecution of members of some ethnic or national groups but not others, the culpability principle becomes of particular importance in ICL because it ensures that the link between the individual defendant and the crime is established beyond doubt.[158]

Similar to the domestic debate, the two positions result from different visions of society – only this time, the question concerns visions of

153 Danner and Martinez, 'Guilty Associations', 79.

154 S. Darcy, 'Imputed Criminal Liability and the Goals of International Justice' (2007) 20 *Leiden Journal of International Law* 377–404, 400–401. Damaška, 'What Is the Point', 348–349. M. Damaška, 'The Shadow Side of Command Responsibility' (2001) 49(3) *The American Journal of Comparative Law* 455, 477–478.

155 Gallant, *Principle of Legality*, 21.

156 B. Roth, 'Moral Disagreement, Sovereign Authority, and the Limits to Extraterritorial Prosecution of Human Rights Violators', in S. Sivakumaran, B. Van Schaack, D. Robinson., T. Meron, and B. Roth (eds.) *The Principle of Legality in International Criminal Law* (American Society of International Law, 2009) 110–112. B. Roth, 'Coming to Terms with Ruthlessness: Sovereign Equality, Global Pluralism, and the Limits of International Criminal Justice' (2010) 8 *Santa Clara Journal of International Law* 231, 235.

157 Damaška, 'What Is the Point', 351.

158 S. Eldar, 'Exploring International Criminal Law's Reluctance to Resort to Modalities of Group Responsibility' (2013) 11(2) *Journal of International Criminal Justice* 331, 346. Damaška, 'What Is the Point', 351.

international society. Significant discrepancies have been observed within the ICL field regarding the meaning of international criminal 'justice' – whether it should be constrained to the minimalistic goal of determining the guilt or innocence of individual accused or whether it should include more ambitious communitarian goals.[159] The notions of morality and ethics have become central to the idea of building an international community of 'humanity' or 'civility' around the condemnation of mass atrocities.[160] From this perspective, morality can have a 'unifying power' in the international arena that otherwise lacks a political community defined by a world state.[161]

By contrast, from the perspective of the liberal critique, the objectification of defendants as means to convey messages to the international community contradicts the Kantian ethic of treating individuals as ends in themselves.[162] Some scholars have maintained that the liberal approach does not ignore the importance of community but simply requires that 'we justify our actions against the individual on behalf of society' by respecting the principles of legality and culpability.[163] From this perspective, because in ICL, just like in domestic criminal law, the object of punishment remains the individual person, the culpability principle is no less applicable in ICL than with respect to ordinary municipal crime.[164] Other scholars problematize the communitarian view that all international crimes 'shock the conscience' of humanity to such an extent that their criminalization is self-evident, and instead understand the international arena as site for moral pluralism.[165] From that perspective, the rule of law is necessary for promoting predictability and accountability in the exercise of power within a society beset by moral differences.[166]

Overall, while the integration of morality and criminal law has gained popularity within the ICL community of practice, especially among NGOs and some academics and practitioners, it has been significantly challenged

159 Sander, 'Unravelling the Confusion', 765.

160 D. Luban, 'The Enemy of All Humanity' (2018) 47(1) *Netherlands Journal of Legal Philosophy* 112, 136. Dubber, 'Common Civility', 924–925.

161 M. Aksenova, 'Solidarity as a Moral and Legal Basis for Crimes against Humanity: A Durkheimian Perspective', in M. Aksenova, E. van Sliedregt, and S. Parmentier (eds.) *Breaking the Cycle of Mass Atrocities: Criminological and Socio-Legal Approaches in International Criminal Law* (Oxford: Hart Publishing, 2019) 73, 88. See also Luban, 'Enemy of All Humanity'135–136. Dubber, 'Common Civility', 926.

162 Robinson, 'Identity Crisis', 926.

163 Robinson, 'Cosmopolitan Liberal Account', 142, emphasis omitted.

164 M. Jackson, 'The Attribution of Responsibility and Modes of Liability in International Criminal Law' (2016) 29(3) *Leiden Journal of International Law* 879, 893.

165 Roth, 'Coming to Terms', 285.

166 Ibid., 236.

in recent years by other legal experts. The latter have stressed the importance of the narrow and predictable application of criminal responsibility laws not just for protecting the defendants' rights, but also for upholding ICL's integrity. The significant dissonance between different sets of shared understandings with the ICL community stems from the dual nature of international criminal justice – as famously observed by George Fletcher, on the one hand, ICL rests on collectivist sentiments, while on the other it relies on liberal individualism to operationalize the idea of criminal responsibility for mass crimes in practice.[167]

3.3 Conclusion

This chapter presented the multiple dimensions of the normative environment within which ICL rules are articulated, contested, and justified. For simplicity, the analysis has outlined opposing sets of shared understandings, but in practice, those sets often overlap as will be demonstrated in the following chapters. Some members of the ICL community of practice evoke customary international law and teleological reasoning to identify a law based on which the defendant could be convicted not only because those members of the ICL community share a humanitarian concern for the victims' welfare, but also because they appear to have already made a moral judgment about the defendant's guilt. Others cherish procedural clarity not only because it protects ICL's integrity but also because of their previous experience in domestic penal systems, which tend to categorize legal rules to a high degree and follow strictly those rules. The schisms between sets of shared understandings also cut across different types of actors within the ICL field. For example, some legal scholars favour the technical application of criminal law principles in ICL, while others are willing to adopt human rights approaches for the purpose of punishing international crimes. Furthermore, respect of the defendants' rights has been advocated not only by states but also by some legal experts on the grounds that the principles of criminal law could protect ICL from excessive politicization more effectively than if legal decisions were guided by moral standards.

The analysis of the internal politics of the ICL field went beyond the commonly identified tension between human rights and criminal law norms to highlight that the latter itself does not present a unified set of shared understandings. While this has often been overlooked, some disagreements among criminal law experts have gained particular prominence at

[167] G. Fletcher, 'Liberals and Romantics'.

the international level, where the purpose of punishment exceeds retribution and includes more ambitious socio-pedagogical goals.[168] Notably, contrary to the 'maturation' thesis, the discussion showed that while the legal epistemic community shares a commitment to the broadly defined principles of criminal law, those principles do not constitute a clear objective standard against which international adjudication can be assessed. Instead, according to the 'practice' framework, the meaning of criminal law principles, such as legality and culpability, is constantly subjected to interpretation and contestation within the legal field.

Overall, the members of the ICL community of practice have been united by virtue of their shared understanding that the perpetrators of mass atrocities should be held criminally responsible and that their punishment should be determined in accordance with the principles of liberal trials. Beyond that consensus, however, significant competition of ideas exists within the ICL field about the meaning and scope of the legal norms that regulate the assessment of the defendant's guilt or innocence. These dynamics inside the ICL field illustrate Shklar's observation that, while the practice of rule-following is not a source of disagreement, the content of the rules is.[169] The diversity of opinion constitutes both a challenge and a favourable development for international courts and tribunals. On the one hand, the ICC cannot satisfy the often-conflicting demands of all members of the ICL community of practice. On the other hand, the availability of various sets of shared understandings regarding individual criminal responsibility for mass atrocities enables the court to choose among a broader set of approaches that are recognized as sound legal reasoning, and thus as within the remit of the 'legalism' norm that binds the ICL field, by at least some members of the ICL community of practice.[170] Critical scholars have observed that this could lead to justifying 'illiberal or hegemonic excess' of ICL.[171] But the 'practice' framework of international law suggests that completely idiosyncratic interpretations of the law, even if attempted by the judges, would likely meet significant criticism. As the following chapters discuss, despite the differences of opinion on the relationship between morality and legality at the post–Second World War tribunals, the UN tribunals, and the ICC, all those institutions have exhibited a stable line of legal reasoning with respect to the assessment of criminal responsibility.

[168] Drumbl, Atrocity, Punishment, and International Law. Ambos, *Treatise on International Criminal Law*, 68–72.

[169] Shklar, *Legalism*, 114.

[170] Vasiliev, 'International Criminal Justice and Injustice'.

[171] Kiyani, 'Legitimacy, Legality', 93.

4

Before Rome

Common Law Influence and the Merging of Morality and Legality

Following the end of the Second World War, the IMT and IMTFE judgments established the foundations of the norm of holding individuals criminally responsible in international law. The nascent community of ICL practice coalesced around the tribunals and began discussing the appropriate interpretation of the principles of legality and personal culpability with respect to international crimes. The UN tribunals for the former Yugoslavia and for Rwanda, established in the 1990s, significantly developed the legal rules regulating the attribution of individual criminal responsibility for mass atrocities. Exploring the practice of the UN tribunals is important for three reasons. Firstly, the tribunals provided the opportunity to consolidate the ICL epistemic community, not only through the tribunals' prolific jurisprudence, but also in terms of the significant engagement of legal academics in commentaries on judicial pronouncements. Secondly, the practice of the UN tribunals polarized the ICL community of practice on questions concerning individual criminal responsibility rules. Finally, the practice of the UN tribunals provides important context for understanding the normative dynamics of the ICL field, which subsequently influenced ICC jurisprudence.

4.1 The Early Days of ICL: Nuremberg and Tokyo

For the first time in international law, individual criminal responsibility was enforced at the Nuremberg IMT.[1] While some aspects of the post-war trials, especially the limited case selection, appeared strongly influenced by the interests of the victorious Allies, a closer look reveals a discernible line of legal reasoning behind the judgments. That reasoning resonated with the set of shared understandings that dominated the emerging ICL community of practice, namely that the perpetrators of atrocities should not go unpunished, even if that required a significant degree of judicial

[1] IMT Nuremberg Judgment, 466.

creativity in determining the applicable law. The IMT and IMTFE judges adopted an outcome-oriented understanding of the legality principle, according to which the law should not be applied in a purely technical manner, regardless of the consequences, but should aim to deliver substantive justice.

4.1.1 State Politics and the Birth of the ICL Field

The IMT Nuremberg and the IMTFE Tokyo were established after the end of the Second World War. The IMT Charter that was annexed to the 1945 London Agreement vested the tribunal with jurisdiction over crimes against peace, war crimes, and crimes against humanity.[2] The IMTFE was created by an order by the Allied Powers' Supreme Commander, US General Douglas MacArthur, and had the same subject matter jurisdiction as the IMT.[3] The influence of the political interests of the Allies were easily observable: the IMT was specifically created for the 'trial and punishment of the major war criminals of the European Axis countries'.[4] Despite the efforts of the Nuremberg Defence, the Allies' actions, such as the deliberate air attacks against civilians in Hamburg and Dresden or the use of the same types of unrestricted submarine warfare as the Axis, could not be raised at the trial.[5] It has been suggested that one of the most contentious issues at the IMT was the presence of the Soviet judge on the bench that would adjudicate the Axis's acts of aggression, when the Soviets had themselves invaded Poland and Finland.[6] Similarly, at the IMTFE, which was led by a US prosecutor, the fact that the American use of atomic bombs was not subject to adjudication raised concerns for one-sided justice.[7] One of the IMTFE judges, Justice Pal, dissented from the Tokyo Judgment, criticizing the idea of having the victorious parties judge the vanquished nations.[8]

2 Cassese, 'From Nuremberg to Rome', 7.
3 Kaufman, 'Nuremberg Tribunal', 754–757.
4 United Nations, Charter of the International Military Tribunal – Annex to the Agreement for the prosecution and punishment of the major war criminals of the European Axis ('London Agreement'), 8 August 1945, Article 1.
5 Tomuschat, 'Legacy of Nuremberg', 833, E. Borgwardt, *A New Deal for the World* (Cumberland, USA: Harvard University Press, 2007) 230–231
6 Borgwardt, New Deal, 230.
7 Nesiah, 'Doing History with Impunity', 106. Borgwardt, New Deal, 230.
8 International Military Tribunal for the Far East, 'Judgment of the Hon'ble Mr. Justice Pal's Dissent', 1984, Part 1 (pp. 1–374), 215.

The selection of individuals accused also revealed the influence of state interests on the post-war proceedings.[9] For instance, the decision to drop the Italian names from the list of suspects has been attributed to the decreasing concerns about the Italian threat after Mussolini's death and the potential difficulties of proving unambiguously Italy's guilt for the war.[10] Much criticism also raised the decision not to indict the Japanese Emperor for waging an aggressive war, which appeared to reflect the Allies' considerations for rebuilding a stable Japan by protecting the Emperor as the symbol of the nation.[11] The selection of the charges also appeared to reflect the Allies' interests. The Nuremberg prosecutors mainly focused on aggression because those crimes had most profoundly affected the Allies' populations, rather than the crimes against humanity committed against the European Jews.[12] The Tokyo trial similarly centred around crimes against peace, despite the evidence of other wartime atrocities.[13]

Overall, the influence of the Allied governments, and especially the United States, over the establishment and the operation of the post-war tribunals and the selection of defendants and charges was significant. Yet, as the following section suggests, a closer look at the Nuremberg and Tokyo judgments reveals that alongside the influence of state politics a line of distinctive legal reasoning is also observable at the tribunals. That legal reasoning resonated with the emerging debates within the still nascent epistemic community of ICL.

4.1.2 Legal Reasoning: Justifying the Trials

The IMT's power to exercise jurisdiction over individual persons was derived partly from occupation law.[14] But to avoid allegations of victors'

9 F. De Vlaming, 'Selection of Defendants', in L. Reydams, J. Wouters, and C. Ryngaert (eds.) *International Prosecutors* (Oxford: Oxford University Press, 2012) 542, 543. A. Gattini, 'A Historical Perspective: From Collective to Individual Responsibility and Back', in A. Nollkaemper and H. van der Wilt (eds.) *System Criminality in International Law* (Cambridge: Cambridge University Press, 2009) 101, 113.

10 D. Hedinger, 'A Global Conspiracy? The Berlin– Tokyo– Rome Axis on Trial and Its Impact on the Historiography of the Second World War' (2016) 14(4) *Journal of Modern European History* 500, 540.

11 De Vlaming, 'Selection of Defendants', 546

12 Borgwardt, New Deal, 223.

13 Y. Totani, 'The Case against the Accused', in Y. Tanaka, T. McCormack, and G. Simpson (eds.) *Beyond Victor's Justice? The Tokyo War Crimes Trial Revisited* (Leiden, Boston: Martinus Nijhoff, 2011) 147, 147–148.

14 H. Jescheck, 'The General Principles of International Criminal Law Set Out in Nuremberg, as Mirrored in the ICC Statute' (2004) 2(1) *Journal of International Criminal Justice* 38, 39.

justice and demonstrate the legality of their judgment, the judges made significant efforts to convince the defence and the international audience: 'The [IMT] Charter is not an arbitrary exercise of power on the part of the victorious nations, but [...] it is the expression of international law existing at the time of its creation.'[15] To prove the pre-existing criminalization of aggression, the IMT heavily relied on the 1928 Kellogg–Briand Pact that renounced the use of war as a tool for resolving international disputes.[16] However, establishing the IMT's jurisdiction over individual persons on a basis other than occupational law was considered controversial in view of the legality principle. The Kellogg–Briand Pact renounced aggressive war waged by states but did not include a provision for prosecuting the individual leaders of aggressive states.[17] Hence, at Nuremberg the illegality of state practice was often interpreted to imply the criminality of individual conduct.[18]

The IMT judges' creative legal findings seemed to be guided by a strong moral impulse to punish the former Nazi generals for the horrors of the war. The Nuremberg Judgment proclaimed that:

> the maxim nullum crimen sine lege is ... a principle of justice. To assert that it is unjust to punish those who ... have attacked neighboring states without warning is obviously untrue, for in such circumstances the attacker *must know* that he is doing wrong, and so far from it being unjust to punish him, it would be unjust *if his wrong were allowed to go unpunished.*[19]

Consequently, the Nuremberg Judgment did not reject the legality principle but understood the principle in specific manner, namely that if legality prevented substantive justice from being delivered, then legality was not a principle of justice, but merely a technical rule devoid of moral value. The IMT judges considered legality to be satisfied in view of the horrendous nature of the crimes, which should have provided notice to the accused that those crimes were criminal despite the scarcity of pre-existing codified law. That line of reasoning was later followed by the IMTFE[20] and the

[15] IMT Nuremberg Judgment, 461

[16] IMT Nuremberg Judgment, 460–461. May, Aggression, 147.

[17] May, Aggression, 147. Tomuschat, 'Legacy of Nuremberg', 833. See also Jescheck, 'General Principles', 41.

[18] Van Schaack, 'Crimen Sine Lege', 128–129.

[19] IMT Nuremberg Judgment, 462, emphasis added.

[20] International Military Tribunal for the Far East Judgment of 4 November 1948 (hereinafter *IMTFE Judgment*) [48] 438–439.

domestic trials against Nazi fugitives, including Eichmann, Barbie, and Finta.[21] The judges in those trials, which marked the birth of ICL, considered that the principles of criminal law should not be followed blindly with disregard of the broader context of the trials. The quality of the process was balanced against the quality of the outcome, and morality and legality were seen as inseparable.

Notably, the reasoning of the judges resonated with the views expressed by members of the nascent ICL community of practice outside the tribunals. Many legal philosophers at the time, including persons who held competing understandings of the law such as Fuller, Hart, and Gustav Radbruch,[22] and state officials, such as Henry L. Stimson, accepted the retroactive application as justified in order to prevent the perpetrators of mass atrocities from enjoying impunity.[23] More recent commentaries on the Nuremberg process similarly considered that the trial would have been a 'travesty of justice' if the judges had acquitted the accused 'merely because no one had previously been convicted of crime against peace'.[24] Hence, the broad interpretation of legality was justified because, even before the trial, the Nazi officials were perceived as evidently guilty.[25] Similarly, despite the seeming presumption of the defendants' guilt, the IMT and IMTFE judges did not reject the principle of personal culpability, thus, demonstrating their commitment to legalism, which they interpreted it in a broad way, so as to establish a link between each defendant and the alleged crimes.

[21] Lamb, 'Nullum Crimen', 739–740.

[22] L. L. Fuller, 'Positivism and Fidelity to Law: A Reply to Professor Hart' (1958) 71(4) *Harvard Law Review* 630. H. L. A. Hart, 'Positivism and the Separation of Law and Morals' (1958) 71(4) *Harvard Law Review* 593, 619–620. G. Radbruch 'Statutory Lawlessness and Supra-Statutory Law (1946), translated by Bonnie Litschewski Paulson, & Stanley L. Paulson' (2006[1946]) 26(1) *Oxford Journal of Legal Studies* 1.

[23] Stimson's remarks were quoted in the *Justice Case* Judgment: Trials of War Criminals before the Nuremberg Military Tribunals under Control Council Law No. 10, Vol. III, 'The Justice Case', October 1946–April 1949, 975.

[24] M. Bassiouni and B. Ferencz, 'The Crime against Peace and Aggression: From Its Origins to the ICC', in M. C. Bassiouni (ed.) *International Criminal Law*, Vol. I, 3rd edition (Leiden: Martinus Nijhoff Publishers, 2008) 207, 214.

[25] D. McGoldrick, 'The Legal and Political Significance of a Permanent International Criminal Court', in D. McGoldrick, P. J. Rowe, and E. Donnelly (eds.) *The Permanent International Criminal Court: Legal and Policy Issues* (Oxford and Portland Oregon: Hart Publishing, 2004) 453, 461. See also Shklar, *Legalism*, 160. T. Meron, 'From Nuremberg to the Hague' (1995) 149(1) *Military Law Review* 107, 109–110.

4.1.3 *Legal Reasoning: Modes of Criminal Responsibility*

4.1.3.1 Nuremberg

As novel institutions, the post-war tribunals faced not only the question of whether they could prosecute the Axis officials, but also how to establish their criminal responsibility in accordance with legal rules. It was here that the debates on individual criminal responsibility began. Colonel Bernays from the United States Department of War has been credited with proposing that the unique magnitude of the Nazi crimes required a special theory of liability that would reflect the *collective* nature of the criminal conduct:[26] 'conspiracy to commit murder, terrorism and the destruction of peaceful populations'.[27] Criminal law commentators have observed that Bernays's strategy did not envision proof of an overt act on behalf of the defendant towards the realization of specific crimes. Rather, mere membership in the conspiracy was deemed sufficient for the allocation of criminal responsibility for the crimes committed in the course of its implementation.[28]

The 'conspiracy' concept triggered controversies during the London negotiations. Bernays drew on the Anglo-American tradition, which recognized the notion of conspiracy, but the French and the Soviet representatives, who were trained in civil law, reportedly expressed strong disapproval of the broad concept of conspiracy that diluted the link between the accused and the crime.[29] Nevertheless, subsequent commentators have observed that the IMT judgment handled the notion of conspiracy cautiously. The judges restrained the scope of the conspiracy charge by determining that it required the existence of a concrete plan for waging war with clearly outlined criminal purposes. Furthermore, the judges considered that only those defendants who had had direct contact with Hitler and had participated knowingly in the preparation of the plans after 1937 could be held liable for conspiring to wage an aggressive

[26] Van Sliedregt, *Individual Criminal Responsibility*, 22–23.

[27] Quoted in L. Yanev, 'A Janus-Faced Concept: Nuremberg's Law on Conspiracy vis-à-vis the Notion of Joint Criminal Enterprise' (2015) 26(3) *Criminal Law Forum* 419, 427.

[28] Yanev, 'Janus-Faced Concept', 427. Van Sliedregt, *Individual Criminal Responsibility*, 22–23. N. Boister, 'The Application of Collective and Comprehensive Criminal Responsibility for Aggression at the Tokyo International Military Tribunal' (2010) 8(2) *Journal of International Criminal Justice* 425, 427.

[29] M. Dubber, 'Comparative Criminal Law' in M. Reimann and R. Zimmermann (eds.) *The Oxford Handbook of Comparative Law*, 1st ed. (Oxford: Oxford University Press, 2006), 1323.

war.[30] Hence, despite the broad language of the Charter, the IMT judges sought to establish a more concrete link between the defendants and the crimes apart from those persons' mere participation in the conspiracy, thus demonstrating the IMT's commitment to legalism. In that regard, it is often noted that only eight of the twenty-two defendants charged with conspiracy were found guilty on that basis.[31]

The IMT judges showed further restraint in the interpretation of the other form of criminal responsibility included in the IMT Charter: participation in a 'criminal organization'.[32] The Charter's drafters criminalized organizational membership per se, without enquiry into the mental state, or the personal culpability, of the accused in relation to the crimes committed by the respective organization.[33] But the judges decided to restrict the application of criminal organization liability only to those persons who had had 'knowledge of the criminal purposes or acts of the organization', despite the absence of such a requirement in the Charter.[34] The judges thus demonstrated restraint in the interpretation of 'criminal organizations' by view of the culpability principle.

The judges' reasoning found approval within the broader ICL community of practice at the time.[35] Even Hans Kelsen, who otherwise expressed reservations regarding the IMT, commended the judges' attempts to restrict liability for membership in criminal organizations.[36] More recently, several legal scholars have commented favourably on the IMT judges' decision to respect the culpability principle when interpreting the law on 'criminal organizations'.[37] Even though the IMT Charter nowhere mentioned that the attribution of criminal responsibility depended on the defendant's personal culpability, the IMT judgment underlined that 'criminal guilt is personal, and that mass punishment should be avoided'.[38] Legal scholars observed that, by restricting the controversial modes of

[30] Boister, 'Collective and Comprehensive Criminal Responsibility', 428. Ambos, *Treatise on International Criminal Law*, 110.
[31] Danner and Martinez, 'Guilty Associations', 116.
[32] Eldar, 'Exploring International Criminal Law', 332–333.
[33] Jescheck, 'General Principles', 44–45.
[34] IMT Nuremberg Judgment, 500.
[35] Q. Wrigth, 'International Law and Guilt by Association' (1949) 43(4) *American Journal of International Law* 746, 754.
[36] H. Kelsen, 'Will the Judgment in the Nuremberg Trial Constitute a Precedent in International Law?' (1947) 1(2) *The International Law Quarterly* 153, 166.
[37] Jain, Perpetrators and Accessories, 23, Van Sliedregt, Individual Criminal Responsibility, 30. Ambos, 'Current Issues', 246.
[38] IMT Nuremberg Judgment, 500.

liability, the IMT delivered convictions without leaving 'any doubt' to the defendants' culpability.[39] As observed by Kirchheimer, despite the influence of the political and military context on the establishment of the Nuremberg tribunal, the IMT was 'not a simulated trial' when it came to the decisions reached for the individual defendants.[40]

This is not to suggest that all Nuremberg judges were equally committed to the culpability principle. Some commentators considered that the Soviet judge, General Nikitchenko, saw the trial as means to *punish* the Nazi leaders, rather than to assess their guilt in accordance with the law.[41] But the final judgment recognized the importance of criminal responsibility principles whether all judges shared that understanding or the majority simply won 'against the protests of the USSR judge'.[42] By paying attention to the principles of criminal law – even those which had not been codified in the IMT Charter, the tribunal laid the foundations of the ICL legal field. And the scope and requirements of individual criminal responsibility for mass atrocities have been a subject of debate within that field ever since.

4.1.3.2 Tokyo

The legal reasoning underlying the interpretation of criminal responsibility laws in the Tokyo Judgment can also be clearly discerned, albeit it displayed a more relaxed interpretation of culpability compared to the Nuremberg Judgment. Chief Prosecutor Keenan alleged the existence of an inner-Japanese conspiracy that aimed to wage aggressive wars to dominate East Asia and the Pacific. According to the prosecutor, the Japanese government officials were responsible for all conducts performed by themselves or by any other person in the execution of the conspiracy.[43] All but two of the 28 defendants were convicted on the conspiracy charge at Tokyo.[44] The availability of evidence illuminates the question of why the IMTFE relied more extensively on the conspiracy charge than did their colleagues at Nuremberg. There was abundant evidence documenting the conducts of the Nazis.[45] By contrast, the IMTFE faced the 'difficulties of

[39] Darcy, 'Imputed Criminal Liability', 399.

[40] Kirchheimer, *Political Justice*, 340.

[41] Gallant, *Principle of Legality*, 79. Bass, *Stay the Hand of Vengeance*, 203.

[42] Kirchheimer, *Political Justice*, 334.

[43] Indictment from the International Military Tribunal for the Far East. Bontecou Papers, World War II File. Japanese War Crimes Trials – general. Harry S. Truman Presidential Museum & Library, 1. Boister, 'Collective and Comprehensive Criminal Responsibility', 429.

[44] Van Sliedregt, *Individual Criminal Responsibility*, 26.

[45] Combs, *Fact-Finding without Facts*, 6.

establishing individual responsibility for action in extensive, complex, fluid and opaque decision-making processes'.[46] It has often been observed that the Tokyo judges used the conspiracy charge to establish an indirect link between the accused and the crimes by, firstly, linking the accused to the conspiracy and, secondly, imputing the crimes that had been committed following the implementation of the conspiracy to the accused in view of that person's membership in the conspiracy.[47]

Another factor that may have influenced the difference in the approaches of the Nuremberg and the Tokyo tribunals was the significant American influence over the latter. The restrained use of conspiracy at the IMT was as a 'partial victory' for the French judge Donnedieu de Vabres[48] who reportedly felt uncomfortable with that common law concept.[49] The fierce criticism of the German defence lawyers against the conspiracy charge may have also influenced the Nuremberg judges in that regard.[50] Despite the dissent of the French judge at the IMTFE who found the conspiracy charge problematic because it obscured the nature of the individual's participation in the crimes,[51] the IMTFE Majority Judgment left 'untouched' the 'broad character and Anglo-American features' of conspiracy.[52] The Tokyo tribunal has been described as 'completely dominated by American personnel, finances, and ideology'.[53]

The reliance on conspiracy to convict such a broad range of defendants, without clearly distinguishing between the degree of responsibility of the different participants within the conspiracy, has been described as concerning by those subscribing to a narrower view of the culpability principle.[54] Nevertheless, the IMTFE Majority demonstrated some restraint

[46] Boister, 'Collective and Comprehensive Criminal Responsibility', 431.

[47] K. Sellars, 'Imperfect Justice at Nuremberg and Tokyo' (2010) 21(4) *European Journal of International Law* 1085, 1093–1094. See also Hedinger, 'A Global Conspiracy', 512. Boister, 'Collective and Comprehensive Criminal Responsibility', 431.

[48] Gallant, *Principle of Legality*, 117.

[49] Ibid., 127.

[50] Ambos, *Treatise on International Criminal Law*, 110.

[51] International Military Tribunal for the Far East, 'Dissenting Judgment of the Member from France of the International Military Tribunal for the Far East, 1948 (hereinafter IMTFE, Judge Bernard's Opinion) 4–5. D. Cohen and Y. Totani, *The Tokyo War Crimes Tribunal: Law, History, and Jurisprudence* (Cambridge: Cambridge University Press, 2018) 392.

[52] Van Sliedregt, *Individual Criminal Responsibility*, 26.

[53] E. Kopelman, 'Ideology and International Law: The Dissent of the Indian Justice at the Tokyo War Crimes Trial' (1991) 23(2) *N.Y.U. Journal of International Law and Politics* 373, 389–390.

[54] Boister, 'Collective and Comprehensive Criminal Responsibility', 438. Ambos, *Treatise on International Criminal Law*, 111.

in the employment of the conspiracy charge. Even though the judges accepted the existence of the inner-Japanese conspiracy charge, they dismissed the charge of the alleged broader German-Japanese conspiracy to secure domination over the world.[55]

In addition to conspiracy, the IMTFE relied on a mode of liability that was not explicitly employed at Nuremberg – the principle of command, or superior responsibility.[56] The norm of holding military commanders accountable for the discipline and conducts of their troops has been traced back centuries.[57] The Tokyo tribunal extended the principle to hold accountable civilian superiors,[58] including cabinet ministers.[59] As construed by the IMTFE Judgment, command responsibility required that the defendants knew or *should have known* about the crimes that were committed by their subordinates, by virtue of their position in charge.[60]

The broad scope of command responsibility triggered criticism from legal experts in view of the culpability principle.[61] The judgment against the former Japanese Foreign Minister Koki Hirota who failed to prevent war crimes committed by Japanese troops has been considered particularly controversial within the ICL field. The Majority Judgment concluded that Hirota's 'inaction amounted to criminal negligence'.[62] Hirota's judgment was criticized for ignoring the accused's inability to do much about

[55] Hedinger, 'A Global Conspiracy', 512.

[56] For an analysis of the 'command'/'superior' responsibility terminology, see G. Mettraux, *International Crimes and the Ad Hoc Tribunals* (Oxford: Oxford University Press, 2006) 144.

[57] B. B. Jia, 'The Doctrine of Command Responsibility in International Law: With Emphasis on Liability for Failure to Punish' (1998) 45(3) *Netherlands International Law Review* 325, 326–327.

[58] R. Cryer, 'The *Ad Hoc* Tribunals and the Law of Command Responsibility: A Quiet Earthquake', in S. Darcy and J. Powderly (eds.) *Judicial Creativity at the International Criminal Tribunals* (Oxford: Oxford University Press, 2010) 159, 160.

[59] G. Boas, J. L. Bischoff, and N. L. Reid, *International Criminal Law Practitioner Library, Vol. I. Forms of Responsibility in International Criminal Law* (Cambridge: Cambridge University Press, 2008) 156.

[60] R. Cryer, 'Then and Now: Command Responsibility, the Tokyo Tribunal and Modern International Criminal Law', in K. Sellars (ed.) *Trials for International Crimes in Asia* (Cambridge: Cambridge University Press, 2015) 64. J. D. Levine, 'The Doctrine of Command Responsibility and Its Application to Superior Civilian Leadership: Does the International Criminal Court Have the Correct Standard?' (2007) 193 *Military Law Review* 52, 64. M. Lippman, 'Humanitarian Law: The Uncertain Contours of Command Responsibility' (2001) 8(2) *Tulsa Journal of Comparative & International Law* 1, 19.

[61] K. Ambos, 'Superior Responsibility', in A. Cassese, P. Gaeta, and J. R. W. D. Jones (eds.) *The Rome Statute of the International Criminal Court* Vol. II (Oxford: Oxford University Press, 2002) 831.

[62] IMTFE Judgment, [49] 791.

the crimes, because the perpetrators had actually worked for another ministry.[63] Minow argued that Hirota's death sentence alleviated the sense of personal responsibility on behalf of the military leaders for the atrocities.[64] Even one IMTFE judge displayed uneasiness with the broad scope of command responsibility, noting that the responsibility of negligent commanders was not of equal gravity with that of the 'immediate author' of the crimes.[65] As will be discussed in Chapter 8, in *Bemba* the ICC has taken a significantly more restrained approach to assessing the material capabilities of commanders to address crimes by subordinates.

The rationale behind the decisions of IMTFE Majority to resort to command responsibility appeared to be the same as their reliance on the conspiracy charge – unlike Nuremberg where there was evidence of the *direct* orders of high-level accused towards their subordinates to commit crimes, at Tokyo the judges had to find a tool to establish the *indirect* link between the leadership level and the crimes.[66] This is illustrated in the IMTFE Majority's attempt to justify their reasoning:

> ... the Tribunal heard evidence ... to atrocities committed in all [theatres] of war on a scale so vast, yet following so common a pattern in all [theatres], that only one conclusion is possible – the atrocities were either secretly ordered or wilfully permitted by the Japanese Government ...[67]

The reasoning of the Tokyo Judgment reflects the shared understanding within the nascent ICL community of practice that the concept of 'culpable conduct' had to be interpreted broadly to avoid impunity for the crimes committed during the war. The IMTFE Majority's intuition was that the crimes were orchestrated from above and, consequently, that the defendants were culpable. From that perspective, to interpret the law narrowly and acquit guilty individuals would have constituted an injustice.

4.1.4 *The Legacy of the Post-War Judgments*

Once the notion of the 'law' is unpacked and examined with reference to the shared understandings held within the community of lawyers and diplomats during the post-war period, one can discern the legal

[63] Boas Bischoff and Reid, *International Criminal Law*, 156.
[64] Minow, *Between Vengeance and Forgiveness*, 41.
[65] IMTFE, *Judge Bernard's Opinion*, 15.
[66] Cryer, 'Then and Now', 60. B. Bonafe, 'Finding a Proper Role for Command Responsibility' (2007) 5(3) *Journal of International Criminal Justice* 599, 601.
[67] IMTFE Judgment, [49] 592.

reasoning, and not just the state influence, behind the Nuremberg and the Tokyo judgments. The modes of liability used at those tribunals might appear sweeping, but the emerging ICL community of practice nevertheless accepted those modes as legitimate for the time being on the grounds of moral arguments, such as the perceived need to avoid impunity for the Axis's wartime atrocities. Another important factor was the influence of common law lawyers in the drafting and interpretation of the Nuremberg Charter. From a common law perspective, the 'conspiracy' concept appeared less controversial in view of the culpability principle than from a civil law perspective. In fact, several years after the Nuremberg Judgment, the *Pinkerton* conspiracy became an accepted doctrine in US domestic law.[68] The IMT and IMTFE judges did not disregard the principles of legality and culpability as pertaining to individual criminal responsibility. Rather, they interpreted those principles in accordance with the normative dynamics of the ICL field at the time, namely the strong moral intuition that the aggressors behind the Second World War should not be allowed to rely on legal loopholes to avoid punishment. It was the judges at the post-war tribunals, rather than the states who drafted the charters, who paid attention to the criminal responsibility principles and the defendants' rights,[69] essentially instituting the ICL field of practice.

4.2 Post–Cold War: The ICTY and ICTR

4.2.1 Putting the Wheels of ICL in Motion

That field of practice was consolidated in the 1990s. The ICTY was established by UN Security Council Resolution 827 of 25 May 1993[70] and the ICTR a year later with Resolution 955 of 8 November 1994.[71] Some commentators have attributed the tribunals' creation to the sense of moral 'guilt' of the global powers for failing to intervene and stop the conflicts in the former Yugoslavia and Rwanda.[72] The Rwandan genocide, in

68 Yanev, 'Janus-Faced Concept', 429.
69 Gallant, *Principle of Legality*, 68.
70 United Nations Security Council, S/RES/827, 25 May 1993.
71 United Nations Security Council, S/RES/955, 8 November 1994.
72 Schiff, *Building the International Criminal Court*, 43–44. See also R. Zacklin, 'The Failings of Ad Hoc International Tribunals' (2004) 2(2) *Journal of International Criminal Justice* 541, 542.

particular, became a symbol of 'the international community's indifference to massive human suffering'.[73] But there was one major challenge to the new tribunals: even though ICL's foundational principles were codified after the Nuremberg proceedings,[74] the system had not advanced significantly during the Cold War. The UN tribunals' statutes were not of particular assistance either. Drafted under time pressure by the Secretary General,[75] the ICTY and ICTR Statutes included little more than general categories of crimes.[76] But instead of surrendering the attempts to end impunity due to the lack of applicable law, the UN tribunals' judges engaged in 'full-scale refashioning of ICL'.[77]

Given the scarcity of pre-existing codified legal rules, the judges turned to alternative sources of law in developing ICL. Commentators observed that customary international law was used at the tribunals 'as a springboard for judicial creativity'.[78] In the tribunals' early days, the term 'laws or customs of war' was often interpreted 'in the broadest possible sense' for the purpose of deriving applicable law.[79] The same has been observed with respect to the UN tribunals' findings on the existence of general principles of law laid down by major legal systems.[80] On occasion, the UN tribunals appeared to 'manipulat[e] the process of abstraction of legal rules from national legal systems, so as to create a legal principle apt for settling the legal issue at hand'.[81] Faced with the potential *non liquet* scenario, i.e. lack of applicable law, the UN tribunals' judges engaged in a practice akin to 'judicial legislation'.[82]

The UN tribunals did not disregard legalism – one of the foundational norms binding the ICL field. They recognized the importance of legality

[73] V. Peskin, *International Justice in Rwanda and the Balkans* (Cambridge: Cambridge University Press, 2008) 155.

[74] United Nations, Principles of International Law Recognized in the Charter of the Nürnberg Tribunal and in the Judgment of the Tribunal. 2005[1950].

[75] Danner, 'When Courts Make Law', 19–23.

[76] Grover, 'Call to Arms', 547. A. Galand, 'The Systemic Effect of International Human Rights Law on International Criminal Law', in M. Scheinin (ed.) *Human Tights Norms in 'Other' International Courts* (Cambridge: Cambridge University Press, 2019) 87, 93.

[77] Van Schaack, 'Crimen Sine Lege', 123.

[78] Powderly, 'Judicial Interpretation', 31.

[79] Lamb, 'Nullum Crimen', 744.

[80] G. Boas, 'Omission Liability at the International Criminal Tribunals – A Case for Reform', in S. Darcy and J. Powderly (eds.) *Judicial Creativity at the International Criminal Tribunals* (Oxford: Oxford University Press, 2010) 204.

[81] Raimondo, 'General Principles of Law', 52, emphasis added. See also Mantovani, 'General Principles', 27–28. Bantekas, 'Reflections on Some Sources', 129.

[82] Darcy, 'Bridging the Gaps', 320.

and culpability for assessing criminal responsibility but interpreted those principles from a specific perspective that integrated morality with legality, displayed humanitarian concern for the victims, and perceived the purpose of domestic criminal law and ICL as fundamentally different. Like their IMT colleagues, the UN tribunals' judges proclaimed the culpability principle to be 'the foundation of criminal responsibility'.[83] Even though the UN tribunals' statutes did not address the accused's *mens rea*, the judges confirmed that as an essential element of criminal responsibility.[84] The ICTY recognized legality and its constitutive principles as 'the solid pillars' of the criminal justice system.[85] But they were generally guided by the shared understanding that at the international level, the preservation of justice and fairness towards the accused had to be 'balance[d]' against 'the preservation of world order'.[86] The tribunals further noted that 'the principles of legality in international criminal law are different from their related national legal systems' because of the distinctive nature of international crimes.[87] The '*immorality* or appalling character' of mass atrocities was considered so great that it should have provided the accused with fair notice that the act was criminal, regardless of the lack of pre-existing codified law proscribing that act.[88] The judicial reasoning behind the early UN tribunals' judgments also appeared to be influenced by a concern for the interest of victims to see justice being served.[89] The ICTY situated itself not merely as a criminal court but as a 'guardian' of 'humanity' within the international political context dominated by sovereign states.[90]

Furthermore, while from the perspective of criminal law the tribunals' judges may have interpreted the legality principle too broadly, from the perspective of public international law that was not necessarily the case.

[83] *Tadić*, Judgment, IT-94-1-A, Appeals Chamber, 15 July 1999 (hereinafter *Tadić* Appeals Judgement), § 186.

[84] W. Schabas, 'Mens Rea and the International Criminal Tribunal for the Former Yugoslavia' (2003) 37(4) *New England Law Review* 1036, 1018.

[85] *Delalić, Mucić, Delić and Landžo*, Judgment, IT-96-21-T, Trial Chamber, 16 November 1998, (hereinafter *Čelebići* Trial Judgment) § 402.

[86] Ibid., § 405.

[87] *Čelebići* Trial Judgment, § 405. See also the ICTR in *Karemera et al. Karemera, Ngirumpatse, Nzirorera, and Rwamakuba*, Judgment, ICTR-98-44-T, Trial Chamber, 11 May 2004, § 43.

[88] *Milutinović, Šainović and Ojdanić*, Decision on Dragoljub Ojdanić's Motion Challenging Jurisdiction – Joint Criminal Enterprise IT_99-37-AR72, Appeals Chamber, 21 May 2003, (hereinafter *Milutinović et al.*, Ojdanić's Motion Decision), § 42, emphasis added.

[89] G. Fletcher, 'New Court', 185–187.

[90] D. Corrias and G. Gordon, 'Judging in the Name of Humanity International Criminal Tribunals and the Representation of a Global Public' (2015) 13(1) *Journal of International Criminal Justice* 97, 103.

One of the former ICTY presidents opined that, compared to international courts such as the International Court of Justice, the ICTY took an 'essentially conservative and traditional approach' towards the identification of the law that did not conflict with legality.[91] It has been observed that the first legal practitioners to engage with ICL in the 1990s mostly came from backgrounds in human rights law and international humanitarian law, which may have influenced their understanding of the limitations imposed by the criminal responsibility principles.[92] As more judges with background in domestic criminal courts were appointed to the ICTY over the years,[93] the practice of interpreting the law at the tribunal came to be conducted in a more restrained manner.[94] Yet, many of the milestone early-days decisions of the UN tribunals were described as 'paradoxical' from the defendant-oriented perspective of criminal law.[95]

From the perspective of intersubjective legalism employed in this book, the reasoning of the UN tribunals was indeed legalist, not only because it followed specific principles, but because it has been recognized as sound reasoning by many members of the ICL community. The tribunals' efforts to develop a system offering legal protection from human rights violations were actively supported in the 1990s.[96] NGOs and human rights advocates saw international trials as a potential contributor to the psychological welfare of victims and societal reconciliation within the affected communities.[97] From the perspective of the human rights organizations monitoring the conflict areas, there was 'little doubt about' the responsibility of certain leadership figures who had 'orchestrat[ed]' the crimes.[98] Similar to the IMT context, rendering impunity for those persons due to the lack of applicable law would have hardly constituted a satisfactory outcome for

[91] T. Meron, 'Revival of Customary Humanitarian Law' (2005) 99(4) *American Journal of International Law* 817, 821.

[92] Robinson, 'Identity Crisis', 928.

[93] L. Swigart and D. Terris, 'Who Are International Judges?' in C. Romano, K. Alter, and Y. Shany (eds.) *The Oxford Handbook of International Adjudication*, 1st ed. (Oxford: Oxford University Press, 2013) 619, 632.

[94] Danner, 'When Courts Make Law', 32. See also Wessel, 'Judicial Policy-Making', 395.

[95] Darcy, 'Bridging the Gaps', 331.

[96] M. Swart, 'Is There a Text in This Court? The Purposive Method of Interpretation and the ad hoc Tribunals' (2010) 70 *ZaöRV* 767, 769.

[97] Amnesty International, 'A Call for UN Human Rights Action on Rwanda and Burundi', 30 April 1994, www.amnesty.org/download/Documents/184000/ior410021994en.pdf, 7.

[98] Amnesty International, 'Rwanda: Mass Murder by Government Supporters and Troops in April and May 1994', 23 May 1994, www.amnesty.org/download/Documents/184000/afr470111994en.pdf, 1. See also P. Hazan, *Justice in a Time of War* (College Station: Texas A&M University Press, 2004), 13.

the UN tribunals' global audience, considering the media publicization of the atrocities in the former Yugoslavia and Rwanda.[99] From that perspective, the UN tribunals' creative interpretation of the law was deemed 'necessary' for the purpose of responding to the challenges of modern inter-ethnic conflict.[100] States were similarly looking forward to successful prosecutions. Supporting the operation of the UN tribunals was expensive.[101] A significant rate of acquittals at the UN tribunals was 'apt to play poorly' in the Western countries that provided 'the bulk of the tribunals' financial and enforcement support'.[102]

But the ICL field is diverse and harbours different beliefs, and many legal scholars and practitioners felt uncomfortable with the tribunals' judicial activism. But even the advocates of narrow interpretations of criminal law principles have recognized the tribunals' reasoning as a sound approach for developing a functional ICL system.[103] As often observed, the ICTY and the ICTR 'put flesh on the bones of modern international law'.[104] In the words of one legal scholar, the UN tribunals' 'impressive achievements and contributions' to the ICL field can hardly be overestimated.[105] Given the scarcity of pre-existing applicable law, it was considered understandable that the tribunals would not be 'the best venue for the expression of a heartfelt belief in the fundamental applicability of legal positivism'.[106] Nevertheless, as will be discussed in the next section, once the foundations of ICL jurisprudence were put in place, many legal scholars from criminal law backgrounds became increasingly critical of the tribunals' practices.

99 Hazan, *Justice in a Time of War*, 8–9.

100 N. Wagner, 'The development of the grave breaches regime and of individual criminal responsibility by the International Criminal Tribunal for the former Yugoslavia' (2003) 85(850) *International Review of the Red Cross* 351, 352.

101 Zacklin, 'Failings of Ad Hoc International Tribunals', 543. See also A. Brannigan, 'Is the Sun Setting on Cosmopolitan Justice?' (2011) 48(5) *Society* 420, 422. Stephen, 'International Criminal Law', 60.

102 Combs, Fact-Finding without Facts, 232.

103 Van Sliedregt, Individual Criminal Responsibility, 14. Danner, 'When Courts Make Law', 52. W. Schabas, *The UN International Criminal Tribunals* (Cambridge: Cambridge University Press, 2006) 236.

104 Grover, 'Call to Arms', 547. See also W. Fenrick, 'The Development of the Law of Armed Conflict through the Jurisprudence of the International Criminal Tribunal for the Former Yugoslavia' (1998) 3(2) *Journal of Armed Conflict Law* 197, 197.

105 G. Sluiter, '*Ad hoc* International Criminal Tribunals (Yugoslavia, Rwanda, Sierra Leone)', in W. Schabas (ed.), *The Cambridge Companion to International Criminal Law* (Cambridge: Cambridge University Press, 2016) 117, 117.

106 Powderly, 'Judicial Interpretation', 18.

4.2.2 *Developing Modes of Liability*

4.2.2.1 Joint Criminal Enterprise

The controversial 'joint criminal enterprise' (JCE) mode of liability was first articulated in 1999 by the *Tadić* AC. The judgment became famous for the AC's 'landmark general findings' on the applicable legal norms, including those regulating the attribution of criminal responsibility.[107] After the 1999 *Tadić* appeal judgment, the JCE doctrine was used in many ICTY trials and some ICRT cases.[108]

In *Tadić*, the judges faced the familiar challenge of establishing individual guilt for a collective crime, which their colleagues at the IMT and IMTFE had dealt with. There was evidence of the accused's presence at the scene of the crimes but not of his direct participation in their commission.[109] Duško Tadić was a member of the armed group that entered the village of Jaskići and killed five Muslim men, but it was not clear that Tadić had personally killed those men.[110] The judges at Nuremberg and Tokyo previously relied on the 'conspiracy' charge to link individual persons to the collective criminal conduct, but that approach proved highly controversial for many criminal lawyers, especially civil law practitioners. By contrast, the *Tadić* AC decided to develop a new mode of liability that would link the accused to the group crime.

The AC judges evoked a teleological interpretation of the ICTY Statute and famously concluded that, since the ICTY Statute aimed to extend its jurisdiction over '*all* ' persons responsible for international crimes, its reach cannot be limited only to those persons who physically committed the crime.[111] Consequently, the AC considered that the term 'committed' under Article 7(1) covered not only direct or physical commission of a crime, but also 'participation in the realisation of a common design or purpose'.[112] Since the ICTY Statute did not specify the elements of the new mode of liability that would become known as 'joint criminal enterprise', the judges resorted to customary international norms for that purpose.[113] The AC concluded that JCE required a) a plurality of persons;

[107] Sassòli and Olson, 'Judgment of the ICTY', 734.

[108] E. Van Sliedregt, 'Joint Criminal Enterprise as a Pathway to Convicting Individuals for Genocide' (2007) 5(1) *Journal of International Criminal Justice* 184.

[109] *Tadić* Opinion and Judgment, IT-94-1-T, 7 May 1997, Trial Chamber (hereinafter *Tadić* Trial Judgment, § 673.

[110] Ibid., § 373.

[111] *Tadić* Appeals Judgment, § 189, emphasis in the original.

[112] Ibid., § 188.

[113] Ibid., § 194.

b) the existence of a 'common plan, design or purpose which amount[ed] to or involve[d] the commission of a crime'; and c) the accused's participation in the common design. Hence, under JCE the prosecutor did not have to prove that the accused had physically carried out the crime. Rather, the accused could be convicted for 'committing' a crime by merely providing 'assistance in, or contribution to, the execution of the common purpose'.[114] The AC found that the notion of participation in a 'common design', or JCE, covered different scenarios. The notorious third scenario (JCE III) imputed liability to the accused for a crime that had been merely 'foreseeable' to them, even if that crime had fallen outside the scope of the common criminal plan.[115]

That development would subsequently polarize the ICL community of practice on questions of criminal responsibility. The creation of JCE, and especially JCE III, quickly triggered debate concerning its statutory basis. Legal scholars expressed concern that to 'foresee' a crime did not fall within the meaning of the term 'to commit' a crime codified in Article 7(1) ICTY Statute.[116] Commentators noted that Article 7(1)[117] already provided the judges with a list of applicable modes of liability, such as planning or ordering the commission of crimes, so the need for articulating a new one was not obvious.[118] The foundations of JCE III in customary international law was also questioned,[119] with some members of the ICL community describing it as the product of 'judicial creativity'.[120]

But many other members of the ICL community of practice justified the development of JCE by reference to the quest to end impunity for mass

[114] Ibid., § 227.

[115] Ibid., § 220.

[116] S. Powles, 'Joint Criminal Enterprise – Criminal Liability by Prosecutorial Ingenuity and Judicial Creativity' (2004) 2(2) *Journal of International Criminal Justice* 606, 611. Darcy, 'Imputed Criminal Liability', 384.

[117] Updated Statute of the International Criminal Tribunal for the former Yugoslavia, adopted 25 May 1993 by Resolution 827, as amended 7 July 2009 by Resolution 1877 (hereinafter ICTY Statute). See also Statute of the International Criminal Tribunal for the Prosecution of Persons Responsible for Genocide and Other Serious Violations of International Humanitarian Law Committed in the Territory of Rwanda and Rwandan Citizens Responsible for Genocide and Other Such Violations Committed in the Territory of Neighbouring States, between 1 January 1994 and 31 December 1994, (hereinafter ICTR Statute), Article6(1).

[118] Powles, 'Joint Criminal Enterprise', 611. Ohlin, 'Three Conceptual Problems', 74.

[119] J. D. Ohlin, 'Joint Intentions to Commit International Crimes' (2011) 11(2) *Chicago Journal of International Law* 693, 712. Darcy, 'Imputed Criminal Liability', 384. Powles, 'Joint Criminal Enterprise', 616.

[120] Fletcher and Ohlin, 'Reclaiming Fundamental Principles', 548.

atrocities. One authoritative judge at the UN tribunals argued that the creative interpretation of Article 7(1) was permissible because the adoption of JCE was 'necessary for the fulfilment of the mission of the ICTY to administer international criminal justice'.[121] As specified by an expert group led by the ICTY's first president, JCE served to prevent individual perpetrators from escaping criminal accountability by hiding behind 'the fog of collective criminality'.[122] For that reason, JCE was defended as a 'useful tool' for establishing the criminal responsibility of those persons who were not directly involved in the violence on the ground, especially the 'high-level perpetrators that use their subordinates' to commit the crimes.[123]

Notably, the UN tribunals' judges considered that JCE did not violate the culpability principle. The ICTY 'took pains' to distinguish JCE from the IMT's broad concepts of conspiracy and criminal organizations.[124] The ICTY judges stressed that JCE was 'not a liability for mere membership or for conspiring to commit crimes'[125] because JCE required not only evidence of an agreement to commit crimes but also proof of the commission of criminal acts in furtherance of that agreement.[126] Hence, the UN tribunals' judges sought to convince the ICL epistemic community that JCE was more compliant with the culpability principle compared to the conspiracy or organizational membership doctrines because it required a more substantial link between the accused and the crimes.[127]

But a growing subgroup within the ICL epistemic community, who understood the principles of criminal law in ICL in a more restrained fashion, remained unconvinced that JCE, and especially its third variant,

[121] M. Shahabuddeen, 'Judicial Creativity and Joint Criminal Enterprise' in S. Darcy and J. Powderly (eds.) *Judicial Creativity at the International Criminal Tribunals* (Oxford: Oxford University Press, 2010) 184, 197.

[122] A. Cassese et al., 'Amicus Curiae Brief of Professor Antonio Cassese and Members of the Journal of International Criminal Justice on Joint Criminal Enterprise Doctrine' (2009) 20(2–3) *Criminal Law Forum* 289, 294.

[123] D. Liu, 'Contribution of the United Nations Ad Hoc Tribunals to the Development of International Criminal Law', in M. Bergsmo, C. W. Ling, S. Tianying, and Yi Ping (eds.) *Historical Origins of International Criminal Law: Volume 4* (Brussels: Torkel Opsahl Academic EPublisher, 2015) 125, 141.

[124] Eldar, 'Exploring International Criminal Law', 333, footnote 6.

[125] *Milutinović et al.*, Ojdanić's Motion Decision, § 26.

[126] Ibid., § 23.

[127] Ohlin, 'Joint Intentions', 696. K. Gustafson, 'The Requirement of an Express Agreement for Joint Criminal Enterprise Liability' (2007) 5(1) *Journal of International Criminal Justice* 134, 140.

complied with the culpability principle.[128] Particularly controversial in that regard was the low *mens rea* requirement of JCE III. Legal scholars expressed concern that the attribution of criminal responsibility for crimes that were merely 'foreseeable' by the accused resembled the attribution of liability without proof of personal culpability.[129] Criminal law scholars argued that JCE III treated so many persons as potential perpetrators that the doctrine experienced difficulties explaining 'why each fish caught deserves punishment for intentional wrongdoing'.[130] Hence, JCE was often called a 'catch-all concept',[131] with one academic proposing that the abbreviation JCE III stood for 'just convict everyone'.[132]

Furthermore, JCE's 'evisceration of the distinction between principals and accomplices' bothered many legal scholars concerned with the principle of fair labelling.[133] Participation in a JCE was considered a more serious form of liability than aiding and abetting a crime at the UN tribunals,[134] but the judges did not appear to distinguish between the gravity of criminal responsibility under JCE III and that under JCE I.[135] Some academics reasoned that a person who merely foresaw the commission of a crime could be considered an aider but to define the participant in JCE III a 'principal' perpetrator breached the fair labelling principle.[136] There is a morally relevant difference, the argument goes, between the militia member who joined the enterprise, despite foreseeing the risk of the ensuing crimes, and the member who personally decided to torture civilians.[137] That line of criticism of JCE displayed a normative approach to criminal responsibility, according to which the terms 'principal' and

[128] Interview with Kevin Heller, 11 August 2002. Interview with Douglas Guilfoyle, 12 August 2020.

[129] Ambos, 'Joint Criminal Enterprise', 174. See also Damaška, 'What Is the Point', 352.

[130] T. Weigend, 'Intent, Mistake of Law, and Co-perpetration in the *Lubanga* Decision on Confirmation of Charges' (2008) 6(3) *Journal of International Criminal Justice* 471, 477.

[131] Van Sliedregt, 'Joint Criminal Enterprise', 1047. Ainley, 'Excesses of Responsibility', 416.

[132] M. E. Badar, '"Just Convict Everyone!" – Joint Perpetration: From *Tadić* to *Stakić* and Back Again' (2006) 6(2) *International Criminal Law Review* 293, 302.

[133] Ohlin, 'Organizational Criminality', 108. See also C. Farhang, 'Point of No Return: Joint Criminal Enterprise in Brđanin' (2010) 23(1) *Leiden Journal of International Law* 137, 140. Robinson, 'Identity Crisis', 940.

[134] *Tadić* Appeals Judgment, § 229.

[135] Olásolo, 'Joint Criminal Enterprise', 286.

[136] Ambos, 'Joint Criminal Enterprise', 168–169. D. Guilfoyle, 'Responsibility for Collective Atrocities: Fair Labelling and Approaches to Commission in International Criminal Law' (2011) 64(1) *Current Legal Problems* 255, 273. Werle and Burghardt, 'Establishing Degrees', 305.

[137] Ohlin, 'Three Conceptual Problems', 83.

'accessory' denote the degree of the accused's blameworthiness.[138] As will be discussed in Chapter 6, the ICC judges placed emphasis on this differentiation between the modes of liability.

The debates surrounding JCE were reminiscent of those around the conspiracy charge at Nuremberg. The low requirements of JCE and the lack of differentiation between the roles within the common enterprise led the critics to conclude that the notion of conspiracy made a 'remarkable comeback' at the UN tribunals, 'wrapped in the cloth' of the JCE doctrine.[139] Also like the Nuremberg debates, the criticism of JCE often reflected the differences between civil and common law approaches to criminal responsibility. The central idea behind JCE, namely the logic of collective perpetration, can be traced back to both common and civil law systems under different names – joint enterprise and co-perpetration, respectively[140] – but the notion of JCE is often associated in the ICL literature with the common law tradition.[141] Indeed, the *Tadić* AC referred to the jurisprudence of the post–Second World War UK and US military courts and to the United States' *Pinkerton* doctrine in support of the existence of JCE.[142] Furthermore, many ICTY judges and legal officers were trained in common law, which has been said to have influenced their interpretation of JCE.[143] By contrast, legal scholars from civil law traditions strongly advocated for inserting a clear standard of differentiation between JCE I and JCE III,[144] or for substituting the doctrine with a more differentiative one altogether.[145]

The JCE doctrine was eventually contested from inside the UN tribunals.[146] In 2003, four years after the *Tadić* AC judgment, the *Stakić* TC substituted JCE with the German-influenced doctrine of indirect co-perpetration, which posed the following requirements: (a) an explicit agreement or silent consent to accomplish a common goal, (b) coordinated co-operation, and (c) joint control over the crime.[147] The *Stakić* TC

138 Werle and Burghard, 'Establishing Degrees', 311. Jackson, 'Attribution of Responsibility', 885.

139 H. Van der Wilt, 'Joint Criminal Enterprise – Possibilities and Limitations' (2007) 5(1) *Journal of International Criminal Justice* 91, 96. See also Ohlin, 'Join Intentions', 721.

140 Van Sliedregt, 'Joint Criminal Enterprise', 190.

141 Ambos, 'Joint Criminal Enterprise', 168.

142 *Tadić* Appeals Judgment, §§ 205–213, § 224, footnote 289.

143 Steer, 'Legal Transplants', 45.

144 Ambos, 'Joint Criminal Enterprise', 171–173.

145 Van der Wilt, 'Joint Criminal Enterprise'.

146 See *Simić, Tadić and Zarić*, Judgment, Separate and Partly Dissenting Opinion of Judge Per-Johan Lindholm, IT-95-9-T, Trial Chamber, 17 October 2003, § 2.

147 *Stakić*, Judgment, IT-97-24-T, 31 July 2003, Trial Chamber (hereinafter *Stakić* Trial Judgment), § 440.

considered that their theory of co-perpetration came 'closer' than JCE to the plain meaning of the term 'committing' under Article 7(1) and, hence, was more compliant with the legality principle.[148] The TC appeared influenced by the German legal tradition, citing the work of the legal scholar Claus Roxin.[149] The professional background of the judges might have also influenced their decision to depart from JCE because the presiding Judge Schomburg previously served as a judge at the German Federal Court of Justice. Later, Judge Schomburg also defended the use of Roxin's theories of co-perpetration and indirect perpetration in ICL in the *Gacumbitsi* case at the ICTR.[150] Notably, all three judges – Schomburg, Argibay from Argentina, and Judge Vassylenko from Ukraine – were appointed as judges at the ICTY between 2001 and 2002.[151] Assuming office after the landmark *Tadić* decision, those judges appeared less convinced by their colleagues of the suitability of JCE for international trials.

But the 2003 *Stakić* TC's findings remained the minority position at the UN tribunals, where the reliance on JCE had become the established practice.[152] On appeal, in 2006 the *Stakić* AC terminated the attempt to substitute JCE with indirect co-perpetration. The AC judges argued that the introduction of a new mode of liability should be consistent with the tribunal's jurisprudence, lest it generated 'uncertainty, if not confusion' about the applicable law.[153] The AC considered that, unlike co-perpetration, JCE constituted a mode of liability that is 'routinely applied in the Tribunal's jurisprudence'.[154]

The TC and AC decisions in *Stakić* present an intriguing clash of ideas in ICL: both decisions cited compliance with criminal law principles but interpreted those principles differently. The TC considered that their theory complied with legality because it came closer to the plain meaning of 'commission'. The AC considered that legality required avoiding the fragmentation of the tribunals' jurisprudence – from that perspective, the defendants already had fair notice about the requirements of JCE. As discussed in Chapter 8, similar dynamics took place at the *Bemba* AC at the ICC.

[148] Ibid., § 441.

[149] Ibid., § 441, footnote 949.

[150] *Gacumbitsi*, Separate Opinion of Judge Schomburg on the Criminal Responsibility of The Appellant for Committing Genocide, ICTR-2001-64-A, Appeals Chamber, 7 July 2006, §§ 16–20.

[151] See ICTY website, 'Former Judges', www.icty.org/en/sid/10572.

[152] Van Sliedregt, Individual Criminal Responsibility, 99.

[153] *Stakić*, Judgment, IT-97-24-A, Appeals Chamber, 22 March 2006 (hereinafter *Stakić* Appeals Judgment), § 59.

[154] Ibid., § 62.

Nevertheless, ICTY judges did not completely disregard the criticism of JCE and, in subsequent decisions, revised the doctrine to reflect the different role of leadership figures and perpetrators on the ground. In 2007 the *Brđanin* AC found that the direct physical perpetrator of the crime did not have to be a member of the JCE in order to impute criminal responsibility for that crime to all JCE members.[155] Instead, it was sufficient that the crime formed part of the common purpose and that one of the JCE members was linked to the physical perpetrator and used the latter as a tool to commit the crime.[156] Van Sliedregt has observed that the *Brđanin* AC's version of JCE somewhat resembled the *Stakić* notion of co-perpetratorship,[157] but there were also differences between the two approaches. It has been suggested that the *Stakić* TC assumed the existence of an overarching criminal apparatus, while the *Brđanin* AC effectively 'delink[ed]' the JCE from the physical perpetrators. Consequently, the latter seemingly imposed less strict requirements for proving the existence of coordinated cooperation between the JCE and the direct perpetrators.[158]

Consequently, those members of the ICL epistemic community who understood the culpability principle in a narrower sense remained unconvinced of the merits of the new JCE version. The 'delinking' between the JCE members and the physical perpetrator was considered to increase the possibility of attributing guilt by association.[159] By contrast, the *Stakić* TC's adoption of co-perpetratorship in 2003 gained the approval of some members of the ICL epistemic community who worried about the broad scope of JCE.[160] As Chapter 6 reveals, the indirect co-perpetration theory eventually gained acceptance at the ICC.

4.2.2.2 Command Responsibility

Like the IMTFE, the UN tribunals have examined the criminal responsibility not only of those persons who participated in the commission of crimes but also of those commanders who, due to inaction, failed to intervene and prevent or punish the crimes of their subordinates. The post–Second World War cases left a disparate legacy concerning the elements of command responsibility, but the UN tribunals clarified the requirements of the doctrine. In a landmark judgment in 1998, the *Čelebići* TC

155 *Brđanin*, Judgment, IT-99-36-A, Appeals Chamber, 3 April 2007, § 410.

156 Ibid., §§ 410–413.

157 Van Sliedregt, Individual Criminal Responsibility, 170.

158 Ibid., 162–163. Farhang, 'Point of No Return', 162.

159 Farhang, 'Point of No Return', 163.

160 Badar, 'Just Convict Everyone', 298. Farhang, 'Point of No Return', 162.

identified three requirements for attributing criminal responsibility to commanders:[161] that (a) a superior-subordinate relationship existed, (b) the superior knew or had reason to know of the commission of the crime, and (c) the superior failed to prevent the crime or punish the perpetrator thereof.[162] While the UN tribunals' judges brought clarity to the command responsibility principle, their interpretation of the law remained contentious among advocates of the restrained interpretation of the culpability principle.

The UN tribunals imposed higher *mens rea* requirements with respect to attributing command responsibility than the IMTFE. In 2001 the *Čelebići* AC concluded that the commander's negligence, i.e. her failure to proactively search for and obtain information about the subordinates' conduct, was insufficient to trigger criminal responsibility.[163] Rather, the term 'had reason to know' was interpreted to require the availability of 'some specific information' to the commander, which should have put the latter on notice about the subordinates' crimes.[164] That interpretation was affirmed in later decisions at the ICTY[165] and the ICTR.[166]

But the UN tribunals' findings on the role of causation in command responsibility proved controversial. The *Čelebići* TC determined that '[n]otwithstanding the central place assumed by the principle of causation in criminal law,' the doctrine of command responsibility did not require proof of causation.[167] The judges considered that it would be impossible to establish a causal link with respect to command responsibility for the failure to punish the crimes of the subordinates because the crimes needed to have already been committed before the commander could fail to punish those conducts.[168] Hence, it cannot be said that by failing to punish the subordinates' crimes, the commander has *caused* the commission of those crimes.

Those members of the ICL epistemic community who were guided by a humanitarian concern for protecting the interests of victims justified the broad scope of command responsibility. One legal scholar argued

161 Ambos, 'Command Responsibility', 129.

162 *Čelebići* Trial Judgment, § 346.

163 *Delalić, Mucić, Delić and Landžo*, IT-96-21-A, Judgment, Appeals Chamber, 20 February 2001 (hereinafter *Čelebići* Appeals Judgment), §§ 224–226.

164 *Čelebići* Trial Judgment, § 393.

165 *Blaškić*, Judgment, IT-95-14-A, Appeals Chamber (hereinafter *Blaškić* Appeals Judgment), 23 July 2004, § 62.

166 *Bagilishema*, Judgment, ICTR-95-1A-A, Appeals Chamber, 3 July 2002, § 36.

167 *Čelebići* Trial Judgment, § 398. See also *Blaškić* Appeals Judgment, § 77.

168 *Čelebići* Trial Judgment, §§ 399–400.

that the commanders who fail to punish the conducts of their subordinates are culpable because they implicitly endorse their subordinates' crimes and thus '*add* to the injury' that is inflicted upon the victims.[169] Reminiscent of the IMTFE Majority's reasoning, other scholars praised command responsibility for providing the prosecution with an opportunity to avoid impunity in those cases where the evidence of the commander's direct orders towards the subordinates to commit crimes was lacking.[170]

The finding of the judges that command responsibility did not require a causal connection between the conduct and the crimes, however, proved controversial with respect to a narrow interpretation of criminal responsibility principles. One ICL scholar opined that by enabling the conviction of a person for an international crime 'without contributing to the crime or having any effect on it', command responsibility breached the principles of culpability and fair labelling.[171] In a well-known article, Mirjan Damaška argued that the stigma of convicting the commander for the crimes committed by the subordinates, such as genocide or war crimes, was disproportionate to the commander's actual conduct, that is the commander's failure to punish those crimes.[172] Hence, command responsibility came 'dangerously close' to imposing liability without proving the culpability of the accused commander.[173]

For that reason, many scholars suggested that the doctrine of command responsibility for failure to punish the subordinates' crimes should constitute a separate offence and not a mode for the attribution of liability for other international crimes. From that perspective, the commander should be punished specifically for her failure to punish the crimes and not for the underlying crimes committed by the subordinates.[174] In fact, the question whether command responsibility for a failure to punish those crimes constituted an offence or a mode of liability triggered ardent debates

169 Sepinwall, 'Failures to Punish', 293–295.

170 G. Vetter, 'Command Responsibility of Non-Military Superiors in the International Criminal Court' (2000) 25(1) *The Yale Journal of International Law* 89, 92. L. Kortfält, 'Sexual Violence and the Relevance of the Doctrine of Superior Responsibility in the Light of the *Katanga* Judgment at the International Criminal Court' (2015) 84(4) *Nordic Journal of International Law* 533, 555.

171 Robinson, 'Identity Crisis', 951.

172 Damaška, 'The Shadow Side', 480.

173 Darcy, 'Imputed Criminal Liability', 397.

174 Ambos, 'Superior Responsibility', 851. Mettraux, International Crimes, 297. B. B. Jia, 'The Doctrine of Command Responsibility: Current Problems' (2000) 3 *Yearbook of International Humanitarian Law* 131, 161–163. Sander, 'Unravelling the Confusion', 125.

among the UN tribunals' judges.[175] However, a review of the UN tribunals' judgments reveals that the commanders were generally convicted for the crimes committed by their subordinates rather than for their dereliction of duty, thus, displaying a broad reading of the culpability principle.[176]

Nevertheless, the UN tribunals attempted to ameliorate the harshness of command responsibility towards the defendant. Schabas observed that the convictions for command responsibility, such as *Strugar*, *Hadžihasanović et al.*, and *Orić*, resulted in short sentences thus suggesting that those cases were 'most definitely not in the category of the most serious crimes'.[177] Furthermore, despite its broad scope, in practice command responsibility charges have generally been successful at the ICTY in cases involving exclusively traditional military-like contexts, where it is easier to demonstrate the commander's effective control over the subordinates.[178] It has also been observed that the UN tribunals' judges preferred to convict the defendant for 'committing' the crimes under Article 7(1)/6(1), rather than based on command responsibility, where the available evidence allowed such findings.[179]

But when the evidence was insufficient to conclude that the defendant had personally participated in the commission of the crime, the UN tribunals often relied on command responsibility as a form of 'fall back liability' under which a conviction could be entered.[180] In fact, command responsibility was applied in rather unconventional situations at the ICTR. Notably, in the *Media* case the defendants – the founders of the *Radio Télévision Libre des Mille Collines* and the editor-in-chief of the *Kangura* newspaper – were convicted under the civilian form of command responsibility of genocides and crimes against humanity for exhorting the Hutu

[175] See the debate in the *Hadžihasanović et al.* case. *Hadžihasanović, Alagic and Kubura*, Decision on Interlocutory Appeal Challenging Jurisdiction in Relation to Command Responsibility, IT-01-47-AR72, Appeals Chamber, 16 July 2003. *Hadžihasanović, Alagic and Kubura*, Partial Dissenting Opinion of Judge Shahabuddeen, IT-01-47-AR72, Appeals Chamber, 16 July 2003. *Hadžihasanović, Alagic and Kubura*, Partial Dissenting Opinion of Judge Hunt, IT-01-47-AR72, 16 July 2003, Appeals Chamber.

[176] See Robinson, 'Identity Crisis', 952.

[177] Schabas, *Introduction to the International Criminal Court*, 222–223.

[178] Bonafe, 'Finding a Proper Role', 602.

[179] Ambos, 'Joint Criminal Enterprise', 166. T. Henquet, 'Convictions for Command Responsibility under Articles 7(1) and 7(3) of the Statute of the International Criminal Tribunal for the Former Yugoslavia' (2002) 15(4) *Leiden Journal of International Law* 805, 819.

[180] S. Manacorda and C. Meloni, 'Indirect Perpetration versus Joint Criminal Enterprise: Concurring Approaches in the Practice of International Criminal Law' (2011) 9(1) *Journal of International Criminal Justice* 159, 161. Ambos, 'Current Issues', 250.

population to kill Tutsis through their media outlets.[181] Consequently, command responsibility appeared to serve as a final resort for avoiding impunity at the tribunals.

The command responsibility principle sits uneasily with the principle of personal culpability. But it is also a special type of criminal responsibility that is peculiar to international crimes, one that was developed in the case law of international tribunals[182] and reflected the mixture of the humanitarian and criminal law goals underlying ICL. The harshness of the doctrine stems from the presumption that the level of authority of commanding figures and the high stakes of their actions or omissions justify the imposition of criminal responsibility, even if the commander did not personally participate in the crimes.[183] Thus, the doctrine is strongly influenced by the concern for enhancing the protection of civilians by incentivizing commanders to keep tighter control over their subordinates. The UN tribunals demonstrated respect for the culpability principle and tried to mitigate the harshness of command responsibility, but the latter still became known as a backup, fail-safe mode for the attribution of liability to the accused, or, as one legal scholar called it, 'the silver bullet of the prosecution'.[184] As Chapter 8 discusses, that practice was put an end to at the ICC.

4.2.3 The Legacy of the UN Tribunals

The UN tribunals were credited with the development of the system of modes of liability in ICL.[185] The articulation of some of those modes of liability, notably JCE, was generally the product of judicial creativity for the purpose of enabling the UN tribunals to 'dispens[e] justice'.[186] It is important to note that the term 'justice' in that context is referred to substantive more than procedural justice. The UN tribunals set out to bring life to ICL after five decades of inactivity and to signal that the perpetrators of mass atrocities would no longer enjoy impunity. That line of reasoning

[181] *Nahimana, Barayagwiza and Ngeze*, Judgment and Sentence, ICTR-99-52-T, Trial Chamber, 3 December 2003.

[182] E. Van Sliedregt, 'Command Responsibility at the ICTY – Three Generations of Case-law and still Ambiguity', in B. Swart, A. Zahar, and G. Sluiter (eds.) *The Legacy of the International Criminal Tribunal for the former Yugoslavia* (Oxford: Oxford University Press, 2011) 377, 394.

[183] May, Crimes against Humanity, 142.

[184] Schabas, *Introduction to the International Criminal Court*, 222.

[185] Liu, 'Contribution', 139.

[186] Shahabuddeen, 'Judicial Creativity', 187.

was generally accepted at the UN tribunals and within the broader ICL community of practice. But when the jurisprudence of the UN tribunals started to settle, when the task of 'putting flesh to the bones' of ICL had been accomplished, many members of the ICL field who favoured strict compliance with criminal law rules, regardless of the trial outcome, started criticizing broad modes of liability, such as JCE and command responsibility. The ICL community was polarized – while some defended the practices of the UN tribunals, other members of that community, both within and outside the UN tribunals, advocated for revising the tribunals' criminal responsibility rules by adopting a more restrained interpretation of the culpability principle. As the Chapters 5 and 6 discuss, those ideas became particularly influential during the process of drafting the ICC's RS and subsequently when the ICC judges interpreted the relevant statutory provisions on individual criminal responsibility.

4.3 Conclusion

The criminal law literature has often criticized the modes of liability used at the post–Second World War tribunals and the UN tribunals for infringing upon the principles of personal culpability. If one looks at the critique of conspiracy, JCE, and command responsibility, it might be tempting to describe the assessment of criminal responsibility at those tribunals as borderline legalism, significantly, and perhaps unjustifiably, expanding the concepts of legality and culpability. But that conclusion can be reached only if one assumes the existence of an objective legal order that the tribunals have fallen short of. By contrast, from the perspective of intersubjective legalism, the ICL field has accommodated a variety of understandings about the nature of the legality and culpability principles. Consequently, while the post–Second World War tribunals and the UN tribunals might have adopted problematic practices from the perspective of those criminal lawyers committed to a dispassionate vision of legalism, a look at the broader ICL field of practice, and the divergent visions of legalism therein, presents a different picture. This chapter showed that those tribunals have displayed sound legal reasoning in the assessment of criminal responsibility because they have engaged in principled reasoning in accordance with *their* understanding of the animating force behind legality – namely morality. From this perspective, the reasoning of those tribunals was sound: firstly, because it followed a consistent normative logic, and secondly, because many judges and outside legal commentators shared that normative logic.

Understanding the context in which the international tribunals operated is key to understanding where that logic came from. This chapter revealed many common aspects of the socio-political contexts in which the post–Second World War and the post–Cold War tribunals operated. Both sets of tribunals faced the challenges of developing and not simply interpreting the criminal responsibility laws in international law. Furthermore, both sets of institutions operated under significant public pressure to respond to specific instances of mass atrocities, which in the case of the ICTY were ongoing. The creation of the IMT and IMTFE enabled the formation of a new community of practice in the international legal field: the ICL community. The establishment of the ICTY and ICTR consolidated the ICL community, with an increasing number of scholars, lawyers, and NGOs engaging in the field.

However, alongside the consolidation of the ICL field of practice came its polarization around criminal responsibility, as the growing ICL community accommodated different, sometimes conflicting, ideas about the construction of criminal responsibility principles. The influence of humanitarian and human rights norms alongside a morality-based perception of legality resulted in broad interpretations of the criminal responsibility rules. The UN tribunals sought a balance between procedural scrupulousness and the moral impulse to punish the perpetrators when developing the laws on criminal responsibility. That line of reasoning was generally accepted as sound given the special context in which those tribunals were established, but it also contributed to the rise of the liberal critique of ICL.[187] The unsuccessful efforts to reform those rules at the UN tribunals left many members of the ICL community frustrated. As Chapters 5 and 6 discuss, those legal scholars and practitioners committed to the dispassionate application of criminal responsibility rules discovered in the ICC a new institutional forum for their visions of criminal responsibility rules.

[187] Chapter 3, Section 3.2.3.2.

5

Drafting the Rome Statute

The Battleground of Ideas about Criminal Responsibility

This chapter offers new insights into the detailed definitions of the general principles of law in the RS, in particular the criminal responsibility provisions. Specifically, the chapter argues that there is more to the drafting history of the RS's criminal responsibility provisions than the interests of states and that these broader dynamics have remained underexamined in the interdisciplinary literature on the ICC. It would be simplistic to present the restrained approach to the assessment of criminal responsibility exhibited in the RS and ICC jurisprudence as the triumph of sovereign states, seeking to shield their nationals from convictions, over non-state actors, such as legal scholars and NGOs, aiming to expand the scope of criminal responsibility provisions to enable easier convictions for the perpetrators of mass atrocities. In fact, authoritative legal experts were among the most ardent proponents of the proposal to codify in detail the general principles of criminal responsibility in the RS, instead of granting discretion to the future judges at the Court to develop the rules of criminal responsibility. From the perspective of those legal experts, the inclusion of a 'General Part' in the Statute marked the progress that ICL had made since its early days towards a coherent penal system. Thus, the politics of the legal field, i.e. the promotion and contestations of different understandings of the law, are crucial for understanding how the principled approach to criminal responsibility became influential in Rome. Notably, the term 'principled' does not suggest that the approach to criminal responsibility that dominated the discourse at Rome was 'more legal' than that of the UN tribunals, even though those members of the ICL field who supported that approach may have understood it to be so. Instead, 'principled' here refers to the dogmatic and technical application of criminal responsibility laws, regardless of the trial outcome.

5.1 Historical Background

The ICC's establishment, described as 'the most significant development' in ICL,[1] was a unique moment in ICL practice for two reasons. Firstly, it provided a forum for contesting the old practices that had previously dominated ICL and for presenting new ideas about criminal responsibility laws. One expert who participated in the drafting process observed that a plurality of states, legal experts from different backgrounds, and hundreds of NGOs participated in the drafting of the future ICC's statute.[2] Secondly, the stakes of influencing the RS drafting process were particularly high. As the statute of 'the first permanent general, future oriented international criminal court',[3] the RS would play a more profound role in the ICL field than the Statutes of the temporary UN tribunals.[4] In other words, the ICC was perceived within the field as the first 'truly' international penal court.[5]

The drafting process took place in several stages. The foundations were placed by the International Law Commission, which produced a report in 1992, followed by a more comprehensive text in 1993, modified in 1994.[6] During that period, earlier ideas about establishing a court that would deal with transnational crimes, such as drug trafficking, gradually faded and the vision of the ICC as the institution that we know now – dealing with the *core* international crimes of concern to humanity as such – took hold.[7] In the mid-1990s and onwards, the negotiations over the establishment of the future ICC took place within the ICL field of practice. Subsequent developments, especially the work of the Preparatory Committee on the ICC statute (PrepCom) from 1996 to 1998,[8] are of crucial importance for tracing the competition of ideas and influence over the drafting of the

1 W. Schabas, 'Editorial: International Criminal Court: The Secret of Its Success' (2001) 12(4) *Criminal Law Forum* 415, 415. See also Charney, 'Progress', 454. B. Broomhall, *International Justice and the International Criminal Court: Between Sovereignty and the Rule of Law* (Oxford: Oxford University Press, 2004) 67.

2 Interview with Kai Ambos, 2 June 2020.

3 H. P. Kaul, 'Ten Years International Criminal Court', 2 October 2012, 5.

4 Van Schaack, 'Crimen Sine Lege', 170. McGoldrick, 'Legal and Political Significance', 454.

5 Jescheck, 'General Principles', 39–40.

6 M. Bassiouni, *The Legislative History of the International Criminal Court: Introduction, Analysis, and Integrated Text of the Statute, Elements of Crimes and Rules of Procedure and Evidence*, Vol. 1 (Ardsley, New York: Transnational Publishers, Inc., 2005), 63.

7 Ibid., 64, emphasis added.

8 M. Bassiouni, *The Legislative History of the International Criminal Court: An Article by Article Evolution of the Statute from 1994–1998*, Vol. 2. (Ardsley, New York: Transnational Publishers, Inc., 2005) xvii–xviii.

future RS. Key documents that provide insights into the RS's drafting history include the 1996 PrepCom report, which comprised the decisions reached on several substantive and procedural issues and the alternative options regarding those issues on which the PrepCom had not been able to reach a consensus.[9] Other documents include reports from the 1997 sessions of the PrepCom, the draft statute named the 'Zutphen Draft' after the city in the Netherlands where it was completed,[10] and the final 1998 draft that was negotiated at the Rome Conference.[11] At that point various working groups were organized to draft different parts of the statute.[12]

Furthermore, legal experts found an additional venue to express their vision of what the law of the future Court should be by holding nine meetings from 1995 to 1998 in Italy and producing the so-called 'Siracusa Draft' statute.[13] The Siracusa Draft became highly influential for the work of the PrepCom with respect to matters of the General Part.[14] Based on an analysis of the official UN documents and the publications of legal academics involved in the RS drafting, the following sections trace the negotiation and subsequent codification of the criminal responsibility provisions in the Statute's General Part to argue that legal experts played a key role in that process.

5.2 Codifying the General Principles of ICL

The drafting of the 'General principles of criminal law', also known as the General Part of the ICC Statute, became a battleground for

9 Report of the Preparatory Committee on the Establishment of an International Criminal Court (Vol. I), UN General Assembly Official Records (GAOR), 51st Sess., Supp. No. 22, U.N. Doc. A/51/22 (1996) (hereinafter PrepCom Report 1996, Vol. I). Report of the Preparatory Committee on the Establishment of an International Criminal Court (Vol. II), UN General Assembly Official Records (GAOR), 51st Sess., Supp. No. 22A, U.N. Doc. A/51/22 (1996) (hereinafter PrepCom Report 1996, Vol. II).

10 Report of the Inter-sessional Meeting from 19 to 30 January 1998 in Zupten, The Netherlands.

11 Report of the Preparatory Committee on the Establishment of an International Criminal Court, United Nations Diplomatic Conference of Plenipotentiaries on the Establishment of an International Criminal Court, A/CONF.183/2/Add.1, 14 April 1998.

12 Bassiouni, Legislative History, Vol. 2, xviii.

13 Draft Statute for an International Criminal Court: Alternative to the ILC-Draft (Siracusa Draft), July 1995, Siracusa/Freiburg (hereinafter Siracusa Draft). Bassiouni, Legislative History, Vol. 2, xix–xx.

14 K. Ambos, 'Establishing an International Criminal Court and an International Criminal Code: Observations from an International Criminal Law Viewpoint' (1996) 7(4) *European Journal of International Law* 519, 521. A. Eser, 'The Need for a General Part' (1993) 11(1) *Nouvelles Études Pénales* 43, 20.

promoting and contesting ideas about the rules that would be used to assess criminal responsibility at the future permanent court. Notably, the very decision to include a General Part in what would become the RS was novel at the time and already displayed the influence of specific ideas, namely that ICL norms required greater categorization than the rules provided in the statutes of previous tribunals. Neither the Nuremberg and Tokyo Charters nor the Statutes of the UN tribunals contained such a section stipulating the general rules that the judges had to follow in assessing criminal responsibility in every case. The ICC draft statute, which was first produced by the International Law Commission, similarly did not include a comprehensive part on the general principles of law.[15] The drafting of the 'General principles of criminal law' section, which dealt with questions of non-retroactivity, individual criminal responsibility, and defences, became a subject of debate later, at the PrepCom.[16]

Some legal experts perceived the detailed codification of the general principles in the RS as a constraint imposed on the future ICC judges by sovereign states.[17] The former ICTY president Antonio Cassese suggested that the restrictive approach of the RS drafters could be explained by the eagerness of states 'to shield their servicemen as much as possible from being brought to trial for, and possibly convicted' at the ICC.[18] There is certainly merit to such arguments. Some state representatives favoured a flexible Statute that would only contain a general mandating clause enabling the judges to elaborate the principles of liability, but the majority of states preferred that the fundamental criminal law principles were clearly articulated in the Statute to avoid conferring 'substantive legislative power' to the future ICC judges.[19] Some former judges at the tribunals, such as Judge Hunt, also viewed the General Part of the RS with a suspicious eye because, 'If it is to fulfil its goals efficiently, international criminal law must be given space to grow, rather than kept in a straightjacket

[15] P. Saland, 'International Criminal Law Principles', in R. Lee (ed.) *The International Criminal Court: The Making of the Rome Statute – Issues, Negotiations, Results* (The Hague: Kluwer Law International, 1999) 189.

[16] PrepCom 1996 Report, Vol. I, 41–47.

[17] Broomhall, 'Article 22', 951. Grover, 'Call to Arms', 552. Charney, 'Progress', 464. Schabas, Introduction to the International Criminal Court, 202. A. Pellet, 'Applicable Law', in A. Cassese, P. Gaeta and J. R. W. D. Jones (eds.) *The Rome Statute of the International Criminal Court* Vol. II (Oxford: Oxford University Press, 2002) 1051, 1058.

[18] Cassese, 'Statute of the International Criminal Court', 526. See also Broomhall, International Justice, 76–77.

[19] PrepCom 1996 Report Vol. I, 42.

imposed by a rigid code.'[20] Indeed, as Chapter 4 discussed, the UN tribunals considered judicial creativity crucial for developing ICL.

But while most states may have preferred a more constrained court, it would be insufficient to attribute the development of the RS General Part only to sovereignty interests and to ignore the variety of competing understandings among legal experts about what the future ICC statute should look like. The view that the detailed codification of criminal responsibility principles would prevent ICL from developing did not constitute a uniform understanding within the ICL epistemic community. The absence of a General Part in the statutes of the earlier international tribunals was attributed to the influential role of the United States in their establishment and the Anglo-American preference for pragmatism over systematization of the law.[21] Consequently, when the RS drafting began, many authoritative legal scholars from civil law backgrounds began advocating for the categorization of the principles of criminal law within a 'General Part' of ICL.[22] That proposition was also incorporated in the Siracusa Draft.[23] According to those legal scholars, the General Part drew on the 'time-honoured' principles of domestic criminal law and contributed towards a more 'sophisticated' ICL.[24] While the codification of the general principles might have reassured some states that their nationals would be shielded from extreme judicial creativity, to criminal law scholars from civil law background, the General Part constituted a necessary component of a *criminal* code, especially at the international level.[25] In the words of one scholar, the General Part 'emancipated' ICL from the 'rudimentary nature of international law and turned it into a mature system of criminal justice.[26] To those legal practitioners who embarked upon the arduous task of synthesizing general criminal law principles across legal systems,[27] the codification of the General Part in the RS was perceived not as a constraint on the judges but as a major achievement of ICL.[28]

The principle of legality is illustrative of the way in which the normative significance of codifying the principles of criminal law in the RS can be

20 D. Hunt, 'The International Criminal Court' (2004) 2(1) *Journal of International Criminal Justice* 56, 59.

21 Ambos, 'Remarks on the General Part', 661. See also R. Clark, 'Mental Element', 296.

22 See Eser, 'Need for a General Part'. Ambos, 'Establishing an International Criminal Court'.

23 Siracusa Draft, 55.

24 Van Sliedregt, 'Pluralism', 852.

25 Eser, 'Need for a General Part', 20.

26 Militello, 'Personal Nature', 943.

27 R. Clark, 'Mental Element', 296–298.

28 Saland, 'International Criminal Law', 191.

neglected if one focuses exclusively on state interests. Commentators have suggested that the principle of legality was used as a justification by drafters to list all crimes in the RS exhaustively and in detail, limiting the gaps in the law and, consequently, judicial discretion.[29] While there is merit to this argument, it presents only part of the story. The principle of legality was incorporated 'as a fundamental principle of criminal law' as early as the 1994 Draft Statute by the International Law Commission.[30] In July 1995, the Siracusa Draft statute – prepared by legal experts, including Cherif Bassiouni, Ambos, Eser, and Triffterer among others – further emphasized the importance of incorporating the legality principle, stressing the benefits of certainty and non-retroactivity in the context of the applicable sources of law.[31] These arguments were made *before* the UN tribunals engaged in expansive interpretations of the law. At that time the ICTY was only beginning to issue indictments.[32] In fact, the expansive decision on the tribunal's jurisdiction in *Tadić*, referred to as a wake-up call for states to define in detail the list of crimes in the RS,[33] was delivered in October 1995[34] – after the International Law Commission and numerous legal experts had already insisted on the importance of incorporating legality in the RS. These observations do not imply that the codification of legality did not favour the sovereign interests of states to constrain the powers of the future Court. But they demonstrate that the exclusive focus on state interests obfuscates an array of other normative dynamics taking place within the legal field that also influenced the development of ICL norms.

For many legal experts, the importance of codifying the general principles of ICL was particularly acute at the ICC. While the perceived purpose of the UN tribunals was to (re)start the engine of international criminal justice, as the first permanent court of its kind, the ICC was expected to provide a 'model' for domestic criminal justice systems worldwide of 'how a criminal court should function'.[35] Consequently, many members of the

[29] Grover, 'Call to Arms', 552. Broomhall, 'Article 22', 950.

[30] International Law Commission, Draft Statute for an International Criminal Court with Commentaries (1994 [2005]) *Yearbook of the International Law Commission*, 1994, vol. II, Part Two (hereinafter Draft Statute for an International Criminal Court 1994), 55.

[31] Siracusa Draft, 55.

[32] See ICTY, 'Timeline', www.icty.org/en/features/timeline.

[33] Schabas, *Introduction to the International Criminal Court*, 202.

[34] *Tadić*, Decision on the Defence Motion for Interlocutory Appeal on Jurisdiction, IT-94-1, Appeals Chamber, 2 October 1995.

[35] Fletcher and Ohlin, 'Reclaiming Fundamental Principles', 540. See also V. Popovski, 'International Criminal Court: A Necessary Step Towards Global Justice' (2000) 31(4) *Security Dialogue* 405, 412.

ICL epistemic community considered that the ICC should move on from considerations of substantive justice and developing legal rules towards the provision of high-quality procedural justice.[36]

These normative dynamics can be identified behind the incorporation of the principle of non-retroactivity codified in Article 24(1) RS. One of the drafters admitted that the principle served a political function, namely to engage those states that had experienced violent pasts and resorted to amnesties for national reconciliation.[37] However, the principle of non-retroactivity also had deep normative legal significance. The ban on retroactivity is a distinctive feature of the RS.[38] The post-war military tribunals were established after the crimes had taken place, which has haunted their legacy ever since. Many of the crimes that the ICTR dealt with also necessitated the retroactive application of the law, because the tribunal was established after the Rwandan genocide. Hence, the ICC stands out as the first international criminal tribunal complying with the non-retroactivity corollary of legality,[39] which signified the development of ICL into a true system of criminal justice. The codification of the general criminal law principles in the RS can, thus, be traced not only to state interests, but more importantly to the shared understanding of many legal scholars at the time about the need for a more principled approach to the assessment of criminal responsibility at the future Court.

Notably, because of the importance of expert authority within the legal field, legal scholars and practitioners became particularly influential actors during the drafting of the General Part, which included the criminal responsibility laws. The General Part was perceived as the 'most technically difficult part of the Statute'[40] because it constituted a novel effort in comparative criminal law.[41] While other RS sections were drafted by military representatives and diplomats, the General Part was mainly the creation of legal experts, including members of justice ministries, who did not always deliberate with the other working groups.[42] The drafting records reveal that the main actors who influenced the content of the

36 Cassese, *International Criminal Law*, 10, 40, 142–143. Grover, 'Call to Arms', 557. D. M. Amann, 'Assessing International Criminal Adjudication of Human Rights Atrocities' (2003) 16 *Third World Legal Studies* 169, 180–181.

37 Saland, 'International Criminal Law', 196

38 Mantovani, 'General Principles', 30.

39 Olàsolo, 'Joint Criminal Enterprise', 291–292.

40 Bassiouni, *Legislative History*, Vol. 1, 95.

41 Schabas, *Introduction to the International Criminal Court*, 194.

42 R. Clark, 'Mental Element', 314.

RS General Part were an 'informal group' of criminal law experts at the PrepCom[43] and the official Working Group on the General Principles of Law at the Rome Conference, both of which were chaired by the Swedish representative Per Saland.[44]

The ideas presented by the working groups of legal experts were of special significance with respect to the laws on criminal responsibility. A notable example of the authority that the working groups of legal experts enjoyed with respect to the drafting of the individual criminal responsibility provisions is the drafting of what would become Article 25(3) RS and the incorporation of the novel provision criminalizing indirect commission of a crime through a non-innocent agent under Article 25(3)(a). In 1996, states contemplated the possibility of differentiating between principals and accessories to the crime by including separate provisions for each in the statute.[45] At the PrepCom, it was proposed that principals should be those who commit the crime by themselves or jointly with other person(s).[46] Notably, two weeks after the submission of state proposals concerning criminal responsibility, the 'informal group' of legal experts at the PrepCom, chaired by Per Saland,[47] proposed a new version of the discussed provisions, but with a few but important differences. Firstly, the informal group added a new type of principal liability to commission and joint commission, namely commission through an *innocent* agent, such as a minor, a person of defective mental capacity, or a person acting under mistake of law.[48] Secondly, the informal group's paper also included a new proposal to draft a single provision that would cover various types of responsibility without specifying which provision constituted principal and which accessory liability.[49] The informal group specified that the 'paper neither represents a text agreed upon among delegations nor suggests that every item should be included in the Statute. This paper identifies possible elements to be included and examples of some possible texts.'[50]

43 PrepCom 1996 Report, Vol. I, 6.

44 R. Lee, *The International Criminal Court: The Making of the RS – Issues, Negotiations, Results* (The Hague: Kluwer Law International, 1999), xviii.

45 State Proposals on General Principles of Criminal Law: Articles A, B, C, D, E, F, G, H, I, J, K, L, M, N, O, P, Q, R, S and T, UD/A/AC-249/1996/WG-2/IP, 13 August 1996 (hereinafter State Proposals 1996), 4–7.

46 Ibid., 4.

47 PrepCom 1996 Report, Vol. I, 6.

48 Informal Group on General Principles of Criminal Law, Proposed New Part [III bis] for the Statute of an International Criminal Court: General Principles of Criminal Law, A/AC.249/CRP.13, 26 August 1996 (hereinafter Informal Group 1996 Proposal), 5.

49 Ibid., 7–8.

50 Ibid., 1.

Nevertheless, it appears that the text of the informal group was highly influential given that the 1996 report of the PrepCom submitted to the 51st General Assembly included both of its suggestions, namely the added form of commission though an innocent agent and the proposal for a single provision on individual criminal responsibility.[51] The report specified that the informal group working on the General Part had had 'the desired degree of wide participation',[52] which possibly explained the incorporation of its proposals into the PrepCom report. Nevertheless, it is intriguing that the notes and the footnotes of neither the informal paper nor the PrepCom report points to the person/s who had suggested the new individual criminal responsibility provisions. Since they had not been recorded as specific proposals submitted by state delegations, it appears that they evolved during the negotiations process within the informal group of legal experts, highlighting the autonomy that expert knowledge enables within the ICL field.

The influence of the ideas proposed by the informal group of experts was evident not only in the 1996 PrepCom report, but also in the subsequent work of the Commission, leading up to the Rome Conference. The informal group's proposals were influential, and at the Rome Conference, the Working Group on the General Part officially agreed that one single article would cover the participation of 'principals and all other modes of participation (except for command responsibility)'.[53] That provision became Article 25(3) RS.

Furthermore, the group of legal experts played a crucial role in the development of one of the most novel statutory provisions: commission through a non-innocent agent under Article 25(3)(a). The concept of indirect perpetration through an innocent agent, such as a minor or a person with a mental disability, which was originally proposed by the informal group, was familiar in many domestic systems.[54] But the expert group subsequently expanded the concept by providing that the indirect perpetrator could bear criminal responsibility for committing the crime even in those cases where the person used to physically perpetrate the crime was fully aware of the criminality of her conduct. This was an important development because, as discussed in Chapters 6–9, the concept of indirect perpetration though a non-innocent agent has been extensively used in ICC jurisprudence over the past 15 years. The drafters entered

[51] PrepCom 1996 Report, Vol. II, 82–85.
[52] PrepCom 1996 Report, Vol. I, 6.
[53] Saland, 'International Criminal Law', 198.
[54] Ambos, 'Article 25', 994.

'controversial waters' by recognizing the expanded form of indirect perpetration[55] because prior to the RS no other international statute explicitly codified that mode of liability.[56]

Notably, the incorporation of the novel RS provision cannot be traced to any state proposals and appears as the creation of the informal group of legal experts at the PrepCom. In 1997, Canada, Germany, the Netherlands, and the UK submitted a joint paper on the question of criminal responsibility to the PrepCom that envisaged the codification of three types of commission liability: commission as an individual, joint commission, and commission through an *innocent* agent,[57] similar to the earlier proposal made by the informal group. Five days after the joint submission, Saland's group of legal experts submitted a new version of the text, which was almost identical with that formally submitted by the state delegations, but with one important change: the concept of indirect commission through an innocent agent was substituted without any explanation by the concept of commission 'through another person, *regardless* of whether that person is criminally responsible'.[58] The writings of legal experts who later joined Saland's working group at Rome may provide some insights as to why the change to the text was made. Kai Ambos, who was part of the German delegation at Rome, noted that the specification of the text represented the drafters' awareness of the complex reality of mass atrocities where the direct executor of the crime is often a person who willingly engages in the crimes, rather than an innocent agent.[59] From that perspective, the expansion of indirect perpetration to the use of non-innocent agents suited the ICL context well because the new mode reflected the organizational dynamics of international crimes.[60] 'Surprisingly enough', the new formulation did not trigger deliberations at Rome and was adopted *en bloc*

[55] Cryer et al., *Introduction to International Criminal Law*, 367.

[56] Eser, 'Mental Elements', 793. G. Werle and B. Burghardt, 'Indirect Perpetration- A Perfect Fit for International Prosecution of Armchair Killers?' (2011) 9(1) *Journal of International Criminal Justice* 85.

[57] Working paper submitted by Canada, Germany, Netherlands, and the United Kingdom. Paper on criminal responsibility submitted by informal group representing various legal systems: Individual Responsibility, A/AC.249/1997/WG.2/DP.1, 14 February 1997 (hereinafter Joint state proposal on criminal responsibility).

[58] Chairman's Text, Article B b., c. and d.: Individual Criminal Responsibility, A/AC.249/1997/WG.2/CRP.2/Add.2, 19 February 1997 (hereinafter Working Group 1997 Proposal), 1, emphasis added.

[59] Ambos, 'Article 25', 994.

[60] F. Jessberger and J. Geneuss, 'On the Application of a Theory of Indirect Perpetration in Al Bashir' (2008) 6(5) *Journal of International Criminal Justice* 853, 866.

with other provisions in the General Part.[61] Thus, one of the most important ICL innovations can be traced not to states' desire to clearly delineate the set of situations in which the future ICC judges can find an accused guilty, but to the shared understanding among the legal experts working on the General Part that ICL required a mode of liability that would reflect the structures of system criminality.

The perceived depoliticization of the questions of technical legal expertise pertaining to criminal responsibility rules seemed to have afforded relative autonomy to the lawyers and academics working on the General Part to express their vision of the laws rather than to promote specific state interests. This conclusion is supported by the most detailed account of the ICC's legislative history, which identifies the parts of the RS concerning international cooperation and judicial assistance as the areas where deference to national sovereignty was most evident on behalf of the drafters.[62] Other authoritative commentators further observed that the most challenging negotiations with respect to states' sovereignty interests concerned the prosecutor's powers, the exercise of jurisdiction,[63] and complementarity and 'opt-out' mechanisms in the RS.[64] Similarly, when the former ICC president Hans-Peter Kaul remarked that the Rome negotiations revealed that states 'did not want a strong court', he referred to the complementarity provisions, rather than the General Part.[65] The historical documents have not recorded significant engagement of state delegations as such in the drafting of the criminal responsibly documents. Specifically concerning the responsibility of principals and accessories,[66] the *actus reus*[67] and the *mens rea*[68] elements of criminal responsibility, only Canada and Japan submitted proposals in 1996.[69] A year later, Canada, Germany,

[61] Jessberger and Geneuss, 'Application of a Theory', 857. T. Weigend, 'Indirect Perpetration', in C. Stahn (ed.) *The Law and Practice of the International Criminal Court* (Oxford: Oxford University Press, 2015) 538, 543.

[62] Bassiouni, *Legislative History*, Vol. 1, 99.

[63] Van Sliedregt, 'International Criminal Law', 1145. See also Deitelhoff, 'Discursive Process'.

[64] Broomhall, *International Justice*, 68.

[65] Kaul, 'Ten Years', 5–6.

[66] UN General Assembly, Summary of the Proceedings of the Preparatory Committee during the Period 25 March-12 April 1996, A/AC.249/1, 7 May 1996, 75–77.

[67] Ibid., 79–80.

[68] Ibid., 81–82. In addition, France submitted a draft Statute which included provisions on individual criminal responsibility. Draft Statute of the International Criminal Court: Working Paper Submitted by France, A/AC.249/L.3, 6 August 1996, 59–60.

[69] Other countries submitted proposals concerning other aspects related to individual criminal responsibility, such as the age of responsibility, mistake of law defence, which fall outside the scope of this study.

the Netherlands, and the UK submitted the joint proposal on the principles of individual criminal responsibility,[70] but as discussed, that proposal was soon overshadowed by the paper of an 'informal group' of experts at the PrepCom.

Similar trends can be observed with respect to the involvement of NGOs in the drafting process. Gaining the reputation of expert knowledge providers, NGOs even entered the negotiations as representatives on behalf of some nations.[71] Yet, the important influence of NGOs on states' decision-making in Rome had generally been discussed with regard to enhancing the powers of the future court vis-à-vis states and the expansion of the list of crimes in view of offering greater protection to the victims of atrocities. One of the main issues on which the CICC, an umbrella organization that united more than 800 NGOs, focused its lobbying efforts was granting the ICC Prosecutor the power to initiate *proprio motu* investigations.[72] The Women's Caucus for Gender Justice was further credited with contributing to the codification of the most comprehensive list of sexual and gender-based crimes in ICL.[73] By contrast, there is far less information about the involvement of NGOs in the drafting of the General Part, apart from the UN Children's Fund and the Children's Caucus's engagement on the issue of the appropriate lower age limit for attributing criminal responsibility. The Children's Fund and the Children's Caucus lobbied hard for setting the age of 18 as the limit under which no criminal responsibility could be imposed at the ICC.[74] The official records do not suggest that NGOs expressed similar interest in the modes of liability.

With states and NGOs preoccupied with other questions, the drafting of the 'technical' General Part of the RS was largely left to legal experts. Consequently, the drafting of the criminal responsibility laws reflected less state interests and more the politics of the legal field – the contestation and justification of different visions of the law by members of the ICL community of practice. The rest of this chapter traces the competition of ideas about the laws on criminal responsibility during the negotiations process specifically with reference to the RS provisions on liability for

[70] Joint State Proposal on Criminal Responsibility.

[71] Boyle and Chinkin, *Making of International Law*, 64–65. Pearson, 'Non-Governmental Organizations', 273.

[72] C. Hall, 'The Powers and Role of the Prosecutor of the International Criminal Court in the Global Fight Against Impunity' (2004) 17(1) *Leiden Journal of International Law* 121, 125.

[73] L. Chappell, 'Conflicting Institutions and the Search for Gender and Justice at the International Criminal Court' (2014) 67(1) *Political Research Quarterly* 183–196, 186.

[74] Saland, 'International Criminal Law', 200.

committing a crime, the command responsibility principle, and the mental elements of criminal responsibility. The main implication from the need to integrate competing visions of the laws on criminal responsibility in the RS was that, rather than being constrained by the detailed codification of modes of liability, the future ICC judges ended up with a variety of tools for establishing criminal responsibility at their disposal, which once again opened the door to the promotion and contestation of different ideas about what the relevant criminal responsibility laws required when the Court began operation.

5.3 Article 25(3) RS: Individual Criminal Responsibility

The drafting history of Article 25(3) reveals that the detailed codification of the criminal responsibility laws did not place significant constraints on future ICC judges. The RS ended up providing a broad range of tools for establishing the accused's criminal responsibility, or modes of liability, resulting from the need to integrate the competing ideas of legal experts from various professional backgrounds. The discretion of the future ICC judges in interpreting the criminal responsibility laws was further enhanced by the ambiguity and overlap between some of the modes of liability listed in Article 25(3).

Article 25(3) presented significantly more detailed codification of the modes of liability compared to Articles 7(1) and 6(1) from the ICTY and ICRT statutes, respectively. Notably, Article 25(3) RS did not leave the term 'commits' a crime undefined but specified in subparagraph (a) that the notion of commission referred to three particular scenarios: commission of a crime 'as an individual', 'jointly with another' person, or 'through another person, regardless of whether that other person is criminally responsible'. Subparagraphs (b)–(d) defined the forms of participation in a crime committed by someone else. Given the level of detail, Article 25(3) has been described as the 'the culmination of a process of specification of criminal participation'.[75]

While the extensive list of modes of liability may be perceived to narrow the discretion of the judges in determining which situation would trigger criminal responsibility, a closer look suggests that there is 'a wide range of individuals who might be considered criminally responsible' at the new court.[76] Firstly, subparagraph (a) may have defined the concept

[75] Van Sliedregt, 'Individual Criminal Responsibility', 74.

[76] Militello, 'Personal Nature', 946.

of 'commission' in a far more detailed manner than the ICTY and ICTY Statutes, but those details did not necessarily constrain the set of situations in which an accused could be found guilty for committing a crime. The expansion of the concept of indirect commission of a crime to cover perpetration through a *non-innocent* agent is telling in that regard.

Secondly, Article 25(3)(b)–(d) listed a variety of other forms of participation in a crime, which enabled the attribution of criminal responsibility even if the accused had not personally committed the crime. Subparagraph (d), in particular, significantly expanded the scope of criminal responsibility in the RS. Because Article 25(3)(d) criminalized contributions to a group crime that were made 'in *any* other way' not covered in subparagraphs (a)–(c), like JCE III it was described as a 'catch-all' provision that provides for 'the weakest form of liability'.[77] The second alternative of the provision, namely that the accused's contribution was made 'in the knowledge' of the group's criminal intentions, presented a particularly low threshold for establishing criminal responsibility.[78] In the context of mass atrocities, many people make contributions to the warring parties, such as the provision of food or clothes, despite their knowledge of those parties' criminal activities.[79] Consequently, some legal experts 'fiercely criticized' the provision[80] for paying 'scant attention' to the culpability principle.[81]

Notably, subparagraph (d) ended up in the RS as a result of a compromise between different legal traditions during the negations.[82] While paragraphs (a)–(c) resembled the continental legal system, subparagraph (d) was a remnant of the common law concept of 'conspiracy' or 'enterprise' liability.[83] In 1996, some delegations at the PrepCom proposed a provision on conspiracy liability drawing upon the Nuremberg IMT's legacy. Some proposals included attributing liability for conspiracy 'even if the object of the conspiracy is impossible or is prevented by a fortuitous event' and punishing the conspirator with the same punishment as the person who actually committed the crime.[84] This is a significantly

77 Werle, 'Individual Criminal Responsibility', 971.

78 Van Sliedregt, 'Individual Criminal Responsibility', 146.

79 Ohlin, 'Three Conceptual Problems', 79.

80 K. Ambos, 'The ICC and Common Purpose – What Contribution Is Required under Article 25(3)(d)?', in C. Stahn, (ed.) *The Law and Practice of the International Criminal Court* (Oxford: Oxford University Press, 2015) 592, 592.

81 Militello, 'Personal Nature', 949.

82 Ambos, 'Article 25', 1010.

83 Jescheck, 'General Principles', 51.

84 State Proposals 1996, 18.

harsh rule of attributing criminal responsibility, requiring a very low *actus reus* – an 'overt act' in furthering of the conspiracy or an act that manifested the shared intent among the conspirators to commit the crime.[85] In the absence of any further clarification, the ICC judges would have been left with wide discretion to decide which acts would be significant enough to merit the attribution of liability. But the proposal was unsuccessful because it caused unease among civil law countries.[86] An agreement on the definition of a mode of liability that would capture the collective nature of international crimes was finally reached after the adoption of the International Convention of the Suppression of Terrorist Bombings of 1997.[87] The language of Article 25(3)(d) is almost verbatim repetition of Article 2(3)(c) of the Convention.[88] To the drafters it appeared 'safe to use' a provision that was already successfully negotiated elsewhere.[89] Civil law scholars, in particular, contested the necessity of incorporating subparagraph (d) in the RS, calling it a 'superfluous' provision.[90] Nevertheless, the pressure to secure consensus among different legal traditions resulted in an expansion of the set of cases in which an accused could be found guilty at the ICC by adding subparagraph (d) to the list of modes of liability and leaving the ultimate decision whether or not to rely on that provision to the future judges.

The incorporation of subparagraph (d) provides some interesting insights into the normative dynamics behind the drafting of the RS criminal responsibility laws. Some of the most ardent critics of the broad provision were legal scholars, concerned with the protection of the culpability principle, rather than states seeking to protect their sovereignty. In fact, at the PrepCom some state delegations proposed an even broader version of criminal responsibility – the infamous conspiracy charge. Consequently, the contestation of the incorporation of subparagraph (d) reflected internal debates within the ICL field, such as the different understandings between common and civil law. The discussion also reflected the disagreement between those members of the ICL

[85] Ibid.

[86] Saland, 'International Criminal Law', 199.

[87] Saland, 'International Criminal Law', 199–200.

[88] International Convention for the Suppression of Terrorist Bombings, New York, 15 December 1997, Article 2(3)(c).

[89] R. Clark, 'Drafting a General Part to a Penal Code: Some Thoughts Inspired by the Negotiations on the RS of the International Criminal Court and by the Court's First Substantive Law Discussion in the *Lubanga Dyilo* Confirmation Proceedings' (2008) 19(3–4) *Criminal Law Forum* 519, 545.

[90] Mantovani, 'General Principles', 35. Eser, 'Individual Criminal Responsibility', 803.

community of practice who considered that a broad form of liability was needed to link individual persons to the collective criminal conduct and those who considered that suggestion potentially dangerous because it risked the attribution of guilt by association. Therefore, as observed by one of the participants in the drafting process, the list of modes of liability in Article 25(3) can be understood as the result of the drafters' attempt to integrate the variety of ideas about the criminal responsibility laws that were presented by the participating legal experts, under the time pressure of international negotiations.[91]

The diverging ideas that states held about the formulation of the rules concerning criminal responsibility is also revealed in what was *not* included in the RS. At the PrepCom some states sought to constrain the assessment of criminal responsibility at the future court by codifying an *actus reus* provision in its statute. Specifically, it was suggested that a provision defining the element of 'omission' should be incorporated 'to set out clearly and carefully in the Statute all conditions under which a crime could be committed, and that this should not be left to the discretion of the Court'.[92] However, the concept of 'omission' presented particular problems for the different legal systems.[93] While Canada and Japan had presented proposals for defining omission, France was particularly opposed to that endeavour.[94] The concept was eventually not included in the RS as a result of the lack of consensus.[95] Some authoritative commentators have suggested that the exclusion of omission liability from the RS could only be understood as the rejection of such kind of liability at the ICC, with the exception of command responsibility, regulated by Article 28.[96] But the recollections of the Chairman of the Working Group on the General Part at the Rome Conference, Per Saland, suggest otherwise. Saland himself proposed that the *actus reus* article should not be included at all and that the question of omission liability be left to the judges to decide. According to Saland, the proposal was not favoured by those 'who wanted to regulate everything in detail' in the Statute but was acceptable to France and other states who had problems with the concept of omission liability. As time pressed the delegates, the suggestion was eventually accepted, and the

[91] Interview with Kai Ambos, 2 June 2020.
[92] PrepCom 1996 Report, Vol. I, 45.
[93] State Proposals 1996, 12.
[94] Saland, 'International Criminal Law', 212.
[95] Eser, 'Mental Elements', 819.
[96] Ibid.

issue of omission was 'left to the Court's case law'.[97] Hence, the question of omission liability other than command responsibility in the RS remained surrounded by uncertainty. Like the debate around the incorporation of enterprise forms of liability, such as Article 25(3)(d), in the RS, the tension around the definition of omission liability reflected the fragmentation of state preferences during the drafting process – a fragmentation that, at least according to some of the drafters, enhanced the powers of the future judges.

The main implication of the challenging endeavour of reconciling competing ideas about the criminal responsibility laws was the conceptual ambiguity and the overlap between some of the provisions in Article 25(3), which left the future judges with discretion to determine the exact meaning of the law. For instance, the Statute did not provide on how to differentiate the notion of 'joint' commission of a crime under subparagraph (a) from, e.g., instigation under (b), aiding and abetting under (c), or contribution to a collective crime under (d). That task was left to the judges, depending on their interpretation of the meaning of the terms 'jointly' and 'committing'.[98] The concepts of indirect perpetration under subparagraph (a) and 'order[ing]' the commission of a crime under (b) were also similar because both the person who orders the crimes and the person who uses another person to commit the crimes exert psychological influence over the direct perpetrator.[99] That overlap also required judicial clarification of the meaning of both provisions.

Overall, Article 25(3) is impressive in its detail compared to statutes of the UN tribunals and the IMT Charter. While that may seem as the result of states seeking to restrain the interpretative space of the ICC judges in assessing the criminal responsibility of their nationals, the drafting process was just as much the product of the competition of legal ideas. Furthermore, the differences of opinion among the legal experts at the working group ended up expanding the interpretative autonomy of the future judges and providing the latter with some very broad scope in modes of liability, such as Article 25(3)(d). As the next section discusses, the negotiations of Article 28 produced similar outcomes, even though states expressed greater interest in that provision.

[97] Saland, 'International Criminal Law', 212–213.

[98] Eser, 'Individual Criminal Responsibility', 789–790.

[99] Van Sliedregt, *Individual Criminal Responsibility*, 107–109.

5.4 Article 28 RS: Responsibility of Commanders and Other Superiors

The drafters included one further provision 'in addition to other grounds of responsibility' in the RS: the command responsibility principle.[100] The drafting history of Article 28 suggests that states expressed more interest in the detailed codification of command responsibility compared to other modes of liability listed in Article 25(3),[101] presumably because they wanted to provide notice about the scope of liability to their military and civilian superiors. But the compromises reached during the negotiations resulted in what was described as 'a very broad' mode of liability.[102]

Article 28 has two subparagraphs: (a) concerning military commanders and (b) concerning non-military or civilian superiors. The article requires, firstly, that a superior-subordinate relationship exist between the accused and the direct perpetrators of the crimes. Next, the military or civilian commander should exercise 'effective command and control', or 'effective authority and control', respectively, over their subordinates. Consequently, the crimes should be the 'result' of the commander's failure to exercise control over her subordinates. This marks a difference with the statutes of the UN tribunals, which did not require a causal connection between the commander's failure to control their subordinates and the crimes committed by the subordinates. Finally, under Article 28 only those commanders who failed to take all 'necessary and reasonable measures' within their powers 'to prevent or repress' the commission of the crimes or 'to submit the matter to the competent authorities for investigation and prosecution' were liable for punishment at the ICC.

At Rome, states were mainly concerned with the question of whether command responsibility should remain restricted to military commanders or should cover civilian superiors as well.[103] According to Saland's recollections, most countries favoured the idea of extending command responsibility to non-military contexts.[104] But the question was contentious considering the differences in the nature and scope of the authority of military and non-military commanders, which led countries like China to object to the expansion of the command responsibility principle.[105]

[100] Rome Statute, Article 28.
[101] Rome Conference Official Records, Vol. II, 136–138.
[102] Ambos, 'Current Issues', 249.
[103] Rome Conference Official Records, Vol. II, 132.
[104] Saland, 'International Criminal Law', 202.
[105] Rome Conference Official Records, Vol. II, 137.

Eventually the United States came up with a compromise solution: command responsibility for civilian superiors would require a higher mental element compared to the cases concerning military commanders. More specifically, the attribution of civilian command responsibility would require that some information about the subordinates' crimes was available to the superior. By contrast, on this account, military commanders could be justly subjected to the harsher negligence standard because those persons were 'in charge of an inherently lethal force' as opposed to a 'bureaucracy'.[106]

The drafting history of Article 28 renders support to the 'practice' framework of international law because it demonstrates that states engaged in the rules of legal discourse when presenting their ideas. The decision to impose a higher mental element standard for civilian commanders can be traced not only to the interests of states for protecting their bureaucrats from prosecution, but also to the normative beliefs of states in the importance of the culpability principle – because, by virtue of their profession, civilian commanders did not possess the same level of control as their military counterparts, the link between civilian officials and the crimes needed to be more explicit. Another observation worth mentioning is the lack of uniformity in states' preferences with respect to the command responsibility principle. While China disagreed with the idea of civilian command responsibility, most states favoured the broader version of the doctrine. Consequently, perceiving the RS modes of liability only as the product of the efforts of 'states' in general to narrow as far as possible the opportunities for convicting a person at the ICC provides an incomplete picture. As actors within the ICL field, states also engaged in a competition of ideas over the determination of the scope of the law on command responsibility.

Notably, the incorporation of Article 28's provision on negligent omissions demonstrated that the competition of ideas provided greater flexibility to the future ICC judges in establishing the accused's criminal responsibility. With respect to the mental element of command responsibility for military commanders, Article 28(a) RS ended up imposing a lower requirement than the UN tribunals. Subparagraph (b), which concerned civilian commanders required that the accused 'either knew [of], or consciously disregarded information which clearly indicated' the subordinates' crimes.[107] This standard appeared similar

[106] Ibid., 136.
[107] Rome Statute, Article 28(b)(i).

to the one found in the UN tribunals' statutes, namely, that the commander 'had reason to know' about her subordinates' crimes.[108] By contrast, subparagraph (a) of Article 28 RS that concerned military commanders required that the commander 'knew or, owing to the circumstances at the time, *should have known*' about the commission of the crimes.[109] The RS drafting records suggest that the drafters understood the words 'should have known' to denote negligence on behalf of the commander.[110] Similar interpretations of the text were made by legal experts when the court began operation.[111] Because the UN tribunals had rejected the negligence standard as applicable,[112] the RS ended up expanding the scope of command responsibility with respect to military commanders.

5.5 Article 30 RS: Mental Element

The politics of promoting and contesting different understandings of the criminal responsibility rules during the RS negotiations can be also observed with the mental element of liability defined in Article 30. The mental element of criminal responsibility could be addressed either as a general matter in the General Part of a criminal code or left to the judges to decide upon in individual cases. The second method is typical of the old common law approach[113] and the post–Second World War and the UN tribunals that were largely influenced by the common law.[114] In fact, the 1994 International Law Commission Draft Statute of the ICC did not include a general regulation concerning the mental element.[115] That question was first contemplated in 1995 when the *Ad Hoc* Committee of the UN General Assembly examining the draft suggested a number of general issues to be discussed, including the mental element.[116] Eventually, Article 30 RS for the first time in ICL standardized the mental element requirements that were applicable to all crimes within the

[108] ICTY Statute, Article 7(3). ICTR Statute, Article 6(3).
[109] Rome Statute, Article28(a)(i), emphasis added.
[110] Rome Conference Official Records, Vol. II, 136.
[111] Ambos, 'Superior Responsibility', 868.
[112] Chapter 4, Section 4.2.2.2.
[113] R. Clark, 'Mental Element', 292.
[114] M. E. Badar, 'The Mental Element in the RS of the International Criminal Court: A Commentary from a Comparative Criminal Law Perspective' (2008) 19(3) *Criminal Law Forum* 473, 473.
[115] Draft Statute for an International Criminal Court 1994.
[116] R. Clark, 'Mental Element', 297.

court's jurisdiction.[117] As with the other RS criminal responsibility provisions, Article 30 demonstrated the desire of the legal experts working on the General Part to codify in detail the elements of liability.[118] But Saland admitted that the drafting of Article 30 was also the subject of a challenging discussion because of the conceptual differences between national systems in relation to the mental element.[119] As with the other RS criminal responsibility provisions, the ambiguity of the legal terms, resulting from the difficulties of reaching consensus during the negotiations, left the future ICC judges with discretion to determine the meaning of the law.

The most important question before the drafters was deciding on the minimum element of a guilty mind that had to be proven on behalf of the accused for the attribution of criminal responsibility at the ICC. The 1996 state proposals submitted to the PrepCom envisaged two options – the common law concept of 'recklessness' and the civil law concept of '*dolus eventualis*'.[120] Eventually, the drafters rejected recklessness as an applicable standard and determined that the attribution of criminal responsibility required the existence of 'intent and knowledge' on behalf of the accused.[121] More specifically, Article 30 RS required that the accused 'mean[t] to engage' in the crime[122] or was 'aware that it will occur in the ordinary course of events' as a result of her actions.[123] At a first glance, it may appear as if the drafters significantly narrowed the scope for serving convictions at the Court by determining that only intentional conduct triggered criminal responsibility, thus deferring to states' interests to protect the freedom of their nationals. Indeed, the ICTY's first president considered the exclusion of recklessness in the RS 'a step backwards' in the development of international criminal justice because, for him, recklessness was sufficient to establish criminal responsibility for some war crimes.[124]

[117] Werle and Jessberger, 'Unless Otherwise Provided', 37. D. Pigaroff and D. Robinson, 'Article 30: Mental Element', in K. Ambos and O. Triffterer (eds.), *Rome Statute of the International Criminal Court: A Commentary*, 3rd ed. (London: Bloomsbury T&T Clark) 1111, 1118.

[118] S. Finnin, 'Mental Elements under Article 30 of the RS of the International Criminal Court: A Comparative Analysis' (2012) 61(2) *International and Comparative Law Quarterly* 325, 326–327.

[119] Saland, 'International Criminal Law', 205.

[120] State proposals 1996, 14.

[121] Saland, 'International Criminal Law', 205.

[122] Rome Statute, Article30(2)(a).

[123] Rome Statute, Article30(2)(b), emphasis added.

[124] Cassese, 'Statute of the International Criminal Court', 508–509.

But on closer inspection, the situation was more complicated. The concepts of 'intentional' conduct and 'knowledge' that a crime 'will occur in the ordinary course of events' are not straightforward terms and can be interpreted to mean different standards, more or less harsh towards the accused. Specifically, the *dolus eventualis* standard, referring to the accused's acceptance of the risk that her conduct may result in the commission of a crime, has been described as the 'borderland' of intentional conduct and does not present the same obstacle to the prosecutor as proving that the accused purposefully aimed at the commission of the crime or was certain that the crime will occur.[125] Notably, the *dolus eventualis* concept was never explicitly rejected in the records.[126] Some legal experts assumed that the RS drafters had dismissed *dolus eventualis* alongside recklessness.[127] But civil law experts have identified subtle differences between the two standards.[128] While both 'recklessness' and '*dolus eventualis*' denote acting with awareness of the risk imposed by one's conduct, it is said that recklessness focuses on the gravity of that risk, while *dolus eventualis* requires personal approval of the risk-taking endeavour or reconciliation with the possible criminal result.[129] Therefore, in some civil law systems, including German and Dutch law, *dolus eventualis* is considered as a form of volitional conduct.[130] Because *dolus eventualis* was nowhere defined in the PrepCom records, nor was it explicitly rejected by the drafters, the question whether the ICC would use the 'borderland' concept of intentional conduct for serving convictions was left to the judges' conceptual understanding of *dolus eventualis*.[131] If they were to interpret *dolus eventualis* as a form of indifference to a substantial risk, then it would be clearly excluded from the RS. But if they were to interpret *dolus eventualis* as an amalgam of volitional and cognitive elements, consistent with the 'intent and knowledge' requirement of the RS, then the judges could consider it applicable at the ICC.

As with other provisions from the General Part of the RS, the ambiguous language of Article 30 reflected a compromise between the common and civil law understandings of the mental element of liability.[132] Concepts

[125] Fletcher and Ohlin, 'Reclaiming Fundamental Principles', 554.
[126] Eser, 'Mental Elements', 932.
[127] R. Clark, 'Mental Element', 301.
[128] K. Ambos, 'Critical Issues in the *Bemba* Confirmation Decision' (2009) 22(4) *Leiden Journal of International Law* 715, 718–719.
[129] Fletcher and Ohlin, 'Reclaiming Fundamental Principles', 554.
[130] Van Sliedregt, Individual Criminal Responsibility', 41.
[131] Ambos, 'Critical Issues', 718.
[132] H. Satzger, 'German Criminal Law and the RS – A Critical Analysis of the New German Code of Crimes against International Law' (2002) 2(3) *International Criminal Law Review* 261, 269.

that were used only in particular domestic traditions, such as *dolus eventualis*, were not explicitly included in the RS. But the search for a neutral language left many questions open to interpretation by the future ICC judges. Thus, even though the codification of the mental element of criminal responsibility rendered the ICC judges more constrained compared to their colleagues at the UN tribunals, the need to reconcile competing understandings of the criminal responsibility laws during the international negotiations granted judicial discretion with respect to determining the meaning and scope of Article 30.

5.6 Conclusion

The detailed codification of criminal responsibility rules in the RS puts the future ICC judges in a more constrained position in relation to the determination of individual criminal responsibility compared to the UN tribunals, which seemingly displays deference to state interests on behalf of the drafters. The meaning of the term 'commission' was specified with reference to three scenarios: commission as an individual, jointly with another person, and through another person, regardless of whether that other person was criminally responsible. The other forms of participation in a crime and the command responsibility principle were similarly codified in detail under Article 25(3)(b)–(d) and Article 28, respectively. Furthermore, while the UN tribunals' Statutes did not specify any rules regarding the mental element of liability, the RS Article 30 required proof of the accused's 'intent and knowledge' in relation to the crimes.

This chapter took a different approach by examining the drafting history of those RS provisions with respect to the competition of ideas that is characteristic of the legal field. This perspective offers several insights into the origins of the RS criminal responsibility provisions. Some modes of liability, such as indirect perpetration through a non-innocent agent, can be traced to the desire of legal experts to reflect the dynamics of system criminality. Other modes, such as Article 25(3)(d), were included by view of balancing civil and common law traditions. Even with respect to more politically sensitive provisions, such as command responsibility, on which state delegations adopted official positions recorded in the archives, the drafting process exhibited sound legal reasoning in the presentation and contestation of ideas. Overall, the impressive level of codification of the RS criminal responsibility laws should be understood not only as due to the interests of states to protect their sovereignty but also due to the understanding, shared among many legal experts in the 1990s, that the general principles of law had to be clearly defined in the RS. The challenges of finding a consensus between the competing ideas about the legal rules that were presented by members of the ICL community during the negotiations further contributed to the detailed listing of criminal responsibility rules.

Furthermore, the analysis demonstrated that state preferences concerning criminal responsibility provisions had been considerably fragmented during the negotiations process, with some state proposals favouring significantly broader forms of liability compared to others. This fragmentation of ideas indicates that states were not guided solely by their self-interest during the negotiations process. States were also guided by their normative understandings about the scope and requirements of criminal responsibility provisions. Hence, states engaged as participants *within* the legal field during the establishment of the ICC.

Notably, as a result of the need to integrate competing ideas about criminal responsibility rules, the ICC judges ended up with a broad variety of provisions pursuant to which they could assess the defendant's guilt or innocence. The revised version of indirect perpetration allowed for a conduct that was committed through a fully responsible person to attract liability for 'commission' of a crime at the ICC. Article 25(3)(d)(ii), which criminalized 'any other contribution' to a group crime that was made merely in 'knowledge' of the criminal purpose of that group, also significantly expanded the scope of liability. Furthermore, Article 28(a) enabled the attribution of criminal responsibility for a negligent conduct. Moreover, many terms that were included within the statutory text required 'judicial construction' to be applied in practice.[133] Article 30 seemingly 'raise[d] more questions than answers'.[134] The ICC judges may have had to take into consideration significantly more statutory text than their colleagues at the UN tribunals, but that also meant that the ICC judges had to engage in that much more legal interpretation.

133 Greenawalt, 'Pluralism', 1080. Steer, 'Legal Transplants', 40.
134 Werle and Jessberger, 'Unless Otherwise Provided', 37.

6

Interpreting the Rome Statute

A Newfound Emphasis on Criminal Law Theory

The ambiguities and overlaps of the RS criminal responsibility provisions meant that the concrete meaning of those legal norms was undetermined. This chapter observes that the competition for delivering an authoritative interpretation of the criminal responsibility provisions in Article 25(3), Article 28, and Article 30 continued when the Court began operation. Some of the developments in ICC jurisprudence, especially the interpretation of Article 25(3)(a) pursuant to the 'control-over-the-crime' theory, have triggered significant academic interest.[1] This chapter contributes to the literature by, firstly, situating these developments within the broader normative context of the ICL field. Specifically, the analysis shows that the interpretation of Article 25(3) should be understood not only as an indication of the growing influence of civil law norms, as has been often suggested,[2] but also with respect to other important overlapping factors, namely the growing dissatisfaction with JCE and the novel institutional environment of the ICC. Firstly, the chapter does not argue that the 'control' theory presented a better picture of mass atrocities or adhered more strictly to the culpability principle than JCE, but that the judges and legal scholars who supported its adoption *perceived* it to be so, at least for the time being. Secondly, this chapter goes beyond the analysis of the early ICC decisions, including those issued by the *Lubanga*, *Katanga and Ngudjolo*, and *Bemba* PTCs, and provides a comprehensive analysis of the (re)construction of criminal responsibility rules at the ICC over a period of 15 years, including recent developments, which took place in 2020–2021 in *Yekatom and Ngaïssona*, *Abd-Al-Rahman*, and *Said*. This approach

1 *See* Sadat and Jolly, 'Seven Cannons'. M. Aksenova, 'The Modes of Liability at the ICC: The Labels That Don't Always Stick' (2015) 15(4) *International Criminal Law Review* 629–644. L. Yanev and T. Kooijmans, 'Divided Minds in the Lubanga Trial Judgment: A Case against the Joint Control Theory' (2013) 13(4) *International Criminal Law Review* 789–828. T. Weigend, 'Perpetration through an Organization: The Unexpected Career of a German Legal Concept' (2011) 9(1) *Journal of International Criminal Justice* 91. Jain, 'Control Theory'.

2 Steer, 'Legal Transplants', 45–46. R. Clark, 'Drafting a General Part', 546–547.

highlights the dynamic nature of ICL norms and allows for tracing the extent to which normative shifts within the broader legal field influence the construction of the criminal responsibility rules in ICC practice. Furthermore, this chapter explores the critique of the 'control' theory raised by advocates of strict compliance with the culpability principle and argues that critique has had a significant impact on the application of Article 25(3)(a) in individual cases, discussed in the Chapters 7, 8, and 9.

6.1 The Interpretative Scope of ICC Practice

Even though the meaning of many terms in Articles 25(3), 28, and 30 of the RS remained ambiguous, the future ICC judges did not enjoy unlimited interpretative discretion. As discussed in Chapter 2, pre-institutionalized norms, including unwritten rules and legal text, simultaneously enable and constrain creative interpretations. Commentators have generally considered that two specific RS provisions may significantly restrain ICC judges from creative interpretations of its rules, including those on criminal responsibility: Article 22 codifying the legality principle[3] and Article 21 listing the applicable sources of law at the Court.[4] But a closer look at those provisions reveals that they could accommodate competing interpretations of the laws on criminal responsibility.

Previous international tribunals sought to balance procedural with substantive justice. The importance of legality was not neglected, but the meaning of the principle was qualified. As observed by one eminent judge at the UN tribunals, the legality principle prohibited idiosyncratic interpretations of the law according to the personal preferences of the judges, but it '[did] not bar the progressive development of the law' aimed at ending impunity for mass atrocities.[5] Consequently, in view of the judicial practices of previous tribunals, some commentators considered it 'unrealistic' that the inclusion of the legality principle in the RS would restrain judicial creativity at the ICC.[6] It was observed that many RS provisions

[3] Broomhall, 'Article 22', 950. Schabas, 'Interpreting the Statutes', 886–887.

[4] R. Cryer, 'Royalism and the King: Article 21 of the Rome Statute and the Politics of Sources' (2009) 12(3) *New Criminal Law Review: An International and Interdisciplinary Journal* 390, 392. Galand, 'Systemic Effect', 128.

[5] M. Shahabuddeen, 'Does the Principle of Legality Stand in the Way of Progressive Development of Law' (2004) 2(4) *Journal of International Criminal Justice* 1007–1017, 1013.

[6] Wessel, 'Judicial Policy-Making', 414. See also G. Werle, 'Do Crimes against Humanity Require the Participation of a State or a "State-Like" Organization?' (2012) 10(5) *Journal of International Criminal Justice* 1158, 1158–1159.

were susceptible to legal 'overreach' if the ICC judges chose to interpret those according to the Statute's 'object and purpose', namely to end impunity for mass atrocities.[7]

Similar observations can be made with respect to Article 21 RS that renders the Statute the primary source of law at the Court[8] and grants only secondary importance to the established 'principles and rules of international law'.[9] Hence, the RS gives precedence to its own provisions, as ratified by the State Parties, over the ambiguous norms of customary international law and general principles of law that the UN tribunals often relied on. The RS also gives weight to the ICC's own interpretations of those provisions.[10] Paragraph (2) provides that the judges may apply the law as interpreted in previous ICC decisions.[11] Similarly to the incorporation of the principle of legality, the decision to list the applicable sources of law in a hierarchical manner in the RS has been perceived by some legal experts as an attempt by states to constrain judicial independence with regard to the determination of the applicable law.[12] Nevertheless, Article 21 gave the ICC judges 'ample opportunities for judicial creativity'.[13] The drafters conceded that the judges could resort to the general principles of law derived from national laws 'as appropriate'.[14] Expert commentators have observed that this left the judges with 'a wide discretionary power' to interpret the general principles of national legal systems.[15] Furthermore, while Article 21 granted primacy to the RS, it could not be read *a contrario* to mean that the ICC should not resort to customary international law or the UN tribunals' jurisprudence under any circumstances.[16] Many legal experts considered that the interpretation of the RS in a consistent manner with the pre-existing ICL jurisprudence and customary international

[7] Sadat and Jolly, 'Seven Cannons', 766.

[8] Rome Statute, Article 21(1)(a).

[9] Rome Statute, Article21(1)(b).

[10] Pauwelyn and Elsig, 'Politics of Treaty Interpretation', 456.

[11] Rome Statute, Article 21(2).

[12] Cryer, 'Royalism and the King', 392.

[13] G. Danilenko, 'The Statute of the International Criminal Court and Third States' (2000) 21(3) *Michigan Journal of International Law* 454, 490. P. Viebig *Illicitly Obtained Evidence at the International Criminal Court* (The Hague: T.M.C. Asser Press, 2016), 25.

[14] Rome Statute, Article21(1)(c).

[15] Pellet, 'Applicable Law', 1075. See also M. DeGuzman, 'Applicable Law', in K. Ambos and O. Triffterer (eds.) *Rome Statute of the International Criminal Court: A Commentary*, 3rd ed. (London: Bloomsbury T&T Clark, 2016) 932, 944.

[16] Van Sliedregt, 'Pluralism', 849–850.

law would be legally convincing[17] because it would avoid the 'fragmentation' of ICL.[18]

Furthermore, if Article 21 is explored not in a legal vacuum but against the background dynamics of the ICL field, it becomes clear that, even though some legal experts considered the restrictive nature of Article 21 a 'serious setback',[19] not all participants in the ICL field felt the same way about the pre-existing practices within the field. As discussed in Chapter 5, the establishment of the ICC provided a unique opportunity for those members of the ICL community who had been dissatisfied with the state of ICL practice to pursue change and promote their vision of international criminal justice. From that perspective, Article 21 constituted a protective barrier that allowed the new court to dissociate itself from previous tribunals, and, as will be discussed, the ICC judges actively used that rule to justify the development of rather novel norms and practices associated with the assessment of criminal responsibility. The explicit authorization of applying principles and rules as interpreted in the ICC's previous decisions further contributed to the creation of an internal normative culture within the Court.

Consequently, from the perspective of the practice framework of ICL, Article 21 did not protect ICC jurisprudence from creative interpretations of the law. Rather, it enabled the judges to pursue novel creative construction of the rules of criminal responsibility and justify their creativity with Article 21's hierarchical structure, which provided precedence to the RS. The ICC judges also had an alternative despite (or maybe because of) the detailed language of that provision. Specifically, they could have sought consistency with previous ICL practices and relied on the vast jurisprudence of the UN tribunals to help in the interpretation of the relevant RS provisions,[20] relying on Article 21's occasional references to making decisions as 'appropriate'. Ultimately, it was largely left to the ICC's judges to decide whether the court's case law would embody pre-existing ICL jurisprudence, depending on how the judges interpreted Article 21 and its purpose.[21] Any young

17 Sadat and Jolly, 'Seven Cannons', 761. H. Satō, 'International Criminal Responsibility Concerning "Control over an Organization" and Command Responsibility Lato Sensu' (2012) 12(2) *International Criminal Law Review* 293, 300. Werle and Jessberger, 'Unless Otherwise Provided', 46. Finnin, 'Mental Elements', 354.

18 R. Cryer, 'The Definitions of International Crimes in the *Al Bashir* Arrest Warrant Decision' (2009) 7(2) *Journal of International Criminal Justice* 283, 295–296. Steer, 'Legal Transplants', 64.

19 Cassese, 'Statute of the International Criminal Court', 512.

20 B. Goy, 'Individual Criminal Responsibility before the International Criminal Court: A Comparison with the *Ad Hoc* Tribunals' (2012) 12(1) *International Criminal Law Review* 1.

21 Greenawalt, 'Pluralism', 1082. Boyle and Chinkin, Making of International Law, 276. B. Van Schaack, 'Legality & International Criminal Law', in S. Sivakumaran, B. Van Schaack,

international legal body makes that interpretative choice: to establish an inward-looking jurisprudence as a 'self-contained regime' or to adopt an outward-looking approach and interpret their treaties with reference to the boarder legacy of international law.[22] Because there existed different sets of shared understandings on these matters within the ICL field, whichever approach the judges would have chosen, it was likely going to receive validation by some subgroups of the ICL epistemic community and criticism from others. This is the simultaneously constraining and enabling nature of the ICL field. In the case of the rules concerning individual criminal responsibility, the ICC judges shared the vision of the Court as a unique and novel system of ICL. The rest of this chapter discusses how that vision played out in the interpretation of Article 25(3), Article 28, and Article 30.

6.2 Interpreting Article 25(3)

The ICC judges took a decidedly self-contained approach to the interpretation of Article 25(3)(a)[23] and cautioned against the mechanical application of the practices associated with the assessment of criminal responsibility derived from the UN tribunals' jurisprudence to the ICC.[24] Instead of the well-established but equally controversial JCE doctrine, the ICC judges at the *Lubanga* and the *Katanga and Ngudjolo* PTCs proposed a novel approach called 'control over the crime' that borrowed heavily from German criminal law scholarship. Like their ICTY colleagues, the ICC judges presented a creative interpretation of the term 'commission'. However, this novel interpretation was underpinned by very different ideas, reflecting the normative shifts within the broader ICL field.

6.2.1 The 'Control over the Crime' Theory

6.2.1.1 A Novel Interpretation

In 2007, the *Lubanga* PTC decided to examine different approaches for differentiating between the modes of principal liability under Article

D. Robinson. T. Meron, and B. Roth (eds.) *The Principle of Legality in International Criminal Law* (American Society of International Law, 2009), 104. B. Perrin, 'Searching for Law While Seeking Justice: The Difficulties of Enforcing International Humanitarian Law in International Criminal Trials' (2008) 39(2) *Ottawa Law Review* 367.

[22] Pauwelyn and Elsig, 'Politics of Treaty Interpretation', 457.

[23] Van Sliedregt, 'Pluralism', 849.

[24] Schabas, *Introduction to the International Criminal Court*, 196.

25(3)(a) and the modes of accessory liability under Article 25(3)(b)–(d). Firstly, the PTC considered the 'objective approach', according to which only the physical perpetrators of the crime were considered principal perpetrators.[25] Next, the judges considered what they called the 'subjective approach', which treated the individuals who shared the intent to commit the crime as principals, regardless of the level of their objective, or physical, contribution to the crime.[26] The PTC described JCE as a 'subjective approach' because of the doctrine's emphasis on the shared intent of the JCE members to commit the crime.[27] The ICC judges concluded that 'unlike the jurisprudence of the [UN] tribunals', the RS embraced a third approach to principal liability, called the 'control over the crime' theory.[28] According to the 'control' theory, the principal liability covered not only the physical perpetrators of the crime, but also the persons who, 'in spite of being removed from the scene of the crime, *control* or *mastermind* its commission', by deciding where and how the crime was committed.[29] The judges noted that the control theory combined both objective elements, namely the factual circumstances enabling the principal perpetrator to control the crime, and subjective elements, namely that person's awareness of such circumstances.[30] Therefore, the ICC judges adopted a theory of criminal responsibility, which they perceived to be *more* objective than the widely criticized JCE.

Based on the control theory, the ICC judges interpreted the language of Article 25(3)(a), finally resolving the ambiguities resulting from the complex drafting negotiations. In 2007, the *Lubanga* PTC focused on the second scenario provided for in subparagraph (a), namely committing a crime 'jointly with another' person. According to the judges, the text referred to situations in which two or more persons jointly shared control over the commission of the crime.[31] The PTC determined that several requirements had to be met to establish the existence of joint control: the 'existence of an agreement or a *common plan* between two or more persons',[32] which included 'an element of criminality',[33] and evidence that each co-perpetrator had made a 'co-ordinated essential contribution'

[25] *Lubanga*, Decision on the confirmation of charges, ICC-01/04-01/06-803-tEN, Pre-Trial Chamber I, 19 January 2007 (hereinafter *Lubanga* Confirmation Decision), § 328.

[26] Ibid., § 329.

[27] Ibid.

[28] Ibid., § 338.

[29] Ibid., § 330, emphasis added.

[30] Ibid., § 331.

[31] Ibid., § 342.

[32] Ibid., § 343, emphasis added.

[33] Ibid., § 344.

towards the common plan.[34] Essential contribution was defined as the power 'to frustrate the commission of the crime by not performing [one's] tasks'.[35] Thus, the *Lubanga* PTC interpreted the 'vague' RS words 'jointly with another' to constitute a theory of co-perpetration that posed very specific requirements.[36] The judges at other ICC chambers subsequently concurred with that interpretation of the Statute.[37]

Arguably, meeting the specific requirements of co-perpetration made the job of the prosecutor more complicated than the plain reading of 'joint conduct' would have. The latter appeared far broader compared to the *Lubanga* PTC's peculiar interpretation of Article 25(3)(a). Already in its first confirmation of charges decision, the ICC demonstrated reluctance to follow the practices exhibited at earlier international tribunals, to establish broad and flexible modes of liability, which would make it easier to link the accused to the crime.[38]

A year later, in 2008, the *Katanga and Ngudjolo* PTC used the control theory to interpret the term commission 'through another person, regardless of whether that other person is criminally responsible' in Article 25(3)(a). Because the legal experts at the PrepCom had not provided interpretative guidance on the novel ICL provision of indirect perpetration through a non-innocent agent, it was up to ICC judges to bestow those words with meaning. The *Katanga and Ngudjolo* PTC found that the provision concerned those instances when a crime was committed through a hierarchical *organization* under the control of the indirect perpetrator.[39] The judges concluded that several requirements had to be met to hold the indirect perpetrator criminally responsible for the crime that was physically committed by a member of that organization: The organization must have a tight hierarchical structure, must accommodate a sufficient number of subordinates in order to guarantee

[34] Ibid., § 346.

[35] Ibid., § 347.

[36] Weigend, 'Intent, Mistake of Law', 479.

[37] See *Katanga and Ngudjolo*, Decision on the Confirmation of Charges, ICC-01/04-01/07-717, Pre-Trial Chamber I, 14 October 2008 (hereinafter *Katanga and Ngudjolo* Confirmation Decision), §§ 480–486. *Bemba*, Decision Pursuant to Article 61(7)(a) and (b) of the RS on the Charges of the Prosecutor Against Jean-Pierre Bemba Gombo, ICC-01/05-01/08-424, Pre-Trial Chamber II, 15 June 2009 (hereinafter *Bemba* Confirmation Decision), §§ 347–348. *Al Bashir*, Decision on the Prosecution's Application for a Warrant of Arrest against Omar Hassan Ahmad Al Bashir, ICC-02/05-01/09-3, Pre-Trial Chamber I, 4 March 2009 (hereinafter *Al-Bashir* Arrest Warrant Decision 2009), § 210.

[38] G. Fletcher, 'New Court'.

[39] *Katanga and Ngudjolo* Confirmation Decision, §§ 512–514.

that the superiors' orders would be carried out, 'if not by one subordinate, then by another',[40] and the accused must have enjoyed 'authority and control' over the organization.[41]

Notably, the *Katanga and Ngudjolo* PTC concluded that the 'co-perpetration' and 'indirect perpetration' modes of liability could be combined into a new mode of liability that the judges called 'joint commission through another person',[42] or 'indirect co-perpetration'.[43] The new mode of liability enabled the attribution of criminal responsibility to each co-perpetrator, even if only one of those persons had exercised control over the physical perpetrators of the crimes.[44]

6.2.1.2 The Novel Interpretation in Context

The *Lubanga* and *Katanga and Ngudjolo* PTCs' interpretation of Article 25(3)(a) essentially did two things. Firstly, it dismissed JCE as the dominant approach to establishing liability for committing a crime in ICL. Secondly, it vested the text of Article 25(3)(a) RS with very specific meaning: 'commission' was interpreted as 'control over the crime'; commission 'jointly with another' person – as making an 'essential contribution' to a 'common plan' resulting in a crime; commission 'through another person' – as commission though a hierarchical 'organization' composed of fungible members ready to obey criminal orders. Sadat and Jolly observe that, given that neither the complete rejection of JCE, nor the adoption of the control approach, was preordained by the statutory language, the ICC's novel approach appeared 'particularly curious'.[45] An enquiry into the normative dynamics of the ICL field at the time reveals that the way in which the *Lubanga* and *Katanga and Ngudjolo* PTCs construed the modes of liability listed in Article 25(3)(a) displayed their shared understandings about the requirements of criminal responsibility for committing a crime.

The *Katanga and Ngudjolo* PTC argued that the notion of 'control over an organized apparatus of power' was 'incorporat[ed] within the legal framework of the Court'.[46] But, as observed later by one ICC judge, Article 25(3)(a) 'only speaks of commission "through another *person*"',

[40] Ibid., § 512.
[41] Ibid., § 513.
[42] Ibid., § 489.
[43] *Al-Bashir* Arrest Warrant Decision 2009, § 213.
[44] *Katanga and Ngudjolo* Confirmation Decision, § 493.
[45] Sadat and Jolly, 'Seven Cannons', 785.
[46] *Katanga and Ngudjolo* Confirmation Decision, § 510. See also *Lubanga* Confirmation Decision, §§ 333–335.

not through an *organisation*.[47] Furthermore, the *travaux préparatoires* nowhere mentioned the control theory.[48] The adoption of the 'control' theory did not present a 'literal interpretation', but a creative interpretation of the RS.[49] The complete rejection of JCE at the ICC was also not self-evident. The notion of 'co-perpetration' under Article 25(3)(a) resembled the basic form of JCE (JCE I), and the concept of 'indirect perpetration' bore similarities with the revised JCE developed in *Brđanin*.[50] Before the ICC judges invoked the control theory, the phrase 'jointly with another' under Article 25(3)(a) RS was interpreted by the Legal Representatives of Victims at the ICC as pertaining to the notion of 'joint criminal enterprise'.[51] Some authoritative commentators also expected the judges at the new court to be 'strongly influenced' by the prolific jurisprudence of the UN tribunals on JCE.[52] Even legal experts, who otherwise considered that there were important differences between the ICC regime and the UN tribunals, acknowledged that insights from the JCE jurisprudence may be relevant for interpreting Article 25(3)(a) RS.[53] The complete rejection of JCE by the *Lubanga* PTC took by 'surprise' some members of the ICL community of practice.[54]

Therefore, the interpretation of Article 25(3)(a) pursuant to the 'control over the crime' theory was creative in two ways. Firstly, it dismissed the pre-existing interpretation of indirect and joint 'commission' found in ICL and took a self-contained approach to the RS's modes of principal liability. Secondly, it adopted a theory that was not explicitly mentioned, whether in the Statute or the *travaux préparatoires*. But, as discussed in Chapter 2, while the ICL field constantly fosters creativity, even novel ideas are always grounded within the shared background understandings among at least some of the participants in the field. Similarly, the adoption

[47] *Ngudjolo*, Judgment pursuant to Article 74 of the Statute, Concurring Opinion of Judge Christine Van den Wyngaert, ICC-01/04-02/12-4, Trial Chamber II, 18 December 2012 (hereinafter *Ngudjolo* Judgment, Judge Van den Wyngaert Opinion), § 52, emphasis in the original. See also Weigend, 'Perpetration through an Organization', 105–106.

[48] The review of all public records at the PrepCom and Rome Conference supports this conclusion. See also Van Sliedregt, Individual Criminal Responsibility, 86. K. J. Heller, 'Lubanga Decision Roundtable: More on Co-Perpetration', *OpinioJuris*, 16 March 2012, http://opiniojuris.org/2012/03/16/lubanga-decision-roundtable-more-on-co-perpetration/. Sadat and Jolly, 'Seven Cannons', 782. Greenawalt, 'Pluralism', 1080–1081.

[49] Weigend, 'Perpetration through an Organization', 109.

[50] Van Sliedregt, 'International Criminal Law', 1156.

[51] *Lubanga* Confirmation Decision, § 325.

[52] Schabas, *Introduction to the International Criminal Court*, 215.

[53] Werle, 'Individual Criminal Responsibility', 961.

[54] Manacorda and Meloni, 'Indirect Perpetration', 165.

of the 'control over the crime' theory can be traced to the ideas that were promoted within the ICL community of practice around the early 2000s.

The adoption of the control theory and the rejection of JCE have often been attributed to the presence of influential civil law-trained judges at the ICC[55] and 'the pleas of (mainly) German legal scholars',[56] and there is merit to such arguments. The *Lubanga* and *Katanga and Ngudjolo* PTCs often referred to German criminal law theory when interpreting the term 'commission' under Article 25(3)(a).[57] The control theory, or the 'domination of the act' theory (*Tatherrschaft*), was developed by the German legal scholar Claus Roxin in 1963. Roxin was also the author of the 'control over an organization' theory (*Organisationsherrschaft*),[58] which the *Katanga and Ngudjolo* PTC relied upon in order to interpret the RS provision on perpetration through a non-innocent agent.[59] Even though the judges argued that the control theory was applied by 'numerous legal systems',[60] it has been generally accepted only in German- and Spanish-speaking literature[61] and applied in national proceedings in Germany, including the trials concerning the shootings at the East German border, and in Latin America, including the trial against the former president of Peru Alberto Fujimori.[62] As observed by one authoritative ICL scholar, it was somewhat of an 'exaggeration' to imply that the control theory was 'widely representative of different legal cultures'.[63]

But the professional background of the judges presents only part of the story behind the rejection of JCE and its substitution by the 'control over the crime' theory. As observed by Van Sliedregt, JCE in fact has a 'hybrid

[55] Steer, 'Legal Transplants', 45–46. R. Clark, 'Drafting a General Part', 546–547.

[56] H. Van der Wilt, 'The Continuous Quest for Proper Modes of Criminal Responsibility' (2009) 7(2) *Journal of International Criminal Justice* 307, 309.

[57] *Lubanga* Confirmation Decision, § 348, footnote 425. *Katanga and Ngudjolo* Confirmation Decision, §§ 482–485 and footnotes 642,645–647, § 489 and footnotes 658–659, § 517 and footnote 684.

[58] C. Roxin, *Täterschaft und Tatherrschaft*, 1st ed. (Hamburg: Cram, de Gruyter & Co., 2011[1963]).

[59] *Katanga and Ngudjolo* Confirmation Decision, § 498.

[60] *Lubanga* Confirmation Decision, § 330. See also *Katanga and Ngudjolo* Confirmation Decision, § 485.

[61] A. G. Gil and E. Maculan, 'Current Trends in the Definition of "Perpetrator" by the International Criminal Court: From the Decision on the Confirmation of Charges in the *Lubanga* case to the *Katanga* judgment' (2015) 28(2) *Leiden Journal of International Law* 349, 354. See also Weigend, 'Indirect Perpetration', 547.

[62] Ambos, 'Article 25', 955.

[63] J. D. Ohlin, 'Co- Perpetration: German Dogmatik or German Invasion?', in C. Stahn, (ed.). *The Law and Practice of the International Criminal Court* (Oxford: Oxford University Press, 2015) 517, 523.

civil/common law heritage' that centres around the idea of joint perpetration, which has been recognized in both penal traditions.[64] Consequently, it is necessary to explore the normative dynamics within the broader ICL field, beyond the civil/common law tension, to provide a more comprehensive assessment of the factors behind JCE's vigorous rejection in the ICC era.

While the idea of 'joint perpetration' might be uncontested in the ICL field, JCE as such was scapegoated as one of the factors leading to unsound legal reasoning at international tribunals. As discussed in Chapter 4, over the early 2000s legal experts increasingly attributed the problems associated with the assessment of criminal responsibility at the ICTY to the broad and flexible nature of JCE. Around the time the ICC Chambers began interpreting Article 25(3) RS, a new vision of 'joint perpetration' was taking hold in the ICL field – a vision premised on the ideas of categorization of legal rules and differentiation between the parties to the crime. It is true that the new vision borrowed from civil law, and specifically from German doctrine, but it constituted more than that – it was constructed and presented in opposition to JCE.

Crucially, the ICC's novel institutional context provided a unique opportunity to materialize this new vision of commission liability in practice – an opportunity that was denied to the UN tribunals. Academic writing and criminal law theory became particularly influential during that process.[65] Prior to the 2007 *Lubanga* PTC's decision, several authoritative scholars who published extensively on questions of ICL, including Kai Ambos, Gerhard Werle, and Albin Eser, had already suggested that *Organisationsherrschaft* was an appropriate legal theory for interpreting Article 25(3)(a).[66] According to Ambos, 'unlike JCE' the *Organisationsherrschaft* theory could convincingly be used by international tribunals to construe the meaning of the term 'committing' a crime.[67] Notably, in the early ICC decisions in *Lubanga* and *Katanga and Ngudjolo*, the judges appeared particularly attentive to such academic analyses of the RS and often referred to the writings of ICL scholars.[68]

[64] Van Sliedregt, 'Joint Criminal Enterprise', 190.

[65] Ohlin, 'Co-Perpetration', 517.

[66] Ambos, 'Remarks on the General Part', 664. G. Werle, *Principles of International Criminal Law* (The Hague: TMC Asser Press, 2005), 124, footnote 196. A. Eser, 'Individual Criminal Responsibility', in A. Cassese, P. Gaeta and J. Jones (eds.) *The Rome Statute of the International Criminal Court* Vol. 1 (Oxford: Oxford University Press, 2002) 767, 796.

[67] Ambos, 'Joint Criminal Enterprise', 182.

[68] See *Lubanga* Confirmation Decision, § 326, footnote 417. *Katanga and Ngudjolo* Confirmation Decision, § 498, footnote 659, § 501, footnote 665. *Mbarushimana*, 'Public

The first AC decision that discussed the matter, in the *Lubanga* case, also noted that the control approach to commission liability was 'supported by academic commentators'.[69] While later decisions did not *explicitly* refer to scholarship analysis, those decisions generally concurred with the theoretically grounded findings of the *Lubanga* and the *Katanga and Ngudjolo* PTCs and the *Lubanga* AC with respect to Article 25(3)(a).[70] The ICC finally presented criminal law scholars with an opportunity 'to develop a comprehensive theory of individual criminal responsibility' in ICL.[71]

Many authoritative academics welcomed the departure from the JCE approach and the ICC's 'path-breaking' decision to interpret Article 25(3) RS in accordance with a detailed criminal law theory.[72] Legal scholars noted the higher degree of precision of the ICC's control theory compared to the approach of the UN tribunals.[73] Even commentators, who were otherwise critical of the expansion of principal liability beyond the physical perpetrators of the crimes, acknowledged that the ICC's approach to commission liability offered more 'sophisticated' justifications for such expansion compared to JCE[74] and possessed the added 'attraction of clarity'.[75]

Redacted Version: Decision on the Confirmation of Charges', ICC-01/04-01/10-465-Red, Pre-Trial Chamber I, 16 December 2011 (hereinafter *Mbarushimana* Confirmation Decision), § 279, footnote 659.

69 *Lubanga*, Public Redacted Judgment on the Appeal of Mr Thomas Lubanga Dyilo against His Conviction, ICC-01/04-01/06-3121-Red, Appeals Chamber, 1 December 2014 (hereinafter *Lubanga* Appeals Judgment), 465, footnote 867, see also footnotes 864–866.

70 See *Bemba* Confirmation Decision, §§ 347–348. *Al-Bashir* Arrest Warrant Decision 2009, § 210. *Ruto, Kosgey and Sang*, Decision on the Confirmation of Charges Pursuant to Article 61(7)(a) and (b) of the Rome Statute, ICC-01/09-01/11-373, Pre-Trial Chamber II, 4 February 2012 (hereinafter *Ruto, Kosgey and Sang* Confirmation Decision), §§ 291-292. *Ongwen*, Decision on the confirmation of charges against Dominic Ongwen, ICC-02/04-01/15-422-Red, Pre-Trial Chamber II, 26 March 2016 (hereinafter *Ongwen* Confirmation Decision), §§ 38–40. *Bemba et al.*, Judgment pursuant to Article 74 of the Statute, ICC-01/05-01/13-1989-Red, Trial Chamber VII, 19 October 2016 (hereinafter *Bemba et al.* Trial Judgment), §§ 62-71. *Gbagbo*, Decision on the Confirmation of Charges against Laurent Gbagbo, ICC-02/11-01/11-656-Red, Pre-Trial Chamber I, 12 June 2014 (hereinafter *Gbagbo* Confirmation Decision), § 230. *Blé Goudé*, Decision on the confirmation of charges against Charles Blé Goudé, ICC-02/11-02/11-186, Pre-trial Chamber I, 11 December 2014 (hereinafter *Blé Goudé* Confirmation Decision), § 134.

71 Jessberger and Geneus, 'Application of a Theory', 867.

72 G. Fletcher, 'New Court'. K. Ambos, 'The First Judgment of the International Criminal Court (Prosecutor v. Lubanga): A Comprehensive Analysis of the Legal Issues' (2012) 12(2) *International Criminal Law Review* 115, 144–146. Jessberger and Geneuss, 'Application of a Theory', 866–867. Granik, M. 2015. 'Indirect Perpetration Theory: A Defence', 28(4) *Leiden Journal of International Law* 977. Werle, 'Individual Criminal Responsibility', 962–963.

73 Manacorda and Meloni, 'Indirect Perpetration', 171.

74 Guilfoyle, 'Responsibility for Collective Atrocities', 279.

75 Ibid., 265.

A Bulgarian diplomat working in the sphere of ICL similarly expressed the view that the 'control over the crime' theory was 'more just' compared to JCE because it 'placed more emphasis on the rights of the person [at trial]' by not allowing 'excess' criminal responsibility to be imputed to the principal perpetrator.[76] In other words, to many members of the ICL field, the notion of control over the crime appeared to be theoretically more rigorous than the notion of participation in a criminal enterprise.

In fact, there are curious similarities between the original purpose for which Roxin developed the control theory and the adoption of his theory in ICL, illustrating the influence of the legal community of practice on the development of criminal responsibility rules at both the domestic and the international level. Roxin's *Tatherrschaft* was developed in attempt to present a new, more 'objectivist' theory for distinguishing between principal and accessory liability.[77] To that point, German courts had generally taken the subjectivist approach to differentiation and examined the accused's intent to commit the crime as the criterion for distinguishing principals from accessories. But the subjective approach triggered concern among legal scholars that the judges were vested with too much discretion to assess the defendant's attitude to the crime.[78] After all, the 'subjective' elements of criminal responsibility, which require an enquiry into the *mind* of a person, appear 'far vaguer and more difficult to prove' than the 'objective' ones.[79]

In a similar manner, the *Lubanga* PTC rejected what the judges defined as the 'subjective' JCE theory in favour of the control theory, which was argued to combine 'objective' with 'subjective' elements. Whether the UN tribunals followed a 'subjective' approach to establishing principal liability in reality is debatable. Some legal experts have opined that such a label did not 'do justice' to JCE because the latter required active contribution to the common design.[80] Since the UN tribunals did not use the 'subjective/objective' terminology in their jurisprudence, the *Lubanga* PTC's categorization of JCE as a 'subjective' approach appeared to be employed in order to differentiate the ICC's control theory from JCE, rather than as an accurate description of

76 Interview with Georgi Minkov, Ministry of Foreign Affairs, Bulgaria, April 2019.

77 Weigend, 'Perpetration through an Organization', 95. Jain, 'Control Theory', 165.

78 Weigend, 'Perpetration through an Organization', 94–95.

79 H. Olásolo, *The Criminal Responsibility of Senior Political and Military Leaders as Principals to International Crimes* (Oxford; Portland, Or.: Hart, 2009), 73.

80 Weigend, 'Intent, Mistake of Law', 478. See also V. Haan, 'The Development of the Concept of Joint Criminal Enterprise at the International Criminal Tribunal for the Former Yugoslavia' (2005) 5(2) *International Criminal Law Review* 167, 195–196.

the UN tribunals' jurisprudence.[81] Moreover, to the extent that the *Lubanga* and the *Katanga and Ngudjolo* PTCs relied on the UN tribunals' jurisprudence in construing the meaning of the term 'commission', they chose the ICTY judgment that tried to substitute JCE with a control-based theory of criminal responsibility – the reformist *Stakić* TC Judgment.[82]

Notably, the ICC did not differentiate itself from all practices of the UN tribunals on the assessment of criminal responsibility, but specifically from those ones, such as the reliance on JCE, that had triggered criticism for infringing upon the culpability principle. Unlike their interpretation of the term 'committing' a crime under subparagraph (a), the ICC judges were more willing to borrow insights from the UN tribunals' jurisprudence when it came to modes of liability that were different from the infamous JCE. Even though the *Mbarushimana* PTC emphasized the differences between the ICC regime and the UN tribunals[83] and subscribed to the control theory of commission liability,[84] the PTC referred to the ICTY's jurisprudence on 'aiding and abetting' a crime when interpreting Article 25(3)(c) RS.[85] Similarly, the *Mudacumura* PTC borrowed from the UN tribunals' jurisprudence in interpreting the terms 'orders, solicits, or induces' the commission of a crime under subparagraph (b).[86] Members of the broader ICL community of practice, who otherwise highlighted the differences between JCE and the modes of principal liability under Article 25(3)(a) RS, supported the idea of relying on the prolific jurisprudence of the UN tribunals when it came to accessory modes of liability, such as Article 25(3)(b) and (c).[87] From that perspective, when it came to modes of liability that did not pertain to the controversial JCE, the ICC could '*legitimately* look at the case law of the [UN] tribunals'.[88]

81 Van Sliedregt, *Individual Criminal Responsibility*, 84.

82 *Lubanga* Confirmation Decision, § 342, footnote 422, § 343, footnote 423, § 346, footnote 424. *Katanga and Ngudjolo* Confirmation Decision, § 506.

83 *Mbarushimana* Confirmation Decision, § 281.

84 *Mbarushimana*, Decision on the Prosecutor's Application for a Warrant of Arrest against Callixte Mbarushimana, ICC-01/04-01/10- 1, Pre-Trial Chamber I, 29 September 2010 (hereinafter *Mbarushimana* Arrest Warrant Decision), § 30.

85 *Mbarushimana* Confirmation Decision, § 279.

86 *Mudacumura* Arrest Warrant Decision, footnotes 129–133. See also Ambos, 'Article 25', 1001–1002.

87 H. Olásolo and R. Carnero, 'Forms of Accessorial Liability under Article 25(3)(b) and (c)', in C. Stahn (ed.) *The Law and Practice of the International Criminal Court* (Oxford: Oxford University Press, 2015) 557, 559. Ambos, 'Article 25', 1008. Werle, 'Individual Criminal Responsibility', 969.

88 Kai Ambos's expert testimony on Article 25(3) RS during the *Mbarushimana* confirmation of charges hearing. Transcript ICC-01/04-01/10-T-8-Red2-ENG, Pre-Trial Chamber I, 20 September 2011, p. 10, lines 13–14, emphasis added.

Unlike JCE, the accessory modes of liability in ICL were generally not considered as a source of much 'controversy or complexity'.[89]

Finally, the attractiveness of the control theory compared to JCE was not merely the result of the theory's perceived objectivity, but also because of its expressivist potential to paint a convincing picture of system criminality.[90] Roxin's theory presented 'juridical acknowledgement of the bureaucratic nature of mass atrocity'.[91] In fact, the notion of organizational control was invoked in well-known cases against former Nazi officials, including the *Eichmann* trial in Israel and the *Justice* trial at the United States court at Nuremberg.[92] The appeal of Roxin's theory was its perceived ability to communicate to the victims and the broader international community 'who was the "real" culprit' behind mass atrocities,[93] namely the mastermind or the leader who used 'ordinary people' to commit the crimes.[94] The *Katanga and Ngudjolo* PTC observed that a person's blameworthiness often increased '*in tandem* with a rise in the hierarchy'.[95] Consequently, the judges argued that their interpretation of Article 25(3)(a) on the basis of the control theory reflected 'the blameworthiness of "senior leaders" adequately'.[96] Roxin's theory of the bureaucracy of atrocities may have been particularly apt to describe Nazi criminality, but it appeared less attuned to modern-day African conflicts that have so far constituted the bulk of ICC investigations.[97] Possibly in anticipation of that challenge, without explanation, the *Katanga and Ngudjolo* PTC modified Roxin's theory by specifying another mechanism apart from the replaceability of the subordinates that could enable automatic compliance with the mastermind's orders. According to the judges, the existence of 'intensive, strict, and violent training regiments', including the abductions of minors and their training to shoot, rape, and pillage, could similarly ensure the indirect perpetrator's control over the organization.[98] Some legal scholars welcomed the ICC's decision to reform what was perceived as the outdated bureaucratic version of the control theory.[99]

[89] Boas, 'Omission Liability', 206.
[90] Steer, 'Legislative Transplants', 52. Granik, 'Indirect Perpetration Theory', 986.
[91] Osiel, Making Sense, 95, emphasis added. Van der Wilt, 'Continuous Quest', 311–312.
[92] Ambos, 'Article 25', 955.
[93] Van Sliedregt, *Individual Criminal Responsibility*, 80.
[94] Jain, 'Control Theory', 196–197. Werle and Burghardt, 'Indirect Perpetration', 88. Weigend, 'Indirect Perpetration', 542.
[95] *Katanga and Ngudjolo* Confirmation Decision, § 503, emphasis in the original.
[96] Ibid., § 492.
[97] Cryer et al., *Introduction to International Criminal Law*, 368.
[98] *Katanga and Ngudjolo* Confirmation Decision, § 518.
[99] Osiel, Making Sense, 103, 111.

Overall, the ICC's creative interpretation of Article 25(3)(a) must be understood both in terms of the acceptance of certain ideas and practices, namely the growing influence of civil law norms in ICL and the heightened concern for the scope of personal culpability, and the rejection of others, specifically, the flexible and pragmatic approach to assessing criminal responsibility embodied by the JCE theory. The novel institutional context at the ICC enabled the new vision of commission liability to take hold over the years. However, as the next section discusses, the dynamic nature of the ICL field has increasingly challenged the stability of the ICC approach.

6.2.1.3 Contesting the ICC's Reliance on the Control Theory

Not all members of the ICL community of practice shared the understanding that the control theory constituted an improvement over JCE. Notably, legal experts within and outside the ICC contested the proposed theory on different grounds. Some, including Judge Fulford who sat at the *Lubanga* TC, considered that the control theory imposed 'an unnecessary and unfair burden on the prosecution'.[100] Instead, Judge Fulford favoured a 'plain' reading of the statutory text and argued that the term 'commits' simply required 'an operative link between the individual's contribution and the commission of the crime', as opposed to proof of the accused's control over the crime and the ability to frustrate its commission.[101] According to Judge Fulford, his plain reading of Article 25(3)(a) involved 'a "lesser" test' for establishing criminal responsibility.[102] Similarly, one of the judges at the UN tribunals, Judge Shahabuddeen, observed with concern that the requirement of establishing the perpetrator's control over the crime meant that in some factual situations a defendant could be convicted under JCE, but not under Roxin's theory.[103] This line of opposition to the 'control over the crime' theory resulted from two overlapping normative premises – firstly, a preference for simplicity as opposed to excessive categorization of the legal rules, and, secondly, a concern for preventing the perpetrators of mass atrocities from escaping justice because of the excessively strict criminal responsibility rules.

[100] *Lubanga*, Judgment pursuant to Article 74 of the Statute, Separate Opinion of Judge Adrian Fulford, ICC-01/04-01/06-2842, Trial Chamber I, 14 March 2012 (hereinafter *Lubanga* Trial Judgment, Judge Fulford Opinion), § 3.

[101] Ibid., § 15.

[102] Ibid., § 21.

[103] Shahabuddeen, 'Judicial Creativity', 200.

By contrast, many other scholars and practitioners criticized the control approach for the opposite reason – they considered that the theory was not restrictive *enough*. More specifically, the *Lubanga* PTC's finding that the 'common plan' between the co-perpetrators did not need to be 'specifically directed at the commission of a crime', but only needed to include an element of criminality,[104] raised concern among those legal experts who advocated for strict compliance with the culpability principle. From that perspective, the PTC's finding could result in charging the defendant with crimes committed in excess of the common plan as long as those crimes were foreseeable, which advantaged the prosecution and disadvantaged the defendant.[105] Even scholars who approved of the control approach argued that the 'common plan' should include a somewhat concrete crime.[106] Another source of concern in view of the culpability principle was the combination of 'co-perpetration' and 'indirect perpetration' into a new mode of liability, 'indirect co-perpetration', by the *Katanga and Ngudjolo* PTC. Some academics considered indirect co-perpetration 'a way to loosen' the concept of co-perpetration.[107] Judge Van den Wyngaert similarly observed that, by enabling the mutual attribution of the crimes to each indirect co-perpetrator, even if only one among those persons had actually controlled the crimes, the indirect co-perpetration mode of liability allowed for confirming the charges against the accused in cases that would not otherwise meet the requirements of either of the modes that were explicitly recognized by the RS, namely, indirect perpetration or co-perpetration.[108]

More recently, in 2021 two judges at the *Ntaganda* AC – Judge Morrison and Judge Eboe-Osuji – similarly criticized the 'control over the crime' theory for expanding the notion of personal culpability and compromising the quality of legal reasoning behind ICC judgments. According to Judge Morrison and Judge Eboe-Osuji, the application of indirect co-perpetration required significant *stretching* of the term 'control' to make the facts of individual cases fit the legal theory.[109] The organizational

[104] *Lubanga* Confirmation Decision, § 344.

[105] Gil and Maculan, 'Current Trends', 360. See also Ohlin, 'Joint Intentions', 724.

[106] Ambos, 'First Judgment', 140.

[107] Manacorda and Meloni, 'Indirect Perpetration', 174.

[108] *Ngudjolo* Judgment, Judge Van den Wyngaert Opinion, § 63.

[109] *Ntaganda*, Annex 2: Separate Opinion of Judge Howard Morrison on Mr Ntaganda's Appeal, ICC-01/04-02/06-2666-Anx2, Appeals Chamber, 30 March 2021 (*Ntaganda* Appeals Judgment, Opinion of Judge Morrison), § 17. *Ntaganda*, Annex 5: Partly Concurring Opinion of Judge Chile Eboe-Osuji, ICC-01/04-02/06-2666-Anx5, Appeals Chamber, 30 March 2021 (hereinafter *Ntaganda* Appeals Judgment, Opinion of Judge Eboe-Osuji), § 77.

complexity and the sheer scale of mass atrocities challenge any conclusive observations that the accused had actually 'controlled' the crimes. As observed by Judge Eboe-Osuji, it is not easy to control a piece of 'mechanical equipment' in the way required by the 'control' theory, 'let alone an aggregate collection of a human multitude under a headman'.[110]

Consequently, some members of the ICL field, including legal academics such as Elies Van Sliedregt, Jens Ohlin, and Thomas Weigend, and judges such as Judge Van den Wyngaert, Judge Morrison, and Judge Eboe-Osuji, criticized the control approach not because they perceived JCE as superior, but because they were concerned that the ICC's preferred theory could have resulted in similar expansion of criminal responsibility like JCE when applied in practice in specific cases.[111] Those scholars were concerned that 'the rationale for the ICC's adoption of control-theory' was to reach 'similar results as would have been possible under JCE without explicitly adopting that much-maligned doctrine'.[112]

The observation that so many legal experts, within and outside the ICC, sought stricter compliance with the culpability principle is important because it demonstrates that the desire to protect the accused from the attribution of guilt by association was shared not only by states, but also by many other actors within the ICL field. Consequently, as demonstrated by both the drafting process of the RS General Part and the *Lubanga* and *Katanga and Ngudjolo* PTCs' interpretation of Article 25(3)(a), the principled approach to the establishment of criminal responsibility was motivated by a particular set of shared understandings within the ICL community of practice that became influential at the ICC, partly as a reaction to the UN tribunals' practices, and partly as a result of the ICC judges' professional background and the growing influence of the civil law tradition in ICL. What is even more intriguing is that much of the criticism of the adoption of the 'control' theory centred around the idea that the ICC had not done enough to depart from the practices of previous tribunals and to protect the integrity of the principle of personal culpability.

110 *Ntaganda* Appeals Judgment, Opinion of Judge Eboe-Osuji, § 93.

111 Interview with Elies Van Sliedregt, 7 May 2020. See also Van Sliedregt, Ohlin and Weigend, 'Assessing the Control Theory', 735–739. A. Gil, 'Mens Rea in Co-perpetration and Indirect Perpetration According to Article 30 of the Rome Statute: Arguments against Punishment for Excesses Committed by the Agent or the Co-perpetrator' (2014) 14(1) *International Criminal Law Review* 82, 89. M. Cupido, 'Pluralism in Theories of Liability: Joint Criminal Enterprise versus Joint Perpetration', in E. van Sliedregt and S. Vasiliev (eds.) *Pluralism in International Criminal Law* (Oxford: Oxford University Press, 2014) 128, 151.

112 Van Sliedregt, Ohlin and Weigend, 'Assessing the Control Theory', 738–739.

6.2.1.4 Reforming the Interpretation of Article 25(3)(a)

Even after the ICC rejected JCE, the push to avoid overstretching the culpability principle for the purpose of making convictions easier continued to dominate the ICL field. The difference is that the new target was not JCE, but rather the very theory that was once hoped would address the problems associated with the ICTY doctrine – the 'control over the crime' theory. Ironically, even though JCE and the 'control' theory have employed very different approaches to the assessment of criminal responsibility – one flexible and one abstract and systematized, respectively – they have ended up being criticized for the same thing, namely infringing upon the principle of personal culpability.

The growing dissatisfaction with the abstract requirements of the 'control' theory and their implications for the quality of legal reasoning behind ICC judgments have appeared to slowly pave the path to reform at the ICC.[113] Departing from established ICC jurisprudence on Article 25(3)(a), in 2019 the *Yekatom and Ngaïssona* PTC did not examine whether the available evidence established the existence of a 'common plan' between the alleged co-perpetrators. Instead of assessing the link between the suspects and the common plan, the judges focused on the link between the suspects and each of the alleged criminal incidents.[114] The PTC concluded that even though the notion of the 'common plan' as a vehicle for imputing criminal responsibility had been a 'recurring feature' of ICC cases, 'the very *compatibility* of the notion of a common plan with the statutory framework and its *usefulness* vis-à-vis article 25 of the Statute [was] far from being a foregone conclusion'.[115] The fact that the *Yekatom and Ngaïssona* PTC judges were mindful of the growing concerns associated with the 'control over the crime' theory among their fellow ICL experts is illustrated by their reference to the earlier remarks of Judge Van den Wyngaert regarding the problems of focusing on the accused's involvement in a 'plan' instead of the actual crimes.[116]

In 2021 the same judges repeated verbatim their conclusion on the questionable benefits of relying on the 'control over the crime' theory and its

[113] L. G. Minkova, 'Control over the Theory: Reforming the ICC's Approach to Establishing Commission Liability?' (2022) *International Criminal Law Review* 1–29, DOI: https://doi.org/10.1163/15718123-bja10129.

[114] *Yekatom and Ngaïssona*, Corrected version of Public Redacted Version of 'Decision on the confirmation of charges against Alfred Yekatom and Patrice-Edouard Ngaïssona', ICC-01/14-01/18-403-Red-Corr, Pre-Trial Chamber II, 14 May 2020 (hereinafter *Yekatom and Ngaïssona* Confirmation Decision), § 60.

[115] Ibid., emphasis added.

[116] Ibid., footnote 106.

'common plan' element in the *Abd-Al-Rahman* case[117] and the *Said* case.[118] Thus, the three most recent confirmation of charges decisions at the ICC have followed this novel approach by dismissing the abstract terminology of the 'control over the crime' theory. In 2021 the matter reached the ICC Appeals Chamber. Like their colleagues at the PTC, the AC judges in *Yekatom* noted that they preferred evidence about the 'role of the accused' in the charges.[119] The AC also found that the 'jointly with another' form of commission under Article 25(3)(a) 'can take a number of forms' depending on the case, and that participation in a 'common plan' pursuant to the 'control' theory was one of those forms.[120] From this perspective, the ICC chambers were not obliged to follow a particular terminology with respect to the modes of liability, aside from the statutory language.[121]

These recent ICC decisions indicate two shifts in the practices associated with the assessment of principal responsibility at the Court, which reflect the growing dissatisfaction with the performance of the 'control over the crime theory'. Firstly, ICC judges have increasingly stressed the importance of assessing the link between the accused and the charges, thus answering the pleas of those members of the ICL community concerned with the overstretching of the culpability principle. Secondly, the ICC judges have tried to downplay the significance that the 'control over the crime' theory has played in ICC jurisprudence. The *Yekatom* AC noted that the ICC chambers have relied on a 'broad spectrum' of approaches to confirm the charges and that, while some decisions have used the 'control-over-the-crime' terminology, others have 'merely track[ed] the language of the Statute', citing decisions in *Katanga and Ngudjolo* and in *Gbagbo* as an illustration of the latter.[122] The AC's conclusion is curious. It is correct that the specific paragraphs of the relevant decisions they cite repeat the

117 *Abd-Al-Rahman*, Corrected version of 'Decision on the confirmation of charges against Ali Muhammad Ali Abd-Al-Rahman ('Ali Kushayb')', 9 July 2021, ICC-02/05- 01/20-433, ICC-02/05-01/20-433-Corr, Pre-Trial Chamber II, 23 November 2021 (hereinafter *Abd-Al-Rahman* Confirmation Decision), § 44.

118 *Said*, Decision on the confirmation of charges against Mahamat Said Abdel Kani, ICC-01/14-01/21-218-Red, Pre-Trial Chamber II, 9 December 2021 (hereinafter *Said* Confirmation Decision), §§ 45–47.

119 *Yekatom and Ngaïssona*, Judgment on the appeal of Mr Alfred Yekatom against the decision of Trial Chamber V of 29 October 2020 entitled 'Decision on motions on the Scope of the Charges and the Scope of Evidence at Trial', ICC-01/14-01/18-874, Appeals Chamber, 5 February 2021, (hereinafter *Yekatom* Appeals Decision), § 44.

120 Ibid., § 58.

121 *Yekatom* Appeals Decision, § 60. *Abd-al-Rahman* Confirmation Decision, § 45.

122 *Yekatom* Appeals Decision, § 48.

language of Article 25(3)(a) RS.[123] But it is also true that other parts of the cited decisions in *Katanga and Ngudjolo* and *Gbagbo* explicitly invoke the 'control-over-the-crime' terminology to analyse the facts of the cases,[124] including the disputed notion of 'common plan'.[125]

The ICC seems to be learning from the mistakes of the ICTY. Citing the fact that the JCE theory had become an established practice in ICTY jurisprudence, the tribunals' judges tried reforming that theory instead of rejecting it altogether. But this strategy did not save the ICTY from criticism from those members of the ICL community who were already concerned with its practice of assessing commission liability.[126] By contrast, the ICC in its recent decisions has not only avoided the use of the 'control over the crime' theory but has actively insisted that there was nothing surprising about the decision not to follow that theory. The recent PTC and AC decisions at the Court have tried to dispose of the troublesome concept of 'control over the crime' without triggering criticism for judicial activism and changing the rules of criminal responsibility in a way that would compromise the defendants' right to fair notice.

It is too early to tell whether this would lead to a permanent dismissal of the practice of relying on the 'control over the crime' theory in ICC jurisprudence. Crucially, both the *Yekatom and Ngaïssona* and the *Abd-Al-Rahman* PTCs avoided the question, citing 'the limited and specific purpose of the confirmation of charges stage of proceedings', which did not extend to deliberations on the interpretation of modes of liability (an intriguing departure from the practice of the *Lubanga* and *Katanga and Ngudjolo* PTCs).[127] The *Yekatom* AC concluded that the 'Trial Chamber will adopt the interpretation it considers to be correct',[128] postponing the question several years in the future. Indeed, reforming or overthrowing an established practice part of the internal culture of a legal body is a challenging task, as demonstrated by the failed attempts to substitute JCE with indirect co-perpetration at the ICTY.

[123] *Katanga and Ngudjolo* Confirmation Decision, §§ 573–581. *Gbagbo* Confirmation Decision, §§ 266, 278.

[124] *Katanga and Ngudjolo* Confirmation Decision, §§ 540–561. *Gbagbo* Confirmation Decision, §§ 230–241.

[125] *Katanga and Ngudjolo* Confirmation Decision, §§ 548. *Gbagbo* Confirmation Decision, §§ 231.

[126] Chapter 4, Section 4.2.2.1.

[127] *Yekatom and Ngaïssona* Confirmation Decision, § 60. *Abd-al-Rahman* Confirmation Decision, § 45.

[128] *Yekatom and Ngaïssona* Appeals Decision, § 47.

Nevertheless, the 2019–2021 developments at the ICC illustrate the normative pressure that the broader ICL community could exert on the development of the legal rules concerning the assessment of criminal responsibility. Earlier that pressure had contributed to the rejection of JCE and the adoption of a highly systematized approach to the assessment of commission liability at the ICC. Now it paves the way towards a new interpretation of Article 25(3) that focuses on the link between the accused and the alleged crimes. As will be discussed in the following chapters, the same tendency can be observed in the ICC cases that have proceeded to trial.

6.2.2 Accessory Liability: Subparagraphs (b)–(d)

The ICC judges' interpretation of the relationship between subparagraph (a) and the rest of the Article 25(3) provisions provides another illustration of the importance of the normative dynamics of the ICL field for the assessment of criminal responsibility at the Court. The ICC jurisprudence fixated mainly on subparagraph (a) and did not attribute significant attention to the rest of Article 25(3),[129] essentially downgrading the significance of subparagraphs (b), (c), and (d). Like the adoption of the 'control' theory, this practice has been influenced in part by the popularity of the German normative approach to the modes of liability, and in part by the dissatisfaction with JCE's tendency to obfuscate the different forms of participation in the crime. Furthermore, the concerns expressed by liberal legalists regarding the broad scope of Article 25(3)(d) have contributed to a series of attempts to limit the scope of that provision beyond the statutory language.

6.2.2.1 A Hierarchy of Blameworthiness

The first chambers that interpreted extensively Article 25(3) at the ICC, including the *Lubanga* and *Katanga and Ngudjolo* PTCs, not only set up rigorous requirements for criminal responsibility under subparagraph (a) but also elevated the normative significance of that mode of liability vis-à-vis the rest of the modes listed in the RS.[130] By contrast to the IMT, IMTFE, and the UN tribunals, in 2012 the *Lubanga* TC Majority subscribed to the idea of differentiating between degrees of criminal responsibility by

[129] *Lubanga* Confirmation Decision, § 321. *Katanga and Ngudjolo* Confirmation Decision, § 471.

[130] *Lubanga* Confirmation Decisions, § 320. *Katanga and Ngudjolo* Confirmation Decision, § 488, § 492, § 503.

interpreting the modes of liability codified in Article 25(3)(a)–(d) as a hierarchy of blameworthiness.[131] Subsequently, the *Lubanga* AC concurred that the distinction between principal liability under subparagraph (a) and accessory modes of liability under subparagraphs (b)–(d) was 'not merely terminological' but carried normative significance.[132] The concept of principal liability was said to 'express the blameworthiness of those perpetrators who are the *most* responsible' for international crimes.[133]

The normative differentiation between modes of liability was not preordained by the Statute. Article 25(3)(a) does not 'expressly' provide for the gradation of criminal responsibility[134] and Article 78 RS, which regulates the ICC's sentencing procedure, does not link the different modes of liability with specific length of punishment.[135] In fact, one of the drafters of the Statute's General Part, Roger Clark, considered that subparagraph (b), which criminalized the ordering of a crime, rather than subparagraph (a), was the provision that would be used to deal with 'the big fry, those typically "most responsible" for what occurs'.[136] But the *Katanga and Ngudjolo* PTC was of the opposing opinion. The PTC concluded that subparagraph (a) carried special significance because it established the indirect perpetrator's principal liability for ordering a crime through a hierarchical organization that ensured almost automatic compliance with the orders, while Article 25(3)(b) concerned merely '*ordinary* cases of criminal ordering' and could be used to attribute only accessory liability to the defendant.[137] Although not explicitly quoted by the PTC, a similar interpretation of Article 25(3) was forwarded earlier in ICL scholarship.[138] Nowhere did the Statute include the terms ordering crimes 'though an organization' or ordering crimes under 'ordinary' circumstances. Yet, the judges bestowed the wording of the provision with meaning by highlighting the significance of principal liability as an exceptionally blameworthy conduct, in effect downgrading the 'ordinary' criminal orders. The mode of liability of aiding and abetting a crime under subparagraph (c) received even less attention in ICC jurisprudence than subparagraph (b). Even though the

[131] *Lubanga*, Judgment pursuant to Article 74 of the Statute, ICC-01/04-01/06-2842, Trial Chamber I, 14 March 2012 (hereinafter *Lubanga* Trial Judgment), §§ 998–999.

[132] *Lubanga* Appeals Judgment, § 462. See also *Bemba et al.* Trial Judgment, § 85.

[133] *Lubanga* Trial Judgment, § 999, emphasis added.

[134] Ambos, *Treatise on International Criminal Law*, 146.

[135] Also observed by Militello, 'Personal Nature', 948. Werle and Burghardt, 'Establishing Degrees', 306.

[136] R. Clark, 'Drafting a General Part', 544.

[137] *Katanga and Ngudjolo* Confirmation Decision, § 517, emphasis added.

[138] See Werle, 'Individual Criminal Responsibility', 974.

mode of aiding and abetting a crime was discussed in some major cases at the UN tribunals,[139] including *Tadić*[140] and *Furundžija*[141] at the ICC subparagraph (c) remained of far lesser importance.

The adoption of the normative approach reflected the judges' shared understandings about the appropriate manner in which criminal responsibility had to be assessed, which played out against the silence of the RS on the matter of differentiation. Legal experts with professional experience mainly in German criminal law defended the normative interpretation of Article 25(3) on the grounds that it displayed respect of the principle of fair labelling.[142] From the perspective of the Germanic system, the practice of 'labelling' the mode of participation of the accused from the outset of proceedings, i.e. from the moment of bringing up the charges, was crucial in civil law system.[143] Several ICC chambers specifically referred to academic publications on the matter to support their conclusion that Article 25(3) constituted a 'value oriented hierarchy of participation'.[144]

Furthermore, the adoption of the normative approach appeared to be influenced by the growing dissatisfaction within the ICL field with the practices of earlier tribunals and a desire to differentiate the ICC from those practices. By introducing the normative distinction between modes of liability to ICL, the AC and the TC Majority in *Lubanga* demonstrated that they shared the concerns of those members of the ICL community of practice that the principle of fair labelling required greater accuracy in describing the accused's criminal responsibility. It was also another way of signalling to the broader ICL field that the ICC had departed from the practices of earlier tribunals: from the use of the conspiracy charge at Nuremberg and Tokyo, to the ICTY's reliance on JCE, international tribunals had been criticized for failing to reflect the different degrees of blameworthiness of the participants in mass atrocities. According to Werle, since international crimes generally involved a vast number of perpetrators, the need to determine the level of individual responsibility was even more pertinent in international than in national criminal law.[145]

139 For an overview see Ambos, 'Article 25', 1003–1008.

140 *Tadić* Trial Judgment, §§ 688–692.

141 *Furundžija*, Judgment, IT-95-17/1-T, Trial Chamber, 10 December 1998, §§ 190–249.

142 Ambos, *Treatise on International Criminal Law*, 147. Werle and Burghard, 'Establishing Degrees', 311–315.

143 Interview with Kai Ambos, 2 June 2020.

144 See *Mbarushimana* Confirmation Decision, § 279 and footnote 659. *Lubanga* Appeals Judgment, § 462, footnote 682. The relevant paragraph of the *Lubanga* Appeals Judgment was also quoted by the *Bemba et al.* Trial Judgment, § 85, footnote 151.

145 Werle, 'Individual Criminal Responsibility', 957.

The normative approach appealed to NGOs too. Influential organizations including Human Rights Watch observed that the precise definition of individual criminal liability was essential for establishing effective accountability mechanisms for human rights abuses.[146]

Finally, the decision of the *Lubanga* and *Katanga and Ngudjolo* PTCs, and the *Lubanga* TC Majority to downgrade the normative significance of the accessory modes of liability under subparagraphs under Article 25(3)(b)–(d), also appeared to be influenced by the growing pressure within the broader ICL field to ensure greater compliance with the culpability principle. The judges recognized that the modes of accessory liability listed in the RS may pose lower requirements than subparagraph (a), but they also mitigated the blameworthiness of those modes, seeking proportionality of punishment, rather than easier convictions.

But because the ICL field accommodates different sets of shared understandings about the law on criminal responsibility, the normative approach of the ICC did not remain uncontested. In 2012, Judge Fulford sitting at the *Lubanga* TC and Judge Van den Wyngaert at the *Ngudjolo* TC rejected the proposition that principal liability for commission of a crime under subparagraph (a) was by default more serious than accessory liability for, for example, ordering, aiding, or otherwise contributing to the commission of a crime under subparagraphs (b), (c), and (d), respectively.[147] In 2021 the same argument was repeated by Judge Morrison and Judge Eboe-Osuji at the *Ntaganda* AC.[148] Judge Morrison argued that the RS was not 'blind to the moral culpability of criminal actors', but it simply allowed for the accused's degree of blameworthiness to be accounted for at the sentencing stage of each individual case instead of being predetermined on the basis of the applicable mode of liability.[149]

This division of opinions at the ICC on the question whether Article 25(3) presents a hierarchy of blameworthiness can be explained in part by the tension between the domestic legal cultures that meet within the ICL field – a tension, which, as Chapter 3 discussed, runs deeper than the common/civil law divide.[150] Specifically, the lack of consensus at the ICC on

[146] Human Rights Watch, 'Justice for Liberia: The Truth and Reconciliation Commission's Recommendation for an Internationalized Domestic War Crimes Court', 10 December 2009, www.hrw.org/news/2009/12/10/justice-liberia#_Definitions, 8.

[147] *Lubanga* Trial Judgment, Judge Fulford Opinion, § 8. *Ngudjolo* Judgment, Judge Van den Wyngaert Opinion, § 22.

[148] *Ntaganda* Appeals Judgment, Opinion of Judge Morrison, §§ 8-9. *Ntaganda* Appeals Judgment, Opinion of Judge Eboe-Osuji, §§ 45–47.

[149] *Ntaganda* Appeals Judgment, Opinion of Judge Morrison, § 11.

[150] *See* Chapter 3, Section 3.2.2.

this matter has been described as 'a clash' between the German/Hispanic tradition of normative differentiation and the French and Anglo-American naturalistic tradition, which generally treats the degree of responsibility as a matter of sentencing to be addressed in each case, rather than a general rule of criminal law.[151]

But important as they might be, domestic legal traditions played only a part in this debate. The contestation of the 'hierarchy of blameworthiness' interpretation of Article 25(3) was also influenced by the preference of some members of the ICL community for a less creative and more textual reading of the RS, in line with their minimalistic vision of legality. From this perspective, the text of Article 25(3) recognized different forms of participation in a crime but nowhere prescribed any normative significance to some of those forms.[152] Even some authoritative German commentators noted that the categorization of accessorial conduct into different subparagraphs could 'perhaps' create a hierarchy between the modes,[153] but nevertheless recommended reading Article 25(3) as a unitary provision which would allow the judges to determine the blameworthiness of each party to the crime on their own on the grounds that the RS provided the same punishment for all parties to the crime.[154] Sadat and Jolly further observed that the importation of the normative differentiation model into ICC jurisprudence did not provide any benefits because the language that the Court had adopted was so 'stunningly complex' that the lay reader of judicial decisions was unlikely to understand much of it.[155]

The contestation of the normative reading of Article 25(3) was further facilitated by a concern for the culpability principle, and specifically the requirement that the punishment is proportionate to the wrong done. Some members of the ICL community shared the opinion that instead of clarifying the rules of assessing criminal responsibility, the excessive categorization of the modes of liability might in practice prevent judgments from reflecting the true nature of a person's participation in the crime. Judge Morrison was concerned that indirect co-perpetration

[151] Van Sliedregt, Ohlin, and Weigend, 'Assessing the Control Theory', 473. See also E. Van Sliedregt, 'The ICC Ntaganda Appeals Judgment: The End of Indirect Co-perpetration?', *Just Security*, 14 May 2021, www.justsecurity.org/76136/the-icc-ntaganda-appeals-judgment-the-end-of-indirect-co-perpetration/.

[152] Van Sliedregt, *Individual Criminal Responsibility*, 108. Van Sliedregt, Ohlin and Weigend, 'Assessing the Control Theory', 744. Gil and Maculan, 'Current Trends', 365.

[153] Eser, 'Individual Criminal Responsibility', 787.

[154] Ibid., pp. 787–788.

[155] Sadat and Jolly, 'Seven Cannons', 783.

under Article 25(3)(a) treated 'very different scenarios in the same way'. Consequently, if that provision is considered the most blameworthy by default, a broad range of persons, ranging from leaders to mid-level commanders and direct perpetrators, could be 'equally' treated as principal perpetrators of the same degree of blameworthiness.[156] The concern here is that, while the normative differentiation approach might work in some domestic systems, given the scale and complexity of mass atrocities, it might have an adverse impact on the 'fair labelling' principle.

Even though the rejection of the 'hierarchy of blameworthiness' argument has been growing in popularity within the ICL field, it is difficult to conclude which side 'won' the battle over the determination of the correct approach to differentiating between the RS's modes of liability. In 2014 the judges at the *Katanga* TC, among whom was Judge Van den Wyngaert, found that the distinction between principles and accessories under Article 25(3) did not constitute a hierarchy of blameworthiness.[157] But subsequent decisions suggest that many ICC judges still subscribed to the normative approach to differentiation.[158] The fact that seven years after the *Katanga* TC judgment, Judge Morrison and Judge Eboe-Osuji made significant efforts to justify the view that Article 25(3) did not constitute a hierarchy of blameworthiness[159] suggests that some of their ICC colleagues still subscribed to the normative approach and the dispute had not been conclusively resolved.

The growing dissatisfaction with the abstract requirements of the 'control over the crime' theory has resulted in a renewed interest in more flexible forms of liability, such as Article 25(3)(d), among some members of the ICL community. Ironically, these suggestions have been made for exactly the opposite reasons to the reasons behind the adoption of JCE at the tribunals. While JCE was seen as a tool for preventing the perpetrators of mass atrocities from escaping punishment, the renewed interest in enterprise forms of liability among some commentators follows an assumption that flexibility enables sound legal reasoning. Specifically,

[156] *Ntaganda* Appeals Judgment, Opinion of Judge Morrison, § 31.

[157] *Katanga*, Judgment pursuant to Article 74 of the Statute, ICC-01/04-01/07-3436-tENG, Trial Chamber II, 7 March 2014 (hereinafter *Katanga* Trial Judgment), § 1386.

[158] *Al-Mahdi*, Judgment and Sentence, ICC-01/12-01/15-171, Trial Chamber VII, 27 September 2016 (hereinafter *Al Mahdi*, Judgment and Sentence), § 58. See also *Ntaganda*, Public with public Annexes A, B, and C Judgment, ICC-01/04-02/06-2359, Trial Chamber IV, 8 July 2019 (hereinafter *Ntaganda* Trial Judgment), § 779.

[159] *Ntaganda* Appeals Judgment, Opinion of Judge Morrison, §§ 8–11. *Ntaganda* Appeals Judgment, Opinion of Judge Eboe-Osuji, §§ 42–45.

flexibility is considered to prevent the overstretching of the culpability principle caused by the reliance on the 'control' theory.

6.2.2.2 Interpreting Subparagraph (d)

The influence of the ICL community of practice also became evident in the *Mbarushimana* PTC and *Mbarushimana* AC's interpretation of the mode of liability that had triggered significant controversy during the RS drafting, namely, Article 25(3), subparagraph (d). By criminalizing contributions to a crime committed by a group acting with a 'common purpose', Article 25(3)(d) appeared reminiscent of the controversial JCE doctrine.[160] In fact, the *Tadić* AC referred to Article 25(3)(d) RS as a legal source that supported the existence of the JCE doctrine in international law.[161] But the judges at the *Mbarushimana* PTC emphasized that, 'as similar as they might appear', JCE and Article 25(3)(d) were not identical because while under JCE the accused's contribution to the collective crime triggered principal liability, under Article 25(3)(d) it triggered merely accessory liability.[162] The *Lubanga* PTC similarly downgraded the normative significance of that mode of liability by calling it a 'residual form of accessory liability'.[163] Thus, ICC judges implicitly suggested that subparagraph (d) was more compliant with the fair labelling principle and avoided escalation of responsibility for participation in a group's crime. Furthermore, the *Katanga* TC argued that JCE could be used to attribute liability for *all* of the crimes committed as part of the common purpose, but subparagraph (d) attracted criminal responsibility only for those crimes to which the accused had *contributed personally*.[164] Thus, the ICC judges implicitly suggested that Article 25(3)(d) presented a mode of liability that was more compliant with the culpability principle than JCE.

Moreover, the ICC judges decided to further restrict the scope of Article 25(3)(d) by adding a criterion that was not included in the RS. The *Mbarushimana* PTC acknowledged the concerns of legal experts, such as Jens David Ohlin, that the statutory language of subparagraph (d) risked the attribution of criminal responsibility to every member of

160 Schabas, Introduction to the International Criminal Court, 217–218. Ohlin, 'Three Conceptual Problems', 77. R. DeFalco, 'Contextualizing Actus Reus under Article 25(3)(d) of the ICC Statute: Thresholds of Contribution' (2013) 11(4), *Journal of International Criminal Justice* 715, 722.

161 *Tadić* Appeals Judgment, § 222.

162 *Mbarushimana* Confirmation Decision, § 282.

163 *Lubanga* Confirmation Decision, § 337.

164 *Katanga* Trial Judgment, § 1619.

a community who simply provided the criminal group with groceries or services.[165] Even though the text of subparagraph (d) did not impose a minimum threshold concerning the accused's contribution,[166] the *Mbarushimana* PTC reckoned that 'it would be inappropriate for such liability to be incurred through *any* contribution to a group crime.'[167] To avoid the possibility of 'overextend[ing]' liability,[168] the PTC judges determined that the contribution to the crime under subparagraph (d) had to be 'at least significant'.[169] Nowhere did the language of the provision include the term 'significant'. As observed by one of the drafters of the RS, Judge Fernández de Gurmendi, who had participated in the Rome Conference, the *Mbarushimana* PTC essentially '*added* a criterion to the wording of article 25(3)(d)'.[170]

Notably, Judge Fernández de Gurmendi did not take issue with the ultimate concern of her colleagues, namely to prevent the overstretching of the culpability principle made possible by the broad language of that provision. Rather, she remained unconvinced that the way in which the *Mbarushimana* PTC proposed to address that problem would have been effective. Specifically, Judge Fernández de Gurmendi was not persuaded that setting a 'significant' contribution requirement would ameliorate the risk of over-expanding the scope of Article 25(3)(d). In her opinion, a conduct, such as supplying a criminal group with food or utilities, could, depending on the context, constitute 'a significant, a substantial or even an essential contribution to the commission of crimes by this group'. Therefore, the judge proposed another way of restricting the scope of Article 25(3)(d), namely to assess 'the normative and causal link' between the accused's contribution and the crime.[171]

Both approaches, that of the *Mbarushimana* PTC and of Judge Fernández de Gurmendi, were developed with the aim of restricting the scope of subparagraph (d), even though neither approach was provided

165 *Mbarushimana* Confirmation Decision, § 277, footnote 656.

166 DeFalco, 'Contextualizing Actus Reus', 716.

167 *Mbarushimana* Confirmation Decision, § 276,emphasis in the original.

168 Ibid., § 277.

169 Ibid., § 283.

170 *Mbarushimana*, 'Judgment on the appeal of the Prosecutor against the decision of Pre-Trial Chamber I of 16 December 2011 entitled "Decision on the confirmation of charges"', Separate Opinion of Judge Silvia Fernández de Gurmendi, ICC-01/04-01/10-514, Appeals Chamber, 30 May 2012 (hereinafter *Mbarushimana* Appeals Judgment, Judge Fernández de Gurmendi Opinion), § 7, emphasis added. See also Ambos, 'ICC and Common Purpose', 598.

171 *Mbarushimana* Appeals Judgment, Judge Fernández de Gurmendi Opinion, § 12.

for by the RS.[172] As observed by Kai Ambos, both approaches appeared to be 'driven by a liberal, culpability-based approach'.[173] Thus, the normative dynamics of the broader ICL field played out in the ICC's interpretation of Article 25(3)(d).

Indeed, without taking into consideration these dynamics, and especially the growing influence of the 'liberal critique' of ICL,[174] the ICC judges' decision to use their interpretative discretion to *narrow* the scope of that mode of liability may appear curious. After all, previous international tribunals, including the IMTFE and the ICTY, had construed broad modes of liability, such as conspiracy and JCE, in order to make it easier to link high-level accused to the crimes. But the analysis of the normative dynamics within the ICL community of practice revealed that the PTCs in *Mbarushimana*, *Katanga and Ngudjolo*, and *Lubanga*, to name a few chambers, understood the culpability principle in a more restrained manner so as to require a more evident link between the accused and the crime compared to the Court's predecessors. The ICC judges also placed greater emphasis on fair labelling of the accused's criminal responsibility. As discussed in Chapter 7, with the notable exception of the *Katanga* TC, the ICC judges have been similarly reluctant to rely on accessory modes of liability for convictions and displayed clear preference for relying on facts that demonstrated the accused's personal involvement, as opposed to remote assistance, in the commission of the crimes.

Notably, the problems that the 'control over the crime' theory and the modes listed under Article 25(3)(a) RS have faced in practice have led some members of the ICL community, including Judge Morrison and Judge Eboe-Osuji, to suggest that Article 25(3)(d) might play a greater role in ICC jurisprudence in the future.[175] In 2021 Judge Morrison argued that that provision allowed for a 'common sense description and appreciation of the role of an individual' in organized forms of criminality, such as mass atrocities.[176] This suggestion again indicates intriguing developments within the ICL field:[177] recent critiques of the 'control over the crime theory' share the concern of the early ICC chambers to respect the principle of personal culpability, but unlike those chambers see the excessive

[172] DeFalco, 'Contextualizing Actus Reus', 729.

[173] Ambos, 'ICC and Common Purpose', 598.

[174] Chapter 3, Section 3.2.3.2.

[175] *Ntaganda* Appeals Judgment, Opinion of Judge Morrison, § 39. *Ntaganda* Appeals Judgment, Opinion of Judge Eboe-Osuji, § 55.

[176] *Ntaganda* Appeals Judgment, Opinion of Judge Morrison, § 40.

[177] See Sections 6.2.1.3 and 6.2.1.4.

categorization of rules of liability as counterproductive. Yet, the lack of consensus on the precise scope and requirements of Article 25(3)(d) in ICC jurisprudence suggests that, if that mode of liability ends up being used more often at the Court, it is likely to trigger just as much debate as Article 25(3)(a) has. The rest of this chapter shows that the interpretation of Article 28 and Article 30 has similarly remained subject to ongoing contestation from inside and outside the Court.

6.3 Interpreting Article 28

The ICC judges have also adopted a restrained approach to the interpretation of command responsibility – another mode of liability that had triggered criticism in view of its compliance with the culpability principles as applied at the IMTFE and the UN tribunals. Notably, the ICC judges referred to the UN tribunals' extensive jurisprudence when elaborating some of the requirements of command responsibility under Article 28 RS, including the notion of 'effective control'.[178] Those elements of command responsibility, as found in the practice of the UN tribunals, were described by legal experts as 'not conceptually controversial' in relation to the culpability principle and were even considered to pose evidentiary challenges for the prosecution.[179] But the main difference in the conceptualization of command responsibility between the UN tribunals and the ICC is the causality requirement. The UN tribunals' jurisprudence on command responsibility did not require proof of a causal relationship between the commander's failure to fulfil her duties and the subordinate's crimes.[180] By contrast, the text of Article 28 stipulated that the crimes must be committed 'as a result of' the commander's failure to discharge her duties and control her subordinates.[181] Some members of the ICL field, such as Amnesty International, tried to contest that requirement out of humanitarian concerns, arguing that it would make it harder to convict commanders and thus it would obstruct the realization of the RS goals to 'end impunity' and prevent 'the most serious international crimes'.[182] But that suggestion was quickly dismissed by the *Bemba* PTC,[183] which affirmed

[178] *Bemba* Confirmation Decision, §§ 414–416.

[179] Danner and Martinez, 'Guilty Associations', 130. See also Osiel, Making Sense, 34.

[180] See *Čelebići* Trial Judgment, § 398. *Blaškić* Appeals Judgment, § 77.

[181] RS of the International Criminal Court, Article 28(a) and (b).

[182] *Bemba*, 'Amicus Curiae Observations on Superior Responsibility Submitted Pursuant to Rule 103 of the Rules of Procedure and Evidence', ICC-01/05-01/08-406, Pre-Trial Chamber II, 20 April 2009 (hereinafter *Bemba Amicus Curiae*), § 31, § 41.

[183] *Bemba* Confirmation Decision, § 423.

the earlier commentaries of legal scholars that the text of Article 28 clearly included a causation requirement.[184]

Apart from the submission of Amnesty International, there appeared to be a consensus within the ICL community of practice that the RS constrained the broad scope of command responsibility by incorporating a causality requirement. The causality requirement would certainly be perceived favourably by sovereign states who seek to shield their commanders from international prosecution. But the desire to limit the scope of command responsibility in such manner also reflected the concerns of those members of the ICL field who advocated for greater respect for the culpability principle. According to one authoritative commentator who shared that concern, the causality requirement in the Rome Statue was not an 'arbitrary limitation' imposed by the drafters, but a 'principle of justice – a fundamental requirement of personal culpability'.[185] From this perspective, the RS had finally resolved a particularly troublesome question regarding the practice of the UN tribunals.

But the RS's definition of command responsibility did not narrow down all aspects of that doctrine compared to the tribunals' jurisprudence. As discussed in Chapter 5, Article 28(a) ended up imposing a lesser mental element of liability than the one accepted at the tribunals. While the UN tribunals' statutes required that the commander 'had reason to know' about the crimes, Article 28(a) RS required only that commander 'should have known' of those crimes, thus bestowing upon the commander a duty to stay informed about their subordinates' conduct in order to avoid criminal responsibility.[186] The normative dynamics of the ICL field, and specifically the growing concern for protecting the culpability principle, appear to have influenced the ICC judges' interpretation of the novel provision. Those members of the ICL field who sought to minimize wartime suffering welcomed the imposition of a lower mental element in the RS, considering that the harsh negligence standard would incentivize military commanders to monitor the behaviour of their subordinates.[187] However,

184 See O. Triffterer, 'Causality, a Separate Element of the Doctrine of Superior Responsibility as Expressed in Article 28 Rome Statute?' (2002) 15(1) *Leiden Journal of International Law* 179. Ambos, 'Superior Responsibility', 860.

185 Robinson, *Justice in Extreme Cases*, 260.

186 Danner and Martinez, 'Guilty Associations', 129–130. Van Sliedregt, 'Command Responsibility', 392. *Kayishema and Ruzindana*, Judgment, ICTR-95-1-T, Trial Chamber, 21 May 1999, § 227.

187 E. Levine, 'Command Responsibility: The *Mens Rea* Requirement' (2005) *Global Policy Forum*, www.globalpolicy.org/component/content/article/163/28306.html. *Bemba* Amicus Curiae, § 8.

from a criminal law perspective, the introduction of a stricter standard sat uneasily with the culpability principle.[188] The *Bemba* PTC seemed to share that uneasiness. The judges noted that the term 'should have known' pertained to 'a form of negligence'[189] because the RS drafters intended to hold military commanders to a stricter standard.[190] Hence, even if the imposition of the negligence standard in ICL had been informed by humanitarian concerns and potentially contradicted the culpability principle, the ICC judges made clear that that was the *drafters*' intentions and not a form of judicial activism. Furthermore, the *Bemba* PTC narrowed the scope of the provision by concluding that the 'form of negligence' provided in Article 28(a) was not that different from the higher 'had reason to know' standard used at the UN tribunals. The *Bemba* PTC determined that the criteria developed by the UN tribunals to meet the 'had reason to know' standard 'may also be useful when applying the "should have known" requirement'.[191] The PTC also considered that the indicia of establishing *actual knowledge* of the crimes were 'relevant' for assessing whether a commander 'should have known' about the crimes. Those indicia provided that the commander 'had general information to put him on notice' of the subordinates' crimes and 'such available information was sufficient to justify further inquiry or investigation'.[192] These criteria rather resembled the higher standard of recklessness, or acting on the basis of available information, instead of a positive obligation to stay informed and discover such information.

Several years later, some ICC judges entered a particularly restrictive interpretation of the command responsibility principle in the 2018 *Bemba* AC judgment. The AC Majority concluded that the key factor in determining whether a commander had taken all necessary and reasonable measures to prevent, investigate, or report the crimes of their subordinates was the commander's 'material ability' to do something about the crimes.[193] To avoid the imposition of strict liability, the Majority

[188] Ambos, 'Superior Responsibility', 851. Van Sliedregt, *Individual Criminal Responsibility*, 200. Manacorda and Meloni, 'Indirect Perpetration', 633. W. Schabas, 'Canadian Implementing Legislation for the Rome Statute' (2000) 3 *Yearbook of International Humanitarian Law* 337, 342.

[189] *Bemba* Confirmation Decision, § 429.

[190] Ibid., § 433.

[191] Ibid., § 434.

[192] Ibid.

[193] *Bemba*, Judgment on the appeal of Mr Jean-Pierre Bemba Gombo against Trial Chamber III's 'Judgment pursuant to Article 74 of the Statute', ICC-01/05-01/08-3636-Red, Appeals Chamber, 8 June 2018 (hereinafter *Bemba* Appeals Judgment), § 167.

considered they had to assess what the commander should have done '*in concreto*' in view of her material capabilities, rather than what she 'might theoretically have done', disregarding the particularities of the situation.[194] Specifically, the *Bemba* AC Majority noted that particular circumstances, such as when the accused had acted as a '*remote* commander' controlling troops abroad, might obstruct their material ability to address the crimes of the subordinates.[195]

The *Bemba* AC Majority's take on the command responsibility principle displayed strong preference for a strict interpretation of the principle of personal culpability and the protection of the rights of the defendant. According to two of the AC judges, even though the strict application of legal principles 'may in some cases lead to *the acquittal of persons who may actually be guilty*' that was 'the price that must be paid in order to uphold fundamental principles of fairness and the integrity of the judicial process'.[196] The AC Majority did not dismiss anti-impunity as a noble cause. Rather, the judges suggested that substantive justice was not the responsibility of a criminal court and that the ICC should be 'relieve[d]' from the 'pressure' to 'secure convictions at all costs'.[197] This statement reflects a principled vision of the scope and mandate of ICL which values procedure over outcome. As Judge Morrison later noted in an interview, 'nobody benefits from an unfair trial'.[198]

The *Bemba* AC Majority's decision triggered a wave of reactions within the broader ICL community of practice regarding the future of the command responsibility principle. Judge Eboe-Osuji argued that the Majority's remarks on the material capabilities of 'remote commanders' to address crimes were merely a factual consideration specific to the case at hand and did not introduce a new *general rule* for command responsibility at the Court.[199] Nevertheless, many legal scholars and practitioners expressed concern about the possibility of introducing such a rule that would treat 'remote' commanders more leniently than commanders on the ground. Some argued that geographical remoteness did not per se make the taking

194 Ibid., § 170.

195 Ibid., § 171, emphasis added.

196 *Bemba*, Separate opinion Judge Christine Van den Wyngaert and Judge Howard Morrison, ICC-01/05-01/08-3636-Anx2, Appeals Chamber, 8 June 2018 (hereinafter *Bemba* Appeals Judgment, Judges Van den Wyngaert and Morrison Opinion), § 5, emphasis added.

197 *Bemba* Appeals Judgment, Judges Van den Wyngaert and Morrison Opinion, § 75.

198 Interview with Judge Howard Morrison, 26 June 2020.

199 *Bemba*, Concurring Separate Opinion of Judge Eboe-Osuji, ICC-01/05-01/08-3636-Anx3, 14 June 2018, Appeals Chamber (hereinafter *Bemba* Appeals Judgment, Judge Eboe-Osuji Opinion), § 258.

up of measures more difficult.[200] Others brought up substantive justice arguments, noting that the introduction of the 'remote commander' principle would shelter from responsibility 'any state, regional organization or even rebel group whose forces cross borders'.[201] According to one authoritative opinion, the Majority's interpretation of command responsibility 'dilut[ed] the very doctrine by which the law may call to account a person who has accepted the burden of high rank'.[202] Notably, even some of the scholars who have actively advocated for greater respect for the culpability principle in ICL found the *Bemba* AC Majority's decision problematic. Darryl Robinson commended the AC judges for interpreting Article 28(a) with empathy for the rights of the defendant and for avoiding a humanitarian 'deterrence-focused' perspective.[203] But he, nevertheless, considered that the Majority had swung too far in their desire to protect the integrity of the culpability principle and '*overestimate[d]*' the degree of restriction that principle required in the assessment of criminal responsibility.[204]

As both Chapters 5 and 6 have discussed, many members of the ICL community have seen the creation of the Court as an opportunity to institutionalize a new, more principled, and defendant-oriented vision of international criminal justice. Despite its efforts to categorize and systematize the legal rules, the ICC is still criticized by experts and judges for not having done enough to prevent the overstretching of the culpability principle in the case of commission liability under Article 25(3)(a).[205] By contrast, the advocates of the criminal law principles within the ICL field seemed to be more content with the Court's interpretation of command responsibility under Article 28. Or at least that was the case until the *Bemba* AC judgment, which triggered concerns even among those experts that the Court might be going *too far*. As Chapter 8 discusses, the restrictive application of command responsibility by the *Bemba* AC Majority and the *Gbagbo* TC Majority resulted in high-profile acquittals.

[200] M. Jackson, 'Geographical Remoteness in Bemba', EJIL: Talk!, 30 July 2018, www.ejiltalk.org/geographical-remoteness-in-bemba/.

[201] L. N. Sadat, 'Fiddling While Rome Burns? The Appeals Chamber's Curious Decision in Prosecutor v. Jean-Pierre Bemba Gombo', EJIL: Talk!, 12 June 2018, www.ejiltalk.org/fiddling-while-rome-burns-the-appeals-chambers-curious-decision-in-prosecutor-v-jean-pierre-bemba-gombo/.

[202] D. M. Amann, 'In Bemba and Beyond, Crimes Adjudged to Commit Themselves', EJIL: Talk!, 13 June 2018, www.ejiltalk.org/in-bemba-and-beyond-crimes-adjudged-to-commit-themselves/.

[203] Robinson, Justice in Extreme Cases, 175.

[204] Ibid., 272, emphasis in the original.

[205] *See* Sections 6.2.1.3 and 6.2.1.4.

6.4 Interpreting Article 30

The interpretation of Article 30 provides another testament to the influence of the normative dynamics within the ICL field, specifically, to the belief of many participants in that field in the importance of strict compliance with the culpability principle in ICL. As discussed in Chapter 5, even though the RS for the first time in ICL codified the mental element for liability, the future ICC judges nevertheless enjoyed interpretative discretion regarding Article 30. Specifically, they had to determine which types of situations fell within the ambit of the conduct that had been committed with 'intent' and 'knowledge'. The RS provided a definition of 'knowledge': 'awareness that a circumstance exists or a consequence *will occur in the ordinary course of events*'.[206] However, the meaning of the terms 'will occur' and 'ordinary course of events' was not straightforward. It remained an open question whether those terms covered all situations of 'substantial risk' that a person's act or omission could result in a crime, or if the provision was restricted to those situations in which only a highly unlikely event would have prevented the commission of a crime.[207]

The first detailed interpretation of Article 30 was conducted in 2007 by the *Lubanga* PTC. The judges identified three degrees of volition that they considered to be compatible with the wording of the RS. Firstly, the PTC found that Article 30 encompassed those cases in which the suspect had undertaken actions or omissions 'with the concrete intent' to commit the crime. The judges defined that situation as '*dolus directus* of the first degree'.[208] Next, the PTC concluded that the volitional element would be satisfied even if the suspect had not had the concrete intent to commit the crime but had known that the commission of the crime would have been 'the *necessary outcome*' of their actions or omissions. That situation was defined as '*dolus directus* of the second degree'.[209] In that scenario, the volitional element gives way to the cognitive element – the perpetrator's intent is inferred from their decision to act despite knowing that their actions would necessarily result in a crime.

Finally, the *Lubanga* PTC judges answered the question that had been debated since the Rome Conference, namely what was the lowest mental element standard that triggered criminal responsibility at the ICC. The PTC considered that Article 30 incorporated the '*dolus eventualis*'

[206] Rome Statute, Article 30(3), emphasis added.

[207] Weigend, 'Intent, Mistake of Law', 482–483.

[208] *Lubanga* Confirmation Decision, § 351.

[209] Ibid., § 352 (i), emphasis added.

standard,[210] which, according to the judges, covered two scenarios. Firstly, in cases where there is a 'substantial' risk of committing a crime and the person 'accepts' that risk and decides to carry out their actions or omissions regardless of it.[211] Secondly, in cases where there is low risk of committing a crime, but the person 'clearly or expressly' accepts the possibility that their actions or omissions might result in the commission of a crime.[212]

The influence of the normative dynamics within the broader ICL field became evident with respect to two aspects of the interpretation of Article 30: the adoption (and subsequent dismissal) of the *dolus* terminology and the acceptance (and subsequent rejection) of *dolus eventualis* as an applicable mental element. The adoption of the *dolus* terminology indicated the influence of German legal norms on the early ICC chambers. That influence had already played out in the *Lubanga* PTC's decision to employ the 'control over the crime' theory when interpreting Article 25(3)(a). Now it played out in the reliance on a German mental element terminology that was nowhere explicitly mentioned in the RS. In fact, it has been observed that during the drafting procedures, many participants with non-civil-law backgrounds found it difficult to distinguish concepts based on the notion of *dolus* within the plain meaning of Article 30.[213] The *Lubanga* PTC's decision to employ the *dolus* terminology might seem curious if one focuses only on the statutory text and the drafting proceedings, but it appears less so when the normative dynamics of the ICL field are taken into consideration.

But because the ICL field is dynamic and subject to cross-cutting beliefs and ideas, the adoption of the *dolus* terminology at the ICC was soon contested, sparking concern among those members of the field who preferred a stricter approach to legality. The adoption of the *dolus* terminology faced two problems for the fair notice requirement of criminal justice: it was not included in the RS and might have been unclear to many non-civil law practitioners. In fact, the meaning of the third variant, *dolus eventualis*, was contested even in Germany.[214] One German ICL expert criticized the *Lubanga* PTC, arguing that 'the fact that some Latin concept *(dolus)* has over the centuries been given different meanings by different writers does not present a solid basis for the interpretation of a statute that does not even mention these Latin words.'[215] Consequently, even though the

[210] *Lubanga* Confirmation Decision, § 352(ii).
[211] Ibid., § 353.
[212] Ibid., § 354.
[213] Clark, 'Mental Element', 302, footnote 37.
[214] Badar, 'The Mental Element', 490.
[215] Weigend, 'Intent, Mistake of Law', 482.

background experience of legal experts within the ICL field plays a role in the sets of shared understandings developing on questions of criminal responsibility, it intersects with the other dynamics taking place within the field, such as ideas about legality and interpretation.

Notably, the *dolus* terminology has been dismissed in favour of the plain language of Article 30 RS in subsequent ICC decisions. The pre-trial and trial chambers issuing those decisions have generally found that Article 30 requires proof of the accused's 'intent and knowledge' to commit the crimes.[216] Unlike the *Lubanga* and *Bemba* PTCs, subsequent ICC chambers have refrained from invoking concepts specific to national penal systems when interpreting the meaning of the terms 'intent and knowledge'.[217] It is possible that the dismissal of the *dolus* terminology from ICC jurisprudence has been influenced at least in part by the negative feedback that earlier chambers received from legal experts outside the Court. It also demonstrates the growing dissatisfaction among part of the ICL field with the invocation of criminal law theory to interpret the RS and a preference for relying on the plain language of the Statute. As discussed, this trend has also been observed in the reluctance of the PTCs in *Yekatom and Ngaïssona* and *Abd-Al-Rahman* to employ the 'control over the crime' theory regarding Article 25(3)(a).[218]

The role of the legal field in the construction of the legal rules concerning the mental element of liability also became evident in the adoption and subsequent rejection of *dolus eventualis* at the ICC. The conclusion of the *Lubanga* PTC judges that *dolus eventualis* was an applicable mental element standard at the ICC was not an idiosyncratic interpretation of the law but reflected the shared understandings held by *some* members of the ICL community of practice. Prior to the *Lubanga* confirmation of charges decision some ICL experts had suggested that Article 30 encompassed the *dolus eventualis* standard.[219] Furthermore, as noted, that standard could also be found in domestic criminal law practice, specifically in Germany.[220] Therefore, *dolus eventualis*, or more generally the punishment of conducts that had been carried out regardless of the perpetrator's awareness of the risks associated with their conduct, was not

[216] *Ntaganda* Trial Judgment, § 735. *Ongwen*, Trial Judgment, ICC-02/04-01/15-1762-Red, Trial Chamber IX, 4 February 2021 (hereinafter *Ongwen* Trial Judgment), § 2782. *Yekatom and Ngaïssona* Confirmation of charges: § 99, § 104, § 112. *Abd-Al-Rahman* Confirmation of Charges: § 95, § 105, § 114.

[217] *Ongwen* Trial Judgment, § 2788.

[218] Chapter 6, Section 6.2.1.4.

[219] Jescheck, 'General Principles', 45.

[220] Badar, 'Mental Element', 490.

alien to domestic criminal law practice. It was also familiar at the international level: the *Tadić* AC had discussed *dolus eventualis*,[221] and the *Stakić* TC – the revisionist chamber that had rejected the notion of JCE for the continental concept of co-perpetration at the ICTY – went further and explicitly adopted *dolus eventualis* as an applicable standard.[222] In fact, some commentators lamented the fact that the *Tadić* AC had not more explicitly adopted the *dolus eventualis* standard that 'no one could object [to]', instead of the broader notion of 'foreseeability' when developing the elements of JCE.[223] In a manner similar to their interpretation of Article 25(3)(a), the ICC judges in *Lubanga* extensively quoted legal academics and the *Stakić* TC Judgment in support of their finding of the applicability of *dolus eventualis*,[224] indicating the importance of the broader ICL field for interpreting the RS.

However, the conclusion of the *Lubanga* PTC that Article 30 incorporated the *dolus eventualis* standard was fiercely contested by other actors with the ICL field who considered that the ICC should apply a more restrained mental element standard to comply with the fundamental principles of criminal law.[225] The first source of contestation were those members of the ICL field who favoured a stricter interpretation of the legality principle. Specifically, the *dolus eventualis* was argued to have been incompatible with a strict interpretation of the RS because Article 30 required knowledge that the crime '*will* occur' and not that it *may* occur in the ordinary course of events.[226] Even the *Stakić* precedent was not accepted to support the incorporation of *dolus eventualis* at the ICC by those who regarded the concept as incompatible with the language of the RS.[227] From this perspective, the disappearance of *dolus eventualis* from the *travaux préparatoires* indicated that the drafters had dismissed it as a standard even though it had not been explicitly rejected. Critics argued that the advocates

[221] *Tadić* Appeals Judgment, § 220.

[222] *Stakić* Trial Judgment, § 587.

[223] Sassòli and Olson, 'Judgment of the ICTY', 750.

[224] *Lubanga* Confirmation Decision, §§ 352–354 and footnotes 434–436.

[225] Eser, 'Mental Elements', 915. See also Van der Vyver, 'International Criminal Court', 66. V. Nerlich, 'Superior Responsibility under Article 28 ICC Statute: For What Exactly is the Superior Held Responsible?' (2007) 5(3) *Journal of International Criminal Justice* 665, 675. R. Clark, 'Mental Element', 301.

[226] Eser, 'Mental Elements', 915, emphasis added. Van Sliedregt, Individual Criminal Responsibility, 47.

[227] J. Van der Vyver, 'Prosecutor v. Jean-Pierre Bemba Gombo' (2010) 104 *American Journal of International Law* 241–247, 243.

of the inclusion of *dolus eventualis* within the meaning of Article 30 'hardly ever give any reason for their position'.[228]

The second source of contestation resulted from a narrower reading of the culpability principle. Some experts were concerned that by adopting *dolus eventualis* the *Lubanga* PTC had 'watered down' the subjective element of criminal responsibility and left the objective 'control' element to do 'all of the heavy lifting' of establishing principal liability at the ICC.[229] Others considered the narrow reading of Article 30 a guarantee that the controversial JCE III would not find its way into ICC jurisprudence. On this account, a narrow reading of Article 30, which excluded the *dolus eventualis* standard, in conjunction with Article 25(3), made JCE III incompatible with the RS.[230] The dismissal of *dolus eventualis* essentially meant that the ICC would end up imposing higher requirements for the attribution of criminal responsibility compared to national systems. But that outcome was justified for some members of the ICL epistemic community in view of the seriousness of international crimes and the nature of the ICC as a court of last resort.[231]

The ardent debates on the question of *dolus eventualis* taking place in ICL academia quickly moved to the courtroom. In 2008 the defence of Germain Katanga argued that *dolus eventualis* was not covered in the RS.[232] Notably, the defence explicitly stated that to support its claim it relied on the work of established legal scholars, including Werle, Jessberger, Van der Wilt, and Ambos.[233] The *Katanga and Ngudjolo* PTC dismissed the question as immaterial to the case at hand.[234] Nevertheless, the ultimate rejection of that standard did not take too long. Two years after the decision delivered by the *Lubanga* PTC, in 2009 the *Bemba* PTC determined that the concept fell outside the ambit of Article 30.[235] Notably, the *Bemba* PTC judges emphasized that they employed a textual interpretation of the RS[236] and concluded, like some legal experts had done, that because Article 30 included the words 'will occur' rather than 'may occur', the provision

[228] Werle and Jessberger, 'Unless Otherwise Provided', 41, footnote 36.
[229] Ohlin, 'Joint Intentions', 724.
[230] Van der Wilt, 'Joint Criminal Enterprise', 100.
[231] Finnin, 'Mental Elements', 349.
[232] *Katanga and Ngudjolo Chui*, Defence Written Observations Addressing Matters that Were Discussed at the Confirmation Hearing, ICC-01/04-01/07-698, Pre-Trial Chamber I, 28 July 2008, § 18.
[233] Ibid., § 31.
[234] *Katanga and Ngudjolo Chui* Confirmation Decision, § 531.
[235] *Bemba* Confirmation Decision, § 358.
[236] Ibid., § 362.

posed a standard that was 'undoubtedly higher' than *dolus eventualis*.[237] According to the *Bemba* PTC, the words 'will occur in the ordinary course of events' required that the occurrence of the criminal result was 'close to certainty'. Consequently, the judges concluded that at the ICC a person can be convicted for committing a crime only if the prosecutor had proven that the accused had acted with 'virtual certainty' or 'practical certainty' that the commission of the crime would follow from her conduct, 'barring an unforeseen or unexpected intervention that prevent[ed] its occurrence'.[238]

The *Bemba* PTC judges emphasized that their restrained interpretation of Article 30 complied with the principles of legality and personal culpability, even if it limited the opportunities for obtaining convictions for mass atrocities. The judges were unwilling to 'wide[n]' the scope of the law by accepting the *dolus eventualis* standard as applicable, only for the sake of 'capturing a broader range of perpetrators.'[239] The *Bemba* PTC also referred to the work of authoritative legal scholars to support the new interpretation of Article 30.[240] Consequently, the interpretation of Article 30 presented by the *Bemba* PTC displayed the judges' understanding that, contrary to the balanced approach to criminal responsibility displayed at the post-Second World War tribunals and the UN tribunals, at the ICC the principles of criminal law had to be applied in a restrained and predictable manner, regardless of the trial outcome.

Even though the *Lubanga* PTC and the *Bemba* PTC reached different conclusions regarding the meaning of Article 30, both interpretations found support among different subgroups of the ICL community of practice. The advocates of the narrow interpretation of the principles of criminal law in ICL welcomed the decision to restrict the scope of the mental element at the ICC.[241] But the possibility that the restrained interpretation of Article 30 by the *Bemba* PTC would have likely resulted in more acquittals triggered concerns among those members of the ICL epistemic community who sought a balance between procedural and substantive criminal justice.[242] One authoritative ICL scholar called upon the ICC to bring back the concept of *dolus eventualis* in the interpretation of Article 30

[237] Ibid., § 363.
[238] Ibid., § 362.
[239] Ibid., § 369.
[240] Ibid., § 636, footnote 455.
[241] See, e.g., Ambos, 'Critical Issues', 718.
[242] S. Wirth, 'Co-perpetration in the Lubanga Trial Judgment' (2012) 10(4) *Journal of International Criminal Justice* 971, 992.

from a humanitarian perspective, and more specifically to ensure greater protection for the civilian population during wartime.[243] After the *Bemba* PTC decision, ICC jurisprudence could have followed either of the two competing understandings of the law that were present within the ICL community of practice.

Three years after the *Bemba* PTC's decision, in 2012, the *Lubanga* TC took a middle approach. The TC followed the *Bemba* PTC and dismissed *dolus eventualis* as an applicable standard at the ICC.[244] However, the *Lubanga* TC provided its own interpretation of the words 'awareness that [...] a consequence will occur in the ordinary course of events'. According to the *Lubanga* TC, those words meant that the suspect had engaged in a prognosis about the consequences of her actions that involved 'consideration of the concepts of "possibility" and "probability", which are inherent to the notions of "risk" and "danger"'.[245] The definition of Article 30 by the *Lubanga* TC essentially substituted the 'virtual certainty' definition forwarded by the *Bemba* PTC with a *prognosis of the risk* that one's conduct could result in the commission of the crime. Arguably, the accused's prognosis of the risk of her conduct was easier to prove in a given case than her virtual certainty of the criminal consequences. The *Lubanga* TC dismissed the controversial *dolus eventualis* standard, thus, appealing to the proponents of legality in ICL. However, it also provided an interpretation of Article 30 that was less harsh on the prosecutor than the one forwarded by the *Bemba* PTC.

Nevertheless, subsequent Trial Chambers and the Appeals Chamber generally endorsed the more restrictive interpretation of Article 30 that was proposed by the *Bemba* PTC, despite its implications in terms of narrowing the opportunities for delivering substantive justice at the ICC. The TCs in *Katanga*,[246] *Bemba et al.*,[247] and *Ntaganda* all found that the correct interpretation of Article 30 required that the accused was 'virtually certain' that the crimes would result from their conduct in the ordinary course of events.[248] Notably, the *Lubanga* AC also affirmed the 'virtual certainty' standard.[249] Not only did those chambers dismiss the notion of

[243] M. E. Badar, 'Dolus Eventualis and the Rome Statute Without It?' (2009) 12(3) *New Criminal Law Review: An International and Interdisciplinary Journal* 433, 467.

[244] *Lubanga* Trial Judgment, § 1011.

[245] Ibid., § 1012.

[246] *Katanga* Trial Judgment, § 776.

[247] *Bemba et al.* Trial Judgment, § 29.

[248] *Ntaganda* Trial Judgment, § 776, footnote 2348.

[249] *Lubanga* Appeals Judgment, § 447.

dolus eventualis, but they also abandoned the balanced approach of the *Lubanga* TC and ultimately signalled to the broader ICL community of practice that protecting the accused from the attribution of guilt by association was of utmost importance at the ICC.

Overall, similar to Article 25(3) and Article 28, the narrow interpretation of Article 30 by the *Bemba* PTC, also adopted by subsequent chambers, affirms the conclusion that the restrained approach to determining the meaning of the law on criminal responsibility exhibited at the ICC can convincingly be traced to the principled belief of members of the ICL community within and outside the ICC in the importance of protecting the integrity of the criminal law process, even if that came at the expense of substantive justice. Both the adoption and the dismissal of *dolus eventualis* could have been justified as sound legal reasoning, with reference to different shared understandings about Article 30 that were held by different members of the ICL community of practice. The *Bemba* PTC's restrained approach reflected the competitive dynamics of the legal field and the dominance of one vision of the law over another.

6.5 Conclusion

This chapter traced the narrow approach to criminal responsibility displayed at the ICC to the understanding shared by many members within the ICL community of practice that, as a criminal justice institution, the Court had to follow strictly the principle of personal culpability and to avoid the attribution of guilt by association to the accused, even if that meant restricting the set of situations in which a conviction can be served. This line of reasoning was displayed both during the drafting of the RS provisions on criminal responsibility and the subsequent interpretation of those provisions at the ICC. Many legal experts sought greater codification of the general principles of criminal law in the RS because they believed that the principled approach to criminal responsibility was the key to a functioning liberal system of justice.

When the Court began operation, the judges at the *Lubanga*, *Katanga and Ngudjolo* and *Bemba* PTCs, and at subsequent chambers that followed their findings, demonstrated that they shared the understanding of the importance of following criminal law principles, regardless of the trial outcome. The ICC judges sought greater compliance with the personal culpability principle, even if that came at the cost of reducing protection to civilians and the ease of convicting perpetrators of mass atrocities. The ICC judges also recognized the importance of fair labelling by explicitly differentiating between the different forms of participation in a crime. In principle, the combined interpretation of Article 25(3)(a) based on the control theory and of Article 30 that excluded the concept of *dolus eventualis* imposed a higher threshold for the attribution of criminal responsibility than JCE. The precise construction of the command responsibility principle is still clouded by uncertainty at the ICC, but the *Bemba* AC Majority decision indicates the preference of some judges for significantly restricting its scope. In effect, the ICC developed 'a reputation for analytical rigor with regard to criminal law theory', something which was largely absent from the pre-existing ICL jurisprudence, which often relied on common law pragmatism.[250] The references to legal scholarship at the ICC were generally made in the first decisions that deliberated on the relevant RS provisions on criminal responsibility, such as the confirmation of charges decisions in *Lubanga* and *Katanga and Ngudjolo* and the TC and AC judgments in *Lubanga*. While subsequent Chambers did not explicitly quote those academic texts, they often strictly followed the theoretically supported legal findings that were made in earlier decisions.

These findings illustrate the importance of examining the internal politics of the ICL field for understanding the assessment of criminal responsibility at the ICC. The time pressure of international negotiations and the challenges of integrating legal norms from different legal traditions left the ICC judges with plenty of opportunities to decide whether they would follow the restrained approach to criminal responsibility and mark a new era in ICL or seek consistency with the jurisprudence of the UN tribunals by interpreting the gaps and overlaps in the RS by view of capturing more harmful conducts. The theoretically rigorous and restrained interpretation of the criminal responsibility laws, especially evident in the findings of the *Lubanga*, *Katanga and Ngudjolo*, *Mbarushimana* and *Bemba* PTCs, reflected the advancement of a new vision of legalism that had become influential within the ICL field: a vision that prioritized the quality of the process before the outcome of that process. That vision was already observable in the idea, promoted by some legal experts long before the Rome Conference, that codifying a comprehensive General Part in the RS would turn it into a sophisticated criminal law system.

But because the ICL field is dynamic, the interpretations of the RS provisions on criminal responsibility by the early ICC chambers have also become the subject of contestation. Notably, the nature of the critical arguments has varied greatly. Some members of the ICL community

[250] Van Sliedregt, Ohlin, and Weigend, 'Assessing the Control Theory', 738.

have expressed a humanitarian concern that the narrow manner in which those provisions have been construed in ICC practice would enable the perpetrators of mass atrocities to escape justice and obstruct the deterrent impact of ICL. Others have expressed concern that the ICC's detailed categorization of the rule of criminal responsibility and invocation of legal theory might be simple window dressing, failing to ensure greater respect for the culpability principle and the rights of the defendant in practice. The judges at subsequent chambers at the ICC seem to have shared the concerns of the latter subsection of the ICL community. The PTCs in *Yekatom and Ngaïssona* and *Abd-Al-Rahman* and the AC in *Yekatom* have avoided the use of complex criminal law theory and employed the plain language of Article 25(3) and Article 30. As will be discussed in the following chapters, ICC chambers have also attempted to interpret the requirements of the modes of liability in a narrow fashion, ensuring that the burden of proof lays on the prosecution. Even in cases where the accused has no politically powerful 'friends' left, the judges have not compromised the quality of the process for the purpose of obtaining easier convictions.

7

An Overview of ICC Cases

Applying the Principled Approach to Criminal Responsibility in Practice

This chapter explores the application of the individual criminal responsibility rules constructed in ICC practice to the facts of individual cases. It looks at the facts and evidence presented by the prosecutor in those cases, as well as, the conclusions of the judges at the pre-trial and trial stage, to ask whether those facts meet the requirements of the RS modes of liability. In view of the practices of the UN tribunals, the challenges of investigating international crimes and the need to demonstrate institutional efficiency, many members of the ICL community of practice expected that the ICC judges would apply the RS in a manner that would render convictions easier.[1] Commentators cautioned that the 'inordinate concern with securing convictions' could come at the expense of producing 'bad law' at the court.[2] Instead, this chapter argues that the assessment of criminal responsibility at the Court has followed a different line of legal reasoning: applying the modes of liability in a restrained manner, regardless of the trial outcome. At the ICC the quality of the process has been cherished as the ultimate prerequisite for 'ending impunity' for those crimes. While this vision of international criminal law has been contested by some members of the ICL community of practice, such as NGOs advocating for victims' rights, it has continued to dominate the ICC approach to assessing criminal responsibility.

7.1 The Modes of Principle Liability in Practice

7.1.1 The 'Common Plan' among the (Indirect) Co-perpetrators

The first aspect of the ICC judges' interpretation of the modes listed in Article 25(3)(a) that could have been interpreted in a broad or narrow

[1] Jessberger and Geneuss, 'Many Faces', 1083. Popovski, 'International Criminal Court', 417.

[2] Greenawalt, 'Pluralism', 1111. See also Bibas, S. and W. Burke-White. 2010. 'International Idealism Meets Domestic-criminal-Procedure Realism', 59(4) *Duke Law Journal* 637, 662.

manner in specific cases, depending on the judges' preferences, was the *Lubanga* PTC's conclusion that the 'common plan' pursuant to which the (indirect) co-perpetrators allegedly committed the crimes did not need to be intrinsically criminal, but only needed to contain an 'element of criminality'.[3] That conclusion triggered concern among some ICC judges and legal scholars because it obfuscated the link between the individual accused who had participated in what could have been a largely political or military plan, and the specific crimes that resulted from the implementation of that plan.[4]

In the first ICC trial, *Lubanga*, which took place from 2009 to 2012, the ICC judges seemed somewhat willing to accept that the commission of the crimes could result from predominantly non-criminal plans, thus easing the burden on the prosecutor. The defendant, Thomas Lubanga Dyilo, was the leader of the *Union des Patriotes Congolais* (Union of Congolese Patriots) (UPC) rebel organization that operated in the Ituri region of North-eastern DRC. Lubanga was convicted under Article 25(3)(a) for co-perpetrating, along with other senior UPC figures, the crimes of conscripting, enlisting, and using child soldiers to participate in hostilities during the 2002–2003 conflict in Ituri.[5] Based on the available evidence, the PTC found that a 'common plan' had existed between Lubanga and other UPC leaders, including Bosco Ntaganda[6] – another ICC suspect who would face trial at the ICC several years later. The pre-trial judges reckoned that the common plan consisted in an agreement 'to further' the organization's war effort by '(i) recruiting, voluntary or forcibly, *young people*', '(ii) subjecting them to military training and iii) using them to participate actively in military operations and as bodyguards'.[7] The judges highlighted that while the UPC's common plan 'did not specifically target *children* under the age of fifteen years', but only young recruits in general, 'in the normal course of events, its implementation entailed the objective risk that it would involve children under the age of fifteen years'.[8] Several years later, the TC judges were similarly unable to establish that Lubanga and the UPC leadership had planned specifically the recruitment and use of child soldiers, but only that the accused had entered an agreement, or a 'common plan', with the other co-perpetrators 'to build an effective army

[3] *Lubanga* Confirmation Decision, § 344.
[4] Chapter 6: Section 6.2.1.3.
[5] *Lubanga* Trial Judgment, §§ 1270–1272.
[6] *Lubanga* Confirmation Decision, § 377(i).
[7] Ibid., § 377(i), emphasis added.
[8] Ibid., § 377(ii), emphasis added.

to ensure the [UPC's] political and military control over Ituri.' The judges considered the crimes of recruiting and using child soldiers merely 'consequences' that were foreseeable 'in the ordinary course of events' by the accused and his co-perpetrators.[9] The judges' conclusion that the accused could be convicted for the crimes resulting from a plan that was generally aimed at political or military goals triggered criticism from some criminal law scholars.[10] Relying on a broad reading of the co-perpetration mode of liability in the first ICC trial seemed to favour the conclusion that the Court had taken advantage of a politically favourable trial against a rebel leader in order to demonstrate its efficiency to punish the perpetrators of mass crimes.

But other ICC chambers have focused specifically on establishing the *criminal* elements of the alleged common plan. For instance, in 2011 the *Banda and Jerbo* PTC confirmed the charges against the accused on the basis of available evidence that they had participated in a common plan of an inherently criminal nature, namely 'to attack' the peacekeeping personnel at the Hashkanita compound in Darfur.[11] In 2012 the *Mudacumura* PTC declined to include charges of principal liability in the arrest warrant because the judges were not convinced of the existence of a common plan with a criminal element, pursuant to which crimes in the DRC's Kivu Provinces had been committed. Specifically, the PTC concluded that the prosecutor had not provided sufficient evidence either of a plan among the alleged co-perpetrators 'to attack the civilian population as its primary target', or that the humanitarian catastrophe in the Kivu Provinces had been 'the product of' any such plan.[12]

Notably, several ICC decisions on the confirmation of charges, delivered in 2019–2021, did not even examine the existence of a common plan as a tool for imputing the crimes to the suspect, but instead focused specifically on the *direct link* between the suspect and the alleged crimes.[13] For example, the *Yekatom and Ngaïssona* PTC's findings on Alfred Yekatom's alleged criminal responsibility under Article 25(3)(a) did not refer to the

[9] *Lubanga* Trial Judgment, § 1136.

[10] Ambos, 'First Judgment', 140. Cupido, 'Pluralism', 147–147.

[11] *Banda and Jerbo*, Corrigendum of the 'Decision on the Confirmation of Charges' ICC-02/05-03/09-121-Corr-Red, Pre-Trial Chamber I, 13 March 2011 (hereinafter *Banda and Jerbo* Confirmation Decision), § 149.

[12] *Mudacumura*, Public Redacted Version: Decision on the Prosecutor's Application under Article 58, ICC-01/04-01/12-1-Red, Pre-Trial Chamber II, 13 July 2012 (hereinafter *Mudacumura* Arrest Warrant Decision), § 62.

[13] *Yekatom and Ngaïssona* Confirmation Decision, § 60. *Abd-Al-Rahman* Confirmation Decision, §§ 44–45. *Said* Confirmation Decision, § 45.

existence of the common plans alleged by the prosecution, but simply to the evidence of the accused having been involved in attacks, issuing 'patently illegal instructions',[14] and being 'in control of the established checkpoints', that were used to terrorize the civilian population.[15] In *Abd-Al-Rahman* the pre-trial judges considered the available evidence alleging that the suspect had been 'present during, directed and personally contributed to the arrest operation' resulting in the commission of some of the crimes listed in the charges[16] and that he had even personally killed a man.[17] Similarly, regarding the charges confirmed under Article 25(3)(a) in the *Said* case, the PTC noted that the suspect had overseen the mistreatment of detainees, instructed his subordinates to engage in such practices, and 'personally participated in the mistreatment of a detainee'.[18] Unlike the *Lubanga* pre-trial and trial chambers, which relied on a broadly construed common plan to impute the crimes to the accused, the *Yekatom and Ngaïssona*, *Abd-Al-Rahman*, and *Said* decisions on the confirmation of charges have specifically engaged with the direct link between the accused and the alleged crimes.

The difference in the style of legal reasoning between the first ICC trial – *Lubanga* – and more recent decisions becomes even more pronounced when the same type of charges is discussed. The *Lubanga* PTC imputed the crimes of recruiting and using child soldiers to the accused on the basis that the alleged crimes were a foreseeable consequence of a military plan that involved targeting 'young people' more generally. By contrast, the *Yekatom and Ngaïssona* PTC's approach to avoid the common plan element enabled the judges to elucidate a more specific link between the accused and the crimes. The judges concluded that Yekatom had been aware of the presence of 'children', in particular, within the forces because 'newly enlisted children were introduced to him as the chief', 'he directly saw the children' when inspecting the ranks, and he gave orders to use children to participate in hostilities.[19]

The discussed 2019–2021 ICC decisions illustrate a tendency to focus on the accused's direct involvement in the crimes, instead of relying on the notion of a common plan or agreement to impute the crimes to the accused. The latter practice somewhat resembled the logic behind the

[14] *Yekatom and Ngaïssona* Confirmation Decision, § 98, § 124.
[15] Ibid., § 139.
[16] *Abd-Al-Rahman* Confirmation Decision, § 108.
[17] Ibid., § 109.
[18] *Said* Confirmation Decision, § 79.
[19] *Yekatom and Ngaïssona* Confirmation Decision, § 154.

controversial JCE doctrine, which imputed the crime committed pursuant to the joint criminal design to all members of the enterprise. The recent ICC approach, by contrast, seems to be, at least in part, provoked by the concerns expressed with the broad scope of the 'common plan' element of liability, expressed by the advocates of the restrained approach to personal culpability in the ICL field.[20] Consequently, the competition of ideas within the ICL field has played a role in the manner in which individual criminal responsibility has been assessed at the ICC.

7.1.2 The Accused's Control over the Crimes

The other aspect of the control theory that could have been interpreted narrowly or broadly, depending on the case, was the question of how the accused's actual control over the crime could be proven. That was a pertinent issue in *Lubanga* because, while the accused was the UPC's leader and the face of its political campaign, his direct involvement in the organization's military wing, the *Forces patriotiques pour la libération du Congo* (Patriotic Forces for the Liberation of Congo) (FPLC), which carried out the alleged crimes of recruiting and using child soldiers, was less evident. The defence argued that Lubanga only enjoyed *de jure* but not *de facto* control over military affairs.[21] The PTC concluded that Lubanga had played 'a key *overall co-ordinating role* in the implementation of the common plan' by maintaining contact with the participants in the common plan, inspecting FPLC training camps and encouraging young recruits, including children, to participate in hostilities and financing the implementation of the common plan.[22] In addition, the PTC found that Lubanga had himself encouraged the civilian population to contribute to the war effort by supplying young recruits, including children, and had personally used children as his bodyguards.[23] Regarding the 'essential' nature of Lubanga's contribution, understood as his power to frustrate the commission of the crimes had he decided to withdraw his contribution, the judges noted that Lubanga was: 'the only person to solve the logistic and financial difficulties that they sometimes had to contend with'.[24] At trial, the TC judges concluded that whether or not Lubanga was involved in day-to-day military

[20] *Yekatom and Ngaïssona* Confirmation Decision, § 60, footnote 106.

[21] *Lubanga*, Prosecution's Reply to the «Conclusions finales de la Défense», ICC-01/04-01/06-2778-Red, Trial Chamber I, 1 August 2011, § 18.

[22] *Lubanga* Confirmation Decision, § 383(ii), emphasis added.

[23] Ibid., § 383(iii).

[24] Ibid., § 401.

affairs was not determinative of his control over the crimes.[25] The TC reasoned that delegation of certain tasks to other UPC members was an 'inevitable result' of Lubanga's leadership position.[26] Instead, the judges focused on the witness testimony, according to which Lubanga had 'the final word on everything'[27] and was regularly informed about the organization's military operations.[28] Based on such evidence, the TC concluded that Lubanga had enjoyed 'ultimate control' over the UPC.[29]

Not all members of the ICL field were convinced that Lubanga's contribution to the crimes, important as it was, amounted to exercising 'control' over those crimes. One authoritative commentator observed that given 'the little evidence presented before it', the PTC's conclusion that Lubanga exercised joint control over the commission of the crimes along with his co-perpetrators was 'a courageous one, to put it mildly'.[30] Other legal experts expressed concern that the trial judges had inferred Lubanga's control over the crimes from his official position rather than from his actual involvement in the crimes.[31]

Notably, states did not display such concerns with the *Lubanga* judgment. At the 2012 ASP several state representatives recognized the *Lubanga* judgment as a step for the ICC towards becoming a fully operational court and contributing to the development of international law.[32] Some states called the judgment a 'milestone' in the fight against impunity for international crimes.[33] Others observed that the judgment would have deterrent impact on commanders by signalling that the recruitment and use of child soldiers would be punished.[34] The DRC similarly welcomed

[25] *Lubanga* Trial Judgment, § 1215.

[26] Ibid., § 1219.

[27] Ibid., § 1056.

[28] Ibid., § 1219.

[29] Ibid., § 1169.

[30] Weigend, 'Intent, Mistake of Fact', 487.

[31] See Jain, Perpetrators and Accessories, 88–89. Cupido, 'Pluralism', 147.

[32] ICC ASP, Statement by H.E. Mr. Yasumasa Nagamine Ambassador of Japan to the Netherlands, The Hague, 15 November 2012, 1. ICC ASP, Intervention de la France de S. E. Monsieur l'Ambassadeur Perre Ménat, Chef de Délégation, 15 November 2012, 1. ICC ASP, Statement by H. E. Dr. Bogdan Aurescu, State Secretary for Strategic Affairs, Ministry of Foreign Affairs Romania, The Hague, 15 November 2012, 2.

[33] ICC ASP, Statement by Denmark, 11th Session of the ASP to the RS of the ICC, The Hague, 15 November 2012, 1. ICC ASP, Statement on behalf of the European Union and its Member States delivered by H. E. Mr. Andreas D. Mavroyiannis, Deputy Minister for European Affairs to the President of the Republic of Cyprus at the 11th Session of the ASP of the ICC, The Hague, 14–22 November 2012, 2.

[34] ICC ASP, Statement on behalf of The Republic of Estonia by H. E. Mr. Urmas Paet Minister of Foreign Affairs of the Republic of Estonia, The Hague, 15 November 2012, 1. ICC ASP, Kingdom of Belgium, 11th Session of the ASP to the RS of the ICC, The Hague, 14 November 2012, 3.

the decision, with a government spokesman calling it a 'positive signal' for peace in the region and even expressing the view that the court should have imposed a longer sentence on Lubanga.[35] The reactions of governments can be explained with reference to states' political interests. In 2012 many states welcomed a sign that the ICC was able to fulfil its mandate and justify the resources it used after 10 years of delivering no judgments. As noted by William Schabas, the *Lubanga* case appeared as a 'win-win' situation for all parties, including the DRC, which relied on the ICC to put on trial a troublesome insurgent commander.[36]

However, a state-centric approach fails to provide insights into the reactions that the *Lubanga* judgment provoked within the ICL field of practice, especially the concerns of some experts. Such reactions indicated that those members of the ICL community who insisted on narrower interpretation of the culpability principle at the ICC compared to earlier tribunals would not be satisfied with the mere articulation of more detailed rules for establishing principal liability. The ICC had set up high expectations among those members of the ICL community that it would depart from the practices of the UN tribunals and specifically from JCE, and there was an understanding that it should now live up to those expectations in practice.

This understanding, shared by groups of experts within the ICL field, appears to have become increasingly influential at the ICC. Notably, other ICC chambers displayed greater preference for evidence of the accused's *direct* involvement in the crimes, rather than the accused's official position. Particularly illustrative in that regard are the 2010 and 2011 confirmation of charges proceedings in the *Abu Garda* and *Banda and Jerbo* cases concerning the 2007 attack on Hashkanita that was carried out by the Justice and Equality Movement splinter group and the Sudan Liberation Army-Unity.[37] The prosecution argued that the alleged commanders of the attacking groups, Bahar Idris Abu Garda, Abdallah Banda Abakaer Nourain 'Banda', and Saleh Mohammed Jerbo Jamus 'Jerbo' bore principal responsibility as co-perpetrators or indirect co-perpetrators for the attack on Hashkanita.[38] With respect to Abu Garda's control over the

[35] BBC, 'DR Congo warlord Thomas Lubanga sentenced to 14 years', 10 July 2012, https://www.bbc.com/news/world-africa-18779726.

[36] Schabas, 'Prosecutorial Discretion', 757.

[37] *Abu Garda*, Decision on the Confirmation of Charges, ICC-02/05-02/09-243-Red, Pre-Trial Chamber I, 8 February 2010 (hereinafter *Abu Garda* Confirmation Decision), § 21. *Banda and Jerbo* Confirmation Decision, § 1.

[38] *Abu Garda* Confirmation Decision, § 22. *Banda and Jerbo* Conformation Decision, § 124.

attack, the prosecutor relied on evidence of the accused's alleged participation in preparatory meetings.[39] But the PTC judges were not convinced of the allegations against Abu Garda,[40] mainly because there was no 'reliable' evidence that the accused had personally participated in the attack.[41] Consequently, the PTC dismissed all charges against Abu Garda.[42] By contrast, the participation of Banda and Jerbo in the preparatory meeting[43] and the fact that Banda and Jerbo had personally led their troops in the attack and participated in the looting of goods at the compound was confirmed by many witnesses.[44] Because the accused's *personal* participation in the attack was established, the PTC judges confirmed the charges of co-perpetration against Banda and Jerbo.[45]

More recently, in 2019, similar dynamics occurred in *Yekatom and Ngaïssona*. Yekatom was a commander of an Anti-Balaka armed group that allegedly committed crimes against the Muslim population in the CAR. Ngaïssona was a senior figure with political and diplomatic functions who held the position of a National General Coordinator of the Anti-Balaka structure.[46] The PTC confirmed the charges under Article 25(3)(a) against Yekatom[47] but were not convinced that Ngaïssona had 'control' over the Anti-Balaka armed groups, which enjoyed 'a high degree of autonomy' in operational matters.[48] The PTC judges noted that, '[c]ontrary to the generic submissions of the Prosecution', the evidence '[did] not allow the Chamber' to conclude that Ngaïssona had been in control of the crime, or that without his involvement, the crimes would not have been committed.[49] Hence, the judges confirmed the charges of principal liability only against the defendant who had been positioned closer to the scene of the crimes.

The confirmation decisions in *Abu Garda*, *Banda and Jerbo*, and *Yekatom and Ngaïssona* strongly suggest that the ICC judges have generally been willing to commit to trial only those persons against whom

[39] *Abu Garda*, Public Redacted Version of Prosecution's 'Document Containing the Charges Submitted Pursuant to Article 61(3) of the Statute' filed on 10 September 2009, ICC-02/05-02/09-91-Red, Pre-trial Chamber I, 24 September 2009, § 126, § 132.

[40] *Abu Garda* Confirmation Decision, § 173.

[41] Ibid., §§ 203–209.

[42] Ibid., § 232.

[43] *Banda and Jerbo* Confirmation Decision, § 131.

[44] Ibid., §§ 146–147.

[45] Ibid., § 162.

[46] *Yekatom and Ngaïssona* Confirmation Decision, § 65.

[47] Ibid., § 99, § 125, § 140, § 155.

[48] Ibid., § 164.

[49] Ibid., § 103.

there was solid evidence of direct involvement in the alleged crimes. The analysis of the influence of legal norms reveals that the ICC judges in those chambers refrained from inferring the accused's 'control' from their rank at least in part because that risked the attribution of guilt by association and, hence, infringed upon the culpability principle. Furthermore, as demonstrated by the case against Ngaïssona, the judges have interpreted the notion of 'control' in a very narrow sense, in line with the conclusion of the *Lubanga* PTC, that one of the elements of control was the perpetrator's 'power to frustrate the commission of the crime by not performing their tasks'.[50]

In fact, the ICC prosecution also seems to have noticed the strict interpretation of the notion of 'control' exhibited by a few ICC chambers and adjusted its strategy accordingly. In the *Abd-Al-Rahman* case, the prosecutor alleged only accessory responsibility for some of the crimes listed in the charges,[51] despite submitting evidence of the accused's active involvement in the alleged criminal incidents, namely evidence that Abd-Al-Rahman had led the planned armed attacks, resulting in the crimes subject to those charges,[52] and had been 'in the front line' of the militia forces.[53] Even the PTC judges expressed their surprise that the prosecutor had not alleged principal liability under Article 25(3)(a) for the alleged charges concerning the incident in Kodoom and Bindisi, considering 'the role played by Mr Abd-Al-Rahman throughout all of the charged events'.[54] While the prosecutor is solely responsible for selecting the charges, this curious decision might partly indicate growing appreciation of the difficulties of meeting the requirements of Article 25(3)(a) in ICC jurisprudence.

7.1.3 *Indirect Co-perpetration in Practice*

Another interpretative decision of the ICC judges that triggered concerns among those members of the ICL field committed to the restrained interpretation of criminal law principles for expanding the scope of principal liability too far was the combination of indirect perpetration with co-perpetration into a new mode of liability. Indirect co-perpetration attributed the crimes committed pursuant to the common plan to each

[50] *Lubanga* Confirmation Decision: § 347.

[51] *Abd-Al-Rahman*, Annex A13-Corr: Summary of Charged Crimes and Modes of Liability, ICC-02/05-01/20-346-AnxA13-Corr, Pre-Trial Chamber II, 21 May 2021.

[52] *Abd-Al-Rahman* Confirmation Decision, § 87.

[53] Ibid., § 88.

[54] Ibid., § 96.

of the co-perpetrators, even if only one of those persons had exercised control over the physical perpetrators of the crimes.[55] At first it may have appeared that indirect co-perpetration introduced the *Brđanin* version of JCE under a different name at the ICC,[56] thus suggesting that the ICC's principled approach to commission liability constituted merely rhetoric, while in reality, the judges at the new court sought to render convictions easier. However, the overview of ICC cases suggests that in practice the ICC judges have demonstrated significant restraint in the application of that mode of liability and required that all elements of both co-perpetration and indirect perpetration be established by the prosecutor. In effect, the incriminating evidence often failed to meet the requirements of indirect co-perpetration.

In *Ngudjolo*, the TC judges were unable to conclude that the accused had controlled the militant group that had attacked a village in North-eastern DRC. The judges considered that the available evidence 'in no way' allowed the Chamber to 'even contemplate' the accused's responsibility as an indirect co-perpetrator.[57] The charges of principal liability under Article 25(3)(a) were also dropped against Ngudjolo's alleged indirect co-perpetrator, Germain Katanga. According to the judges, the prosecutor failed to establish key elements of indirect co-perpetration, such as Katanga's ability 'to ensure the execution of orders' through the organization or the existence of any 'centralised command' within the militia.[58]

The ICC judges have also dismissed the prosecutor's charges of indirect co-perpetration before a case even reached the confirmation of charges proceedings. For instance, in *Mbarushimana*, already in the decision to issue an arrest warrant, the PTC judges concluded that the prosecutor had failed to establish that the accused had 'had the power, by not performing his tasks, to frustrate the commission of the crimes'.[59] Thus, the PTC demonstrated that indirect co-perpetration did not risk the attribution of guilt by association to the accused. On the contrary, the judges showed that indirect co-perpetration posed requirements that were hard to meet in practice.

As will be discussed in Chapter 9, in those cases in which the ICC judges have entered a conviction based on indirect co-perpetration, namely

[55] *Katanga and Ngudjolo* Confirmation Decision, § 493, §§ 519–520.

[56] Van Sliedregt, 'International Criminal Law', 1156.

[57] *Ngudjolo*, Judgment pursuant to article 74 of the Statute, ICC-01/04-02/12-3-tENG, Trial Chamber II, 18 December 2012 (hereinafter *Ngudjolo* Judgment), § 110.

[58] *Katanga* Trial Judgment, § 1419.

[59] *Mbarushimana* Arrest Warrant Decision, § 36.

Ntaganda and *Ongwen*, they have not only meticulously assessed whether the evidence supported each element of that mode of liability, but also paid special attention to the accused's personal involvement in the alleged criminal conducts to establish a link between them and the crimes.

7.1.4 Conclusions on Principal Liability

The *Lubanga* TC appeared more willing compared to other ICC chambers to rely on a generally non-criminal common plan for imputing criminal responsibility to the accused and to infer the latter's control over the crimes from, inter alia, evidence of his position. Notably, *Lubanga* was the first ICC trial in which Article 25(3) was applied to deliver a verdict. As one commentator put it, the *Lubanga* judgment inaugurated the adolescent period of ICL.[60] Consequently, for many legal experts, the significance of the trial lay in the interpretation of the applicable law by the judges, rather than in the factual findings of the case.[61] The successful outcome for the prosecutor in the first ICC trial was moreover of symbolic importance for the human rights community, as it signalled the 'first step' to combatting impunity at the new court.[62] This is not to argue that the *Lubanga* judgment was legally unfounded, as suggested by some legal experts who favour the principled approach to criminal responsibility.[63] Indeed, the TC spent some 150 pages in discussing the link between Lubanga and the crimes. Notably, other ICC Chambers have been even more restrictive in the application of the control theory in practice even if that meant the dismissal of some or all charges against the accused, as was the case in *Abu Garda*, *Ngaïssona*, and *Ngudjolo*.

7.2 The Mental Element in Practice

The rejection of *dolus eventualis* as an applicable standard at the ICC and its substitution by the requirement of 'virtual certainty' on behalf of the accused further narrowed the scope of criminal responsibility and reaffirmed the Court's commitment to the principled assessment of criminal

[60] C. Kaoutzanis, 'A Turbulent Adolescence Ahead: The ICC's Insistence on Disclosure in the Lubanga Trial' (2013) 12(2) *Washington University Global Studies Law Review* 263, 311.

[61] W. Schabas and C. Stahn, 'Introductory Note: Legal Aspects of the Lubanga Case' (2008) 19(3) *Criminal Law Forum* 431, 431.

[62] The New Humanitarian, 'Lubanga Verdict "A First Step"', 14 March 2012, www.thenewhumanitarian.org/report/95073/drc-lubanga-verdict-"-first-step".

[63] Interview with Kevin Heller, 11 August 2020.

responsibility, regardless of the trial outcome. The *Yekatom and Ngaïssona* provide an illustration. Regarding the charges of recruiting child soldiers by the Anti-Balaka groups, the prosecutor submitted that Ngaïssona was 'aware of the presence of child soldiers among the Anti-Balaka' and that the situation was 'widely reported' by media, NGOs, and international organizations.[64] But the PTC judges were not convinced by the evidence, which they considered 'too general' to establish the accused's 'knowledge' of the crimes under Article 30.[65] The judges noted that media coverage and reporting of crimes were 'of very limited relevance' for making conclusive findings on whether the accused intended and knew about the crimes.[66] Media coverage might be indicative of a person's awareness of the commission of crimes. Such awareness comes close to the *dolus eventualis* standard, which was dismissed by the *Bemba* PTC, but does not meet the 'virtual certainty' standard, which was accepted by several ICC chambers.[67] Consequently, the PTC dismissed the charges of recruiting child soldiers against Ngaïssona.[68]

By contrast, the evidence concerning Yekatom's alleged intent and knowledge to recruit and use child soldiers in hostilities appeared more solid. The PTC observed that the children were present at 'locations under Yekatom's control or where Yekatom was present as well'.[69] Furthermore, witness testimony suggested that children were mobilized to participate directly in hostilities 'because Yekatom considered that "children had to be involved" in it'.[70] The PTC was satisfied by the abundant evidence and confirmed the child soldier charges against Yekatom.

The PTC's assessment of the facts and evidence points to a stable line of legal reasoning regarding the application of Article 30 RS in practice – accepting only solid evidence that the accused *intended and knew of* the crimes and dismissing allegations that the accused was probably *aware* of the commission of the crimes. Even though the *Yekatom and Ngaïssona* PTC did not employ the '*dolus*' terminology when discussing the requirements of Article 30, in practice it rejected the lower *dolus eventualis* standard and applied a stricter mental element. Thus, the judges demonstrated faithfulness in practice to the standard established by the *Bemba* PTC and

[64] *Yekatom and Ngaïssona* Confirmation Decision, § 158.
[65] Ibid., §§ 160–161.
[66] Ibid., § 159.
[67] *See* Chapter 6, Section 6.4.
[68] *Yekatom and Ngaïssona*, Confirmation Decision, § 163.
[69] Ibid., § 146.
[70] Ibid., § 149.

subsequent chambers. As will be discussed in Chapter 9, evidence of the accused's personal involvement in the crimes has been crucial for establishing the mental element of liability at the ICC.

7.3 The Modes of Accessory Liability in Practice

Despite the difficulties of meeting the requirements of Article 25(3)(a), the ICC judges were left with a variety of modes of accessory liability pursuant to which an accused could be convicted. The judges adopted a restrained approach to the modes of commission liability under Article 25(3)(a), but they could still rely on subparagraphs (b)–(d) or Article 28 in order to punish the accused and, thus, demonstrate efficiency in politically favourable cases. But the Court has generally refrained from such practices, reflecting the influence of the shared understanding among members of the ICL community within and outside the ICC that the modes of accessor liability should not be used as a safety net for delivering convictions.

Despite the availability of a wide range of accessory modes of liability, as of February 2022 only one person, Germain Katanga, had been convicted for mass atrocities on the basis of accessory liability at the ICC. Even in that case, which concluded in 2014, the TC judges appeared hesitant to rely on Article 25(3)(d)(ii), the provision that had already triggered much criticism among the advocates of strict compliance with the criminal responsibility principles. One of the judges, Judge Van den Wyngaert, dissented from the judgment and argued that she would have acquitted Katanga from all charges because she did not think that the prosecutor's evidence met the requirements of Article 25(3)(d)(ii).[71] The dissenting Judge considered that subparagraph (d) posed fundamentally *different*, and not lower, requirements from subparagraph (a) and that the evidence that the prosecutor had relied on with respect to subparagraph (a) could not be forced to fit the requirements of Article 25(3)(d).[72] Put simply, Judge Van den Wyngaert did not consider that subparagraph (d) could be used as a less demanding version of subparagraph (a) for obtaining convictions.

The TC Majority were less harsh towards the prosecutor and concluded that there was sufficient evidence to convict Katanga under Article 25(3)(d)(ii), but not for all charges that were brought against him. More

71 *Katanga*, Minority Opinion of Judge Christine Van den Wyngaert, ICC-01/04-01/07-3436-AnxI, Trial Chamber II, 7 March 2014 (hereinafter *Katanga* Judgment, Judge Van den Wyngaert Opinion), § 6.

72 Ibid., §§ 18–20.

specifically, the Majority acquitted Katanga of rape and sexual slavery.[73] Those judges found that Katanga had contributed to the common purpose of a militia to attack a civilian village by providing the combatants with weapons.[74] But the Majority concluded that in order to avoid the imposition of guilt by association, Katanga could only be held criminally responsible for those crimes which he had known, and not merely foreseen, that the militia would commit during the attack.[75] The judges specified that the accused's knowledge must be established in view of 'each specific crime' and that 'general criminal intention' to support the militia would be insufficient for conviction.[76] The Majority concluded that when he armed the militia for the attack Katanga knew that the militia would murder civilians and pillage their property during that attack, but he did not know with certainty that the combatants would also rape and sexually enslave the civilians.[77] Thus, the *Katanga* judgment applied in a restrained fashion the mode of liability, which had triggered concerns among some members of the ICL community for overstretching the principle of personal culpability.

Another illustration of that trend was the 2011 confirmation of charges proceedings in *Mbarushimana*. The suspect, Callixte Mbarushimana, was among the leadership of the *Forces démocratiques pour la libération du Rwanda* (Democratic Forces for the Liberation of Rwanda) (FDLR), a militia operating in Eastern DRC, partly constituted of exiled Rwandans but drawing most recruits from Congolese Hutu communities.[78] The prosecutor alleged that Mbarushimana had contributed to the FDLR's common purpose to create a 'humanitarian catastrophe' in Eastern DRC in order to attract international attention to the political demands of the group.[79] More specifically, the OTP alleged that Mbarushimana's contribution, as understood under Article 25(3)(d), consisted of denying FDLR's responsibility for the attacks and portraying the organization as a peaceful actor in front of the international public.[80] But the PTC Majority remained unconvinced by the prosecution's arguments and declined to confirm the charges against Mbarushimana. The first obstacle to confirming the charges was the judges' concern that the OTP had established 'no

[73] *Katanga* Judgment, §§ 1643–1644.
[74] Ibid., § 1680.
[75] Ibid., §§ 1620–1621.
[76] Ibid., § 1642.
[77] Ibid., § 1663.
[78] *Mbarushimana* Confirmation Decision, § 3.
[79] Ibid., § 6.
[80] Ibid., § 8.

link' between the accused and the FDLR soldiers on the ground who had allegedly committed the crimes.[81] The judges noted that many former FDLR soldiers said that they had never heard of Mbarushimana when asked.[82] The second obstacle was the requirement that the PTC *added* to Article 25(3)(d) in order to restrain its broad scope, namely that the accused's contribution to the group's crime had to be at least 'significant'.[83] The Majority found that 'by far' the most significant responsibility Mbarushimana had within the FDLR was issuing press releases, but that this was insufficient to prove that he had contributed to the organization's alleged common plan to attack civilians.[84] The Majority concluded that 'the Suspect did not provide any contribution' to the commission of the crimes, 'even less a "significant" one', and dropped all charges against Mbarushimana.[85] Hence, the *Mbarushimana* PTC's decision demonstrated a desire to narrow the scope of Article 25(3)(d) liability not only in theory, but also when applying that provision in practice.

In 2021, the prosecution similarly failed to proceed with the charges under accessory modes of liability in the *Said* case. The prosecution had alleged that the accused, Mahamat Said Abdel Kani, was responsible, *inter alia*, as an accessory under Article 25(3)(c) or (d) for crimes related to the imprisonment and mistreatment of detainees, allegedly committed at the *Comité Extraordinaire pour la Défense des Acquis Démocratiques* (CEDAD) compound in Bangui, CAR.[86] However, the PTC concluded that the Prosecutor had 'failed to identify any discernible link between the alleged facts and Mr Said'[87] and declined to confirm those charges against the accused.[88] The discussion of *Gbagbo and Blé Goudé* and *Bemba* cases in Chapter 8 provides further illustration of the judges' restraint in the application of the modes of accessory liability under Article 25(3)(b)–(d) and Article 28 RS.

Nevertheless, not all accessory liability charges have remained unsuccessful at the ICC. Where the prosecutor has provided more solid evidence of the link between the accused and the crimes, the judges have

[81] Ibid., § 297.
[82] Ibid., § 322.
[83] Ibid., § 283.
[84] Ibid., § 299.
[85] Ibid., § 292.
[86] *Said*, Public Redacted Version of 'Document Containing the Charges, ICC-01/14-01/21-144-Conf', dated 16 August 2021, ICC-01/14-01/21-144-Red, dated 17 October 2021, ICC-01/14-01/21-144-Corr2, Pre-Trial Chamber II, 27 October 2021, § 28, §§ 68–74.
[87] *Said* Confirmation Decision, § 135.
[88] Ibid., § 153.

confirmed the charges. For example, in 2019 the *Yekatom and Ngaïssona* PTC confirmed some of the charges brought against Ngaïssona under Article 25(3)(c) and 25(3)(d).[89] The judges were satisfied that the accused had 'structure[d]' and 'financed' the organization involved in the commission of the alleged crimes.[90] Yet, the PTC stressed that the evidentiary standard of the confirmation of charges proceedings was lower than that of the final verdict,[91] meaning that the TC will decide whether or not the prosecutor's charges will lead to conviction.

The restrained application of the modes of accessory liability at the ICC did not remain uncontested within the ICL community of practice. Gender justice advocates were particularly dissatisfied with the *Katanga* judgment.[92] NGOs also considered the failure to sustain the charges against Mbarushimana a 'great loss for victims/survivors' in Eastern DRC 'who may not have other opportunities to access justice'.[93] A Human Rights Watch official observed that the failure of the proceedings against FDLR commanders 'for their grave crimes' had 'encouraged further attacks against civilians'.[94] This line of reasoning displays humanitarian concerns for the deterrent impact of international criminal justice and for enabling the victims to see justice being served. By contrast, those judges and legal scholars who prioritized strict compliance with the criminal responsibility principles considered the acquittal as an indication that the ICL system was functioning properly.[95] The latter understanding has generally dominated the ICC, although that vision of the criminal responsibility laws continues to be contested by actors within and outside. Similar remarks were made by state diplomats in The Hague, namely that the ICC acquittals' rate 'in no way' compromised the legitimacy of the Court because those outcomes were a normal part of the functioning of an independent judicial body.[96]

[89] *Yekatom and Ngaïssona* Confirmation Decision, § 104, § 112, § 128, § 143.

[90] Ibid., § 101, § 112.

[91] Ibid., § 102.

[92] Kortfält, 'Sexual Violence', 579. Women's Initiatives for Gender Justice, 'Partial Conviction of Katanga by ICC: Acquittals for Sexual Violence and Use of Child Soldiers', 7 March 2014, 2. C. Stahn, 'Justice Delivered or Justice Denied?' (2014) 12(4) *Journal of International Criminal Justice* 809, 821.

[93] Women's Initiatives for Gender Justice, 'Legal Eye on the ICC 2012'.

[94] G. Mattioli-Zeltner quoted in Human Rights Watch, 'ICC: Pursue Case Against Rwandan Rebel Leader', 1 June 2012, www.hrw.org/news/2012/06/01/icc-pursue-case-against-rwandan-rebel-leader.

[95] Interviews with Judge Howard Morrison, Elies Van Sliedregt, and Kai Ambos.

[96] Interviews with H. E. Rumen Alexandrov, Ambassador of Bulgaria to The Netherlands and Nadia Zhivkova-Vaneva, Legal Advisor and Second Secretary of the Bulgarian diplomatic mission at The Hague, 14 May 2019.

7.4 Assessment of Evidence

The belief in the importance of high-quality criminal law process, regardless of the trial outcome or the background of the accused, is further illustrated in the unwillingness of many ICC chambers to rely on incriminating evidence of questionable credibility. The prosecutor supports her arguments, including with respect to the accused's form of criminal responsibility, by presenting the judges with evidence. In turn, the judges have the authority to rule on the 'relevance and admissibility' of all evidence submitted by the prosecutor.[97] Many members of the ICL community of practice have expressed concern that the difficulties of investigating mass atrocities and the lack of documented orders to commit crimes prompted the UN tribunals to use 'distortive methods' in the evaluation of the available evidence, such as relying on eyewitness testimony that is harder to verify than documentary or forensic evidence.[98] The UN tribunals have also relied on the reports of human rights NGOs, the validity of which has been questioned by criminal law experts.[99] The reason is the different aims and 'professional culture' of human rights monitoring organizations and criminal investigators – while the former, driven by concerns for protecting the victims, focus on demonstrating that crimes have been committed, the latter in addition search for evidence for the specific link between the suspect and those crimes.[100] Consequently, the influence of human rights and humanitarian ideas at the ICTR and ICTY played out not only in the articulation of broad modes of liability but also in the occasionally lenient approach towards the available inculpatory evidence.

Compared to its predecessors, the ICC seems to have placed greater emphasis on the defendant's rights to a fair trial and intolerance towards the investigatory hurdles of the prosecutor. This became evident already in the first ICC trial – *Lubanga*. Despite the broad interpretation of some of the elements of 'control' under Article 25(3)(a), the *Lubanga* TC appeared eager to demonstrate that the Court was not willing to compromise the quality of proceedings for the purpose of delivering a conviction, despite the high stakes of the first ICC judgment. The TC stayed the proceedings twice to deal with issues concerning evidence and, as one expert commentator observed, the *Lubanga* judgment 'devoted a hundred pages to painstaking

97 ICC Rules of Procedure and Evidence, Rule63(2).

98 Combs, Fact-Finding without Facts, 20. Y. McDermott, 'Strengthening the Evaluation of Evidence in International Criminal Trials' (2017) 17(4) *International Criminal Law Review* 682, 684–685. Zahar, 'Pluralism'.

99 Bergsmo and Wiley, 'Human Rights Professionals', 9.

100 Ibid., 3, 6.

assessment of witness testimony that it would in the end reject'.[101] One of the main issues the TC had to deal with was the quality of the prosecution's evidence. Due to the difficulties of conducting investigations in North-eastern DRC, the prosecution resorted to the assistance of 'intermediaries', or informants who often were not ICC employees but acted as informal agents of the court.[102] The TC judges found that problematic, arguing that due to a lack of oversight by the prosecution, the intermediaries were able to 'take advantage of the witnesses'[103] and even encouraged some witnesses to give false testimony.[104] The intermediaries issue put into question the continuation of proceedings twice. The TC stayed the proceedings on the eve of the trial because it found that Lubanga's rights had been compromised by the prosecution's failure to disclose the sources of potentially exculpatory evidence obtained based on the condition of confidentiality.[105] The TC emphasized the importance of upholding the quality of procedure in criminal law, justifying its decision with the statement: 'the trial process has been ruptured to such a degree that it is now impossible to piece together the constituent elements of a fair trial.'[106] The TC subsequently imposed another stay in proceedings on the grounds that the prosecutor declined to disclose the identity of an intermediary, which the judges considered to affect the defendant's rights.[107] The TC was highly critical of the prosecution for failing to supervise the intermediaries who, according to the judges, had tampered with witness testimony.[108] The relations between the prosecution and the judges had reached a stage at which one authoritative commentator of the court called them 'ugly and unhealthy'.[109] The rupture between the judges

101 D. M. Amann, 'International Decisions: Prosecutor v. Lubanga', (2012) 106 *American Journal of International Law* 809–817, 816.

102 C. De Vos, 'Prosecutor v. Lubanga – Someone Who Comes between One Person and Another: Lubanga, Local Cooperation and the Right to a Fair Trial' (2011) 12(1) *Melbourne Journal of International Law* 217, 218.

103 *Lubanga* Trial Judgement, § 482.

104 Ibid., § 483.

105 *Lubanga*, 'Decision on the consequences of non-disclosure of exculpatory materials covered by Article 54(3)(e) agreements and the application to stay the prosecution of the accused, together with certain other issues raised at the Status Conference on 10 June 2008', ICC-01/04-01/06-1401, Trial Chamber I, 15 June 2020, §§ 92–94.

106 Ibid., § 93.

107 *Lubanga*, 'Redacted Decision on the Prosecution's Urgent Request for Variation of the Time Limit to Disclose the Identity of Intermediary 143 or Alternatively to Stay Proceedings Pending Further Consultations with the VWU', ICC-01/04-01/06-2517-Red, Trial Chamber I, 8 July 2010, § 31.

108 *Lubanga* Trial Judgment, § 482.

109 W. A. Schabas quoted in M. Simons, 'For International Criminal Court, Frustration and Missteps in Its First Trial', *New York Times*, 21 November 2010, www.nytimes.com/2010/11/22/world/europe/22court.html.

and the prosecutor on the issue of intermediaries was so significant that, as one commentator observed, Lubanga's conviction was put into question.[110]

Eventually, the second stay of proceedings was overturned by the Appeals Chamber, which considered the stay a 'drastic remedy'[111] and the case reached the verdict stage. But the issue of intermediaries and its potential implications for the perception of the fairness of the trial remained a major concern for the judges, who devoted 130 pages of their judgment to examine the issue.[112] The TC concluded that despite the security challenges it faced, the prosecution should not have delegated investigative activities to the intermediaries in the manner it did.[113] Consequently, the TC judges dismissed the testimony of nine former child soldiers as unreliable.[114] But even this step was considered insufficient by some members of the ICL community, who placed great emphasis on the quality of procedural justice. On appeal, Judge Ušacka argued that she would have reversed the conviction.[115] Judge Ušacka was concerned with the fact that, after the TC had dismissed the testimonies of the nine former child soldiers, the Chamber had nevertheless entered a conviction on the grounds of the evidence demonstrating the *pattern* of the children's victimization. In effect, according to Judge Ušacka, Lubanga was convicted on the basis of allegations that did not include reference 'to a single identified victim' and were framed in 'unacceptably broad terms such as "[d]uring 2002 and 2003" and "throughout Ituri".'[116] The judge concluded that the TC had thus 'violated [Lubanga's] right to be informed in detail of the nature, cause and content of the charges against him'.[117] In *Lubanga*, Judge Ušacka's position was not shared by the Majority and the conviction was not overturned. However, as will be discussed in Chapter 8, several years later the *Bemba* AC Majority, citing the importance of the quality of proceedings and the rights of the accused, overturned the conviction entered earlier by the TC.

[110] J. Freedman, *A Conviction in Question: The First Trial at the International Criminal Court* (Toronto: University of Toronto Press, 2017).

[111] *Lubanga*, 'Judgment on the appeal of the Prosecutor against the decision of Trial Chamber I of 8 July 2010 entitled "Decision on the Prosecution's Urgent Request for Variation of the Time-Limit to Disclose the Identity of Intermediary 143 or Alternatively to Stay Proceedings Pending Further Consultations with the VWU"', ICC-01/04-01/06-2582, Appeals Chamber, 8 October 2010, § 55.

[112] See pages 90–220 from the *Lubanga* Trial Judgment.

[113] Ibid., § 482.

[114] *Lubanga* Trial Judgement, § 479.

[115] *Lubanga*, Appeals Judgment, § 1.

[116] Ibid., § 2.

[117] Ibid., § 10.

Other ICC Chambers displayed a similarly strict approach to the evaluation of evidence. The *Ngudjolo* TC criticized the evidence presented by the prosecutor. Specifically, the judges were concerned that in the absence of forensic findings, the prosecution had relied heavily on witness statements, reports by investigators from the UN peacekeeping mission to the DRC, or NGO representatives.[118] As noted, similar practices had been employed at the UN tribunals, triggering criticism from criminal law experts. The judges did not find credible the testimony of the prosecutor's key witnesses[119] and expressed particular concern in relation to OTP's reliance on hearsay evidence.[120] Notably, the TC judges personally travelled to the DRC with the goal to verify *in situ* certain specific points and evaluate the geography of locations referred to by witness testimony.[121] The TC emphasized their familiarity with the contextual background of that case, which enabled them to assess the evidence presented. Throughout that acquittal, the judges stressed the importance of the findings made during their visit to the DRC and suggested that the prosecutor could have benefited from examining in more depth the background of its witnesses and the sociocultural framework of the Ituri region.[122]

The *Mbarushimana* PTC was even more critical of the prosecution. In *Mbarushimana* the prosecution submitted that the judges should not discount evidence because it was 'ambiguous, subject to more than one interpretation, or potentially inconsistent with other evidence'. Rather, the prosecution reasoned, any evidence which was 'not incredible on its face' should be accepted by the judges.[123] The judges, however, vigorously opposed that logic, which they reckoned incompatible with the criminal law process. The judges emphasized that there was no provision in the RS that expressly stated that ambiguities in the evidence should be resolved in favour of the prosecution.[124] Furthermore, the PTC criticized the prosecution for supporting its reasoning with reference to the procedures before the ad hoc tribunals, which they considered 'fundamentally different' from those at the ICC.[125] Regarding the specific evidence brought by the prosecution against Mbarushimana, the judges expressed concerns with the technique followed by the prosecution investigators. According to them, the transcripts of the

118 *Ngudjolo* Trial Judgment, § 117.

119 Ibid., § 343.

120 Ibid., § 496.

121 Ibid., §§ 68–70.

122 *Ngudjolo* Judgment, §§ 121 and 123.

123 *Mbarushimana*, 'Prosecution's written submissions on the confirmation of charges', ICC-01/04-01/10-448-Red, Pre-Trial Chamber I, 6 October 2011, § 32.

124 *Mbarushimana* Confirmation Decision, § 45.

125 Ibid., § 45.

interviews with witnesses often left the impression that the investigator had been 'so attached' to her theory that she would put leading questions or even show 'resentment, impatience[126] or disappointment' whenever the witness's replies did not match her expectations. The judges '*deprecat[ed]* such techniques' and assigned low probative value to that evidence.[127] As will be discussed, the TC Majority in *Gbagbo and Blé Goudé* approached with similar 'hypersceptical' attitude the prosecutor's incriminating evidence.[128]

More recently, in 2021 the *Said* PTC similarly dismissed part of the evidence submitted by the prosecutor. The judges noted that, even though 14 out of the 15 incidents cited by the prosecutor were based on the statements of direct victims of the crimes, none of those statements mentioned the accused. This was deemed problematic by the judges, especially because the witnesses had named other Séléka leaders. The *Said* decision is illustrative of the differences between human rights and a criminal law approach to investigations – while the prosecutor's evidence demonstrated the suffering inflicted upon the victims, it failed to specify the accused's alleged participation in that suffering. Because the criminal trial is concerned with assessing the criminal responsibility of the defendant, evidence of the victims' suffering alone is insufficient.

Not every member of the ICL community of practice was convinced by the ICC's meticulous approach to evidence. Some legal experts outside the Court expressed concerns that the ICC judges advanced 'the goal of a fair trial *at the expense* of future convictions'[129] by precluding 'the possibility of easier future investigations'.[130] In *Mbarushimana* Judge Monageng dissented from the Majority decision, which dismissed the charges against the suspect. The judge emphasized that he did not object to any of the 'main legal principles' enunciated by the PTC[131] but disagreed with how the Majority had handled the evidence. In other words, Judge Monageng did not object to his colleagues' idea of restraining the scope of Article 25(3)(d) liability by adding the 'significant contribution requirement', but to their harsh attitude towards the prosecution's evidence. According to Judge Monageng, the judges had on occasion made conclusions without discussing 'critical pieces of evidence' presented by

126 *Said* Confirmation Decision, § 127.
127 *Mbarushimana* Confirmation Decision, § 51, emphasis added.
128 Robinson, 'Other Poisoned Chalice'. Robinson, 'International Criminal Law'.
129 Kaoutzanis, 'Turbulent Adolescence Ahead', 306, emphasis added.
130 Ibid., 310.
131 *Mbarushimana* Confirmation Decision, Dissenting Opinion of Judge Sanji Mmasenono Monageng, § 1.

the prosecution.[132] Overall, Judge Monageng considered that while the totality of evidence did not establish that Mbarushimana had been a 'linchpin' figure at the FDLR,[133] the Majority had failed consider evidence that the accused's contribution to the crimes had been 'significant'.[134]

But many others considered the strict control over the prosecution's investigative practices as 'important and necessary'.[135] As observed by one ICC judge, the burden of proof clearly rested with the prosecutor.[136]

7.5 The Politics of the Legal Field, Evidence, and State Cooperation

The shared understanding among ICC chambers that the burden on the prosecutor in establishing the defendant's link to the crimes should not be eased can influence trial outcomes in conjunction with other factors, such as the availability of evidence and of state cooperation with investigations. A thorough analysis of these other factors falls beyond the scope of this book, not least because, as discussed in Chapter 1, they have been examined in detail in the scholarship on international criminal justice. Nevertheless, this section provides a brief illustration of the way in which the lack of state cooperation can affect trial outcomes in conjunction with the ICC's restrained approach to the assessment of criminal responsibility.

The cases against Kenyan nationals present an interesting illustration in that regard. The prosecution went after representatives of both sides to the 2007 post-election conflict in Kenya. The case against Uhuru Muigai Kenyatta, Francis Kirimi Muthaura, and Mohammed Hussein Ali concerned crimes allegedly committed by the Mungiki group and pro-Party of National Unity (PNU) youth and aided by the failure of the Kenyan police to intervene.[137] The case against William Samoei Ruto, Henry Kiprono Kosgey, and Joshua Arap Sang concerned crimes that were allegedly committed by a rival organization called the 'Network', belonging to the Kalenjin community and comprised eminent representatives of the Orange Democratic Movement (ODM).[138]

132 Ibid., § 65.

133 Ibid., § 102.

134 Ibid., § 112.

135 C. Safferling, *International Criminal Procedure* (Oxford: Oxford University Press, 2012), 430.

136 Interview with Judge Morrison, 26 June 2020.

137 *Kenyatta, Muthaura and Ali*, Decision on the Confirmation of Charges Pursuant to Article 61(7)(a) and (b) of the RS, ICC-01/09-02/11-382-Red, Pre-Trial Chamber II, 29 January 2012 (hereinafter *Kenyatta, Muthaura, and Ali* Confirmation Decision), § 102.

138 *Ruto, Kosgey and Sang*, Public Document Containing the Charges, ICC-01/09-01/11-261-AnxA, Pre-Trial Chamber II, 15 August 2011 (hereinafter *Ruto, Kosgey and Sang* Amended DCC), § 25, §§ 43–44.

Even though the suspects appeared voluntarily at the Court,[139] in practice the OTP's investigation faced significant opposition by the Kenyan government.[140] The prosecution submitted that it had 'expended considerable efforts' to attempt to obtain cooperation from the Kenyan government and had had to 'overcome various tactics employed to stall, delay, or altogether thwart the Prosecution's collection of certain evidence in Kenya'.[141] A member of the ICC's ASP Kenya even set out to amend some of the Rules of Procedure and Evidence of the Court, which could have affected the ongoing proceedings against its nationals.[142] Notably, two of the indicted persons – Kenyatta and Ruto – entered a coalition and won the 2013 Kenyan elections. It has been observed that part of their electoral campaign involved attacking the ICC as a neo-colonial court on a variety of public platforms.[143]

Combined with the increasingly strict rules of assessing the evidence concerning criminal responsibility at the ICC, the scarcity of available evidence contributed to the termination of all cases and precluded the judges from delivering a final verdict. The PTC declined to confirm the charges against two of the suspects – Ali and Kosgey. The prosecution alleged that Ali had contributed to the commission of the crimes by instructing the Kenyan Police not to obstruct the attack by the Mungiki and the pro-PNU youth, including by failing to arrest the perpetrators.[144] However, the judges found that the evidence was insufficient to establish that the Kenyan Police had participated by inaction in the attack[145] and concluded that there was no conduct on the basis of which to attribute responsibility to Ali.[146] The PTC judges stressed that their approach was in compliance with the 'fundamental principles of criminal law'.[147] Similar developments occurred in the *Ruto, Kosgey, and Sang* case. Kosgey was charged together with Ruto

[139] *Kenyatta, Muthaura and Ali* Confirmation Decision, § 4.

[140] Peskin, 'International Justice', 413–422.

[141] *Muthaura and Kenyatta*, Public redacted version of the Additional Prosecution observations on the Defence's Article 64 applications, filed in accordance with order number ICC-01/09-02-11-673, ICC-01/09-02/11-683-Red, Trial Chamber V, 8 March 2013, § 24.

[142] Woolaver and Palmer, 'Challenges to the Independence', 646–651.

[143] G. Lugano, 2017. 'Counter-Shaming the International Criminal Court's Intervention as Neocolonial: Lessons from Kenya', 11(1) *International Journal of Transitional Justice* 9–29, 11.

[144] *Kenyatta, Muthaura and Ali*, Document Containing the Charges, ICC-01/09-02/11-280-AnxA, Pre-Trial Chamber I, 2 September 2011, (hereinafter *Kenyatta, Muthaura and Ali*, DCC), § 99.

[145] *Kenyatta, Muthaura and Ali* Confirmation Decision, § 425.

[146] Ibid., § 426.

[147] Ibid., § 424.

as an indirect co-perpetrator of the crimes committed by the Network.[148] The evidence against Kosgey, however, was not strong enough to convince the ICC judges. The prosecution had primarily relied on the testimony of one anonymous witness to prove the allegations concerning Kosgey's role within the organization. Mindful of the lower probative value of anonymous testimony the judges examined potential corroborative evidence.[149] However, they concluded that the allegations of Kosgey's involvement in the post-election violence, including the provision of funding, were only made 'in general terms' and did not corroborate the anonymous testimony.[150] For the PTC judges, general allegations of 'involvement' were not sufficient to meet the requirements of the 'control over the crime' theory. Furthermore, the judges noted one witness's testimony that Kosgey 'never challenged Ruto on any issue'.[151] The hierarchy among the co-perpetrators mattered for demonstrating the ability of each co-perpetrator to frustrate the commission of the crimes as required by the 'control' theory.[152] As the prosecutor's evidence regarding Kosgey's role in the crimes was deemed insufficient, the judges declined to confirm the charges against him.[153]

Eventually, in 2013 the OTP withdrew the charges against Muthaura and Kenyatta. The prosecutor concluded that the available evidence provided 'no reasonable prospect of a conviction'.[154] Indeed, Ngudjolo's acquittal, the difficulties experienced in *Katanga*, and the criticism regarding the quality of evidence that the prosecution endured in *Mbarushimana* had demonstrated that the ICC judges were not willing to lessen the burden of proof on the prosecutor. The prosecution needed strong and clear evidence, but none seemed to be available. In the *Kenyatta and Muthaura* case, one key witness had recanted a significant part of his incriminating evidence and had admitted accepting bribes. Furthermore, many potential witnesses were unwilling to testify. The prosecution explained its decision to drop the charges with reference to the Kenyan government's failure to assist the investigations, arguing that:

148 *Ruto, Kosgey and Sang* Confirmation Decision, § 285.

149 Ibid., § 293.

150 Ibid., § 295.

151 Ibid.

152 See Yanev and Kooijmans, 'Divided Minds', 824.

153 *Ruto, Kosgey and Sang* Confirmation Decision, § 293.

154 *Muthaura and Kenyatta*, Prosecution notification of withdrawal of the charges against Francis Kirimi Muthaura, ICC-01/09-02/11-687, Trial Chamber V, 11 March 2013 (hereinafter *Muthaura and Kenyatta*, Withdrawal of Charges against Muthaura), § 9. See also *Kenyatta*, Notice of withdrawal of the charges against Uhuru Muigai Kenyatta, ICC-01/09-02/11-983, Trial Chamber V(B), 5 December 2014, § 2.

> … Despite assurances of its willingness to cooperate with the Court, the Government of Kenya has in fact provided only limited cooperation to the Prosecution, and has failed to assist it in uncovering evidence that would have been crucial, or at the very least, may have been useful in the case …[155]

In 2016 the charges against Ruto and Sang were vacated by the trial judges[156] on the grounds that there was 'hardly' any concrete evidence that showed the existence of either the Network organization or their common plan to commit the alleged crimes.[157] Nevertheless, the majority of the judges did not *acquit* the accused but merely discharged those 'without prejudice to their prosecution afresh in future'.[158] Judge Fremr noted that 'in a normal state of affairs' he would have acquitted the accused but given 'the *special circumstances* of the case', namely the fact that the accused profited from the witness interference, the judge agreed to only vacate the charges.[159]

Given the lack of co-operation by the Kenyan government, one may suggest that the proceedings against the Kenyan defendants were terminated (partly) because of political pressure on the Court, which played out in the inability to collect evidence. Therefore, in the trials resulting from the Kenyan investigation state politics had an indirect impact on the outcome of proceedings by obstructing the prosecutor's efforts to collect evidence. Given the principled belief of many ICC judges that the burden of proof on the prosecutor should not be eased, such difficulties resulted in the dismissal of the charges against the accused. Indeed, the converse situation can also be observed in which states have an indirect impact on the outcome of proceedings by providing abundant evidence to the prosecutor when the case concerns a rebel commander, as seen in *Ongwen*.[160]

But the impact of state politics is not the only factor influencing trial outcomes, and an enquiry into the judges' principled understanding about what the laws on criminal responsibility require can provide additional insights. Rather, the analysis of the normative dynamics behind the construction of criminal responsibility rules and practices provides new insights into those aspects of the operation of ICL that remain neglected from a state-centric international relations perspective. As will be

155 *Muthaura and Kenyatta*, Withdrawal of Charges against Muthaura, § 11.

156 *Ruto and Sang*, 'Decision on Defence Applications for Judgments of Acquittal', ICC-01/09-01/11-2027-Red-Corr, Trial Chamber V(A), 5 April 2016 (hereinafter *Ruto and Sang* Trial Decision), § 131, § 143.

157 *Ruto and Sang* Trial Decision, Reasons of Judge Fremr, § 33.

158 *Ruto and Sang* Trial Decision, § 1.

159 *Ruto and Sang* Trial Decision Reasons of Judge Fremr, § 148, emphasis added. See also *Ruto and Sang* Trial Decision, Reasons of Judge Eboe-Osuji, § 8.

160 Chapter 9, Section 9.2.

discussed in Chapter 8, despite the availability of government cooperation in *Gbagbo and Blé Goudé* and the observation that the *Bemba* case appeared politically expedient for the CAR and DRC government,[161] the collected evidence still proved insufficient to meet the high criminal responsibility standards enforced by the TC and AC majorities, respectively.

Furthermore, in many of the cases discussed, where some or all the charges had been dropped before trial, the accused comprised rebel commanders who had lost, or never enjoyed, significant political backing. Banda and Jerbo were members of insurgent groups who fought against the Sudanese government forces in Darfur.[162] The ousting of the Al-Bashir government in Sudan in 2019 provided further opportunities for apprehending more of the suspects indicted as part of the Darfur investigation, including Abd-Al-Rahman. He had fled to the CAR before surrendering himself to the ICC in a move that commentators described as an attempt to avoid arrest by Sudan's new leadership.[163] Abd-Al-Rahman's apprehension was welcomed by Western powers, such as France, which even agreed to transfer the suspect to the Court.[164] The apprehension of the suspects from the CAR investigation likewise did not appear to trouble the government. Yekatom and Ngaïssona, commanders of Anti-Balaka groups in the CAR, which were reportedly loyal to the deposed president François Bozizé,[165] were surrendered to the Court in 2018, with Yekatom surrendered by the CAR government,[166] and Ngaïssona arrested by the French authorities.[167] Said, a former commander of the rival Séléka rebel

[161] W. Wakabi, 'Reactions to Bemba's Conviction', International Justice Monitor, 31 March 2016, www.ijmonitor.org/2016/03/reactions-to-bembas-conviction/.

[162] *Banda and Jerbo*, Second Decision on the Prosecutor's Application under Article 58, ICC-02/05-03/09-1, Pre-Trial Chamber I, 15 June 2010, §§ 11–14.

[163] R. Grey, 'Gender-based Persecution against Men: the ICC's Abd-al-Rahman Case', 35 May 2021, *OpinioJuris*, http://opiniojuris.org/2021/05/30/gender-based-persecution-against-men-the-iccs-abd-al-rahman-case/.

[164] Ministère de l'Europe et des Affaires Étrangères, 'International Criminal Court – Surrender of Ali Muhammad Ali Abd-Al-Rahman (Ali Kushayb) to the International Criminal Court', 9 June 2020, www.diplomatie.gouv.fr/en/french-foreign-policy/international-justice/news/article/international-criminal-court-surrender-of-ali-muhammad-ali-abd-al-rahman-ali.

[165] W. Wakabi, 'Judges Confirm Charges Against Two Former Central African Militiamen', International Justice Monitor, 2 January 2020, www.ijmonitor.org/2020/01/judges-confirm-charges-against-two-former-central-african-militiamen/.

[166] ICC, 'Situation in Central African Republic II: Alfred Yekatom surrendered to the ICC for crimes against humanity and war crimes', 17 November 2018, www.icc-cpi.int/Pages/item.aspx?name=pr1418.

[167] ICC, 'Situation in Central African Republic II: Patrice-Edouard Ngaïssona arrested for crimes against humanity and war crimes', 12 December 2018, www.icc-cpi.int/Pages/item.aspx?name=PR1425.

group, was likewise surrendered to the Court by the CAR government in January 2021 against the backdrop of continuing political instability in the country, and growing criticism of the CAR authorities for failing to prosecute 'higher-level Séléka leaders'[168] and government figures.[169] The existing international relations scholarship discussed in Chapter 2 helps explain why those persons may have ended up at the ICC, namely because their arrests did not infringe upon the interests of powerful actors, but falls short of enquiring what happened within their trials afterwards.

An analysis of the legal reasoning in those cases reveals that most ICC judges shared the understanding that the 'common plan' element of (indirect) co-perpetration required being handled in cautiously, lest it become a vehicle for imputing guilt by association to the accused. This shared understanding has implications for the outcome of proceedings in that most ICC chambers specifically looked to the relationship between the accused and the *crime*, rather than between the accused and the *common plan* – an arguably more challenging standard for the prosecutor to meet. The *Yekatom and Ngaïssona* PTC judges even referred to the concerns expressed by Judge Van den Wyngaert with respect to the common plan element of liability when explaining their decision to focus specifically on the link between the accused and the criminal incidents.[170] This is not to say that there were no other factors, including but not limited to the availability of evidence, which affected the outcomes of those proceedings; rather, this is to shed light on one of the contributing factors, namely the judges' understanding of how the criminal responsibility laws should be applied.

7.6 Conclusion

The ICC judges in *Lubanga* and *Katanga and Ngudjolo* sought to provide greater clarity and limit discretion by building upon the language of the RS and developing in detail the requirements of the modes of liability applicable at the Court. Nevertheless, the ICC judges were still left with

[168] E. Tambay, 'ICC Should Pursue Higher-Level Seleka from Central African Republic', Human Rights Watch, 11 October 2021, www.hrw.org/news/2021/10/11/icc-should-pursue-higher-level-seleka-central-african-republic.

[169] Amnesty International, 'Central African Republic: Dozens Suspected of Criminal Responsibility for War Crimes and Crimes against Humanity Remain atLarge', 8 December 2021, www.amnesty.org/en/latest/news/2021/12/central-african-republic-dozens-suspected-of-criminal-responsibility-for-war-crimes-and-crimes-against-humanity-remain-at-large/.

[170] *Yekatom and Ngaïssona* Confirmation Decision, § 60, footnote 106.

considerable room to manoeuvre in practice. The question whether a particular accused had exercised 'control' over the crime, and therefore could be convicted, ultimately rested with the judges' discretion in applying the concepts of 'control', 'essential contribution' to the crime, 'common plan' among the co-perpetrators, and 'virtual certainty' of the criminal result, to the facts and evidence presented in specific cases. The question of what type and quality of evidence the judges would deem sufficient to meet those requirements was crucial for operationalising the modes of liability in practice. As discussed in Chapter 2, precisely this indeterminacy of legal concepts has prompted critical scholars to suggest that international law risks collapsing into a mere 'apology' for politics when applied in practice.[171] By contrast, in accordance with the 'practice' framework of ICL, which this book employs, the decisions of judges are influenced by identifiable legal norms, even if the meaning of those norms is constantly subject to contestation and revision.

The findings of this chapter do not negate that a variety of other factors, not least state interests, may influence trial outcomes in both direct and indirect ways, but the findings do provide novel insights into trial outcomes. The analysis revealed that different sets of shared understandings about the meaning of criminal responsibility rules have gained authority at the UN tribunals versus the ICC. The ICC's approach to criminal responsibility can be understood as influenced by the understanding, shared by many ICC judges, including in the *Mbarushimana* PTC, the *Ngudjolo* TC, and the *Said* PTC, that, as a criminal justice institution, the ICC foremost needs to protect the defendant's rights. This line of legal reasoning has featured in the strict assessment of evidence and the application of the RS modes of liability in practice, and has been especially prominent after the *Lubanga* PTC and TC endured criticism from members of the ICL field of practice for overstretching the notion of 'control over the crime'. Consequently, the outcomes of ICC trials need to be understood not only with respect to state interests, which may explain the selection of suspects and the available evidence, but also in relation to the competition of ideas about the meaning and purpose of the criminal responsibility laws that are promoted by various actors within the ICL field.

[171] Koskenniemi, *From Apology to Utopia*.

8

The Road to Acquittals

Bemba and *Gbagbo and Blé Goudé*

This chapter explores the legal and political dilemmas arising from the assessment of individual criminal responsibility in two ICC cases, which ended in acquittals: *Bemba* and *Gbagbo and Blé Goudé*. It offers an illustration of the distinctive and predominant line of legal reasoning with respect to the assessment of criminal responsibility at the ICC, a line of legal reasoning that prioritizes the quality of the process through the narrow application of the modes of liability and the meticulous assessment of evidence, all regardless of the trial outcome. The *Bemba* AC Majority and *Gbagbo and Blé Goudé* TC Majority have adopted an internal shared understanding about the role of the court in the international society, according to which procedural excellence upholds the integrity of the liberal system of criminal justice and provides an antidote to the false information dominating the modern political world. Nevertheless, the strict approach to the assessment of evidence and the application of the RS modes of liability has been contested from both inside the Court, in the form of dissenting opinions to the final judgments, and outside the Court, from NGOs and legal experts. This analysis focuses on the dynamics taking place within the legal field while situating those dynamics within the broader international political context of the *Bemba* and *Gbagbo and Blé Goudé* trials.

8.1 Bemba

The *Bemba* case provides a stark illustration of the significance that ICC judges have attached to the quality of legal procedure when it comes to the assessment of individual criminal responsibility. Over the span of a decade, the case presented a series of surprises, from the decision of the PTC to recharacterize Bemba's mode of liability from principal liability (Article 25(3)(a)) to command responsibility (Article 28(a)), to the decision of the AC Majority to overturn the conviction. The line of reasoning that underpinned the appeals judgment indicated that some ICC judges had become even more committed to procedural justice than its advocates within the broader ICL field.

8.1.1 Case Background

The *Bemba* case resulted from the first ICC investigation in the CAR, concerning the 2002–2003 conflict between the forces of Ange-Félix Patassé, CAR's President at the time, and the former Army Chief of Staff of the CAR armed forces François Bozizé, who attempted to unseat Patassé in a coup.[1] Bozizé's 2002 coup attempt failed, but he was eventually elected as president of the CAR.[2] In 2004 the CAR Government made a self-referral to the ICC concerning the 2002–2003 armed conflict. The prosecution noted that it had also received 'significant communications' from NGOs and international organizations concerning the situation in the CAR, and in 2007 it initiated an investigation.[3]

The OTP's investigation and the selection of suspects reflected the complex political reality on the ground. The OTP did not start proceedings against Bozizé or members of his forces for alleged crimes committed by those forces during subsequent conflicts in the CAR, which broke out in 2005, although the prosecution gave indication that it was closely monitoring those conflicts.[4] Instead, the prosecutor requested an arrest warrant against Jean-Pierre Bemba Gombo, whose troops had aided the former CAR president Patassé in his attempt to hold on to power in the conflict against Bozizé. During the 2002–2003 CAR conflict, Bemba was the President and Commander-in-Chief of the *Mouvement de Libération du Congo* (Movement for the Liberation of the Congo) (MLC)[5] – a movement established by Bemba himself with the proclaimed aim of restoring democracy in the DRC through both political and military means.[6] The prosecution alleged that Patassé had requested Bemba to provide

1 *Bemba*, Public Redacted Version of the Amended Document containing the charges filed on 30 March 2009, ICC-01/05-01/08-395-Anx3, Pre-Trial Chamber III, 30 March 2009 (hereinafter *Bemba* Amended DCC) § 13.

2 M. Glasius, 'What Is Global Justice and Who Decides?: Civil Society and Victim Responses to the International Criminal Court's First Investigations', (2009), *Human Rights Quarterly* 31: 2, 496–520, 500.

3 ICC, 'Background: Situation in the Central African Republic', 22 May 2007, www.icc-cpi.int/NR/rdonlyres/B64950CF-8370-4438-AD7C-0905079D747A/144037/ICCOTPBN20070522220_A_EN.pdf.

4 Glasius, 'What Is Global Justice', 504.

5 *Bemba* Amended DCC, § 5.

6 Ibid., §§ 4–5.

MLC troops to assist him in exchange for significant benefits, including securing the CAR as the MLC's strategic rear base and deterring potential threats to his movement from the DRC government.[7] Thus, the ICC OTP focused on the crimes allegedly linked to the former CAR regime, rather than the ones allegedly linked to the sitting government at the time. The first CAR investigation had high stakes for other political actors in the region as well. Bemba was a DRC national and an active political figure, who in 2003 became one of the four vicepresidents of the DRC Transitional Government.[8] It has been suggested that the ICC case against Bemba, the 'main political rival' of the DRC's president at the time, Kabila, helped solidify his position in power.[9]

Expert commentators have observed that the cooperation of Bozizé's government in the CAR and Kabila's government in the DRC had aided, even enabled, the ICC prosecution to conduct investigations and collect evidence.[10] And indeed, evidence was plentiful, as the MLC forces were implicated in a considerable number of crimes committed against the civilian population in the CAR in 2002–2003. For instance, a medical charity had reported 316 cases of rape in the CAR at the relevant time and the Prosecutor of the Republic in Bangui had received more than 300 reports of rape from surviving victims.[11] Operating within a seemingly favourable political situation, the ICC OTP was able to collect abundant evidence about the crimes committed in the CAR. The major challenge in front of the prosecutor was to convince the ICC judges that the evidence also established a clear link between those crimes and the defendant.

8.1.2 *Pre-trial: From Principal Liability to Command Responsibility*

The difficulties of linking Bemba to the crimes committed by MLC soldiers in the CAR were observable already at the pre-trial stage. In 2008 the prosecution alleged that Bemba was responsible as a co-perpetrator under Article 25(3)(a) and convinced the PTC to issue an arrest warrant pursuant to that mode of liability.[12] The PTC judges were satisfied that there were reasonable grounds to believe that the suspect had participated in a

7 Ibid., § 14.

8 Ibid., §§ 1 and 6.

9 Clark, Distant Justice, 98.

10 Clark, Distant Justice, 270.

11 *Bemba*, Decision on the Prosecutor's Application for a Warrant of Arrest against Jean-Pierre Bemba Gombo, ICC-01/05-01/08-14-tENG, Pre-Trial Chamber III, 10 June 2008 (hereinafter *Bemba* Arrest Warrant Decision), § 34.

12 *Bemba*, Arrest Warrant Decision, § 71.

common agreement with Patassé to provide the latter with military assistance in exchange for securing the support of the CAR government for the MLC.[13] The judges further concluded that Bemba had made an essential contribution to his common plan with Patassé by providing logistical support to the combatants and that, without his contribution, the MLC operation in the CAR would not have taken place.[14]

However, to sustain the charges of principal liability at the confirmation of charges stage of proceedings, the prosecutor had to overcome two difficulties. Firstly, unlike the decision to issue an arrest warrant, which required 'reasonable grounds to believe', the confirmation of charges decision relied on the higher 'substantial grounds to believe' evidentiary threshold. Secondly, at the confirmation of charges stage, the *Bemba* PTC decided to adopt a very strict interpretation of Article 30 RS that elevated the mental element of liability to 'virtual certainty' that the crime would be committed.[15] The latter development was particularly challenging for the OTP, considering the available evidence. In the 2008 arrest warrant decision, the PTC had concluded that Bemba 'knew that, in such a climate of impunity, sending his troops to the CAR would lead in the normal course of events to the commission of crimes' and nevertheless 'took [that] risk'.[16] While the judges did not use the *dolus* terminology or refer to the *Lubanga* jurisprudence, the invocation of the notion of risk and the suspect's acceptance of that risk suggests that the available evidence satisfied the lower *dolus eventualis* mental element rather than the 'virtual certainty' one. However, after the wave of criticism that the incorporation of *dolus eventualis* in ICC jurisprudence triggered and the decision of the *Bemba* PTC to choose a more restrained interpretation of Article 30,[17] the charges of principal liability against Bemba appeared less solid.

Nevertheless, the judges considered that the case was not without merit and decided to intervene in the work of the prosecution by suggesting an alternative mode of liability. Article 61(7) of the RS provided the PTC with the power to adjourn the hearing and request the prosecutor to conduct further investigations or to amend the charges if the evidence presented 'appears to establish a different crime'.[18] The *Bemba* PTC interpreted the

13 Ibid., § 73.

14 Ibid., § 79.

15 *See* Chapter 6, Section 6.4.

16 *Bemba* Arrest Warrant Decision, § 82.

17 Chapter 6, Section 6.4.

18 *Bemba*, Decision Adjourning the Hearing Pursuant to Article 61(7)(c)(ii) of the RS, ICC-01/05-01/08-388, Pre-Trial Chamber III, 3 March 2009, § 1.

latter provision to include not only the offences listed in the RS, but also the modes of liability.[19] Specifically, the PTC requested the prosecution to include command responsibility under Article 28 as a mode of liability in the DCC.[20] With some hesitancy, the prosecutor agreed to include Article 28 charges in the DCC 'as an alternative to, not in substitution of' principal liability[21] and argued that the choice between the two modes should be ultimately left to the TC to decide.[22]

The PTC, however, was resolved that the evidence presented did not meet the high requirements of principal liability nor of the new strict approach to the mental element established by the *Bemba* PTC itself. The prosecution had inferred Bemba's intention and knowledge concerning the crimes from, inter alia, the prior behaviour of the MLC in the CAR and Bemba's continuation of the implementation of the common plan despite being informed of the commission of MLC crimes via international media and internal communication channels.[23] It is possible that under the *dolus eventualis* standard the PTC might have confirmed the charges against Bemba as a co-perpetrator of the MCL crimes. However, the judges considered the available evidence insufficient to meet the 'virtual certainty' standard, which they had added to the requirements of Article 30.[24] Specifically, the PTC remained unconvinced that the facts provided sufficient grounds to infer that when sending MLC troops to the CAR, Bemba had been virtually certain that in the ordinary course of events those troops would commit murder, rape, and pillaging. According to the judges, even if Bemba knew that the MLC had previously committed such crimes, that alone was insufficient to infer that he was certain that the MCL would commit them again during the 2003 mission in the CAR.[25] Similarly, the judges were unable to infer from Bemba's decision to continue to implement his plan with Patassé, despite the media warning of MLC's behaviour, that the accused was 'virtually certain' that the alleged crimes would be committed. According to the judges, Bemba 'may have foreseen the risk of occurrence of such crimes as a mere possibility and accepted it' for the sake of helping Patassé retain power, but that mental

[19] Ibid., § 26.

[20] Ibid., § 49.

[21] *Bemba*, Prosecution's Submission of Amended Document Containing the Charges, Amended List of Evidence and Amended In-Depth Analysis Chart of Incriminatory Evidence, ICC-01/05-01/08-395, Pre-Trial Chamber III, 30 March 2009, § 9.

[22] Ibid., § 10.

[23] *Bemba* Confirmation Decision, § 373.

[24] Ibid., § 272.

[25] Ibid., § 377.

state did not meet the requirements of Article 30.[26] Thus, the new strict interpretation of Article 30 RS at the ICC precluded the confirmation of the charges of principal liability against the accused.

Nevertheless, the *Bemba* PTC resorted to a mode of liability which it considered to require a lower cognitive element: command responsibility. According to the judges, 'knowledge' in the context of command responsibility did not require 'virtual certainty', as in the context of principal liability.[27] The PTC's decision to change the mode of liability from principal liability to command responsibility was supported by authoritative commentators.[28] Regarding the objective elements of liability, the judges found that as the military commander of the MLC, Bemba had had effective authority and control over the troops,[29] which granted him the power to prevent and repress the commission of their crimes.[30] In support of that conclusion, the judges pointed to the fact that during the 2002–2003 mission Bemba had resorted to his powers to investigate MLC crimes[31] and even travelled to the CAR to address his troops, threatening them with punishment for misconduct.[32] Following their reasoning that 'knowledge' of the crimes under Article 28(a) was distinct from the 'intent and knowledge' requirement of Article 30, the judges confirmed Bemba's liability pursuant to the first alternative, concluding that as a commander Bemba 'knew' of the commission of MLC crimes in the CAR,[33] despite the fact that throughout the period of the mission he had been primarily stationed in the DRC.[34] The judges gave particular weight to the widespread nature of MLC crimes, Bemba's visit to the CAR, his statement cautioning his troops against misbehaviour, the fact that he was informed by members of his circle of the crimes, and the existence of media broadcasts covering those.[35] Nevertheless, the judges considered that the measures taken by Bemba in terms of investigating and punishing the crimes committed by his troops in the CAR were 'disproportionate'.[36] Because the PTC concluded that Bemba had failed to take all the 'necessary or reasonable'

[26] Ibid., § 400.
[27] Ibid., § 479. For a critique of this point see Ambos, 'Critical Issues'.
[28] See Ambos, 'Critical Issues', 720.
[29] *Bemba* Confirmation Decision, § 446.
[30] Ibid., § 461.
[31] Ibid., § 469.
[32] Ibid., § 471.
[33] Ibid., § 478.
[34] Ibid., § 485.
[35] Ibid., § 489, emphasis added.
[36] Ibid., § 495.

measures within his material ability to repress or punish the crimes, they confirmed the charges of command responsibility against him.[37]

Thus, the *Bemba* PTC demonstrated reluctance to expand the scope of principal liability by accepting the evidence pointing to Bemba's 'awareness' of the crimes as sufficient to fulfil the requisite mental element: virtual certainty. Rather, they considered the evidence sufficient for the purpose of referring the case to trial only under command responsibility. While some questioned the PTC's activist decision to substitute one mode of liability with another,[38] others considered that were it not for the PTC's intervention, 'the case would not even have made it past the confirmation stage'.[39]

Yet, as the subsequent developments in the case would reveal, even a mode of liability such as command responsibility could prove too demanding for the prosecution in a court committed to procedural justice and protecting the defendant's rights. During the later stages of proceedings, the main source of contention turned out to be not whether Bemba knew of the crimes, but whether he had had the material capabilities to do something about those crimes.

8.1.3 *Trial and Appeal: Overturning the Conviction*

8.1.3.1 Trial

In 2016 the TC convicted Bemba for the war crimes of murder, rape, and pillaging, committed by the MLC troops during their 2002–2003 stay in the CAR. The trial judges were satisfied by the available evidence that as a commander Bemba had known about the MLC's crimes.[40] The TC noted the evidence of radios, mobile telephones, and other communications equipment that enabled MLC commanders to communicate with Bemba throughout the mission[41] and the availability of reports by intelligence services and media to the accused.[42] The crucial evidence for establishing Bemba's knowledge of MLC crimes ironically proved to be his very efforts

[37] Ibid., § 490.

[38] Ambos, 'Critical Issues', 724–726.

[39] K. J. Heller, 'Why Bemba's Conviction Was Not a "Very Good Day" for the OTP (Updated)', OpinioJuris, 22 March 2016, http://opiniojuris.org/2016/03/22/a-few-thoughts-on-bembas-conviction/.

[40] *Bemba*, Judgment pursuant to Article 74 of the Statute, ICC-01/05-01/08-3343, Trial Chamber III, 21 March 2016, §§ 717–718.

[41] Ibid., § 707.

[42] Ibid., §§ 708–709.

to investigate and punish those crimes. In particular, the judges found that Bemba had set up several commissions of enquiry and a court martial.[43] Since Bemba had tried to address the crimes, the judges reasoned, he knew of those crimes. The measures taken by Bemba with regard to the MLC crimes would eventually prove a source of significant disagreement between the TC and the AC regarding the responsibility of the accused.

The trial judges reckoned that a conviction was warranted because the measures taken by Bemba to address the MLC's crimes were 'grossly inadequate' and 'not genuine'.[44] The judges noted that only public allegations of MLC crimes had prompted a response by Bemba,[45] and even those responses were 'limited in mandate, execution, and/or results'.[46] Thus, even though there was evidence that as a commander Bemba had taken steps to repress the crimes of his subordinates and initiate investigations, the motivations behind those steps – mainly 'to counter public allegations and rehabilitate the public image of the MLC'[47] – convinced the judges that Bemba's attempts were insufficient to absolve him from criminal responsibility. In fact, the judges listed a number of actions that, in their opinion, Bemba could have taken to address the crimes, including ensuring that MLC troops were properly trained in the rules of international humanitarian law, conducting 'genuine and full' investigations, and issuing clear orders to commanders in the CAR to prevent the commission of crimes.[48] Consistent with the causality element of command responsibility, the trial judges concluded that, had Bemba taken such measures, the crimes 'would have been prevented or would not have been committed in the circumstances in which they were'.[49] Consequently, Bemba was convicted as a commander for the crimes committed by MLC troops under his command in the CAR.

Bemba's conviction and the TC's reasoning were generally well-received within the broader ICL community. NGOs welcomed the first ICC conviction that featured gender-based crimes.[50] A Human Rights Watch official called the conviction 'a bright moment in achieving all-too-rare accountability for commanders who permit rape and sexual violence

[43] Ibid., §§ 711–713, 715.
[44] Ibid., § 727.
[45] Ibid.
[46] Ibid., § 720.
[47] Ibid., § 728.
[48] Ibid., § 729.
[49] Ibid., § 741.
[50] W. Wakabi, 'Reactions to Bemba's Conviction', *International Justice Monitor*, 31 March 2016, www.ijmonitor.org/2016/03/reactions-to-bembas-conviction/.

by their troops'.[51] Other commentators further noted that the *Bemba* judgment for the first time in ICL recognized sexual violence against men as instances of rape, as opposed to torture or outrages upon personal dignity.[52]

Some legal scholars who advocated for greater respect for the principle of personal culpability and criticized the UN tribunals for their handling of some of the elements of command responsibility commended the *Bemba* trial judgment for providing 'the most sophisticated judicial analysis to date' on those matters.[53] Considering the significant criticism that command responsibility had triggered for overstretching the culpability principle from the Tokyo Judgment to the UN tribunals, the reactions to the *Bemba* TC judgment demonstrate the normative shift that has occurred at the Court – from substantive to procedural justice, from a moral intuition of fairness to neutral and predictable application of legal rules, regardless of the outcome. But the trial judgment was not the end of the story.

8.1.3.2 Appeal

That normative shift reached its culmination in the decision delivered by majority at the appeals stage of proceedings. In April 2016 Bemba's defence appealed the conviction decision and sought an acquittal on each charge.[54] More than two years after the judgment, in June 2018 the AC delivered a decision acquitting Bemba of all charges by majority of three out of five judges at the appeals bench.[55] The rationale for acquittal was a strong concern on behalf of the Majority that the interpretation of the facts by the TC had been coloured by the trial judges' personal conviction of the accused's faulty *character traits*, which had prevented them from making a fair assessment of his culpability in accordance with the legal rules. The AC Majority included Judge Eboe-Osuji, Judge Morrison, and Presiding Judge Van den Wyngaert. Notably, Judge Van den Wyngaert had already demonstrated her preference for a strict interpretation of the legality and culpability principles in *Katanga and Ngudjolo* and, as will be

[51] G. Mattioli-Zeltner, 'Dispatches: High-Profile ICC Warning to Commanders on Rape', Human Rights Watch, 21 March 2016, www.hrw.org/news/2016/03/21/dispatches-high-profile-icc-warning-commanders-rape.

[52] N. Hayes, 'The Bemba Trial Judgement – A Memorable Day for the Prosecution of Sexual Violence by the ICC', PhD Students in Human Rights, 21 March 2016, humanrightsdoctorate.blogspot.com/2016/03/hayes-bemba-trial-judgement-memorable.html.

[53] Robinson, Justice in Extreme Cases, 257.

[54] *Bemba*, 'Defence Notice of Appeal against the Judgment pursuant to Article 74 of the Statute, ICC-01/05-01/08-3343', ICC-01/05-01/08-3348, Appeals Chamber, 4 April 2016.

[55] *Bemba* Appeals Judgment.

discussed, dissented from the decision to confirm the charges against the former Ivoirian President Laurent Gbagbo out of similar concerns. The three judges preferred to acquit the accused, despite the fact that Bemba's conviction had received generally favourable comments, than to compromise on their understanding of a high-quality legal process.

Specifically, the AC Majority took a novel approach to reviewing the findings of the TC, which enabled it to reach a different conclusion regarding the guilt of the appellant. The pre-existing standard of appellate review at the ICC was instituted by the *Lubanga* AC in 2014[56] and corresponded to the established practice of the UN tribunals.[57] The *Lubanga* AC concluded that the Appeals Chamber would not 'interfere' with the factual findings of the Trial Chamber unless 'it cannot discern how the Chamber's conclusion could have reasonably been reached from the evidence before it'.[58] This traditional standard of review, thus, gave 'a margin of deference' to the factual findings of the TC[59] and precluded the AC from assessing the evidence *de novo* with a view of determining whether it would have reached the same conclusion as the TC.[60] The *Bemba* AC Majority, however, were concerned with the impact of the traditional standard of review on the legality of proceedings[61] and highlighted that the RS nowhere provided for the notion of appellate deference.[62] In particular, the Majority did not share the opinion that the AC might interfere *only* when it could not discern how the TC reached its factual conclusions. Rather, according to the *Bemba* AC Majority, the appeals judges had the power to interfere with the factual findings of the TC to ensure the quality of the legal process.[63] Even though the AC Majority argued that the standard of review did not allow for simply substituting the TC's findings with those of the AC,[64] their novel approach enhanced the review powers of the appeals judges in a manner that proved decisive for the outcome of *Bemba*.

Based on this new standard of review, established in accordance with Majority of judges' understanding of the appropriate legal procedure, the

[56] *Bemba,* Dissenting Opinion of Judge Sanji Mmasenono Monageng and Judge Piotr Hofmański, ICC-01/05-01/08-3636-Anx1-Red, Appeals Chamber, 8 June 2018 (hereinafter *Bemba* Appeals Judgment Dissenting Opinion), § 3.

[57] *Lubanga* Appeals Judgment, § 27.

[58] Ibid., § 21.

[59] Ibid., § 22.

[60] Ibid., § 27.

[61] *Bemba* Appeals Judgment, § 38.

[62] Ibid., § 40.

[63] Ibid., § 40, emphasis added.

[64] Ibid., § 46.

AC overturned two major factual findings of the TC, resulting in Bemba's acquittal. The first issue concerned the precise scope of the charges. The Majority criticized the TC for entering a conviction based on what appeared as an exceptionally broad conduct – crimes perpetrated 'in the CAR' from '26 October 2002 to 15 March 2003'. According to the Majority, the broad language of the conviction appeared to cover 'potentially, *all* such crimes committed by MLC soldiers in a territory of more than 600,000 square kilometers and over a period of more than four and a half months'.[65] The Majority determined that Bemba should have been convicted only for those specific acts of murder, rape, and pillaging, which the TC had examined.[66] This emphasis on specificities and intolerance of general allegations echoed the concerns expressed several years earlier by Judge Ušacka at the *Lubanga* AC.[67] While Judge Ušacka expressed the minority position at the time, in *Bemba* the situation was reversed. Furthermore, the *Bemba* AC Majority concluded that not all of the specific criminal acts presented before the TC could be legitimately relied upon for the purpose of conviction. The prosecution had added evidence of further specific acts at trial.[68] The defence objected, arguing that because those acts were not included in the DCC or confirmed by the PTC, the defendant's right to fair notice was abrogated.[69] The TC had sided with the prosecution on the grounds that in cases in which the accused has been geographically remote from the scene of the crimes, 'it may not be possible to plead evidential details concerning the identity or number of victims, precise dates, or specific locations' in the DCC.[70] The AC Majority overthrew that reasoning and dismissed the 18 specific acts added by the prosecution at trial.[71] Thus, overall, the AC concluded that the correct scope of Bemba's conviction was limited to one murder, the rape of 20 persons, and five acts of pillaging, rather than the overall conduct of the MLC committed in the CAR in 2002–2003.[72]

Next, the AC Majority considered the link between the accused and those specific crimes.[73] As noted in Chapter 6, the *Bemba* AC considered that the key factor in determining whether a commander had taken all necessary and reasonable measures was their 'material ability' to do

[65] *Bemba* Appeals Judgment, § 103, emphasis in the original.
[66] Ibid., §§ 104–105.
[67] Chapter 7, Section 7.4.
[68] *Bemba* Trial Judgment, § 48.
[69] Ibid., § 38.
[70] Ibid., § 43.
[71] *Bemba* Appeals Judgment, §§ 115–116.
[72] Ibid., § 119.
[73] Ibid., § 194.

something about the crimes.[74] In particular, with regard to the Bemba, the Majority found that the TC had paid 'insufficient attention to the fact that the MLC troops were operating in a foreign country with the attendant difficulties on Mr Bemba's ability, as *a remote commander*, to take measures'.[75] The judges reasoned that the TC had disregarded certain pieces of information, which has resulted in an 'unrealistic assessment of the "wide range of available measures at his disposal"'.[76]

The Majority criticized the TC not merely for neglecting specific aspects of the case, but for allowing their personal convictions about Bemba's character to influence their assessment of his acts, namely, whether he had taken all necessary and reasonable measures concerning MLC crimes. The Majority criticized the TC for 'inappropriately' taking Bemba's motives into consideration when determining whether his measures were necessary and reasonable.[77] According to the Majority, the TC's 'preoccupation' with the idea that Bemba had only taken measures with regard to the MLC in order to protect the organization's public image had made Bemba's motives 'determinative, in and of themselves' of the adequacy of his measures.[78] Unlike the TC's 'inappropriate' approach, the AC Majority's 'dispassionate' and 'objective' assessment considered Bemba's motivations as irrelevant. From the Majority's perspective, Bemba's motives were neither 'intrinsically "negative"' nor necessarily preclusive of the effectiveness of the measures taken.[79] The Majority observed that while the TC seemed to imply that the limited effectiveness of the investigatory commissions was the result of Bemba's lack of genuine desire to address MLC's crimes, the trial judges made 'no such finding as to the sham nature of the measures'.[80] Rather, from the perspective of the Majority, the 'sham nature' seemed to be presumed by view of Bemba's dishonourable motives. Furthermore, the Majority noted that the TC had disregarded evidence of a letter by Bemba addressing the CAR Prime Minister and requesting an international commission of enquiry to be set up.[81] Once again, the Majority suggested that the reasons for dismissing that evidence were rooted in the trial judges' personal 'doubts' about its validity.[82]

[74] Ibid., § 167.
[75] Ibid., § 171, emphasis added.
[76] Ibid., § 731.
[77] Ibid., § 176.
[78] Ibid., § 178.
[79] Ibid., § 179.
[80] Ibid., § 181.
[81] Ibid., § 174.
[82] Ibid., § 175.

> Finally, the Majority recalled its previous finding that Bemba could have only been legitimately convicted for a limited number of specific crimes and not for the overall criminal conduct of the MLC in the CAR. Consequently, the Majority considered that a finding that a commander's measures were insufficient to address an 'extended crime wave' did not mean that those measures were also insufficient to address 'the limited number of specific crimes […] for which that commander is ultimately convicted'.[83]

Overall, the Majority concluded, the TC judges had led their preoccupation with Bemba's motivations and character traits to influence their assessment of the measures he had taken. For the AC Majority, this had resulted in a failure to appreciate that his actual ability to address MLC crimes had been significantly constrained due to the fact that he had acted as a 'remote commander'.[84] Consequently, the AC Majority determined that one of the elements of command responsibility – failure to take all necessary and reasonable measures – was not established beyond reasonable doubt[85] and so reversed the conviction.[86] A decade after the charges against him were confirmed, Bemba was acquitted.

In the context of the debates discussed in Chapter 3, The AC Majority's vision of the mandate and purpose of international criminal law reflects a strong desire to dissociate the practice of ICL from the influence of moral considerations and to assess criminal responsibility in a manner that the judges understood as dispassionate, rational, and detached from any considerations of the trial outcome. The Majority's reasoning presents a highly formalistic assessment of the facts. From this perspective, the identity or character of the individual accused might play a role in the moral judgments made in personal affairs but should not bear any implications on the assessment of their criminal responsibility by a public court.

The AC Majority's formalistic approach dismissed several factors that could have otherwise influenced an assessment of the defendant's guilt based on moral intuition. Bemba's concern for the MLC's public image was not the only morally questionable act of the accused that the Majority refused to take into consideration when assessing his criminal

[83] Ibid., § 183.
[84] Ibid., § 191–192.
[85] Ibid., § 194.
[86] Ibid., § 197.

responsibility. While in court, Bemba and members of his defence team also became involved in a witness tampering scandal, which resulted in the first ICC case for offences against the administration of justice under Article 70 RS.[87] The alleged plan between Bemba and members of his defence team involved bribing witnesses in exchange for false testimony and forging documents related to the main *Bemba* case. The prosecution claimed that Bemba evaded the ICC monitoring system and orchestrated the plan from the Detention Centre.[88] The TC convicted the accused of giving false testimony, presenting false evidence, and corruptly influencing witnesses. With the exception of the charge of presenting false testimony, which was reversed, the AC upheld the rest of the convictions against Bemba and the members of his defence team in March 2018.[89] Yet, only three months later the AC, with almost the same composition (with the exception of Judge Fernández de Gurmendi who was now replaced by Judge Van den Wyngaert), did not even mention the witness tampering case nor its potential impact on assessing whether Bemba had taken all necessary and reasonable measures to address the MLC's crimes. The prosecution filed a motion arguing that the 'toxic effects of the corrupt and tainted evidence' adduced by Bemba and his defence team influenced the decision of the AC to acquit him.[90] However, the TC in *Bemba et al.* noted that the witness tampering case had been 'clearly understood as independent from the Main Case' and found 'absolutely no indication' that the AC Majority had relied on evidence by the corrupted witnesses in acquitting Bemba. Rather, the TC recalled, the Majority had found 'other problems in the Main Case trial judgment'.[91] The fact that Bemba had tried to present a more favourable image of himself at trial through illegal means does not suggest that he was guilty of the crimes subject to the trial. However, from a moral or character-based perspective,[92] a conviction for giving false

[87] For a commentary see J. Nilsson, 'Prosecutor v. Bemba et al. Case No. ICC-01/05-01/13' (2018) 112(3) *American Journal of International Law* 473.

[88] *Bemba et al.*, Public Redacted version of 'Document Containing the Charges', ICC-01/05-01/13-526-AnxB1-Red, Pre-Trial Chamber II, 3 July 2014, §§ 3 and 23.

[89] *Bemba et al.*, Judgment on the appeals of Mr Jean-Pierre Bemba Gombo, Mr Aimé Kilolo Musamba, Mr Jean-Jacques Mangenda Kabongo, Mr Fidèle Babala Wandu and Mr Narcisse Arido against the decision of Trial Chamber VII entitled 'Judgment pursuant to Article 74 of the Statute', ICC-01/05-01/13-2275-Red, Appeals Chamber, 8 March 2018.

[90] *Bemba et al.*, Prosecution Detailed Notice of Additional Sentencing Submissions, ICC-01/05-01/13-2296, Trial Chamber VII, 2 July 2018, § 4.

[91] *Bemba et al.*, Decision Re-sentencing Mr Jean-Pierre Bemba Gombo, Mr Aimé Kilolo Musamba and Mr Jean-Jacques Mangenda Kabongo, Trial Chamber VII, 17 September 2018, §§ 23–24.

[92] Chapter 3, Section 3.2.3.

testimony and corrupting witnesses casts a shadow over the defendant, which could easily influence the perception of his responsibility for the underlying crimes, casting him as a person of questionable moral character. As discussed in Chapter 4, the moral intuition about the defendant's criminal responsibility and the reluctance to let them escape punishment through legal loopholes has been a major driver behind the development of ICL at previous tribunals. By leaving aside the witness tampering controversy, the AC judges demonstrated that their assessment of the facts was guided by nothing but strict procedure. What mattered were the specific acts or omissions of the accused in relation to the charges, and any consideration of his general behaviour seemed to be excluded.

8.1.4 The Politics of the Legal Field

8.1.4.1 Reactions to the AC Judgment

The *Bemba* AC Judgment quickly became one of the most discussed topics within the ICL field, triggering comments by ICC judges, legal experts outside the courts, and NGOs. The first ground for contestation turned out to be the novel standard of appellate review introduced by the AC Majority. Two of the AC judges, Judge Monageng and Judge Hofmański, dissented from the Majority decision. The dissenting judges preferred the pre-existing standard of appellate review, which gave a margin of deference to the findings of the TC, because they considered that the trial judges, having heard all the evidence presented at trial were better situated to assess the facts of the case compared to the AC.[93] Similar views were expressed by commentators outside the Court.[94] Judge Monageng and Judge Hofmański were concerned that the new standard introduced by the AC Majority in practice turned the appeal stage into 'a second trial'.[95]

The disagreement at the *Bemba* AC over the appropriate standard of appellate review reflects two different understandings of the legality principle: one prioritized the predictability of legal rules and the other one fairness towards the defendant. Judge Monageng and Judge Hofmański argued that 'predictability of the law' was 'essential for any court', and even more so at the ICC with its complex legal framework and a limited number of cases.[96]

[93] *Bemba* Appeals Judgment Dissenting Opinion, §§ 6–7.

[94] J. Trahan, 'Bemba Acquittal Rests on Erroneous Application of Appellate Review Standard', *OpinioJuris*, 25 June 2018, http://opiniojuris.org/2018/06/25/bemba-acquittal-rests-on-erroneous-application-of-appellate-review-standard/.

[95] *Bemba* Appeals Judgment Dissenting Opinion, § 7.

[96] Ibid., § 5.

The dissenting judges stressed that they were unaware of any international tribunal that applied a standard of review differently from the one previous affirmed by the *Lubanga* AC.[97] Legal commentators outside the Court similarly lamented that the *Bemba* AC Majority had not paid sufficient attention to the 'adherence to principles of certainty, consistency, and predictability'.[98] NGOs were similarly concerned about the new standard of review. In an interview, the Executive Director of WIGJ Melinda Reed noted that the innovative approach of the *Bemba* AC had raised significant uncertainty within the ICL field as to the applicable rules of appellate review.[99] By contrast, the *Bemba* AC Majority prioritized the protection of the defendant's right to a fair assessment of their alleged criminal responsibility over the desire to avoid the fragmentation of jurisprudence. The Majority argued that a more detailed engagement with the factual findings of the TC was required when 'the failure to interfere may occasion a miscarriage of justice'.[100] From this perspective, while the predictability of legal rules was important, it should not come at the expense of the quality of the legal process. One sympathetic commentator noted that, because unlike in national penal systems there is no further appellate body in ICL, the standard of review of the ICC AC 'needs to be designed in a way that protects the rights of the accused most effectively'.[101]

The *Bemba* AC Majority considered that *their* vision of ICL adjudication was the most consistent one with the requirements of criminal law trials:

> [T]he strong divergence in how we evaluate the Conviction Decision is not just a matter of difference of opinion, but appears to be a fundamental difference in the way we look at our mandates as international judges. ... While we do not presume to speak for our colleagues, it is probably fair to say that we attach more importance to the strict application of the burden and standard of proof. We also seem to put more emphasis on compliance with due process norms[.][102]

The bold exchanges between the AC Majority and the dissenting judges, thus, highlighted the tension between different visions coexisting within

97 Ibid., § 3.

98 J. Powderly, 'Introductory Note to Prosecutor v. Jean-Pierre Bemba Gombo: Judgment on the Appeal of Mr. Jean-Pierre Bemba Gombo against Trial Chamber III's "Judgment Pursuant to Article 74 of The Statute" (Int'l Crim. Ct.)' (2018) 57 *American Journal of International Law* 1031–1079, 1032.

99 Interview with Melinda Reed, Women's Initiatives for Gender Justice, The Hague, 15 May 2019.

100 *Bemba* Appeals Judgment, § 40, emphasis added.

101 A. Heinze, 'Some Reflections on the Bemba Appeals Chamber Judgment', OpinioJuris, 18 June 2018, http://opiniojuris.org/2018/06/18/some-reflections-on-the-bemba-appeals-chamber-judgment/.

102 *Bemba* Appeals Judgment Separate Opinion, § 4.

the ICL field of the mandate and purpose of international criminal justice. Notably, both sides of the debate advocated for greater respect for the principle of legality, but their understandings of what that principle entailed in practice led to competing interpretations of the applicable legal rules.

The second ground for contesting the Majority's decision was its approach to assessing Bemba's alleged criminal responsibility under Article 25(3)(a). One former member of the ICC prosecution team described the Majority's decision as 'a naïve and pointless act of formalism'.[103] Other legal experts criticized the Majority for articulating their version of command responsibility and applying it anew to the facts of the case.[104] Criticism of the AC judgment was particularly acute among those members of the ICL field interested not only in procedural, but also in substantive justice. NGOs concerned with the outcome of the trial for the affected communities, in terms of both reparations and the recognition of their suffering, called the decision 'a devastating outcome'[105] and 'an insult to the thousands of victims'.[106] More balanced reactions noted that while an acquittal was a 'legitimate outcome', given the limited number of cases going to trial at the ICC, the Majority's judgment raised questions regarding the functioning of the court in the eve of the 20th anniversary of the RS.[107] From this perspective, the mandate of the Court was understood in broader humanitarian terms – as having implications for the fate of the victims and the prevention of future atrocities.

By contrast, the *Bemba* AC Majority saw their mandate in very different terms. According to Judge Van den Wyngaert and Judge Morrison:

> Some may find our approach overly demanding and may think that it undervalues considerations of substantive justice. It is true that the strict application of, for example, the standard of proof, may in some cases lead to the acquittal of persons *who may actually be guilty* [...] While such instances are regrettable, we believe that they are *the price that must be paid* in order to uphold fundamental principles of fairness and the integrity of the judicial process.[108]

[103] A. Whiting, 'Appeals Judges Turn the ICC on Its Head with Bemba Decision', Just Security, 14 June 2018, www.justsecurity.org/57760/appeals-judges-turn-icc-head-bemba-decision/.

[104] See Amann, 'In Bemba and Beyond'. Sadat, 'Fiddling While Rome Burns'.

[105] REDRESS, 'Efforts to Afford Justice for Sexual Crimes in CAR Must Not Stop with Bemba's Acquittal', 8 June 2018, https://redress.org/news/efforts-to-afford-justice-for-sexual-crimes-in-car-must-not-stop-with-bembas-acquittal/.

[106] FIDH, 'Acquittal of Jean Pierre Bemba on Appeal: An Affront to Thousands of Victims', 8 June 2018, www.fidh.org/en/region/Africa/central-african-republic/acquittal-of-jean-pierre-bemba-on-appeal-an-affront-to-thousands-of.

[107] E. Keppler, 'No Redress for Central African Victims', Human Rights Watch, 11 June 2018, www.hrw.org/news/2018/06/11/no-redress-central-african-victims.

[108] *Bemba* Appeals Judgment, Judges Van den Wyngaert and Morrison Opinion, § 5, emphasis added.

This constitutes an exceptionally frank statement of the trade-off between procedural and substantive justice and a clear summary of one of the major normative cleavages dividing the ICL field. The judges clarified that their approach did not mean that they had failed to 'empathise with the pain and loss of the victims', but simply that such 'emotions' had no place in a legal assessment of the accused's alleged criminal responsibility.[109] In fact, the ICC took some measures to address victims' suffering. In 2018 the Trust Fund for Victims announced plans to launch a programme in the CAR aiming to assist the victims of the crimes subject to the *Bemba* case as well as gender-based crime victims throughout the country.[110] From the perspective of the *Bemba* AC Majority, concerns about the fate of the victims were important, but they were independent of the assessment of criminal responsibility.

The ardent contestation of the *Bemba* AC Judgment might detract attention from the fact that the AC Majority's reasoning found support from within the broader ICL field. Amnesty International commended the AC Majority for highlighting numerous 'concerning practices' by the PTC and the TC, which threatened the 'fairness' of ICC trials.[111] Some legal experts similarly concurred that the acquittal was the correct decision.[112] During interviews, criminal law experts upheld the reasoning forwarded by the Majority that an acquittal should not be perceived as a failure for the ICC but as a normal outcome and indication of the proper functioning of a criminal court.[113] From that perspective, the main problem with the *Bemba* case was the quality of the investigation. NGOs called on the OTP to enhance its efforts to conduct thorough investigations before initiating cases.[114] Other commentators focused on the investigative techniques of the former ICC prosecutor who had managed the *Bemba* investigation.[115]

[109] Ibid., § 79.

[110] ICC ASP, 'Report to the Assembly of States Parties on the Projects and the Activities of the Board of Directors of the Trust Fund for Victims for the Period 1 July 2017 to 30 June 2018', ICC-ASP/17/14, 23 July 2018, www.trustfundforvictims.org/sites/default/files/reports/ICC-ASP-17-14-ENG.pdf, 10.

[111] Amnesty International, 'Bemba Judgment Warrants Better Investigations and Fair Trials – Not Efforts to Discredit the decision', 19 June 2018, https://hrij.amnesty.nl/bemba-verdict-warrants-better-investigations-and-fair-trials/.

[112] Heinze, *Some Reflections*. K. J. Heller, 'Bim, Bam, Bem-Boom!', *OpinionJuris*, 12 March 2019, http://opiniojuris.org/2019/03/12/bim-bam-bemb-oom/.

[113] Interviews with Elies Van Sliedregt and Kai Ambos. *See also* Heinze, *Some Reflections*. Jackson, 'Commanders' Motivations' and Kai Ambos's commentary below the post.

[114] Amnesty International, 'Bemba Judgment Warrants Better Investigations'.

[115] J. H. Anderson, 'Ocampo's Shadow Still Hangs over the ICC', *International Justice Tribune*, 18 June 2018, www.justicetribune.com/blog/ocampos-shadow-still-hangs-over-icc.

Such comments indicated that the ICC judges' lack of sympathy for the prosecutor's evidentiary hurdles, discussed in Chapter 7,[116] was increasingly shared by members of the broader ICL field.

8.1.4.2 The Politics of the Legal Field v. State Politics

Even if it is difficult to assess the interests of all states in the region concerning the *Bemba* trial, as noted earlier in this chapter it appeared politically expedient for the DRC and CAR governments.[117] After the trial judgment, some commentators observed that Bemba's conviction prevented him from going back home and mobilizing political opposition in the DRC.[118] It was also speculated that Bemba's arrest was welcomed by the European states that were involved in the political dynamics of Central Africa.[119] Why did a case, which had been considered as expedient for both governments and the ICC, ended up in an acquittal after decade-long proceedings?

The simple legalist answer is that the evidence was insufficient to sustain the conviction. However, the analysis of the normative dynamics taking place within the ICL field suggests that the availability of evidence does not provide the full picture. Indeed, based on that same evidence in 2016, the TC unanimously convicted Bemba. The trial judgment, which did not trigger controversy within the ICL field at the time, rendered the 2018 acquittal a 'surpris[e]'.[120] The acquittal appears less surprising, however, when examined against the background of the normative tensions within the ICL field. The decision was firmly positioned in favour of strict criminal law procedure and against the incorporation of humanitarian concerns that, from the AC Majority's perspective, risked infringing upon the rights of the defendant.

[116] *See* Chapter 7, Section 7.4.

[117] Wakabi, 'Reactions to Bemba's Conviction'.

[118] T. Carayannis, 'Making Justice Work: The Bemba Case and the ICC's Future', Foreign Affairs, 5 April 2016, www.foreignaffairs.com/articles/central-african-republic/2016-04-05/making-justice-work. L. Seayand M. Broache, 'A Congolese Warlord Was Just Convicted. So Why Isn't Everyone Thrilled about It?', *Washington Post*, 24 March 2016, www.washingtonpost.com/news/monkey-cage/wp/2016/03/24/a-congolese-warlord-was-just-convicted-so-why-isnt-everyone-thrilled-about-it/.

[119] Carayannis, 'Making Justice Work'.

[120] M. Peniguet, 'CPI: Jean-Pierre Bemba, chronique d'un acquittement surprise', *Dalloz: Actualité*, 22 June 2018, www.dalloz-actualite.fr/flash/cpi-jean-pierre-bemba-chronique-d-un-acquittement-surprise#.XVJpfC2Q0zU. L. N. Sadat, 'Prosecutor v. Jean-Pierre Bemba Gombo. Case No. ICC-01/05-01/08. Appeals Judgment' (2018) 113(2) *American Journal of International Law* 353, 356.

Crucially, what might be less obvious is that the *Bemba* AC Judgment also reflected the normative tensions existing *within* criminal law practice. Notably, the common/civil law division did not play a significant role with respect to the *Bemba* AC decision – the AC Majority included representatives of both traditions. However, the Majority's approach reflected possibly the most pronounced separation to date of moral intuition and 'emotions' from 'rational' and impersonal criminal law in ICL. The Majority's decision reflected an understanding of the nature of criminal responsibility that clearly distinguished the acts or omissions of the defendant from any inquiries into the quality of their moral character. From that perspective, criminal responsibility was attributed based upon a person's wrongful choice (to act or omit an action), and it was not the purpose of criminal law to inquire whether that wrongful choice resulted from a bad character or not. As will be discussed in the next chapter in the context of the *Ongwen* case, the rationalistic, or choice-based, approach to criminal responsibility adopted at the ICC could also result in the opposite outcome – convicting the accused regardless of his prior victimization and its implications for the development of his moral character.

Thus, Bemba's acquittal illustrates the role of the internal politics of the ICL field, the debates concerning criminal responsibility, for the outcomes of ICC trials. The rest of this chapter discusses the equally intriguing dynamics that contributed to the acquittals of Gbagbo and Blé Goudé.

8.2 Gbagbo and Blé Goudé

The *Gbagbo and Blé Goudé* case presented a particularly politically favourable environment and a unique opportunity to hold accountable a high-profile defendant. The former Ivoirian president, Laurent Gbagbo, lost the support of other African or European governments, and the new Ivoirian government assisted the ICC investigation against him. But the majority of ICC judges were committed to a restrained application of the modes of liability and proved uncompromising in relation to the quality of the incriminating evidence. The prosecutor faced challenges already during the confirmation of charges proceedings. Eventually, the OTP was unable to convince the judges that Gbagbo or his former aid Charles Blé Goudé had participated in any way in the alleged crimes.

8.2.1 Case Background

The ICC has a long history of involvement in Côte d'Ivoire. After in 2003 the UN High Commissioner for Human Rights publicly mentioned the possibility of an ICC investigation into alleged human rights abuses in the country, the president Laurent Gbagbo personally requested the UN Security Council to refer the situation to the ICC for a 'competent' investigation that, he insisted, would clear him.[121] Even though Côte d'Ivoire was not an ICC State Party at the time, in a special Declaration the country accepted ICC jurisdiction over crimes committed after 19 September 2002.[122] Throughout the following years, Gbagbo's presidency was marked by significant domestic political polarization and increasingly deteriorating international legitimacy,[123] a situation that was described as 'neither war, nor peace'.[124]

When Gbagbo lost the 2010 elections to his opponent Alassane Ouattara and refused to cede power, violence rapidly escalated in Côte d'Ivoire and the ICC intervened.[125] During the post-election crisis, at least 3,000 people were killed, and more than 150 women were raped.[126] On 30th March 2011, the Security Council passed Resolution 1975 authorizing the UN Operation in Côte d'Ivoire (UNOCI) to take any measures necessary to protect civilians and on 11 April Gbagbo, his wife, and members of his staff were apprehended in the presidential residency.[127] In June 2011 the prosecutor requested an authorization to start a *proprio motu* investigation into the crimes committed during the period of post-election violence in Côte d'Ivoire.[128]

The request was granted by the PTC[129] and the court soon issued arrest warrants against Laurent Gbagbo,[130] his wife Simone Gbagbo,[131] and

121 M. McGovern, 'Proleptic Justice: The Threat of Investigation as a Deterrent to Human Rights Abuses in Côte d'Ivoire', in K. M. Clarke and M. Goodale (eds.) *Mirrors of Justice: Law and Power in the Post-Cold War Era* (New York: Cambridge University Press, 2009) 67, 71–72.

122 Situation in Côte d'Ivoire, Prosecution's provision of further information regarding potentially relevant crimes committed between 2002 and 2010, ICC-02/11-25, Pre-Trial Chamber III, 3 November 2011, § 1.

123 B. Charbonneau, 'War and Peace in Côte d'Ivoire: Violence, Agency, and the Local/International Line' (2012) 19(4) *International Peacekeeping* 508, 512–516.

124 M. MacGovern, *Making war in Côte d'Ivoire* (London: Hurst, 2011), 203–204.

125 Rosenberg, 'International Criminal Court', 477.

126 Human Rights Watch, '"They Killed Them Like It Was Nothing" The Need for Justice for Côte d'Ivoire's Post-Election Crimes' (2011) www.hrw.org/sites/default/files/reports/cdi1011webwcover_0.pdf, 4.

127 A. Novosseloff, 'United Nations Operation in Côte d'Ivoire (UNOCI)', in J. A. Koops, T. Tardy, N. MacQueen, and P. D. Williams (eds.) *The Oxford Handbook of United Nations Peacekeeping Operations* (Oxford: Oxford University Press, 2015) 707, 713–714.

128 Situation in Côte d'Ivoire, Request for authorisation of an investigation pursuant to article 15, 23 June 2011, ICC-02/11-3, Pre-Trial Chamber III, 23 June 2011, § 1.

129 Situation in Côte d'Ivoire, Corrigendum to 'Decision Pursuant to Article 15 of the RS on the Authorisation of an Investigation into the Situation in the Republic of Côte d'Ivoire', ICC-02/11-14-Corr, Pre-Trial Chamber III, 15 November 2011, § 212.

130 *Gbagbo*, Warrant of Arrest for Laurent Koudou Gbagbo, ICC-02/11-01/11-1, Pre-trial Chamber III, 23 November 2011.

131 *Simone Gbagbo*, Warrant of Arrest for Simone Gbagbo, ICC-02/11-01/12-1, Pre-Trial Chamber III, 29 February 2012.

Charles Blé Goudé.[132] Simone was a 'prominent figure' within Gbagbo's political party, the *Front populaire ivoirien* (Ivorian Popular Front) (FPI).[133] Charles Blé Goudé was Minister of Youth during Gbagbo's presidency and controlled youth organizations such as the *Fédération estudiantine et scolaire de Côte d'Ivoire* .[134] Blé Goudé was surrendered to the Court in March 2014.[135]

The only suspect who did not reach the ICC was Simone Gbagbo. The Ivoirian government initially provided full assistance to the ICC investigation but refused to surrender Simone Gbagbo to the Court and held two domestic trials against her instead. Some commentators observed that Simone's eventual acquittal by the Ivoirian court appeared as an attempt by the government to 'foster appeasement' among the political opposition in Côte d'Ivoire.[136] Others suggested that by suddenly positioning itself in favour of domestic proceedings, the Côte d'Ivoire government indirectly tried to shelter key members of the ruling coalition from future ICC indictments.[137]

The complex political environmental enabled the ICC to proceed with the trials of only two of the three suspects. Nevertheless, those persons provided the Court with a unique opportunity to demonstrate that high-level political figures were not immune to criminal responsibility. But given the ICC's restrained approach to criminal responsibility, despite the lack of political opposition towards the trials of Gbagbo and Blé Goudé, the question of the defendants' guilt was far from resolved.

8.2.2 *Pre-trial: Myriad of Inferences*

The *Gbagbo and Blé Goudé* case presented a clear illustration of the difficulties created for the prosecutor by the ICC judges' narrow reading of the

[132] *Blé Goudé*, Warrant of Arrest for Charles Blé Goudé, ICC-02/11-02/11-1, Pre-Trial Chamber III, 25 December 2011.

[133] *Simone Gbagbo*, Decision on the Prosecutor's Application Pursuant to Article 58, ICC-02/11-01/12-2-Red, Pre-Trial Chamber III, 2 March 2012, § 15.

[134] *Blé Goudé*, Decision on the Prosecutor's Application Pursuant to Article 58 for a warrant of arrest against Charles Blé Goudé, ICC-02/11-02/11-3, Pre-Trial Chamber III, 06 January 2012 (hereinafter *Blé Goudé* Arrest Warrant Decision), § 15.

[135] *Blé Goudé* Confirmation Decision, § 4.

[136] E. A. Semien, 'Simone Gbagbo Acquitted by the Abidjan Assize Court: Between the Independence of the Judiciary and a Political Twist to Save the Day', International Justice Monitor, 5 May 2017, www.ijmonitor.org/2017/05/simone-gbagbo-acquitted-by-the-abidjan-assize-court-between-the-independence-of-the-judiciary-and-a-political-twist-to-save-the-day/.

[137] S. Straus, '" It's Sheer Horror Here': Patterns of Violence During the First Four Months of Côte d'Ivoire's Post-Electoral Crisis' (2011) 110(440) *African Affairs* 481, 178–179. P. Clark, Distant Justice, 291.

'control' theory. The cases against Laurent Gbagbo and Blé Goudé involved almost identical charges of crimes against humanity, including murder, rape, persecution, and inhumane acts.[138] The charges involved several major accidents, including the attack on demonstrators at the building of the state-sponsored radio-television *Radiodiffusion Télevision Ivoirienne* (RTI), which was carried out by the Ivorian Defence and Security Forces (FDS), the attack against a pro-Ouattara women's demonstration in the Abobo commune in Abidjan, the shelling of a densely populated area near the Abobo market by the security forces under Gbagbo's alleged command, and the attack on civilians in the Yopougon commune in Abidjan by youth organizations, militia, and mercenaries.[139] Subsequently, another attack on Yopougon was added to the charges against Blé Goudé.[140]

Establishing the link between high-level officials such as the former Ivoirian president and the crimes on the ground, however, proved particularly challenging to the prosecutor. There was no conclusive evidence that Gbagbo was *directly* involved in the alleged crimes. For example, the prosecution relied on evidence that Gbagbo had told the armed forces during the RTI demonstration to 'Deal with the situation'[141] and had 'declared that the FDS must not lose Abobo'.[142] Yet, none of those statements constituted explicit orders from Gbagbo to the forces on the ground to commit specific crimes.[143] Considering the preference of ICC judges for specificity rather than general allegations, the prosecution's evidentiary hurdles presented an important obstacle to sustaining the charges.

Notably, the prosecutor relied on the 'control over the crime' theory to build a complex case against Laurent Gbagbo that aimed to link the accused to the physical perpetrators of the crimes. The OTP alleged that the former president was an indirect co-perpetrator, who had planned and executed the crimes alongside Blé Goudé, Simone Gbagbo, and other members of

138 *Gbagbo*, Public redacted version of 'Decision on the Prosecutor's Application Pursuant to Article 58 for a warrant of arrest against Laurent Koudou Gbagbo', ICC-02/11-01/11-9-Red, Pre-Trial Chamber III, 30 November 2011, § 4. *Blé Goudé* Arrest Warrant Decision, § 4.

139 *Laurent Gbagbo*, 'Annexe 1 Publique Document amendé de notification des charges', ICC-02/11-01/11-592-Anx1, Pre-Trial Chamber I, 13 January 2014 (hereinafter *Gbagbo* Amended DCC), § 217–219.

140 *Blé Goudé* Confirmation Decision, § 26.

141 *Gbagbo*, Confirmation of Charges Hearing, Transcript 17, ICC-02/11-01/11-T-17-Red-ENG, 22 February 2013, Pre-Trial Chamber I (hereinafter *Gbagbo* PTC Hearing (Transcript 17)), p. 10, lines 14–16.

142 Ibid., p. 13, line 10.

143 *Gbagbo*, Decision on the Confirmation of Charges against Laurent Gbagbo, Dissenting Opinion of Judge Christine Van den Wyngaert, ICC-02/11-01/11-656-Anx, Pre-Trial Chamber I, 12 June 2014 (hereinafter *Gbagbo* Confirmation Decision, Dissenting Opinion), 7.

his entourage,[144] or 'inner circle'.[145] The physical perpetrators of the crimes that Gbagbo and his inner circle allegedly controlled were generally identified as the 'pro-Gbagbo forces' and included the FDS, which comprised the National Armed Forces of Côte d'Ivoire, the Gendarmerie, the Republican Guard, the Security Operations Command Centre, and the Police,[146] pro-Gbagbo youth organizations, militias, and mercenaries.[147]

Thus, the OTP linked Gbagbo to the alleged common plan among him and his 'inner circle' rather than to specific crimes. The rationale behind that approach was the *Lubanga* PTC's finding that the 'common plan' did not have to be itself criminal but could be aimed at a political goal and only include an element of criminality.[148] While Gbagbo's direct involvement in the crimes on the ground was hard to establish, there was abundant evidence of Gbagbo's intention to stay in power as the President of Côte d'Ivoire,[149] including numerous public statements made by him and Simone.[150] The fact that Gbagbo had refused to accept the 2010 electoral results and had boycotted the domestic political opposition and the international community for months, until he was forced out of power, further demonstrated his intent to stay in power. Consequently, the OTP alleged that once the former president and his inner circle realized that they were about to lose the elections, they agreed to a common plan to retain power by all means, including through the use of force against civilians.[151] Specifically, the prosecution argued: 'Even if Mr Gbagbo did not always issue concrete orders, or express orders, he was at the center of all decisions that led to the implementation of the common plan and to the commission of the crimes charged'.[152] Notably, the prosecution relied in this line of reasoning to link Gbagbo even to events that had taken place after his arrest, namely the 12 April attack in Yopougon. The prosecution submitted that those crimes had occurred as 'the continuation of the implementation of the common plan' Gbagbo had allegedly set in motion[153] and consequently, argued that Gbagbo bore

[144] *Gbagbo* Amended DCC, §§ 74–78.
[145] *Gbagbo* Confirmation Decision, § 78.
[146] *Gbagbo* Amended DCC, § 40.
[147] *Gbagbo* Amended DCC, § 4.
[148] *See* Chapter 6, Section 6.2.1.1.
[149] *Gbagbo* Confirmation Decision, § 110.
[150] Ibid., §§ 111–116.
[151] *Gbagbo* Amended DCC, § 39. *Gbagbo and Blé Goudé,* Trial Hearing, Transcript ICC-02/11-01/15-T-9-ENG, Trial Chamber I, 28 January 2016, p. 57, lines 7-9.
[152] *Gbagbo* PTC Hearing (Transcript 17), p. 8, lines 7–9.
[153] *Gbagbo and Blé Goudé,* Trial Hearing, Transcript ICC-02/11-01/15-T-10-ENG, Trial Chamber I, 29 January 2016, p. 34, line 18.

principal liability under Article 25(3)(a) RS for the crimes. Therefore, the prosecution's case relied on a broad interpretation of the notion of 'common plan': a political plan that accepted the risk of harming civilians in the pursuit of its main goal – to keep Gbagbo in power.

Another challenge that the prosecution had to address was establishing that Gbagbo had enjoyed control over the various groups that allegedly comprised the pro-Gbagbo forces. As the president, Gbagbo enjoyed authority over the FDS.[154] But no similar links seemed to exist between Gbagbo and the youth organizations, the militias, and the mercenaries. The OTP relied on the indirect co-perpetration mode of liability to link the accused to those crimes that were committed by persons who were not under Gbagbo's direct control. The indirect co-perpetration mode enabled the mutual attribution of the crimes to each indirect co-perpetrator, even if only one of them had enjoyed control over the physical perpetrators of the crimes.[155] Specifically, the OTP alleged that Gbagbo had 'controlled' the youth organizations 'through Blé Goudé.'[156] Blé Goudé was presented as the leader of the pro-Gbagbo youth who had extraordinary power to mobilize them.[157] Furthermore, Blé Goudé was allegedly involved with the militias[158] and the recruitment and funding of mercenaries to support the pro-Gbagbo forces.[159] Hence, Blé Goudé's link with those elements of the pro-Gbagbo's forces was used to infer Gbagbo's control over the crimes. Another alleged co-perpetrator, Gbagbo's wife Simone, also played an important role in the prosecution's arguments. The testimony of several witnesses and Simone's diary, seized from the Presidential Residence, suggested a 'direct relationship' between her and youth and militia leaders.[160] On this line of reasoning, it seemed reasonable that Simone had coordinated her activities with her husband[161] and that the crimes committed by forces under her control could be attributed to Gbagbo. Thus, a key element of the prosecution's arguments were Laurent Gbagbo's links to other persons who had been in close contact with the direct perpetrators of the crimes.

[154] *Gbagbo* Confirmation Decision, § 96.

[155] *Katanga and Ngudjolo* Confirmation Decision, § 493, §§ 519–520.

[156] *Gbagbo* PTC Hearing (Transcript 17), p. 15, lines 14–15.

[157] *Blé Goudé*, 'Annexe 1 Publique Version corrigée de ICC-02/11-02/11-124-Anx1 Document de notification des charges', ICC-02/11-02/11-124-Anx1-Corr, Pre-Trial Chamber I, 27 August 2014 (hereinafter *Blé Goudé* DCC), 231.

[158] *Blé Goudé* DCC, § 236.

[159] Ibid., § 257.

[160] *Gbagbo* Confirmation Decision, para, 82.

[161] Ibid., § 80.

Thus, the prosecution stretched the notion of 'control over the crime' to bring charges of principal liability against Gbagbo and his aid Blé Goudé. Nevertheless, presumably sensing the ICC judges' increasingly restrained approach to principal liability, the OTP attempted to rely on modes of accessory liability as a back-up for securing the charges in case the judges dismissed the charges under Article 25(3)(a). In the *Gbagbo* DCC, the prosecutor listed several alternative modes of liability pursuant to which the accused could be linked to the crimes, including accessory liability under Article 25(3)(b) and (d) and command responsibility under Article 28.[162] Similarly, the *Blé Goudé* DCC proposed that, in the alternative, the defendant's responsibility could be examined under Article 25(3)(b)–(d).[163] Essentially, the prosecutor used 'every possible liability mode' at her disposal to link the accused to the crimes.[164]

Even though the charges against the accused were eventually confirmed,[165] the PTC judges did not make that easy for the prosecutor, thus, demonstrating their commitment to protecting the defendants' rights. Like their colleagues in *Mbarushimana* and *Ngudjolo*, the PTC judges in *Gbagbo* were very demanding of the quality of the incriminating evidence. The *Gbagbo* PTC expressed 'serious concern' that the prosecution had 'relied heavily on NGO reports and press articles', generally based on anonymous hearsay,[166] which placed a burden on the defence in assessing the trustworthiness of that information.[167] While previous international tribunals had occasionally relied on evidence of questionable quality, the ICC PTC considered that type of evidence unfit for criminal proceedings. The judges concluded that the prosecution's evidence was 'apparently insufficient' to proceed to trial and adjourned the confirmation of charges hearing until the OTP collected more evidence.[168] Only after the OTP submitted an amended DCC,[169] in 2014 the PTC confirmed, by majority, the charges against Gbagbo.[170]

[162] *Gbagbo* Amended DCC, § 6.

[163] *Blé Goudé* DCC, § 171.

[164] G. Knoops, 'Introductory Note', in G. Z. Capaldo (ed.) *The Global Community of International Law and Jurisprudence 2015* (New York: Oxford University Press, 2016) 379, 389.

[165] *Gbagbo* Confirmation Decision. *Blé Goudé* Confirmation Decision.

[166] *Gbagbo*, Decision adjourning the hearing on the confirmation of charges pursuant to article 61(7)(c)(i) of the RS, ICC-02/11-01/11-432, Pre-Trial Chamber I, 3 June 2013, § 35.

[167] Ibid., § 29.

[168] Ibid., § 15.

[169] *Gbagbo* Confirmation Decision, § 11.

[170] Ibid., § 230.

The OTP also faced challenges in the *Blé Goudé* case, this time resulting from the judges' strict interpretation of the notion of 'control'. Unlike the former head of state, Blé Goudé appeared more directly connected to some of the physical perpetrators of the crimes, especially to the pro-Gbagbo youth. The prosecution argued that Blé Goudé controlled the actions of the pro-Gbagbo youth: 'When he called upon them, the youth, they acted'.[171] To support the allegation that Blé Goudé controlled the youth, the prosecution emphasized his 'charisma' and 'oratorical skills'.[172] The prosecution alleged that Blé Goudé used those skills to incite the youth to commit violence. There was available evidence of Blé Goudé's 'inflammatory and xenophobic statements' against the internal opposition, namely the pro-Ouattara supporters, and against external actors, including France, the European Union, the United States, the UN, and the Economic Community of West African States (CEDEAO).[173] Consequently, the PTC Majority confirmed the indirect co-perpetration charges against the accused in relation to the crimes that were committed by the youths and militias who had been allegedly acting under Blé Goudé's control during the two attacks on Yopougon.[174] Yet, the facts submitted by the prosecution left unclear whether Blé Goudé's alleged charismatic influence over the pro-Gbagbo youth amounted to actual 'control' over an organized apparatus. While the evidence managed to convince the PTC Majority to refer the case to trial, as will be discussed, the prosecution's inability to establish a more specific link between Blé Goudé and the criminal incidents proved an obstacle to sustain the charges at trial.

Blé Goudé's link to another element of the pro-Gbagbo forces, the FDS, was even less evident. The prosecutor argued that the accused had participated in the integration of some of the pro-Gbagbo youth into the armed forces. Blé Goudé allegedly 'played a key role in recruiting, arming, training and integrating thousands of volunteers and enlisting them into the FDS chain of command'.[175] The prosecution noted that youths had been incorporated within the FDS in 2003 to form the so-called 'contingent Blé Goudé'.[176] According to the prosecution, the members of Blé Goudé's

171 *Gbagbo and Blé Goudé,* Trial Hearing, Transcript ICC-02/11-01/15-T-9-ENG, Trial Chamber I, 28 January 2016 (hereinafter *Gbagbo and Blé Goudé,* Trial Hearing (Transcript 9)), p. 45, lines 2–3.

172 Ibid., p. 59, lines 15–17, *Blé Goudé,* Arrest Warrant, § 15.

173 *Blé Goudé* Confirmation Decision, §§ 96–97.

174 *Blé Goudé* Confirmation Decision, § 158.

175 *Blé Goudé,* Arrest Warrant Decision, § 33. *See also Blé Goudé* DCC, § 179.

176 *Blé Goudé* DCC, § 179.

contingent were 'the most violent elements within the forces' who they enjoyed impunity for their crimes.[177]

But the PTC judges were not convinced that Blé Goudé had enjoyed control over the alleged FDS crimes. The obstacle to confirming the charges was the judges' narrow interpretation of the 'essential contribution' element of the 'control over the crime' theory. Consistent with the findings of the *Lubanga* PTC,[178] the pre-trial judges in *Blé Goudé* considered that the notion of control required proof that without the accused's contribution the commission of the crime would have been frustrated. The PTC concluded that the crimes committed during 'primarily FDS operations', including the repression of the RTI demonstration and the Abobo attacks, would not have been frustrated without Blé Goudé's contribution.[179] Nevertheless, the PTC Majority confirmed the charges related to those incidents under modes of accessory liability pursuant to Article 25(3)(b)–(d).[180] But one of the three PTC judges remained sceptical that the prosecutor's evidence was sufficient to sustain those charges in future proceedings.

Judge Van den Wyngaert issued dissenting opinions in both the *Gbagbo* and the *Blé Goudé* cases. In *Gbagbo*, Judge Van den Wyngaert argued that in view of the persistent evidentiary deficiencies in the *Gbagbo* case, there was 'no point in confirming the charges' against the accused.[181] Reluctant to employ a broad interpretation of the 'common plan' element of liability, the Judge expressed concern that there was an 'explici[t] or implicit[t]' criminal element of the alleged common plan between Gbagbo and his inner circle.[182] Furthermore, she was not persuaded that Gbagbo's public statements merited the conclusion that he had given his supporters a carte blanche to commit crimes and noted that there was no evidence of orders emanating directly from Gbagbo concerning those crimes.[183] Finally, the Judge was unconvinced that the evidence had met the restrained interpretation of Article 30 accepted in ICC jurisprudence. She noted that the evidence might have been sufficient to conclude that by deploying armed forces Gbagbo had 'created a risk' that civilians might be harmed and 'accepted' that risk, which Judge Van den Wyngaert considers an example

[177] *Gbagbo* PTC Hearing (Transcript 17), p. 20, lines 12–14.
[178] *See* Chapter 6, Section 6.2.1.1.
[179] *Blé Goudé* Confirmation Decision, § 148.
[180] Ibid., § 161, § 171, § 181.
[181] *Gbagbo* Confirmation Decision Dissenting Opinion, § 4.
[182] Ibid., § 5.
[183] Ibid., §§ 5–6.

of the *dolus eventualis* standard. However, the Judge reasoned that since *dolus eventualis* was not accepted at the Court and the evidence was insufficient to conclude that the rapes and murders were foreseeable 'in the ordinary course of events', the mental element of Gbagbo's liability had not been established.[184]

Judge Van den Wyngaert was also unconvinced that Blé Goudé could be considered a principal perpetrator under Article 25(3)(a) in relation to any of the crimes that constituted the charges, including those involving the pro-Gbagbo youth,[185] because, in her words, Blé Goudé had not been 'at the appropriate level' to control the commission of those crimes.[186] Furthermore, Judge Van den Wyngaert was unpersuaded that Blé Goudé bore any form of responsibility, either principal, or accessory, for the crimes committed by the FDS units in Abobo.[187] In her opinion, the evidence did not provide 'any meaningful information' as to Blé Goudé's involvement in those incidents[188] or to his powers over the FDS.[189]

Demonstrating a belief in the separation of morality from legality, Judge Van den Wyngaert stressed that she did not deny that 'horrendous crimes' were committed by forces loyal to Laurent Gbagbo. But in her opinion, the mandate of the judges at the ICC was limited to assessing whether the allegations against the accused, 'as formulated by the prosecutor' were sufficiently strong to go to trial.[190] Hence, Judge Van den Wyngaert upheld the understanding that, as a criminal court, the ICC should be first and foremost concerned with the defendant's right to a fair trial and not with the plight of the victims, an understanding that was also shared by the *Gbagbo and Blé Goudé* TC Majority.

8.2.3 *Trial: No Case to Answer*

In March 2015 the cases against Gbagbo and Blé Goudé were joined.[191] Over the course of two years, from January 2016 to January 2018, the OTP

[184] Ibid., §§ 5–6 and footnote 6.

[185] *Blé Goudé*, Confirmation of Charges Decision, Partly Dissenting Opinion of Judge Christine Van den Wyngaert, ICC-02/11-02/11-186-Anx, PTC I, 11 December 2014, § 2.

[186] Ibid., § 7.

[187] Ibid., §§ 3–4.

[188] Ibid., § 4.

[189] Ibid., § 7.

[190] *Gbagbo* Confirmation Decision Dissenting Opinion, § 12.

[191] *Gbagbo and Blé Goudé,* Decision on Prosecution requests to join the cases of The Prosecutor v. Laurent Gbagbo and The Prosecutor v. Charles Blé Goudé and related matters, ICC-02/11-01/15-1, Trial Chamber I, 11 March 2015.

presented its arguments against the accused.[192] Following the prosecutor's presentation, the defence teams of both accused filed requests to acquit their clients from all charges on the grounds that the OTP had not proven their allegations.[193] Notably, the prosecution also seemed to be aware that the available evidence could not support all charges and agreed with the defence that the charges against Blé Goudé concerning the Abobo attacks can be dismissed.[194]

The TC Majority's narrow approach to criminal responsibility, displaying the judges' determination to comply strictly with the culpability principle, resulted in the dismissal of the rest of the charges. In January 2019 the TC Majority decided that the prosecution's evidence was insufficient to establish beyond reasonable doubt any of OTP's allegations.[195] Notably, the judges were so sceptical of the OTP's complex arguments that they dismissed the charges without even providing the Defence with the opportunity to refute the prosecution's allegations.[196] The judges considered that there was 'no need for the Defence to submit further evidence as the Prosecutor has not satisfied the burden of proof in relation to several core constitutive elements of the crimes as charged'.[197] In other words, the ICC judges concluded that there was 'no case' for the defendant to 'answer' because the OTP had not succeeded in presenting convincing arguments against the accused. The written reasons for the Majority's decision were filed half a year later. The reasons presented by Judge Henderson[198] and the opinion of Judge Tarfusser, who concurred with his

[192] *Gbagbo and Blé Goudé*, 'Reasons for oral decision of 15 January 2019 on the Requête de la Défense de Laurent Gbagbo afin qu'un jugement d'acquittement portant sur toutes les charges soit prononcé en faveur de Laurent Gbagbo et que sa mise en liberté immédiate soit ordonnée, and on the Blé Goudé Defence no case to answer motion', ICC-02/11-01/15-1263, Trial Chamber I, 16 July 2019, § 20.

[193] *Gbagbo and Blé Goudé*, 'Version corrigée de la «Requête de la Défense de Laurent Gbagbo afin qu'un jugement d'acquittement portant sur toutes les charges soit prononcé en faveur de Laurent Gbagbo et que sa mise en liberté immédiate soit ordonnée».', ICC-02/11-01/15-1199-Corr, Trial Chamber I, 25 September 2018. *Gbagbo and Blé Goudé*, 'Public Redacted Version of "Corrigendum to the 'Blé Goudé Defence No Case to Answer Motion' (ICC-02/11-01/15-1198-Conf), 23 July 2018," 3 August 2018, ICC- 02/11-01/15-1198-Conf-Corr', ICC-02/11-01/15-1198-Corr-Red, Trial Chamber I, 28 September 2018.

[194] *Gbagbo and Blé Goudé*, 'PUBLIC: With Confidential Annex 1 and Confidential Annexes A and B Prosecution's Response to Defence No Case to Answer Motions', ICC-02/11-01/15-1207, Trial Chamber I, 10 September 2018, § 25.

[195] *Gbagbo and Blé Goudé*, Delivery of Decision, ICC-02/11-01/15-T-232-ENG ET WT, Trial Chamber I, 15 January 2019.

[196] Ibid., p. 3 lines 2–4.

[197] Ibid.

[198] *Gbagbo and Blé Goudé* Reasons of Judge Henderson.

colleague's findings,[199] comprised more than a thousand pages, demonstrating that, despite the delay, the Majority had not taken an impulsive decision acquitting the accused and had given sufficient thought regarding the evidence presented by the prosecution.

Like in *Bemba*, an analysis that focuses only on the state-politics context of the *Gbagbo and Blé Goudé* trial fails to provide insights into their outcome. The Ivoirian government had cooperated with the OTP and the Court could have used the trial to demonstrate its capability to hold accountable high-profile persons in front of state parties and human rights advocates. An inspection of the normative dynamics of the ICL field provides insights into the decision to acquit the two accused. The analysis of the reasons for the acquittal, presented by Judge Henderson, Judge Tarfusser concurring,[200] supports the conclusion that many ICC judges had developed an internal shared understanding about the role of the court in the international society. From the perspective of the judges, procedural excellence, regardless of the trial outcome, constituted the antidote to false information. Judge Henderson explained that in the era of 'fake news' it was important that the judiciary maintained its 'rationality and transparency' by giving sound and well-reasoned decisions.[201] A similar comment was made in 2018 by the *Bemba* AC Majority.[202] Hence, unlike previous international tribunals, which had sought to balance procedural with substantive justice, many ICC judges considered that a criminal court should be concerned only with the quality of the process, regardless of the trial outcome. As the following sections discuss, the *Gbagbo and Blé Goudé* TC Majority employed a narrow approach to criminal responsibility that resulted in the accused's acquittal, despite the availability of state cooperation during the investigations.

8.2.3.1 The Charges of Principal Liability

The TC Majority, first, expressed concern about the quality of the presented evidence. The judges concluded that the prosecutor's case suffered from 'pervasive' evidentiary problems[203] and noted that most

[199] *Gbagbo and Blé Goudé* 'Opinion of Judge Cuno Tarfusser', ICC-02/11-01/15-1263-AnxA Trial Chamber I, 16 July 2019 (hereinafter *Gbagbo and Blé Goudé*, Opinion of Judge Tarfusser), § 1.

[200] *Gbagbo and Blé Goudé*, Opinion of Judge Tarfusser, § 1.

[201] *Gbagbo and Blé Goudé* Reasons of Judge Henderson, § 4.

[202] See *Bemba Appeals Judgment*, Judges Van den Wyngaert and Morrison Opinion, § 5.

[203] *Gbagbo and Blé Goudé* Reasons of Judge Henderson, § 36. See also *Gbagbo and Blé Goudé* Opinion of Judge Tarfusser, § 89.

documentary exhibits would not have passed 'even the most rudimentary admissibility test in many domestic systems',[204] especially considering that an 'extraordinary amount of evidence' rested upon anonymous hearsay.[205] Thus, consistent with their colleagues in *Mbarushimana* and *Ngudjolo*, the TC Majority in *Gbagbo and Blé Goudé* was reluctant to ease the burden of proof on the prosecutor by view of the challenges of investigating mass atrocities. From this perspective, a criminal trial had to comply with strict standards of procedure, regardless of whether it took place at the domestic or the international level.

Like Judge Van den Wyngaert, the TC Majority were also concerned that the available evidence did not match the requirements of the 'control' theory. The Majority were critical of the fact that '[u]pon the pretext that the Common Plan/policy must not be exclusively' criminal, the OTP had presented a lot of evidence regarding the non-criminal aspects of Gbagbo's alleged plan to stay in power, but offered nothing to specifically prove the criminal elements of that plan.[206] The TC Majority were determined not to let the prosecutor play a 'cat and mouse game with the content (and putative criminality)' of the common plan on which depended the imputation of crimes to the accused.[207]

Judge Henderson was also not convinced that the prosecutor's evidence demonstrated Gbagbo's 'control' over the 'pro-Gbagbo forces', which the accused had allegedly exercised through the main FDS chain of command and through 'parallel' structures.[208] The Judge considered such claims paradoxical. In his opinion, if the FDS was an organized apparatus that ensured automatic compliance with the leadership's orders, there would be no need for a parallel structure of command. Conversely, if the establishment of the parallel structure was necessary to ensure the 'inner circle's' control over the troops, then all FDS crimes that were not commanded through the parallel structure of control could not be attributed to the accused.[209] The judges were also not convinced that the accused had been to control the variety of groups, such as youths and militias, that had allegedly 'complemented' the FDS.[210] Consequently, while the notion of 'control' may seem abstract and broad, in *Gbagbo and Blé Goudé* the

[204] *Gbagbo and Blé Goudé* Reasons of Judge Henderson, § 36.
[205] Ibid., §§ 42–43.
[206] Ibid., § 85.
[207] Ibid., § 85.
[208] *Gbagbo* Amended DCC, § 143. *Gbagbo* Confirmation Decision, § 96.
[209] *Gbagbo and Blé Goudé* Reasons of Judge Henderson, § 1923.
[210] Ibid., § 1902.

judges interpreted all inconsistencies in the OTP's allegations concerning the accused's control over the crimes in favour of the accused, following their narrow understanding of criminal responsibility rules.

In effect, the prosecutor failed to meet key requirements of the indirect co-perpetration mode of liability.[211] Advocates of the narrow interpretation of the culpability principle, from both inside and outside the Court, had previously expressed concern that indirect co-perpetration was a tool for relaxing the link between the accused and the crime.[212] However, the *Gbagbo and Blé Goudé* TC demonstrated significant restraint with respect to that mode of liability and did not accept the prosecution's submissions, which relied on a very broad interpretation of the term 'control over the crime'.

8.2.3.2 The Charges of Accessory Liability and Command Responsibility

The TC could have, nevertheless, sustained the charges of accessory liability, including under Articles 25(3)(b)–(d) and 28 RS, which posed lower requirements than the modes of principal liability. Indeed, Article 28 appeared particularly relevant for describing the responsibility of a high-level official, such as the former head of state, who had not personally taken part in the criminal activities. But while Judge Herrera-Carbuccia found that approach legally sound, the TC Majority remained committed to strict compliance with the principles of criminal law and dismissed the charges of accessory liability against the two accused.

The Majority was unwilling to rely on broad modes of accessory liability, which had previously triggered concern among the proponents of strict legality in the ICL field, such as Article 25(3)(d), for securing conviction. Judge Henderson noted that the prosecutor's arguments with respect to Article 25(3)(d), namely that the accused had contributed to the crimes of a group acting with a 'common purpose', were identical with the OTP's arguments in relation to Article 25(3)(a).[213] Since the alleged 'common purpose' of the group appeared to be the same as the alleged 'common plan' between Gbagbo and his inner circle, the judges concluded that the charges under subparagraph (d) were equally unsupported as those under subparagraph (a).[214] That was a notable departure from the 2014 *Katanga* Judgment where the TC Majority had convicted the accused under

211 Ibid., § 1908.

212 *See* Chapter 6, Section 6.2.1.3.

213 *Gbagbo and Blé Goudé* Reasons of Judge Henderson § 1954.

214 Ibid., § 1955.

subparagraph (d) after determining that the prosecutor's evidence had not met the requirements of indirect co-perpetration. The *Gbagbo and Blé Goudé* TC seemingly took note of Judge Van den Wyngaert's dissent in *Katanga*, where she opined that Article 25(3)(d) codified a fundamentally different type of criminal responsibility and not simply a less demanding version of subparagraph (a).[215] The *Gbagbo and Blé Goudé* decision signalled to those members of the ICL community of practice, who called for narrow and predictable application of criminal responsibility rules that Article 25(3)(d) was not a safety net for obtaining a conviction.

The judges in *Gbagbo and Blé Goudé* were also unable to establish the accused's liability under the modes that did not require the existence of a common plan or common purpose. With regard to liability under subparagraph (b), namely, for ordering or inducing the commission of the crimes, the OTP had itself acknowledged the lack of evidence that Gbagbo had issued criminal orders or that his orders had been directly transmitted to the physical perpetrators of the crimes.[216] Specifically, with regard to Gbagbo's numerous public speeches, which featured prominently in the prosecution's case, the judges noted that no effort was made to demonstrate that those speeches had reached the physical perpetrators, much less how the perpetrators had interpreted them.[217] It was concluded that the prosecution had failed to establish any causal connection between Gbagbo's actions and those of the physical perpetrators to support the claims that Gbagbo had encouraged his subordinates to commit violence.[218] Consequently, Gbagbo's liability under subparagraph (b) was not established.[219] Regarding Blé Goudé, the prosecution acknowledged that during his speeches Gbagbo had not explicitly called upon his audience to use violence.[220] The judges noted that, while Blé Goudé's speeches might have contained inflammatory passages as interpreted within a given context, such an effect could not be *assumed*, rather, it needed to be established.[221] According to the Majority, the prosecution had failed to give examples of perpetrators who were 'demonstrably influenced' by Blé Goudé's speeches.[222] Judge Henderson was also critical of the fact that the prosecution had relied on the same evidence regarding subparagraph

215 Chapter 7, Section 7.3.

216 *Gbagbo and Blé Goudé* Reasons of Judge Henderson, § 1971.

217 Ibid., § 1976.

218 Ibid., § 1981.

219 Ibid., § 1983.

220 Ibid., § 1984.

221 Ibid., § 1994.

222 Ibid., § 1995.

(c) liability for aiding and abetting the crimes as it had done regarding subparagraphs (a) and (b) liability.[223] The Judge opined that the prosecutor's arguments appeared so 'abstract and generic' that the causal link between the accused's contribution and the crimes had become so 'tenuous', to the point that it was 'difficult to imagine that any of the physical perpetrators was conscious of Mr Blé Goudé's alleged generic contributions'.[224]

The TC Majority was similarly critical of the prosecutor's attempt to use Article 28 'as a fall-back to secure a conviction at any cost'.[225] That impression resulted from the OTP's 'half-hearted' efforts to present clear arguments against Gbagbo that met the specific requirements of command responsibility.[226] Similar to the *Bemba* AC Majority, the *Gbagbo and Blé Goudé* TC Majority placed significant emphasis on Gbagbo's material capability to do something about the behaviour of his subordinates. According to Judge Henderson, the OTP had failed to specify what particular measures Gbagbo should have taken in that regard.[227] Judge Tarfusser added that the prosecution did not explain how, even though Gbagbo fell in captivity in April 2011, he was expected to have prevented, repressed, or investigated the crimes that were committed '*following* his arrest'.[228] Thus, the *Gbagbo and Blé Goudé* TC Majority joined the efforts of their colleagues at the *Bemba* AC to rebuke the image of command responsibility as a legally controversial doctrine that was only used for the purposes of convicting the defendants in cases lacking evidence of the accused's personal involvement in the crimes.

Overall, the Majority refused to treat Articles 25(3)(b)–(d) and 28 RS as a back-up for obtaining convictions. They emphasized that each of those provisions posed requirements that were different from, and not merely lower than, the requirements of subparagraph (a). While the IMT, IMTFE, and the UN tribunals had relied on enterprise-type modes of liability and command responsibility to balance the moral impulse of punishing high-level officials who intuitively seemed guilty for the crimes perpetrated by their subordinates, the vision of legalism that dominated the ICC, namely the idea that the rules of criminal law must be applied in a technical manner, regardless of the trial outcome, was cautious that such imputations of criminal responsibility might lead to unsound legal reasoning.

223 Ibid., § 2017.
224 Ibid., § 2020.
225 Ibid., § 2032.
226 *Gbagbo and Blé Goudé* Reasons of Judge Henderson, § 2030. See also *Gbagbo and Blé Goudé* Opinion of Judge Tarfusser, § 17.
227 *Gbagbo and Blé Goudé* Reasons of Judge Henderson, § 2031.
228 *Gbagbo and Blé Goudé* Opinion of Judge Tarfusser, § 17, emphasis in the original.

8.2.3.3 Judge Herrera-Carbuccia's Dissent

Notably, some ICC judges contested that vision of international criminal justice and sought a different approach to the assessment of criminal responsibility. Judge Herrera-Carbuccia considered that the evidence presented against Gbagbo could have met the requirements of Article 28[229] and that Blé Goudé could have been convicted for inducing the crimes under Article 25(3)(b).[230] Her approach demonstrated due regard to the fundamental principles of criminal law but also a humanitarian concern for the inability of the victims in Côte d'Ivoire to see justice being served.

Like her colleagues, Judge Herrera-Carbuccia refrained from concluding that Gbagbo or Blé Goudé had committed the alleged crimes under Article 25(3)(a),[231] thus, maintaining a narrow reading of the 'control' theory. Nevertheless, Judge Herrera-Carbuccia considered that the trials concerning mass atrocities had to balance the technical application of the rule of law with the interests of victims to see justice being done.[232] In her opinion, the command responsibility principle was an 'original creation' of ICL and international human rights law that departed from the 'traditional' criminal law principles.[233] The purpose of that departure was reportedly 'to prevent impunity for those in power – those who, by traditional criminal law standards, would have escaped justice'.[234] From that perspective, the *Gbagbo* case was an example of the goal of including Article 28 in the RS, namely to hold commanders criminally responsible for the acts committed by their subordinates.

Judge Herrera-Carbuccia was mindful of the culpability principle. She noted that Gbagbo could not be held criminally responsible for failing to prevent or punish those crimes that were committed after his arrest.[235] Nevertheless, unlike her colleagues, Judge Herrera-Carbuccia considered that the accused could have been convicted for the rest of the charges under Article 28. According to her, the ICC should not 'allow' a president 'to target citizens' and 'commit crimes against humanity with impunity'.[236] Hence, from Herrera-Carbuccia's perspective, the ICC's mandate

[229] *Gbagbo and Blé Goudé*, 'Dissenting Opinion Judge Herrera Carbuccia (Public redacted version)', ICC-02/11-01/15-1263-AnxC-Red, Trial Chamber I, 16 July 2019, § 486.

[230] Ibid., § 18.

[231] Ibid., § 17–18.

[232] Ibid., § 7.

[233] Ibid., § 492.

[234] Ibid., § 493.

[235] Ibid., § 17.

[236] Ibid., § 6.

was not limited to the assessment of individual criminal responsibility but also included broader goals, such as deterrence and social restoration.

Like the *Bemba* AC, the *Gbagbo and Blé Goudé* TC Majority rejected that balanced position and prioritized the narrow and predictable application of the law. Judges Henderson and Tarfusser considered their mandates to be limited to assessing the available evidence and stressed that in their role as judges they could not take 'position on the accused's moral or political responsibility'.[237] Thus, *Gbagbo and Blé Goudé* became another illustration of the understanding shared among many ICC judges that their judgments cannot be guided by 'political or even humanitarian goals', lest the ICC was to become 'a court in name only'.[238]

The Majority's reasoning and the dissenting opinion illustrate two different visions of international criminal justice, promoted within the ICL community of practice. Both of those visions respect the main shared understandings of the ICL field – that the perpetrators of mass atrocities need to be punished through a fair trial. But the two positions disagreed on the relationship between the moral impulse to punish and the legal requirements of fair trial. The outcome of the trial suggested that the principled approach to criminal responsibility, understood as the technical application of the law, regardless of the trial outcome, dominated the ICC.

8.2.4 *The Politics of the ICL Field v. State Politics*

Gbagbo and Blé Goudé's acquittal demonstrated the importance of taking into consideration the internal dynamics of the ICL field if one wants to go beyond an analysis of the selection of suspects and to examine what happens within the case – the assessment of the accused's guilt or innocence. The critical international relations literature on the ICC provides important insights into the selection of suspects in the Ivoirian investigation. By the time Gbagbo was arrested, a consensus had been reached among African states that he had to be ousted from the presidency.[239] The new Ouattara government sent two letters to the ICC that declared its support for international investigations in the country.[240] The proceedings against members of the former regime appeared politically favourable to

[237] *Gbagbo and Blé Goudé* Reasons of Judge Henderson, § 8. See also *Gbagbo and Blé Goudé* Opinion of Judge Tarfusser, § 124.

[238] *Gbagbo and Blé Goudé* Reasons of Judge Henderson, § 10.

[239] C. T. Hunt, 'Côte d'Ivoire', in A. J. Bellamy and T. Dunne (eds.) *The Oxford Handbook of the Responsibility to Protect* (Oxford: Oxford University Press, 2016) 693, 700.

[240] *Côte d'Ivoire*, Decision to Open Investigation, §§ 11–12.

the new government. It was observed that Gbagbo's transfer to the Court two weeks before the legislative elections in Côte d'Ivoire weakened the political opposition there.[241] Furthermore, the prosecutor did not start proceedings against members of the new government even though abuses by pro-Ouattara forces were documented,[242] which left the impression of 'one-sided justice'.[243] Some commentators suggested that the ICC merely prioritized the case against Gbagbo as more expedient,[244] while others opined that the OTP was too dependent on the cooperation of the Ivoirian government for the investigation to target its officials.[245] In any case, the lack of proceedings against government members seemed to open an opportunity for successfully prosecuting Gbagbo. The Ouattara government provided the prosecutor with a vast amount of evidence, including documents seized from Gbagbo's private residency,[246] government documents, video footage, visitor logbooks from Gbagbo's presidential palace,[247] and evidence from many insider witnesses.[248]

Consequently, the selection of suspects from the Ivoirian investigation renders support to the argument that state politics affect ICL proceedings. But it fails to inquire into the subsequent developments of the case. While it falls beyond the scope of this book to disentangle the complex web of state interests surrounding the trial, it is interesting to note that the Ivoirian government opposed Gbagbo's release on the grounds that his return home would destabilize the country.[249] Some news agencies even proposed that Gbagbo's acquittal 'pave[d] the way for his possible return to political life in Côte d'Ivoire'.[250]

241 M. Ricard, 'Historicity of Extraversion in Côte d'Ivoire and the 'Post-conflict' (2017) 35(4) *Journal of Contemporary African Studies* 506, 517.

242 Human Rights Watch, 'Côte d'Ivoire: Ouattara Forces Kill, Rape Civilians During Offensive' (2011) www.hrw.org/news/2011/04/09/cote-divoire-ouattara-forces-kill-rape-civilians-during-offensive. Straus, 'It's Sheer Horror Here', 487.

243 M. Segun and D. Traoré, 'A Shrinking Window for Justice in Côte d'Ivoire', Human Rights Watch 30 January 2019, www.hrw.org/news/2019/01/30/shrinking-window-justice-cote-divoire.

244 Rosenberg, 'International Criminal Court', 472.

245 C. Hillebrecht and S. Straus, 'Who Pursues the Perpetrators?: State Cooperation with the ICC' (2017) 39(1) *Human Rights Quarterly* 162, 180.

246 *Gbagbo* PTC Hearing (Transcript 17), p. 6, lines 15–16.

247 *Gbagbo and Blé Goudé*, Trial Hearing (Transcript 9), p. 46, lines 14–18.

248 Ibid., p. 64, lines 1–3.

249 W. Wakabi, 'Government Says Gbagbo's Return Would Destabilize the Ivory Coast', *International Justice Monitor*, 31 January 2020, www.ijmonitor.org/2020/01/government-says-gbagbos-return-would-destabilize-the-ivory-coast/.

250 A. Aboa, 'Ivorian Dresident Does Not Rule Out Running for Third Term in 2020', Reuters, 26 January 2019, www.reuters.com/article/us-ivorycoast-politics/ivorian-president-does-not-rule-out-running-for-third-term-in-2020-idUSKCN1PK0J8.

To understand what happened next in the case, one has to look to the politics of the legal field, and more specifically, to the understanding shared among the Majority at the *Gbagbo and Blé Goudé* TC that providing a high-quality process, regardless of the outcome, was of key importance for safeguarding the integrity of ICL. The ICC judges not only abstained from convicting a former head of state with seemingly no friends left among governments, but they openly criticized the prosecutor for presenting a 'rather one-sided version of the situation in Côte d'Ivoire' by focusing only on the crimes committed by Gbagbo's supporters.[251] Judge Henderson was dissatisfied with the prosecutor's uncritical acceptance of the statements of the Ivoirian authorities that no one had tampered with the documents found in the Presidential Palace, which were used as evidence against Gbagbo and Blé Goudé.[252] Judge Tarfusser expressed concern that the prosecution started conducting interviews in Abidjan merely four days after the PTC authorized the investigation and that contacts with key witnesses predated the authorization.[253] These remarks implicitly suggested that the prosecution was guided by a particular understanding of the events from the outset that affected its selective approach to evidence – an unacceptable practice for a court that, as the TC Majority claimed, aimed to provide rational assessment of the facts and combat 'fake news'.

The acquittals of Gbagbo and Blé Goudé reflected the complex politics of the legal field, that is, the internal debates between different subgroups of the ICL community of practice regarding the meaning and purpose of the law. The Majority's reasoning resonated with those members of the ICL community of practice, such as Judge Van den Wyngaert, Judge Morrison, and legal scholars including Kai Ambos, Elies Van Sliedregt and Kevin Heller, who advocated for a narrower interpretation of the criminal responsibility principles in international trials.[254]

By contrast, Judge Herrera-Carbuccia's dissent displayed the humanitarian concern for the plight of the victims that was shared by many human rights advocates. Major NGOs called the decision to acquit the accused 'a bitter pill to swallow'[255] and a 'crushing disappointment' for

[251] *Gbagbo and Blé Goudé* Reasons of Judge Henderson, § 66, §§ 105–108. See also *Gbagbo and Blé Goudé* Opinion of Judge Tarfusser, § 116.

[252] *Gbagbo and Blé Goudé* Reasons of Judge Henderson, § 35.

[253] *Gbagbo and Blé Goudé* Opinion of Judge Tarfusser, § 116.

[254] Interview with Elies Van Sliedregt, 7 May 2020. See also Twitter posts by Barrie Sander: https://twitter.com/Barrie_Sander/status/1085140843525230592 and Kevin Heller: https://twitter.com/kevinjonheller/status/1085294583104327681.

[255] Segun and Traoré, 'Shrinking Window'.

the victims in Côte d'Ivoire who had invested their hopes in the trial.[256] That opinion was shared by the Ivoirian national coalition for the ICC.[257] Commentators also expressed concern about the Court's capabilities to prosecute high-level accused.[258] The Executive Director of the International Bar Association argued that in comparison with the ICTY's record of convictions, the ICC was 'struggling to sustain any perceptible notion of success'.[259]

Eventually those concerns would be somewhat relieved by the convictions of Bosco Ntaganda and Dominic Ongwen. But as the following chapter discusses, the conviction did not mark a change in the perception of many ICC judges of their mandates or a tendency to lower the burden of proof for the purpose of delivering a conviction in a politically convenient case. Rather, because there was significant evidence available of Ntaganda's and Ongwen's personal involvement in the alleged criminal conducts, the prosecutor finally convinced judges in the accused's criminal responsibility.

8.3 Conclusion

The analysis of the *Bemba* and *Gbagbo and Blé Goudé* cases points to several observations. Firstly, the majority of ICC judges have remained reluctant to impute liability to persons removed from the scene of the crimes when the prosecutor has failed to establish a clear link between those persons and the crimes. Specifically, in *Bemba* the AC Majority were unconvinced that the accused had had the material capacity to address the MLC crimes. In *Gbagbo and Blé Goudé* the TC Majority refused to rely on the 'common plan' element of principal liability as a vehicle for imputing liability for the crimes allegedly committed by the pro-Gbagbo

256 Amnesty International, 'Cote d'Ivoire: Acquittal of Gbagbo and Blé Goudé a crushing disappointment to victims of post-election violence', 15 January 2019, www.amnesty.org/en/latest/news/2019/01/cote-acquittal-of-gbagbo-a-crushing-disappointment-to-victims/.

257 Coalition for the ICC, 'Côte d'Ivoire: Laurent Gbagbo and Charles Blé Goudé Acquitted by ICC and Released on Conditions', 16 January 2019, www.coalitionfortheicc.org/news/20190116/cote-divoire-laurent-gbagbo-and-charles-ble-goude-acquitted-icc.

258 B. Batros, 'The ICC Acquittal of Gbagbo: What Next for Crimes against Humanity', Just Security 18 January 2019, www.justsecurity.org/62295/icc-acquittal-gbagbo-crimes-humanity/.

259 M. Ellis, 'The Latest Crisis of the ICC: The Acquittal of Laurent Gbagbo', OpinioJuris, 28 March 2019, http://opiniojuris.org/2019/03/28/the-latest-crisis-of-the-icc-the-acquittal-of-laurent-gbagbo/. See also L. Moffett, 'Why Gbagbo Acquittal Is a Bigger Blow for the ICC than the Bemba Decision', *The Conversation*, 15 January 2019, https://theconversation.com/why-gbagbo-acquittal-is-a-bigger-blow-for-the-icc-than-the-bemba-decision-109913.

forces to the accused. Secondly, in both cases the majority of the judges entered a very strict interpretation of command responsibility. Since the Tokyo Judgment, command responsibility has enabled international prosecutors to link high-level persons to the crimes, lacking evidence of their direct involvement. For that reason, command responsibility has been praised from a humanitarian perspective and criticized by those members of the ICL community who advocated for stricter interpretation of the culpability principle. The *Bemba* and *Gbagbo and Blé Goudé* decisions changed the reputation of command responsibility – into a mode of liability designed for a specific context, namely the special responsibilities of persons in command who have the ability to hold their subordinates accountable, and not for easing the burden of proof on the prosecutor. Finally, both cases demonstrated that, while state power politics play an important role in international criminal justice, they alone cannot provide a comprehensive picture of ICC trial outcomes. Even if state cooperation provides the OTP with significant amount of evidence that establishes the commission of the crimes, what the ICC judges are ultimately concerned with is whether that evidence is sufficient to link the person on trial to those crimes. The restrained interpretation of legal rules in both cases significantly raised the bar for establishing that link and ultimately resulted in acquittals.

A look at the internal dynamics of legal practice, or the politics of the legal field, reveals the importance of norms and socially validates standards of competence for the assessment of criminal responsibility at the Court. Both cases illustrate a normative shift in ICL practice – from substantive to procedural justice, from a moral intuition of fairness to neutral and predictable application of legal rules, regardless of the outcome, from emotion to rationalism.

9

The Road to Convictions

Ntaganda and *Ongwen*

This chapter examines the normative legal dynamics behind the assessment of criminal responsibility in two ICC cases that have ended in conviction: *Ntaganda* and *Ongwen*. Unlike the *Bemba* and *Gbagbo and Blé Goudé* cases, which ended in acquittal, the persons standing trial in *Ntaganda* and *Ongwen* had been actively involved in the hostilities that have resulted in the commission of the crimes. Both Bosco Ntaganda and Dominic Ongwen were charged with direct personal commission of some of the crimes listed in the charges. The accused's proximity to the crimes and their willingness to engage personally in criminal conducts convinced the judges of their criminal responsibility as well as enabled the imputation of criminal responsibility to the accused for the crimes that they had committed 'indirectly' through their troops. Apart from two appeals judges, who expressed concern with the reliance on the 'control over the crime' theory in *Ntaganda*, the meticulous assessment of the facts in the judgments left little room for contestation within the ICL field.

9.1 Ntaganda

After the 2012 *Lubanga* judgment, in 2019 the ICC convicted another UPC member, Bosco Ntaganda. The decision is pending appeal, but for the time being the judgment constitutes a landmark for the court, because it marks the conviction for the highest number of charges at the ICC yet, namely 18 counts of crimes against humanity and war crimes. The most notable difference between the *Ntaganda* case and the cases which ended in acquittal was that, unlike Bemba and Gbagbo, Ntaganda had been personally involved in the alleged crimes. In fact, Ntaganda had personally committed some of those crimes. Ntaganda's proximity to the crimes convinced the judges that the accused had exercised control over the crimes. Consequently, the *Ntaganda* TC did not lower the requirements of the control theory to obtain a conviction. Instead, the prosecutor finally managed to meet those requirements. The comparison between *Gbagbo and*

Blé Goudé and *Ntaganda* demonstrates a stable line of legal reasoning across ICC judgments, regardless of the defendant's political position.

9.1.1 *Case Background*

The *Lubanga* and *Ntaganda* cases originated from the OTP's investigation into crimes that were committed during the 2002–2003 conflict in the Ituri region in Northeastern DRC. The ethnic tensions in the region exacerbated in 1998–1999 when the Hema and the Lendu ethnic groups created self-defence forces. From 1999 to the middle of 2003 a number of opposing rebel groups struggled to gain control of Ituri, including through violent means.[1] In 2000, the organization UPC was created,[2] mostly comprising Hema members.[3] In September 2002 a UPC-controlled government took hold of Ituri under Lubanga's leadership.[4]

The DRC ratified the Rome Statute in April 2002 and referred the situation on its territory in 2004.[5] In 2006 the OTP submitted a joint application for two arrest warrants for war crimes against members of the UPC leadership, namely the President Thomas Lubanga and Bosco Ntaganda.[6] The latter had served as the Deputy Chief of Staff of the UPC's armed wing, the *Forces Patriotiques pour la libération du Congo* (FPLC).[7] Bosco Ntaganda ranked third in the UPC hierarchy – he was a subordinate to the Chief of Staff Floribert Kisembo, who answered to Thomas Lubanga. Ntaganda only took over Kisembo's position as the FPLC's Chief of Staff in December 2003, at the very end of the period covered by the charges.[8]

Lubanga was available for transfer to the ICC immediately when the arrest warrant against him was issued because he was already in custody in the DRC.[9] But Ntaganda's situation was different. After leaving the UPC/FPLC, Ntaganda went on to lead other armed groups in the North Kivu region of the DRC, including the *Congrès national pour la défense*

1 *Lubanga* Trial Judgment, §§ 74–80.
2 Ibid., § 81.
3 *Lubanga*, Public Redacted Version Document Containing the Charges, Article 61(3)(a), ICC-01/04-01/06-356-Anx2, Pre-trial Chamber I, 28 August 2006, § 12.
4 Ibid., § 9.
5 *Ntaganda*, Case Information Sheet ICC-01/04-02/06, ICC-PIDS-CIS-DRC-02-016/19_Eng Updated: February 2020, 1.
6 *DRC*, First Arrest Warrants Decision.
7 Ibid., § 78.
8 Ibid., § 79.
9 ICC, Office of the Prosecutor, Report on the Activities Performed during the First Three Years (June 2003–June 2006), 12 September 2006, 8–9.

du peuple , that were allegedly implicated in numerous crimes. For a long time, the DRC government was reluctant to hand him over to the ICC, claiming that Ntaganda was a crucial figure in the peace process in Eastern DRC. Ntaganda was even integrated into the DRC army and rose to the position of a colonel in 2004.[10] It was not until 2012 when Ntaganda defected from the DRC army and created the rebel group *Mouvement du 23 mars* (M23), that President Kabila called for his arrest. Following the loss of a power struggle within the M23, in 2013 Ntaganda finally surrendered himself to be transferred to the court in what was described as 'an act of self-preservation'.[11]

9.1.2 Pre-trial: Direct and Indirect Perpetration

9.1.2.1 Revising the Charges

The six-year time lapse between the apprehensions of Lubanga and Ntaganda proved crucial for collecting evidence against the latter suspect. Originally, the arrest warrants against Lubanga and Ntaganda included the same charges, namely for the war crimes of enlistment, conscription, and the use of children to participate actively in hostilities, that were allegedly committed by the UPC/FPLC between July 2002 and December 2003.[12] But after the *Lubanga* judgment was issued, the prosecutor decided to bring new charges against Ntaganda.[13] The prosecutor explained that decision with the significant amount of evidence concerning UPC activities that was gathered during the *Lubanga* proceedings.[14]

The DCC against Ntaganda, which was filed after his apprehension by the prosecutor in 2014, further included UPC/FPLC crimes that were allegedly committed during two attacks on civilian villages in Ituri in 2002–2003. In relation to the first attack, the prosecutor argued

[10] P. Clark, Distant Justice, 226.

[11] P. Dale, 'Bosco Ntaganda – the Congolese 'Terminator'', BBC, 8 July 2019, www.bbc.com/news/world-africa-17689131.

[12] *Ntaganda*, Decision on the Prosecution Application for a Warrant of Arrest, ICC-01/04-02/06-1-Red-tENG, Pre-Trial Chamber I, 6 March 2007 (hereinafter *Ntaganda* 2007 Arrest Warrant Decision), § 47. *Lubanga*, Warrant of Arrest, ICC-01/04-01/06-2-tEN, Pre-Trial Chamber I, 10 February 2006, 2–3.

[13] *Ntaganda*, Second Corrigendum of the Public Redacted Version of the Prosecutor's Application under Article 58 filed on 14 May 2012, ICC-01/04-611-Red-Corr2,16 May 2012 (hereinafter Ntaganda Second Arrest Warrant Application).

[14] ICC, Office of the Prosecutor, 'Statement ICC Prosecutor on New Applications for Warrants of Arrest DRC Situation' (2012).

in the DCC that Ntaganda had commanded the takeover of the town of Mongbwalu and personally participated in the battle and instructed the UPC brigades. Under his leadership, the troops allegedly killed, raped, and displaced civilian members, pillaged and destroyed their property.[15] With respect to the second attack, the prosecutor alleged that Ntaganda and his co-perpetrators had launched a large-scale attack on over 40 villages. Ntaganda allegedly served as the overall operational commander of the attacks,[16] during which troops under his control killed, raped, and sexually enslaved civilians; pillaged homes; and destroyed houses and protected objects.[17] Gender-based crimes featured prominently in the charges,[18] including atrocities that were committed against girl soldiers within the UPC/FPLC.[19]

9.1.2.2 Ntaganda's Personal Involvement in the Crimes

The prosecutor brought a broad range of charges against Ntaganda that reflected the spectrum of the UPC/FPLC's criminal conduct. But the OTP also had to link Ntaganda to those crimes. The key difference between *Ntaganda* and other cases, such as *Bemba* or *Gbagbo*, was that the latter concerned persons who were removed from the scene of the crimes. By contrast, as the commander of a military brigade, Ntaganda's personal involvement in the alleged crimes was more easily discernible. Overall, the prosecution submitted 69,000 pages of evidence for consideration by the judges.[20]

Notably, much of the available evidence pointed to crimes that were allegedly perpetrated by Ntaganda himself. There was evidence that during the first attack listed in the charges Ntaganda had personally committed crimes, including murder, persecution, pillaging and attacking protected objects.[21] For instance, Ntaganda had allegedly shot dead the

[15] *Ntaganda*, Public Document Containing the Charges, ICC-01/04-02/06-203-AnxA, 10 January, 2014 (hereinafter *Ntaganda* DCC), §§ 64 67.

[16] Ibid., § 77.

[17] Ibid., § 78.

[18] *Ntaganda* Second Arrest Warrant Application, §§ 100–115.

[19] *Ntaganda* DCC, §§ 103–105.

[20] Women's Initiatives for Gender Justice, 'Legal Eye on the ICC – September 2014 – Special Issue – Ntaganda Confirmation of Charges' (2014), https://4genderjustice.org/home/publications/eletters/legal-eye-on-the-icc-september-2014-special-issue-ntaganda-confirmation-of-charges/.

[21] *Ntaganda*, Decision Pursuant to Article 61(7)(a) and (b) of the RS on the Charges of the Prosecutor against Bosco Ntaganda, ICC-01/04-02/06-309, Pre-Trial Chamber II, 14 June 2014 (hereinafter *Ntaganda* Confirmation Decision), § 36.

priest of Mongbwalu,[22] used child soldiers as bodyguards[23] and personally recruited child soldiers to participate actively in hostilities.[24] Furthermore, there was available evidence that Ntaganda himself raped and sexually enslaved women in the UPC/FPLC, which the DCC described as an act of official approval of such crimes that furthered their commission by Ntaganda's subordinates.[25] Hence, Ntaganda's personal criminal conduct was used to infer that the accused knew of and even encouraged the commission of such crimes by the UPC/FPLC. The allegations against Ntaganda were also supported by evidence of similar crimes that were committed by the accused on other occasions but fell outside the scope of the charges.[26] Even though the crimes that were allegedly committed during Ntaganda's stay at the CNDP and the M23 were not prosecuted at the ICC, the OTP referred to those crimes as an indication of 'a continuing pattern of conduct' by the accused.[27]

But the OTP was also cautious to avoid the impression that Ntaganda was merely one of the soldiers on the ground, which could have led the judges to conclude that the UPC/FPLC crimes were controlled by a more senior figure and that Ntaganda's role was not essential to their execution. In fact, the main challenge to the prosecutor's allegations was the defence's claim that Ntaganda merely held a deputy position throughout most of the period relevant to the charges and did not have significant authority within the organization.[28] The prosecution countered those claims with the observation that, in addition to his military duties, Ntaganda also engaged in devising and implementing the UPC's policy[29] and that he was a trusted officer and adviser of Lubanga.[30]

Hence, unlike previous cases, Ntaganda's position within the UPC/FPLC provided the prosecutor with an opportunity to link the accused to the crimes. Unlike the top leadership figures that are generally removed from the crimes, Ntaganda's position within the UPC's military wing

[22] *Ntaganda*, Trial Hearing Transcript, ICC-01/04-02/06-T-23-ENG, Trial Chamber VI, 2 September 2015 (hereinafter *Ntaganda*, Trial Hearing (Transcript 23), p. 41, lines 6–18.

[23] *Ntaganda* DCC, § 99.

[24] Ibid., § 8.

[25] Ibid., § 105.

[26] *Ntaganda*, Trial Hearing (Transcript 23), p. 44, lines 15–17.

[27] *Ntaganda* DCC, § 140.

[28] *Ntaganda*, Trial Hearing Transcript, ICC-01/04-02/06-T-24-ENG, Trial Chamber VI, 3 September 2015 (hereinafter *Ntaganda*, Trial Hearing (Transcript 24)), p. 40, lines 5–9, p. 70, lines 8–12.

[29] *Ntaganda, Second Arrest Warrant Application*, § 120.

[30] Ibid., § 122.

rendered him at the forefront of many operations. At the same time, the accused was not an ordinary soldier but a commander in power, which enabled the court to examine his alleged criminal responsibility for the broader conduct of the FPLC troops, rather than simply for his own criminal conducts. Consequently, in the DCC the prosecutor argued that the accused could be held accountable not only as a direct perpetrator of his own crimes, but also as a direct/indirect co-perpetrator under Article 25(3)(a) of the crimes committed by UPC/FPLC troops.[31]

Regarding the charges of (indirect) co-perpetration, the OTP argued that the UPC/FPLC crimes were committed pursuant to the same 'common plan' that was outlined in *Lubanga*, namely that the UPC leadership sought to assume military and political control of Ituri.[32] But this time, the *Ntaganda* DCC clearly set out the *criminal* elements of that plan. The prosecutor alleged that the implementation of the UPC's plan envisaged the occupation of non-Hema dominated areas and the expulsion of the civilian population there, including by means of murder, rape, sexual slavery, persecution, pillaging, and using child soldiers.[33] The *Ntaganda* DCC, thus, marked a notable departure from the prosecutor's complex and abstract arguments concerning the 'common plan' among the co-perpetrators in *Gbagbo and Blé Goudé*.

Other requirements of indirect co-perpetration, such as the accused's 'essential contribution' to the common plan and his 'control' over the physical perpetrators of the crimes, were also easier to deduce from the facts in *Ntaganda*, compared to other ICC cases, such as *Ngudjolo* or *Katanga*. Ntaganda's alleged contribution to the implementation of the UPC's plan involved planning attacks, issuing orders to the UPC/FPLC soldiers and Hema civilian supporters to commit crimes, and recruiting and training young persons into the FPLC.[34] The OTP also noted that by personally committing some of the crimes, Ntaganda acted as a criminal 'role model' for his subordinates.[35] With regard to the control over the UPC/FPLC troops, the DCC observed that unlike many other rebel organizations where the locus of control was hard to identify, the FPLC 'mirrored the conventional structure of a traditional army' with a straightforward chain of command and control and that Ntaganda 'discharged significant military functions' within the organization.[36]

[31] *Ntaganda* DCC, § 109.
[32] Chapter 7, Section 7.1.1.
[33] *Ntaganda* DCC, § 1.
[34] Ibid., § 126.
[35] Ibid., § 2.
[36] Ibid., § 123.

The availability of evidence of Ntaganda's direct involvement in the alleged crimes made that case more promising for the prosecutor compared to the complex arguments presented in *Gbagbo and Blé Goudé*. As the following section discusses, the evidence was sufficient to support each of the elements of criminal responsibility as construed in the ICC jurisprudence, even though the judges applied those elements to the facts of the case in same restrained manner as they had done in other ICC cases.

9.1.3 Trial: The Commander on the Ground

9.1.3.1 Ntaganda's Direct Perpetration of Crimes

Unlike the *Gbagbo* case where there was no evidence that the accused had directly committed by himself any of the alleged crimes, Ntaganda's personal involvement in the FPLC's military activities enabled the TC judges to find Ntaganda guilty as a direct perpetrator with respect to eight counts of charges, including for murder, attacking and persecuting civilians, pillaging, and recruiting child soldiers.[37] Notably, the judges found that Ntaganda had committed those crimes 'as an individual', rather than 'jointly with another' person. In other words, Ntaganda had 'personally' carried out the crimes, rather than having contributed to a common effort to commit the crimes.[38]

This constituted the first time at the ICC when the accused was found guilty of physically carrying out the crimes by himself, pursuant to the first alternative of Article 25(3)(a).[39] The TC in the *Al-Mahdi* case made similar findings based on the available evidence of the accused's personal participation in the destruction of five buildings of protected cultural heritage in Mali[40] and Al-Mahdi's own admission of his guilt.[41] But the judges concluded that Al-Mahdi's criminal responsibility would most accurately be described as direct *co*-perpetration because his personal conduct constituted an 'essential contribution' to the collective effort of the Ansar Dine insurgent group to destroy 10 protected buildings of cultural heritage.[42] In 2019 during the confirmation of charges procedure against another Malian citizen, Al-Hassan, the prosecutor also submitted

[37] *Ntaganda* Trial Judgment, § 734.
[38] Ibid., § 735.
[39] See Chapter 5, Section 5.3.
[40] *Al Mahdi*, Judgment and Sentence, § 40.
[41] Ibid., § 43.
[42] Ibid., § 61.

evidence that the suspect had personally committed some of the crimes listed in the charges.[43]

Notably, neither Ntaganda, nor Al-Mahdi or Al-Hassan were among the 'big fish' of international suspects. Al-Mahdi was described as a 'little-known defendant'[44] and even though Al-Hassan's role within Ansar Dine evolved over time, the suspect never became one of its senior figures.[45] Initially, in 2006, Ntaganda's case was dismissed by the ICC judges on the grounds that he was not 'a core actor' during the Ituri conflict.[46] The PTC finally agreed to issue an arrest warrant against Ntaganda a year later, in 2007.[47] While some called Ntaganda an 'important player in the conflict' in Ituri,[48] he largely rose into prominence after he left the UPC/FPLC.[49] Whether in the future the prosecutor is likely to establish the criminal responsibility of a more high-profile defendant, such as a leadership figure or a state official, ultimately depends on the quality of evidence obtained and the possibilities for conducting investigations. In the meantime, several commentators have already suggested that the OTP is likely to be more successful when it pursues 'rebel leaders' on 'a relatively narrow group of charges'.[50] As will be discussed, that also turned out to be a successful strategy in *Ongwen*.

9.1.3.2 Ntaganda's Indirect Co-perpetration of Crimes

Ntaganda's active role on the ground during the UPC/FPLC attacks enabled the prosecutor to link the accused not only to the crimes that

[43] *Al-Hassan*, 'Rectificatif à la Décision relative à la confirmation des charges portées contre Al Hassan Ag Abdoul Aziz Ag Mohamed Ag Mahmoud', ICC-01/12-01/18-461-Corr-Red, Pre-Trial Chamber I, 13 November 2019 (hereinafter *Al Hassan*, Confirmation Decision), 709.

[44] Sterio, M. 2017. 'Individual Criminal Responsibility for the Destruction of Religious and Historic Buildings: The *Al Mahdi* Case', 49(1–2) *Case Western Reserve Journal of International Law* 63, 66–67.

[45] *Al Hassan*, Confirmation Decision, § 766.

[46] *DRC*, First Arrest Warrants Decision, § 87.

[47] *Ntaganda* 2007 Arrest Warrant Decision.

[48] O. Bueno, 'Between Hope and Skepticism: Congolese Await the Trial of Ntaganda', *International Justice Monitor*, 2 September 2015, www.ijmonitor.org/2015/09/between-hope-and-skepticism-congolese-await-the-trial-of-ntaganda/.

[49] See V. Tampa, 'A Brutal Warlord Has Been Convicted – So Why Doesn't It Feel Like a Triumph?', *The Guardian*, 8 July 2019, www.theguardian.com/commentisfree/2019/jul/08/warlord-bosco-ntaganda-democratic-republic-of-the-congo-congolese.

[50] D. Guilfoyle, 'A Tale of Two Cases: Lessons for the Prosecutor of the International Criminal Court? (Part I)', EJIL: Talk!, 28 August 2019, www.ejiltalk.org/a-tale-of-two-cases-lessons-for-the-prosecutor-of-the-international-criminal-court/. See also M. Sterio, 'The International Criminal Court: Current Challenges and Prospect of Future Success' (2020) Cleveland State University: *Law Faculty Articles and Essays* 1136, 467–478, 475.

the latter had directly committed, but also to the ones that were indirectly perpetrated through the soldiers under his control.[51] In *Ngudjolo*, *Katanga*, and *Gbagbo and Blé Goudé*, indirect co-perpetration proved to be a mode of liability with particularly challenging requirements. But in *Ntaganda*, there was sufficient evidence to establish the existence of the 'common plan' among the co-perpetrators, the accused's 'essential contribution' to the crimes, his 'control' over the direct perpetrators thereof, and his 'intent and knowledge' with respect to the crimes. The *Ntaganda* TC did not have to lower the requirements of the control theory to convict the defendant – rather, the prosecutor's evidence met those requirements.

In *Lubanga*, the evidence with respect to the existence of a 'common plan' among the UPC/FPLC leadership primarily focused on the group's establishment and its aspirations to take control over Ituri.[52] But the *Ntaganda* TC was able to make considerably more specific conclusions about the criminal aspects of the UPC/FPLC's 'plan':

> [T]he co-perpetrators meant the destruction and disintegration of the Lendu community, which inherently involved the targeting of civilian individuals by way of acts of killing and raping, as well as the targeting of their public and private properties, via acts of appropriation and destruction.[53]

Furthermore, based on the prosecutor's submissions, the judges observed that the 'ethnical claims' bound the UPC/FPLC leadership to the implementation of the common plan.[54] The available evidence convinced the judges that the commission of the crimes was an integral part of the UPC/FPLC's strategy, rather than an unfortunate consequence of an otherwise legitimate political campaign.

With respect to the requirement that the accused had made an 'essential contribution' to the implementation of the common plan of crucial significance was the evidence of Ntaganda's 'proximity to the commanders and soldiers deployed' during the attacks and 'his own personal violent conduct towards civilians'.[55] The judges noted that Ntaganda had issued direct orders to target and kill civilians, but also 'illustrated for his troops how the orders were to be implemented' by committing such crimes

[51] *Ntaganda* Trial Judgment, § 764.
[52] *Lubanga* Trial Judgment, §§ 1128–1136.
[53] *Ntaganda* Trial Judgment, § 809.
[54] Ibid., § 808.
[55] Ibid., § 855.

himself.[56] Furthermore, the judges found that the first attack listed in the charges was 'launched and conceived' by Ntaganda.[57] In relation to the second attack, the judges noted that even though Ntaganda had not participated on the ground, the accused still made an essential contribution by participating in the planning of the attack[58] and maintaining contact with the commanders in the field during the attack.[59] Finally, it was established that the accused had been 'personally and actively involved' in the recruitment of child soldiers.[60] The evidence demonstrated that Ntaganda regularly visited training camps[61] and 'personally' taught recruits.[62] Thus, the prosecutor accomplished in *Ntaganda* what it could not accomplish in *Gbagbo*, namely to convince the judges in the existence of the common plan that included an evidently criminal goal, and in the accused's essential role in the implementation of that plan.

With regard to the other crucial element of indirect co-perpetration – the control over the physical perpetrators of the crimes – the TC in *Ntaganda* noted that the operations on the ground were executed in line with the orders issued by Ntaganda and his co-perpetrators and that the leadership could rely on the UPC/FPLC troops to implement those orders.[63] Contrary to the defence's argument that Ntaganda's superior, Floribert Kisembo, had been the one in charge, the judges concluded based on the available evidence that in practice Ntaganda had enjoyed 'control over *military* planning and operations', while the role of Kisembo had been 'predominantly administrative or political'.[64] The judges also recalled evidence that Ntaganda had 'inspired fear' and respect amongst the troops, which ensured compliance with his orders.[65]

Furthermore, the TC judges did not take for granted that the Hema civilians who had participated alongside the troops in the killings and lootings[66] were similarly controlled by Ntaganda. Instead, the judges carefully examined whether those civilians, like the UPC/FPLC soldiers, were used 'as a tool of the co-perpetrators', because otherwise the crimes of the Hema civilians could not be attributed to Ntaganda and his

56 Ibid., § 851.
57 Ibid., § 836.
58 Ibid., § 837.
59 Ibid., § 846.
60 Ibid., § 830.
61 Ibid., § 365, §§ 369–370.
62 Ibid., § 372.
63 Ibid., § 816.
64 Ibid., § 322, emphasis added.
65 Ibid., § 322.
66 Ibid., § 820.

co-perpetrators.[67] The judges were satisfied in that regard because the evidence suggested that the Hema civilians were so strictly controlled by the UPC/FPLC soldiers that the former's personal will had become 'irrelevant'.[68] Thus, the factual findings of *Ntaganda* closely resembled the strict requirements of Roxin's *Organisationsherrschaft* theory. Consequently, the ICC employed a more principled and theoretically rigorous approach to the assessment of criminal responsibility than the UN tribunals not only in words, that is by substituting 'JCE' with *Organisationsherrschaft*, but also in practice, by construing the requirements of that theory in a narrow fashion. In some cases that resulted in acquittal but because Ntaganda was situated closer to the operation on the ground, compared to the more senior UPC/FPLC leadership that generally dealt with political matters, it was easier to establish the accused's control over the troops and the supporting civilian groups.

Finally, Ntaganda's active involvement in the military campaign rendered sufficient evidence for the prosecutor to meet the high mental element standard that was set by the *Bemba* PTC's interpretation of Article 30 RS. The *Ntaganda* TC concluded that 'the occurrence of these crimes was not simply a risk that [the co-perpetrators] accepted, but crimes they foresaw with virtual certainty'.[69] Hence, the *Ntaganda* TC demonstrated fidelity in practice to the strict legal findings of the *Bemba* TC. The judges were not interested in whether Ntaganda had simply foreseen the risk that the troops under his command would commit the crimes, but whether he had been certain they would do so.

Overall, the *Ntaganda* judgment demonstrated that the ICC judges were willing to convict the accused as an indirect co-perpetrator only after a careful assessment of the available evidence in relation to each of the requirements of that mode of liability. Consequently, Ntaganda's conviction did not appear as the opportunistic conviction of a former rebel commander against whom there was no substantial evidence available. On the contrary, the meticulous assessment of the facts by the judges clearly established the link between the accused and the crimes.

9.1.3.3 Reactions to the Judgment

The *Ntaganda* judgment was well-received by advocates of procedural justice and advocates of substantive justice alike. On the one hand, the judges' 'methodically, even dully' assessment of the facts demonstrated

[67] Ibid., § 822.

[68] Ibid., § 824.

[69] *Ntaganda* Trial Judgment, § 811.

that the ICC was 'acting as a court, and nothing more'.[70] The judgment reassured some of those members of the ICL epistemic community who expressed concern that the indirect co-perpetration mode of liability infringed upon the principle of personal culpability. One of those legal scholars praised the *Ntaganda* TC's 'extensive' explanations and 'transparent approach' regarding the evaluation of evidence.[71]

On the other hand, the judgment received positive reactions among civil society organizations. After a series of acquittals, the judgment was called 'a rare sweeping win' for the OTP.[72] Human Rights Watch observed the potential deterrent impact of Ntaganda's conviction, calling it a 'strong message that justice awaits those responsible for grave crimes' in the DRC,[73] and Amnesty International noted the positive outcome for the victims of the UPC/FPLC crimes.[74] Furthermore, commentators noted that if the conviction was upheld on appeal, it would become the first ICC conviction for gender-based crimes.[75] Women's organizations also welcomed the *Ntaganda* trial,[76] but other commentators lamented that the crimes that were allegedly committed by the M23 under Ntaganda's command were not included in the charges.[77] It was also observed that, apart from Ntaganda, many of those persons who were responsible for the violence in Ituri were still at large.[78]

Consequently, after the trial, the conviction appeared as a favourable outcome to the entire community of ICL practice – both those who prioritized high-quality process and those who sought substantive

70 K. Carlson, 'Why the Ntaganda Judgment Shows that the ICC Has Found Its Footing', *The Conversation*, 16 July 2019, https://theconversation.com/why-the-ntaganda-judgment-shows-that-the-icc-has-found-its-footing-120433.

71 Guilfoyle 'A Tale of Two Cases'.

72 S. Van den Ber and C. Sengenya, 'Ntaganda's Conviction, a Sweeping Win for the ICC Prosecutor', *Justiceinfo*, 9 July 2019, www.justiceinfo.net/en/tribunals/icc/41897-ntaganda-s-conviction-a-sweeping-win-for-the-icc-prosecutor.html.

73 Human Rights Watch, 'ICC: Congo Warlord Guilty of Crimes against Humanity', 8 July 2019, www.hrw.org/news/2019/07/08/icc-congo-warlord-guilty-crimes-against-humanity.

74 Amnesty International, 'DRC: ICC Conviction of Ntaganda Provides Long Awaited Justice for Victims of Grotesque Crimes', 8 July 2019, www.amnesty.org/en/latest/news/2019/07/drc-icc-conviction-of-ntaganda-provides-long-awaited-justice-for-victims-of-grotesque-crimes/.

75 R. Grey, 'Gender-Based Crimes: A Monumental Day for the ICC', *IntLawGrrls*, 8 July 2019, https://ilg2.org/2019/07/08/gender-based-crimes-a-monumental-day-for-the-icc/.

76 Women's Initiatives for Gender Justice, 'Statement on the Sentencing of Bosco Ntaganda', 7 November 2019, https://4genderjustice.org/statement-on-the-sentencing-of-bosco-ntaganda/.

77 Tampa, 'A Brutal Warlord'.

78 Human Rights Watch, 'ICC: Congo Warlord Guilty'. Van den Ber and Sengenya, 'Ntaganda's Conviction'.

justice – but also a reminder of the limited capacity of the ICC to hold accountable the perpetrators of mass atrocities. Notably, those limitations resulted not only from the OTP's dependence on state cooperation but also from the difficulties of meeting strict criminal responsibility requirements when mass atrocities, involving numerous perpetrators, are concerned.

9.1.4 Appeal: Contesting the 'Control' Theory

Like in *Bemba*, the main source of contestation concerning the *Ntaganda* trial judgment came from judges at the AC who placed significant emphasis on the quality of legal reasoning and criminal law procedure. Notably, both judges who questioned the TC's reliance on the 'control over the crime' theory to deliver a conviction – Judge Morrison and Judge Eboe-Osuji – had also been members of the AC Majority that had acquitted Bemba three years earlier.

According to the two judges, the concerns that the 'control' theory could lead to unsound legal reasoning were clearly illustrated in the *Ntaganda* case. Judge Morrison did not object to the findings that Ntaganda was guilty but questioned the reasoning behind some of the findings based on the 'control' theory. Specifically, Judge Morrison did not consider that the evidence went as far as to establish that the Hema civilian had been 'under the control' of Ntaganda, nor that the civilians' personal will had become 'irrelevant' and they had acted as mere tools that Ntaganda used to commit the crimes. Judge Morrison also observed that there was insufficient evidence about the command structure or the way the Hema civilians were organized, which rendered the conclusion that Ntaganda had *controlled* those civilians unsound.[79] Judge Eboe-Osuji's comments clearly illustrate the difficulties of making the facts from the real world fit the abstract requirements of the 'control' theory in the *Ntaganda* case:

> It is not easy to control an articulated piece of mechanical equipment in that way [as required by the control theory], let alone an aggregate collection of a human multitude under a headman.[80]

This led Judge Eboe-Osuji to conclude that the 'control' theory was 'dangerous' for the Court because it led to unsound reasoning which damaged the authority of the judgments.[81]

[79] *Ntaganda* Appeals Judgment, Opinion of Judge Morrison, §§ 19–21.
[80] *Ntaganda* Appeals Judgment, Opinion of Judge Eboe-Osuji, § 93.
[81] Ibid., § 94.

The difference with the *Bemba* AC Judgment was that this time the Majority upheld the conviction,[82] and the evidence of Ntaganda's personal involvement in some of the crimes and in the UPC's conduct more generally appear to have influenced that decision. Notably, Judge Morrison also did not question the decision to convict Ntaganda for the crimes he had perpetrated personally and for his participation in the crimes of the UPC troops and the Hema civilians. The judge also did not argue that the TC had exaggerated the degree of responsibility of Ntaganda. Judge Morrison stated from the outset: 'I am convinced that Mr Ntaganda was responsible for the crimes of which he was convicted and that his sentence reflected the gravity of his conduct'.[83] Consequently, Judge Morrison was concerned that the invocation of the nebulous notion of 'control' led to unnecessary complications in the judicial reasoning and risked casting a shadow over an otherwise legitimate trial outcome.

Judge Eboe-Osuji, who had previously expressed his preference for strict rules of procedure, was more cautious and concurred with only part of the conviction judgment. Specifically, Judge Eboe-Osuji was satisfied that the available evidence had established Ntaganda's criminal responsibility for the charges of murder and persecution in the commission of which the latter had directly participated, as well as the crimes of recruiting and using child soldiers, in which Ntaganda had also been directly involved.[84] The Judge's dissent concerned the rest of the conviction, which relied on the indirect co-perpetration mode of liability. For those charges Judge Eboe-Osuji said that his preference would have been to refer the case back to the TC to assess the evidence pursuant to alternative modes of liability, which did not rely on the broad notion of 'control over the crime'.[85]

The major difference between the *Bemba* and the *Ntaganda* cases turned out to be the available evidence, which established in a more explicit way the accused's involvement in the crimes on the ground in the latter case. Even though two AC judges criticized the TC for relying on the nebulous notion of 'control', the Trial Chamber did not display a more lenient approach to the prosecution to help it secure a conviction. In fact, the *Ntaganda* TC has been one of the most commended ICC chambers for its meticulous assessment of the available evidence.[86]

[82] *Ntaganda*, 'Judgment on the Appeals of Mr Bosco Ntaganda and the Prosecutor against the Decision of Trial Chamber VI of 8 July 2019 Entitled "Judgment"', ICC-01/04-02/06-2666-Red, Appeals Chamber, 30 March 2021.

[83] *Ntaganda* Appeals Judgment, Opinion of Judge Morrison, § 2.

[84] *Ntaganda* Appeals Judgment, Opinion of Judge Eboe-Osuji, § 168.

[85] Ibid., § 169.

[86] *See* Guilfoyle, 'Lacking Conviction', 36. Sterio, 'International Criminal Court', 475.

9.1.5 Conclusions from the Ntaganda Trial

Overall, the Ntaganda judgment constituted a notable example of a case in which a variety of interests coincided. Firstly, the political interests of the DRC government coincided with the interest of the ICL community to put Ntaganda on trial. Even though the defendant had reportedly enjoyed his freedom in the DRC and was even promoted in the DRC army despite the standing ICC arrest warrant against him for several years,[87] when he defected from the Congolese army, Ntaganda lost his political support. Next, the interests of various groups within the ICL epistemic community also coincided, namely those who favoured the dispassionate implementation of criminal law principles and those who were influenced by moral considerations for the plight of the victims. Because of Ntaganda's position within the UPC/FPLC – high enough in the command chain to be held responsible for the conduct of its troops, but not so high that he would be removed from the scene of the crimes – the prosecutor was able to convince the judges in the accused's criminal responsibility. Consequently, Ntaganda's conviction sent a message that military commanders did not enjoy impunity, but also presented a methodologically reasoned legal decision.

Therefore, the case is important because, as Chapter 10 suggests, it may show the way in which the OTP can adapt to the judges' principled approach to criminal responsibility. The state-centred literature has examined how the OTP has 'accommodated' towards the political dynamics of the Court's environment in the selection of cases.[88] The analysis of the assessment of criminal responsibility at the Court makes the important observation that the prosecutor will also have to adapt to the understanding, shared by many ICC judges, such as the *Bemba* AC Majority, the *Gbagbo and Blé Goudé* TC Majority, and the *Ntaganda* TC, that the culpability principle should be interpreted and applied narrowly, regardless of the trial outcome.

The *Ntaganda* case also bears implications for the expectations of those members of the ICL community of practice who understand the term 'end impunity' to mean not only fair process, but also punishment of the perpetrators of mass atrocities. The conviction can unrealistically raise the expectations of NGOs and scholars who seek to see the Court deliver substantive justice in the form of convictions. A closer analysis of the judgment reveals that the *Ntaganda* TC did not change its principled approach

[87] P. Clark, Distant Justice, 226.
[88] Bosco, Rough Justice, 20. Vinjamuri, 'International Criminal Court', 340.

to the assessment of criminal responsibility to render convictions easier. If anything, the *Ntaganda* judgment demonstrates the lowered expectations that human rights advocates should have in relation to seeing convictions delivered at the ICC, lest the prosecutor becomes more efficient in the collection of high-quality evidence. The small number of judgments at the ICC makes projections difficult, so it remains for future research to examine what the ICC trial record would look like. Nevertheless, the *Ntaganda* case has been followed by another success for the prosecution in a case concerning mid-level rebel commander, who had been directly involved in hostilities – that of Dominic Ongwen.

9.2 Ongwen

The case against Dominic Ongwen, a former member of the Lord's Resistance Army (LRA), which operated in Northern Uganda and the wider region, has followed a similar pattern to the case against Ntaganda. Just as Ntaganda, Ongwen had served as a military commander involved in the organization's day-to-day affairs on the ground. Also like in *Ntaganda*, the defendant was apprehended by the ICC years after the arrest warrant against had been issued, which provided the OTP with significant time to collect evidence supporting a long list of additional charges. Of crucial importance for the prosecutor's investigation was the cooperation of the Government of Uganda, which provided a major amount of evidence against the former rebel commander. All those factors contributed to the prosecution's success at trial.

9.2.1 Case Background

The investigation in Uganda marked the beginning of what would become an established practice at the Court, namely states referring the situations on their own territory to the ICC – known as self-referrals) – and illustrated the political implications of that approach. Specifically, in 2003 the OTP received a referral letter from the Government of Uganda about 'the situation concerning the Lord's Resistance Army', in which the government accused the LRA of committing crimes against humanity.[89] The referral concerned the conflict in Acholiland, Northern Uganda, where the LRA, acting under the leadership of the self-proclaimed spirit medium Joseph Kony, had led an armed rebellion against the government and

89 Nouwen, Complementarity in the Line of Fire, 114.

terrorized the local civilian population for over a decade. In 2005, a year and a half after the official start of the investigation, the Court issued five arrest warrants against top LRA commanders: Joseph Kony, Vincent Otti, Raska Lukwiya, Okot Odhiambo, and Dominic Ongwen.[90]

The referral of the situation in Uganda from the outset triggered concerns about the political 'instrumentalization' of the ICC by governments to suppress domestic opposition.[91] The fact that the ICC prosecutor announced the referral at a joint conference with the President of Uganda further contributed to that perception.[92] Sarah Nouwen has described the referral as 'the wedding ring in an arranged marriage of convenience between Uganda and the ICC'.[93] The Ugandan government's policy of forcibly relocating the Acholi population into camps for internally displaced persons (IDPs) had had devastating consequences[94] and the Ugandan People's Defense Force (UPDF)'s abuses had been well documented.[95] The OTP officially opened an investigation concerning the situation in Uganda and not 'concerning the Lord's Resistance Army', as the government had tried to frame it. But in practice, the prosecution issued arrest warrants only against LRA members, emphasizing that their crimes were of 'dramatically higher gravity' than those of the government.[96]

Ensuring the cooperation of the Government of Uganda was crucial for the OTP's ability to conduct investigations and collect evidence. Among the most crucial pieces of evidence were intercepted LRA radio communications, including sound recordings and handwritten logbooks.[97] The recordings were made by the Internal Security Organization of the Ugandan government, the UPDF, and the Ugandan Police.[98] Furthermore, the prosecution relied on witnesses from those units to break the codes

[90] *Ongwen*, Decision on the Prosecutor's Application for Warrants of Arrest, ICC-02/04-01/05-1-US-Exp, Pre-Trial Chamber II, 8 July 2005, (hereinafter *Ongwen* Arrest Warrant Decision).

[91] Branch, Displacing Human Rights, 187, 191.

[92] M. Happold, 'The International Criminal Court and the Lord's Resistance Army' (2007) 8(1) *Melbourne Journal of International Law* 159–184, 170.

[93] Nouwen, Complementarity in the Line of Fire, 113.

[94] Branch, 'Uganda's Civil War', 181.

[95] Human Rights Watch, 'Uprooted and Forgotten: Impunity and Human Rights Abuses in Northern Uganda', 24–35 (2005), www.hrw.org/sites/default/files/reports/uganda0905.pdf.

[96] ICC, Statement at the Informal Meeting of Legal Advisors of Ministries of Foreign Affairs, 24 October 2005, 7.

[97] *Ongwen*, Trial Hearing Transcript ICC-02/04-01/15-T-26-ENG, Trial Chamber IX, 6 December 2016 (hereinafter *Ongwen* Trial Hearing (Transcript 26)) p. 42, lines 19–22.

[98] Ibid., p. 47, lines 7–9.

used by the LRA and identify commanders by their voices.[99] This evidence proved crucial at the Court, which had exhibited increasing reluctance to tolerate the prosecution's investigatory hurdles in other cases. Dominic Ongwen was apprehended in 2015 with the assistance of the CAR, where he had surrendered himself to Séléka rebels.[100] With one former LRA commander being transferred to the Court after a decade-long wait, the ICC prosecution could finally use the vast amounts of available evidence and pursue a successful case.

9.2.2 *Pre-trial: ICC's Longest List of Charges*

In the 2005 arrest warrant Dominic Ongwen was charged with seven counts of crimes allegedly committed during the attack on the Lukodi IDP Camp in May 2004.[101] But the situation had changed dramatically ten years later when the ICC apprehended him. The OTP stressed that there was 'a great deal of evidence' that merited the expansion of the list of charges against Ongwen to 70.[102] Specifically, the prosecution added charges related to three other LRA attacks on IDP camps: on the Pajule IDP Camp on 10 October 2003,[103] the Odek IDP Camp on 29 April 2004,[104] and on the Abok IDP Camp on 8 June 2004.[105] During those attacks, LRA troops had committed a range of crimes against the civilian population, including murder, cruel treatment, enslavement, and pillaging.[106] Notably, the prosecution submitted that Ongwen had personally participated in some of those attacks, including 'personally committing acts of violence against civilians' during the attack on the Pajule IDP Camp,[107] and 'commanding and coordinating the Odek attack on the ground'.[108] The available evidence also suggested that, regarding the Lukodi attack, Ongwen had instructed his subordinates to kill indiscriminately, burn houses, and return with food.[109] Similarly, a brigade officer who had participated in the

99 Ibid., p. 47, lines 24–25, p. 48, lines 1–4.

100 Branch, 'Dominic Ongwen', 30–31.

101 *Ongwen*, Warrant of Arrest for Dominic Ongwen, ICC-02/04-01/05-10-US-Exp, Pre-Trial Chamber II, 8 July 2005 (hereinafter *Ongwen* Arrest Warrant) §§ 13–14.

102 *Ongwen* Trial Hearing (Transcript 26), p. 41, lines 15–19, line 22.

103 *Ongwen*, Document Containing the Charges, ICC-02/04-01/15-375-AnxA-Red, Pre-Trial Chamber II, 22 December 2015 (hereinafter *Ongwen* DCC), § 15.

104 Ibid., § 27.

105 Ibid., § 54.

106 Ibid., § 15, § 27, § 41, § 54.

107 Ibid., § 17.

108 Ibid., § 29.

109 *Ongwen* Conformation Decision, § 78.

Odek attack told the prosecution that Ongwen had ordered the killing of people in the camp who were perceived as 'enemies' of the LRA.[110]

In addition, the prosecution added charges concerning broader patterns of the LRA's violent campaigns, namely the recruitment and use of child soldiers in hostilities[111] and the commission of sexual and gender-based crimes.[112] The latter set of charges turned the case into one of great symbolic significance for the human rights organizations advocating for gender justice because, for the first time at an international court, the crime of 'forced marriage' was explicitly formulated, as a form of 'other inhumane acts' within the meaning of Article 7(1)(k) of the RS.[113]

Notably, the prosecution's charges for gender-based crimes against Ongwen included not only evidence of the crimes committed by the LRA troops under his command, but also those that the accused had personally committed against women in his household. Regarding the latter, the PTC accepted the testimonies of seven women who had been abducted by the LRA, distributed to Ongwen's household, and made his 'wives' immediately or after a period of serving as domestic servants. The Chamber noted that all the women had been deprived of their personal liberty, regularly forced to have sexual intercourse with him and, with the exception of one woman, become pregnant as a result of the rapes.[114] The available evidence also indicated that the defendant had personally used child soldiers as his 'escorts who participated in hostilities alongside him' and ordered his subordinates 'to abduct children to replenish the ranks of his troops'.[115] The Prosecution noted that when meeting one of the witnesses during the peace talks in 2006, Ongwen refused to release the two children carrying heavy items and escorting him[116] with the words: 'You call them children. I call them my soldiers.[117]

The availability of such evidence was of crucial importance for the prosecutor's allegations because, as illustrated in *Ntaganda*, the ICC chambers

[110] *Ongwen* Trial Hearing (Trial Transcript 26), p. 65, lines. 20–23.

[111] *Ongwen* Conformation Decision, § 139.

[112] Ibid., § 129.

[113] Women's Initiatives for Gender Justice, 'Trailblazing ICC Judgment on SGBC – Ongwen Verdict Advances International Accountability for Forced Marriage and Forced Pregnancy', 4 February 2021, https://4genderjustice.org/trailblazing-icc-judgment-on-sgbc-ongwen-verdict/.

[114] *Ongwen* Confirmation Decision, § 104.

[115] Ibid., § 139.

[116] *Ongwen*, Trial Hearing Transcript ICC-02/04-01/15-T-27-ENG, Trial Chamber IX, 7 December 2016 (*Ongwen* Trial Hearing (Transcript 27)), p. 38, lines 18–23.

[117] Ibid., p. 38, lines 24–25.

had been more willing to impute crimes committed through an organization to the accused when there was evidence of the accused's personal participation in at least some of those conducts. Presumably in view of the difficulties it had experienced in sustaining the charges of principal liability in other cases, the OTP listed several alternative modes of liability pursuant to which Ongwen's criminal responsibility could be characterized: accessory liability for ordering the crimes under Article 25(3)(b) or contributing to their commission under Article 25(3)(d) and command responsibility under Article 28(a). Consequently, if the charges under Article 25(3) were not sustained during the course of proceedings, the prosecutor could have still argued that Ongwen was criminally responsible for failing 'to take the necessary and reasonable measures to prevent or repress the commission of the charged crimes' or 'to submit the matter to the competent authorities for investigation and prosecution'.[118] However, the abundant evidence enabled the PTC to confirm all 70 counts of charges that the prosecutor had brought against Dominic Ongwen under Article 25(3)(a), concluding that the accused had perpetrated some of the crimes directly and others indirectly, though the LRA.

Notably, the PTC also confirmed the charges under command responsibility on the grounds that confirming alternative modes of liability had become an established ICC practice[119] but made it clear that its 'own understanding of the relevant facts' did not coincide with that of the prosecutor.[120] The judges observed that:

> … the narrative of the relevant events as emerging from the available evidence is such that Dominic Ongwen's conduct cannot be seen as a mere *failure* to prevent or repress crimes committed by other persons. To the contrary … the Chamber finds that it is precisely the *deliberate* conduct of Dominic Ongwen that resulted in the realization of the objective elements of the crimes.[121]

The PTC thus highlighted the contradiction in the prosecution's narrative, which had resulted from the apparent desire to provide several different avenues for securing the charges. It appeared illogical to argue that a person was criminally responsible for, on the one hand, attacking civilians and ordering their abduction and maltreatment, and on the other hand, for failing to prevent and punish those same crimes. The judges thus once again reminded the prosecution that Article 28 RS constituted a special

118 *Ongwen* DCC, §§ 17, 29, 43, 56, 133, 139.
119 *Ongwen* Confirmation Decision, § 148.
120 Ibid., § 149.
121 Ibid., § 147, emphasis added.

form of responsibility with its own requirements, and not merely a form of backup liability. As discussed, the *Gbagbo and Blé Goudé* case demonstrated that when the evidence was insufficient to link the accused to the crimes, the ICC judges would not convict the accused under any mode of liability, including Article 28. Conversely, as the *Ongwen* trial showed, when the evidence was abundant, the judges did not hesitate to enter a conviction based on principal liability.

9.2.3 Trial

9.2.3.1 Ongwen's Direct Perpetration of Crimes

Ongwen became the second ICC trial after *Ntaganda* in which the accused was convicted for perpetrating some of the charges himself. The TC was presented with abundant testimony concerning the crimes that Ongwen had personally perpetrated against women in his household. The evidence suggested that those women had been 'distributed' to the accused and one had been 'personally abducted' by him.[122] Ongwen's forced 'wives' had been placed under 'heavy guard' and threatened that they would be killed if they tried to escape.[123] The available evidence also pointed to the conclusion that some of those women had been subjected to beating 'at Ongwen's command at any time' and, as a result of those beatings, had been left unconscious or permanently scarred.[124] Some of the women had also been raped by the accused 'on a repeated basis'[125] and subsequently gave birth.[126] The TC judges noted that 'the sustained character of the acts' committed by Ongwen 'over a long period of time' indicated that the accused had not only carried out the objective elements of the crimes, but also 'meant' to engage in those criminal conducts.[127] Consequently, the TC convicted Ongwen for directly perpetrating the crimes of forced marriage, forced pregnancy, rape, sexual slavery, enslavement, torture, and outrages upon personal dignity.

Notably, the TC emphasized that the evidence of Ongwen's personal engagement in sexual and gender-based crimes was also indicative of his intent to commit such crimes *through* the LRA troops under his command

[122] *Ongwen* Trial Judgment, § 3022.
[123] Ibid., § 3022.
[124] Ibid., § 3028.
[125] Ibid., § 3040.
[126] Ibid., § 3057.
[127] Ibid., § 3060.

by ordering the abductions of women to be distributed as 'wives' within his brigade.[128] The evidence of Ongwen's personal engagement in the variety of criminal conducts listed in the charges thus also facilitated his conviction for the crimes that had been committed by the LRA troops from his brigade.

9.2.3.2 Ongwen's Indirect (Co-)perpetration of Crimes

Most of the charges brought against Ongwen concerned allegations that he had perpetrated crimes indirectly, through the LRA soldiers under his command. Specifically, Ongwen was charged as an indirect perpetrator of crimes committed during the attacks on the Lukodi and Abok IDP camps,[129] and as an indirect co-perpetrator, alongside Kony and other LRA commanders for the crimes committed during the attacks on Pajule and Odek IDP camps, for committing gender-based crimes through the LRA, and for recruiting and using child soldiers.[130] The proximity of the accused to the crimes and the peculiar structure of the LRA proved crucial for establishing Ongwen's criminal responsibility for those crimes.

The LRA has built a notorious reputation for the abduction of children, ruthless responses to defections, and the fear instilled within the organization by the cult of Kony's personality and his self-proclaimed mystical powers.[131] Those specificities of the LRA enabled the prosecution to convince the judges that the evidence met the requirements of the 'control over the crime' theory. The undisputed leadership of Kony and the organization of the four LRA brigades, in turn composed of battalions each led by a 'commander', convinced the judges that the LRA had the required 'hierarchical structure'.[132] Furthermore, the TC made 'a number of factual findings' concerning the availability of a vast number of interchangeable subordinates to carry out criminal operations. Those findings included the continuous supply of abductees, who were then 'taught military discipline', 'forced to brutally kill', threatened with beating and execution for disobedience, and subjected to 'a violent disciplinary system'.[133] As discussed in Chapter 6, the *Katanga and Ngudjolo* PTC had concluded

[128] Ibid., § 3097.

[129] *Ongwen* DCC, § 42 and § 55, respectively.

[130] Ibid., §§ 15, 27, 129, 136, respectively.

[131] *See* L. Cakaj, 'The Lord's Resistance Army of Today', Enough Project, November 2010, 6. T. Allen and M. Schomerus, 'A Hard Homecoming: Lessons Learned from the Reception Center Process in Northern Uganda: An Independent Study', 2006.

[132] *Ongwen* Trial Judgment, § 2856. *See also* §§ 123–124.

[133] Ibid., § 2856.

that the automatic compliance with criminal orders could be established based on the existence of 'intensive, strict, and violent training regiments', including the abductions of minors and their training to shoot, rape, and pillage.[134] Consequently, the *Ongwen* TC judges concluded that the LRA leadership had had 'a reliable pool of persons' from which they could choose hundreds of soldiers to carry out any particular attack.[135] The notorious coercive environment of the LRA thus convinced the judges that the organization met the specific requirements of indirect perpetration, namely a strict hierarchical structure and the availability of a sufficient number of subordinates to ensure almost automatic compliance with criminal orders.

Those findings mark a noticeable departure from *Gbagbo and Blé Goudé*, where the prosecutor had failed to establish a discernible link between the accused and the direct perpetrators of the crimes.[136] Unlike the pro-Gbagbo forces, which allegedly comprised a broad range of actors from military personnel to violent youth groups, the LRA with its hierarchical structure and harsh disciplinary measures made it easier for the judges to trace back criminal orders to the accused at trial. Furthermore, unlike in the *Ntaganda* case, where the participation of Hema civilians in the attacks alongside UPC troops had led some judges to question the accused's 'control' over the crimes, in *Ongwen* the accused had relied only on the strictly trained and disciplined troops under his command.

The judges made two types of findings: one concerning Ongwen's overall control over his troops and the other concerning his control over specific criminal conducts. Regarding Ongwen's overall control as a brigade commander, the TC relied on evidence that the accused had 'personally ordered disciplinary measures, issued threats to LRA members that they would be killed if they attempted to escape, and ordered killings of abductees in front of LRA members to illustrate this threat'.[137] Thus, the evidence suggested that Ongwen had not only relied on the coercive environment of the LRA to commit crimes, but that he had also actively participated in sustaining that coercive environment. That finding was complemented by evidence of Ongwen's control over the attacks on IDP camps. Regarding the Pajule attack, in which Ongwen had participated on the ground, the judges observed that the accused had 'carried out a commanding role'

[134] *Katanga and Ngudjolo* Confirmation Decision, § 518.
[135] *Ongwen* Trial Judgment, § 2858.
[136] Chapter 8, Section 8.2.
[137] Ibid., § 2860.

and 'personally determined' the specific criminal actions of his troops.[138] Similarly, they concluded that Ongwen had had 'full operational control on the attack on the Odek IDP camp'.[139] Ongwen's role in the attacks on the Lukodi IDP camp was even more pronounced. The available evidence suggested that the accused had personally 'decided' to attack the Lukodi camp and afterwards 'took responsibility' for the attack in front of other LRA commanders.[140] Similar findings were made regarding the attack on the Abok camp.[141] The available evidence of Ongwen's active role in the LRA's violent campaigns enabled the judges to conclude that the accused had enjoyed 'control' over the crimes.

The accused's personal involvement in the crimes and the peculiar structure of the LRA also enabled the judges to establish the 'co-perpetration' elements of the indirect co-perpetration mode of liability, including the existence of a 'common plan' among the co-perpetrators – in this case, the LRA leadership. The arrest warrants against LRA commanders issued back in 2005 briefly noted that the group had carried out an insurgency against the government, its army, and local defence units, and that 'in pursuing its goals, the LRA has engaged in a cycle of violence and established a pattern of "brutalization of civilians"'.[142] That broad description of the LRA's goals, however, was unlikely to satisfy the preferences of ICC judges to seek evidence of the concrete criminal elements of the alleged common plan between the co-perpetrators – a preference that in 2019 had resulted in the acquittals of Laurent Gbagbo and Charles Blé Goudé. But the prosecution was better prepared in *Ongwen* – the OTP not only underlined the exclusively criminal nature of the LRA's conduct, but even distinguished between *several* criminal plans among the LRA leadership, which had resulted in the commission of the crimes. In particular, the Prosecution alleged that the accused and other LRA commanders committed the crimes according to the following common plans: to attack the Pajule and Lapul IDP camps,[143] to attack the Odek IDP camp,[144] to abduct women and girls to be subjected to SGBC,[145] and to abduct children and conscript them into the Sinia brigade to ensure the constant supply of

[138] Ibid., § 2862.
[139] Ibid., § 2917.
[140] Ibid., § 2963.
[141] Ibid., § 3010.
[142] *Situation in Uganda*, Warrant of Arrest for Joseph Kony Issued on 8 July 2005 as Amended on 27 September 2005, ICC-02/04-01/05-53, 13 October 2005, § 5.
[143] *Ongwen* DCC, § 15.
[144] Ibid., § 27.
[145] Ibid., § 129.

fighters.[146] In *Gbagbo and Blé Goudé* the TC Majority remained unconvinced that the violence against civilians had been the natural result of the alleged plan to keep Gbagbo in power. By contrast, in *Ongwen* there was no need to establish that the crimes would have occurred as a consequence of the LRA's plans in the ordinary course of events – the commission of the crimes constituted the very essence of those alleged plans. For example, the *Ongwen* TC concluded that the LRA leadership's plans to attack IDP camps had been '*specifically directed*' at the commission of criminal conducts.[147] Thus, the notorious public image of the LRA as a particularly violent organization that had terrorized the civilian population in Northern Uganda for years enabled the prosecution to convince the judges of the criminal nature of their plans and to establish one of the key elements of the indirect co-perpetration mode of liability.

The other element of indirect co-perpetration – the accused's 'essential contribution' to the crimes – was established based on the available evidence of Ongwen's active participation in the LRA's criminal plans. Regarding the alleged common plan to abduct women and commit sexual and gender-based crimes, the TC noted evidence that the accused had 'personally decided on the "distribution" of abducted women and girls' and 'used his authority as LRA commander to enforce the so-called "marriage"' between abductees and LRA soldiers in his brigade.[148] The judges concluded that Ongwen had been a 'crucial and indispensable' figure who had 'helped define' and 'sustain' the system of abducting women and girls at the organization.[149] Similarly, regarding the alleged plan to recruit child soldiers, the TC noted evidence that Ongwen had 'abducted children himself' and ordered his soldiers to abduct children, and that children had participated in all four attacks relevant to the charges.[150]

Finally, the abundant evidence of Ongwen's involvement in the crimes enabled the prosecution's allegations to meet the strict mental element requirements adopted in ICC jurisprudence. The prosecution argued that Ongwen 'initiated operations autonomously and *enthusiastically*. Joseph Kony and Vincent Otti frequently described Dominic Ongwen as an example for other LRA commanders to follow'.[151] Notably, many

146 Ibid., § 136.

147 *Ongwen* Trial Judgment, § 2853, emphasis added. *See also* § 2912.

148 *Ongwen* Trial Judgment, § 3093.

149 Ibid., § 3094.

150 Ibid., § 3110.

151 Trial Transcript 26, *supra* note 27, p. 61, lines 14–17, emphasis added. The prosecution used the term 'enthusiastically' in other parts of its opening statement, *see also* Trial Transcript 27, *supra* note 88, lines 17–18.

observations about Ongwen's state of mind were based on recordings of his statements from intercepted radio communications, which once again demonstrated the crucial importance of government cooperation for collecting evidence. As the Prosecution acknowledged at the opening of the trial, the materials:

> ... represent a unique opportunity to step inside the mind of Dominic Ongwen and other LRA commanders at a time before any prospect of Prosecution could possibly have influenced their thoughts or their actions. The Chamber will be able to hear Dominic Ongwen's voice recorded over ten years ago claiming responsibility for the Odek, Lukodi and Abok IDP camp attacks.[152]

The prosecution also relied on another indication of Ongwen's intent and knowledge of the crimes subject to the charges, namely his rapid promotions at the LRA. During the October 2003 attack on the Pajule IDP Camp, Ongwen was still serving as a commander of the Oka battalion, part of the Sinia brigade. After that he became a commander of the whole Sinia brigade[153] and by the latter half of 2005 Ongwen became the most senior LRA commander in Uganda.[154] The prosecution attributed those promotions to Ongwen's 'unwavering loyalty and ferocity'.[155] Based on the available evidence, the TC judges concluded that Ongwen's conducts were such that, by their 'nature', they 'could only have been undertaken intentionally'.[156]

Notably, the prosecution also relied on the evidence of Ongwen's enthusiastic engagement in criminal campaigns to argue that the accused had personally enjoyed control over the crimes, rather than merely complying with Kony's commands. The Prosecution argued that the available evidence

> makes it clear that far from Ongwen being under Kony's thumb, simply having to follow precisely the orders given, they each had preferred tactics to optimize the effectiveness of attacks. They were able to converse, to discuss, to exchange ideas, as one commander to another. Dominic Ongwen had a full measure of discretion about *how* to carry out the attacks that his troops conducted.[157]

152 *Ongwen* Trial Hearing (Transcript 26), p. 54, lines 1–6.
153 Ibid., p. 24, lines 19–21.
154 Ibid., p. 59, lines 17–24.
155 Ibid., p. 26, lines 15–16.
156 *Ongwen* Trial Judgment, § 2865., § 2919, § 2965, § 3012.
157 *Ongwen* Trial Hearing (Transcript 27), p. 9, lines 24–25, p. 10, lines 1–5, emphasis added.

Like in the *Ntaganda* case, the prosecution made an effort to demonstrate that the person at trial bore criminal responsibility for his personal criminal conduct and not merely for contributing to the execution of the crimes planned by his superior. Ironically, in both *Ntganda* and *Ongwen* the fact that might have put in question the accused's ultimate authority within the respective organization, namely their subordinate roles and participation in the crimes on the ground, was also the fact that satisfied the ICC judges' preference for evidence of the accused's direct personal involvement in the concrete criminal conduct. From the perspective of a strict interpretation of the culpability principle, evidence of personal involvement in the crimes was of crucial importance for imputing those crimes to the defendant.

9.2.3.3 Ongwen's Victim-Perpetrator Status and Reactions to the Judgment

Despite the similarities with the *Ntaganda* case, *Ongwen* was nevertheless different from other ICC cases in one important regard: as a child, the defendant had personally suffered some of the crimes that he had later perpetrated as an adult. Ongwen had been abducted by the LRA at an early age and subjected to the organization's harsh training and disciplinary systems.[158] Having grown up in the LRA's coercive environment, Ongwen considered himself one of its victims.[159] Commentators have observed that some among the population of Northern Uganda 'sympathize[d]' with Ongwen because of his abduction as a child.[160] The Defense relied on Ongwen's former victimization to seek his exclusion from criminal responsibility pursuant to Article 31 RS. Specifically, the Defense argued that Ongwen should have been excluded from criminal responsibility on two grounds: mental disease or defect and duress.[161]

Faithful to their preferred approach, the ICC judges treated any considerations of the defendant's morality, character, and personal background as separate from the assessment of their *criminal* responsibility, and in this case, the grounds for excluding such. That approach had previously

158 For an analysis of Ongwen's childhood and life at the LRA see K. Anderson, 'Dominic Ongwen: It Is Very Difficult to Balance All That', *Justice in Conflict*, 2 February 2021, https://justiceinconflict.org/2021/02/02/dominic-ongwen-it-is-very-difficult-to-balance-all-that/.

159 *Ongwen* Trial Hearing (Transcript 26), p. 17, lines 12–13.

160 S. K. Kasande and J. Mugero, 'The Ongwen Verdict: A Step Closer to Acknowledgment and Justice for Victims in Northern Uganda', International Center for Transitional Justice, 2 August 2021, www.ictj.org/news/ongwen-verdict-step-closer-acknowledgment-and-justice-victims-northern-uganda.

161 *Ongwen* Trial Judgment, § 2448.

resulted in the acquittal of Bemba, when the AC Majority criticized their TC colleagues for allowing their perception of the accused's personal motivations to cloud their judgment regarding his ability to address the crimes of his subordinates.[162] By contrast, in *Ongwen* the 'dispassionate' and devoid of 'emotion' approach to assessing criminal responsibility worked in favour of the prosecution.

The TC observed in a highly formalistic manner that 'Dominic Ongwen's childhood experience in the LRA [was] not central to the issue' at hand, namely 'whether a threat relevant under Article 31(1)(d) of the Statute existed at the time of the conduct relevant for the charges' that would have excluded him from criminal responsibility on the grounds of duress.[163] The judges, employing a rationalist, choice-based approach to criminal responsibility,[164] were interested in whether Ongwen had had sufficient autonomy to exercise his free will and make autonomous choices with respect to the specific criminal conducts listed in the charges. Considering the available evidence that at the time relevant to the charges Ongwen had already become an LRA commander with authority who 'personally' threatened and victimized new abductees,[165] the judges concluded that the elements of 'duress' under Article 31(1)(d) RS were not met and the defendant was not excluded from criminal responsibility.[166] Based on the submissions of expert witnesses, who did not identify a mental disease or illness in the defendant, the TC also dismissed the other potential basis for excluding criminal responsibility raised by the Defense.[167]

While the TC's findings that the accused had committed the crimes for which he was convicted did not turn into a significant subject of dispute within the ICL field, members of the ICL community debated whether Ongwen's prior victimization should have somehow been taken into account when assessing his criminal responsibility. Some considered the judgment convincing because 'legal examination of difficult cases such as Ongwen's should not merely be emotional, abstract exercises. It must be grounded in a full canvassing of all the relevant facts, … and most

[162] Chapter 8, Section 8.1.3.2.

[163] *Ongwen* Trial Judgment, § 2592. The *Ongwen* PTC has previously approached the question in a similarly formalistic manner. *See* M. Drumbl, 'Victims Who Victimise' (2016) 4 *London Review of International Law* 217, 242. L. G. Minkova, 'Expressing What? The Stigmatization of the Defendant and the ICC's Institutional Interests in the Ongwen case' (2021) 34 *Leiden Journal of International Law* 223–245, 241–243.

[164] Chapter 3, Section 3.2.3.

[165] *Ongwen* Trial Judgment, § 2591.

[166] Ibid., § 2585.

[167] Ibid., § 2580.

importantly of all: the evidence.'[168] On this account, while the defendant's background and its role in the formation of his character might have been a mitigating factor for the length of punishment, it was a separate issue from the question of whether or not that person bore criminal responsibility for his conducts. The reason is that 'former child soldiers are not devoid of agency' and are able to make their own choices.[169] The emphasis on choice, free will, and agency suggests that, like the ICC judges, many of the participants in the ICL field adopted a choice-based rather than a character-based understanding of criminal responsibility. From this perspective, criminal responsibility is attributed for a wrongful act or choice, and considerations of the defendant's background, beliefs, and morals bear no consequence for determining whether that person is guilty or not.

Other legal experts were critical of the fact that the ICC judges had focused exclusively on Ongwen's 'free will', 'choices, and how he elected to exercise his agency'.[170] From that perspective, it was important to address the question 'how just it is to hold someone criminally responsible if he or she was never taught the wrongfulness of certain conducts'.[171] This type of argument follows the reasoning that acts and choices cannot be understood in the abstract, but rather that they constitute a reflection of the underlying morals of a person. By contrast, premised on the notion of free will and choice, the ICC judges treated Ongwen's prior victimization and his crimes as an adult as unrelated questions.

Notably, not all commentators who found the judges' formalistic reasoning problematic argued that Ongwen should have been acquitted. The general debate was not whether the accused's background should have determined whether he was guilty or not, but whether it should have

[168] P. Bradfield, 'The Moral and Legal Correctness of Dominic Ongwen's Conviction', *Justice in Conflict*, 10 February 2021, https://justiceinconflict.org/2021/02/10/the-moral-and-legal-correctness-of-dominic-ongwens-conviction/. See also E. Keppler, 'Litany of Horrors by LRA Leader: Ongwen Was No "Puppet on a String"', Justice in Conflict, 8 February 2021, https://justiceinconflict.org/2021/02/08/litany-of-horrors-by-lra-leader-ongwen-was-no-puppet-on-a-string/.

[169] B. Sander, 'We Need to Talk about Ongwen: The Plight of Victim-Perpetrators at the ICC', Justice in Conflict, 19 April 2016, https://justiceinconflict.org/2016/04/19/we-need-to-talk-about-ongwen-the-plight-of-victim-perpetrators-at-the-icc/.

[170] M. Drumbl, '"Getting" an Unforgettable Gettable: The Trial of Dominic Ongwen', Justice in Conflict, 5 February 2021, https://justiceinconflict.org/2021/02/05/getting-an-unforgettable-gettable-the-trial-of-dominic-ongwen/.

[171] N. E. Pieters and T. Kirabira, 'The Ongwen Judgement at the ICC: A Missed Opportunity for Former Child Soldiers?', International Law Blog, 22 June 2021, https://internationallaw.blog/2021/06/22/the-ongwen-judgement-at-the-icc-a-missed-opportunity-for-former-child-soldiers/.

somehow featured in the judges' analysis of the facts related to his criminal responsibility. Generally, those members of the ICL field argued that the TC judges could have convicted Ongwen and nonetheless addressed the complexities of the culpability of victim-perpetrators by discussing those complexities in the judgment.[172]

Some critical commentators perceived the TC's restrained and formalistic approach as an indication of the judges' lack of confidence in engaging with the complexities of the case and their desire to validate the Court as an institution able to hold accountable the most notorious international criminals.[173] The *Ongwen* judgment indeed seemed to vindicate the OTP's decade-long investigation in Uganda, which had failed to produce any other outcomes. But from the perspective of this book, the judges' approach does not appear as an indication of their desire to make their task simpler. Rather, it appears as a reflection of their normative belief, also shared by some outside commentators, that in principle considerations of the accused's character had no place in assessing whether the defendant was guilty or not. The debate spurred by the *Ongwen* case, thus provides an illustration of Duff's argument discussed in Chapter 3, namely that the character-based and the choice-based accounts of criminal responsibility reflected different understandings of society and the role of criminal law in it. While some considered that further engagement with Ongwen's prior victimization would have enhanced the didactic, or expressive, function of the trial and contributed to establishing a comprehensive record of the events, the ICC judges interpreted their mandates in a more restrained and formalistic manner. For the latter, the purpose of the judgment at a criminal court was confined to determining whether the accused was guilty or not, thus excluding moral considerations that might be deeply relevant in other social settings.

Furthermore, the ICC trial record shows that the judges have not been afraid to acquit the accused even after decade-long proceedings where they had concerns around the quality of the legal process. While institutional considerations certainly play a role at the Court, the 'institutional interest' of the ICC is itself a contestable issue: while some certainly see convictions as an indication that the ICC is fulfilling its mandate to 'end impunity' for mass atrocities, this book has demonstrated that many other members of the ICL field have considered fair process, regardless of the trial outcome, the ultimate benchmark for assessing the Court's performance. The same

172 Pieters and Kirabira, 'Ongwen Judgment'.
173 Drumbl, '"Getting" an Unforgettable Gettable'.

line of legal reasoning – a dispassionate, emotionless assessment of criminal responsibility – that led to the acquittals of other accused was one of the factors underpinning Ongwen's conviction.

9.2.4 Conclusions from the Ongwen Trial

The *Ongwen* case provides an example of the combined impact of state politics and the normative dynamics of the ICL on trial outcomes. In this case, state politics played out in the decision of the Ugandan government to cooperate with the ICC OTP and to provide a wealth of evidence of the accused's conducts. That evidence, including 'the voluminous intercept evidence' available,[174] proved decisive at the ICC, which had increasingly prioritized strict procedure and refused to tolerate the prosecutor's investigatory challenges, regardless of the trial outcome. While some experts called for a more cautious approach towards assessing the reliability of intercepted communications evidence,[175] overall the available evidence in *Ongwen* appeared more solid than in previous cases in which the prosecution had built its arguments mainly on anonymous testimony, hearsay, and NGO reports. A crucial factor for the success of the prosecution's arguments was also the fact that the LRA was already internationally recognized as a particularly brutal and violent organization.

State politics also played an important role. A common perception is that, as one commentator noted, 'without President Museveni's nod, the ICC would not have delivered judgment against Ongwen'.[176] The *Ongwen* verdict also marked a rare instance of US approval of ICC actions. The United States officially 'welcome[d]' the verdict and offered 'up to $5 million' for cooperation regarding the arrest of the LRA's leader, Joseph Kony.[177] Considering the otherwise tense relationship between the Court and the United States, which culminated in US sanctions against ICC officials following the opening of the Afghanistan investigation,[178] the *Ongwen* verdict presents another illustration of the ICC's embeddedness in state politics.

[174] *Ongwen* Trial Judgment, § 614.

[175] *See* D. Marchesi, 'Intercepted Communications in the *Ongwen* Case: Lessons to Learn on Documentary Evidence at the ICC' (2021) *International Criminal Law Review* 1-21, DOI: https://doi.org/10.1163/15718123-bja10104.

[176] Drumbl, '"Getting" an Unforgettable Gettable'.

[177] United States Department of State, 'Welcoming the Verdict in the Case against Dominic Ongwen for War Crimes and Crimes against Humanity', Press Statement, 4 February 2021, www.state.gov/welcoming-the-verdict-in-the-case-against-dominic-ongwen-for-war-crimes-and-crimes-against-humanity/.

[178] *See* Chapter 1, Section 1.3.

Nevertheless, while state politics might have been key to holding the trial in the first place, their impact on the trial outcome was indirect, occurring through the normative dynamics of the legal field. The availability of vast amounts of incriminating evidence was needed in order to reach the high threshold established by the ICC judges' belief, shared by many participants in the broader ICL field, that the burden of proof on the prosecution should not be lowered despite the challenges specific to the investigations of mass atrocities. Thus, like *Ntaganda*, the *Ongwen* trial found the balance between the demands of different actors within the legal field, both those who strictly prioritized procedural justice and some of those who cherished the opportunity to enable the victims to see justice being served.

Unlike in *Ntaganda* or any other ICC conviction, those upholding the interests of the victims expressed mixed reactions towards the *Ongwen* judgment. Human rights NGOs welcomed the judges' recognition of the gravity and the variety of sexual and gender-based crimes suffered by the LRA victims.[179] One commentator described the judges' findings on forced marriage and forced pregnancy '[t]he most noteworthy parts of the decision'.[180] But other commentators were concerned by the ICC judges' formalistic approach, which had instituted a solid separation between the defendant's own prior victimization and his subsequent criminal acts as an adult.

As with the rest of the ICC trials discussed in this book, the dynamic nature of the ICL field resulted in the validation of the *Ongwen* judgment by some actors and its contestation by others. The trial also demonstrated the difference between the validation of the judgment outside and inside the ICL field. The reaction of the US government and the support of the Ugandan government reflected the interests of politically powerful actors in prosecuting members of a declared terrorist organization, in the case of the former and to further stigmatize a rebel organization. By contrast, both validation and contestation of the judgment within the ICL field were made based on specific liens of legal reasoning – appraising the soundness of the judges' approach to assessing criminal responsibility in view of the different visions of their mandates and the role of ICL in the international community.

179 Women's Initiatives for Gender Justice, 'Trailblazing ICC Judgment'. Coalition for the ICC, 'Trial Chamber IX Found Mr Dominic Ongwen Guilty of 61 Counts of Crimes against Humanity and War Crimes', 4 February 2021, www.coalitionfortheicc.org/news/20210204/Ongwen-verdict.

180 T. Kirabira, 'Ongwen at the International Criminal Court', 19 May 2021, American Society of International Law, www.asil.org/insights/volume/25/issue/7.

9.3 Conclusion

The analysis of *Ntaganda* and *Ongwen* suggests that the confirmation of charges and convictions decisions in those cases followed the same line of legal reasoning as those decisions that acquitted other accused, such as Bemba and Gbagbo. Consequently, the ICC judges do not appear to have lowered the burden on the prosecutor for the purpose of delivering convictions. Rather, in those cases such as *Ntaganda* and *Ongwen* where the accused had been actively involved in the criminal conduct and had personally committed some of the crimes, the prosecutor was more successful in convincing the judges that the facts met their strict requirements. The proximity of the accused to the crimes provides support for establishing both the *actus reus* and *mens rea* elements of principal liability constructed in ICC jurisprudence: that those persons had exercised some form of control over the crimes and that they had intended the commission of those crimes. Nevertheless, while the findings of the TCs in those cases have generally been praised for their meticulous assessment of the facts and evidence, some members of the ICL community expressed concern with the continuing reliance on the 'control over the crime' theory. The criticism of Judge Morrison and Judge Eboe-Osuji in *Ntaganda* displayed their belief that the 'control over the crime' theory constituted a problematic importation into ICC jurisprudence. And, as discussed, one PTC has dismissed the 'control' theory in several ICC cases.[181] It remains to be seen whether future trial chambers will follow suit in their judgments.

[181] Chapter 6, Section 6.2.1.4.

10

Concluding Remarks

In the aftermath of the Nuremberg and Tokyo trials, Judith Shklar observed that 'legalism' was an ideology – specifically, the belief that a certain course of conduct involving the adjudication of criminal responsibility in a courtroom setting was the appropriate response to mass atrocities.[1] Several decades later, the practice of the UN tribunals and the ICC has revealed the existence of a variety of 'sub-ideologies' *within* legalism, which ultimately rest on different visions of international society. Throughout the course of this book, two have become particularly apparent. One of those visions favours the communitarian idea that ICL and its trials should reflect an emerging global morality that binds together the international community of mankind. The other follows a more minimalistic idea of the international society, in which the rule of law serves to institute stable order with clearly defined rules but not to deliver specific substantive justice outcomes in the short term. This concluding chapter draws out the implications of the main findings of this book concerning the internal politics of the ICL field and discusses how the clash between these two different visions of legalism may play out in the future.

10.1 The Variety of Legalist Ideologies

The findings of this book have revealed the importance of understanding the dynamics taking place within the ICL field, namely the intersubjective legal norms that regulate the assessment of criminal responsibility, for analysing trial outcomes at the Court. The claim that 'law matters' has often been uttered with respect to international criminal justice, but it generally rests on a bifurcated view of law and politics as two separate realms. By contrast, this book examined the internal politics of the legal field and, more specifically, the constant struggle for the promotion of different visions about what the legal rules concerning criminal

[1] Shklar, *Legalism*.

responsibility should require. While all those visions demonstrate commitment to liberal legalism, they display significant variation in terms of the perceived role of ICL in international society – some aim at building a stable and predictable international legal order, other at strengthening the moral community of mankind. Nevertheless, the political struggle over the meaning of the criminal responsibility laws is unique to the legal field in that the politics of ICL are both constrained and enabled by the intersubjective rules of practice that govern that field.

Responsibility on Trial makes several important observations with regard to the internal politics of the ICL field. Firstly, while the ICL community of practice enforces specific norms that define what constitutes sound legal reasoning, those norms vary across time and place, even on short time scales – for instance, from the ICTY and ICTR, which started operating in the early 1990s, to the ICC which was established in the late 1990s and began operating in the 2000s. The devastation caused by the Second World War and the widespread publicization of the atrocities committed in the former Yugoslavia and in Rwanda fuelled the moral impulse to prevent the perpetrators of those crimes from escaping justice due to a lack of applicable codified law or because those persons had been removed from the scene of the crimes. That normative impulse, coupled with the influence of common law pragmatism and strong advocacy for protecting the victims, enabled loose interpretations of the culpability principle and broad modes of liability. However, the establishment of the permanent ICC and the drafting of the RS marked a shift in the expectations of many members within the ICL community of practice, with an increasing number of legal experts in the mid-1990s calling for codification of the principles of criminal law in the RS and strict compliance with those principles at the new court, even if the result were more acquittals. Consequently, the detailed text of the criminal responsibility provisions that ended up in the RS needs to be understood in view of the principled beliefs about the meaning of the law that were presented by various members of the ICL community of practice during the RS negotiations, and not simply as the result of states' attempts to shield their nationals from convictions by narrowing the scope of the criminal responsibility laws in the Statute. Furthermore, many ICC judges chose to interpret the RS provisions regulating the attribution of criminal responsibility in a manner that, *in their view*, restricted the scope of situations in which the defendant could be found guilty, perhaps even going further than what had been intended by some of the RS drafters. The *Lubanga* PTC strongly disassociated the new court from the 'joint criminal enterprise', or JCE, mode of liability that had often been used at the ICTY but had triggered criticism from many legal experts for infringing upon the criminal law principles of personal culpability and fair labelling. Instead, the ICC judges adopted what they perceived to be a more 'objective' theory of liability, known as 'control over the crime', and borrowed heavily from the continental legal tradition. Echoing the concerns expressed by some ICC judges and external commentators that the notion of 'control' was, nevertheless, quite broad, the PTC in *Yekatom and Ngaïssona*, *Said*, and *Abd-Al-Rahman* focused exclusively on the link between the accused and the crimes, even if that meant the dismissal of some of the charges. Furthermore, the *Bemba* AC Majority presented a highly restrained interpretation of the command responsibility principle, which significantly narrowed the scope of what was otherwise one of the broadest modes of liability in ICL. Finally, the ICC judges imposed a very strict mental element standard of liability, which several chambers, including the *Bemba* PTC, *Lubanga* Appeals Chamber, and *Ntaganda* Trial Chamber, defined as 'virtual certainty' that one's conduct would result in a crime. In short, ICC jurisprudence on criminal responsibility confirms the earlier predictions of some scholars that while the international trials during the immediate post–Cold War period had been often result-oriented, at the ICC the focus would need to shift the technical application of legal rules, regardless of the trial outcome.[2]

Secondly, this book highlighted a stable line of legal reasoning behind the application of the Rome Statute criminal responsibility provisions in individual cases. The detailed comparison between the cases that have ended up in acquittals, such as *Bemba* and *Gbagbo and Blé Goudé*, and those where the accused was convicted, such as *Ntaganda* and *Ongwen*, revealed that the ICC judges applied the modes of liability in an equally restrained manner in both types of cases. With the possible exception of the first ICC trial, *Lubanga*, where the trial judges appeared willing to infer the accused's control over the crimes from his position of authority over the direct perpetrators of those crimes, other ICC chambers have applied the modes of liability listed in the Rome Statute in a significantly narrow fashion. Consequently, the final verdict in ICC cases appeared to be foremost influenced by the ability of the prosecutor's evidence to meet the high criminal responsibility requirements that were followed in ICC jurisprudence. Furthermore, the empirical analysis does not offer support for the proposition that the judges lowered those requirements for the purpose of convicting certain persons and tightened the requirements

[2] Amann, 'Assessing International Criminal Adjudication', 180–181.

in order to others. Instead, Chapters 7 to 9 reveal that the strict criminal responsibility requirements enforced by the ICC judges allowed for the confirmation of charges and convictions in cases, including *Ntaganda*, *Ongwen*, *Banda and Jerbo*, *Al-Hassan*, and *Yekatom*, where there was clear evidence of the defendant's personal engagement in the criminal conduct. Conversely, the cases against individuals who were distant from the scene of the crimes, such as former political figures like Bemba and Gbagbo, have experienced difficulties meeting the ICC judges' requirements and often resulted in acquittals. Overall, by analyzing the understandings about the meaning of the law that are shared by the majority of ICC judges, this book sheds light on an important factor that influences the outcomes of ICC trials: namely, the technical and narrow application of criminal responsibility laws, which, from the perspective of ICC judges, serves the purpose of protecting the integrity of the judicial process and upholding the liberal values that underpin international criminal justice. Without claiming that legal norms are the only factor determining trial outcomes, the findings of this book nevertheless provide new insights into the question of why, in several cases, the ICC prosecutor has failed to convince the judges that the defendant should bear criminal responsibility.

Thirdly, this book observes that the difference between the assessment of criminal responsibility at the post–Second World War trials and the UN tribunals on the one hand, and the ICC on the other, should not be interpreted as a sign that the practice of ICL has become more 'legal' as the discipline 'matures'. The concept of 'legal norms' is revealed as a socially bounded intersubjective phenomenon, not as an objective standard against which the ICC scores *better* compared to previous tribunals. It cannot be said that earlier tribunals have not followed the law, while the ICC has. Rather, those tribunals have followed different visions of criminal responsibility rules. The IMT at Nuremberg, the IMTFE at Tokyo, and the UN tribunals often perceived morality as the animating force behind legality. From that perspective, if legal rules did not follow the dictates of moral conscience, namely to prevent the perpetrators of mass atrocities from escaping punishment by staying away from the scene of the crimes, those legal rules obstructed the process of serving justice. By contrast, the majority of ICC judges, including at the *Bemba* AC and the *Gbagbo and Blé Goudé* TC, along with some criminal law scholars have considered that the law should be applied in a dispassionate manner despite the horrendous nature of international crimes. From that perspective, the narrow and predictable interpretation of legal rules, regardless of the trial outcome, carries its own normative significance, namely to ensure a law-based system of international governance.

Finally, the overview of ICC cases demonstrated that the analysis of the normative dynamics within the ICL field complements the insights from the existing literature on the functioning of the ICC in the international political arena. State politics could indirectly affect the proceedings, for instance by creating obstacles to the collection of evidence as in the Kenyan trials or providing evidence as in the Ugandan trial. But this book revealed that the assessment of the defendants' guilt or innocence is also guided by a distinguishable line of legal reasoning, one that understands the criminal responsibility laws in a strict and narrow manner. The legal norms that guide the ICC judges' reasoning are 'political' in the sense that they present a variety of intersubjectively held beliefs about the meaning and purpose of the law that are being promoted by different subgroups of the ICL community of practice. Consequently, the different visions of legalism discussed in this book comprise different visions of international political order. This is why the debates taking place inside the ICL community of practice are political debates and not merely technical debates on criminal law procedure. But these are the internal 'politics' of the legal field where every idea about the law needs to be justified with respect to pre-existing sets of shared understandings. In the context of the ICC, the advocates of strict compliance with the criminal law, both within and outside the Court, proved particularly influential. Given the challenges of obtaining reliable evidence in relation to mass atrocities, this trend has rendered the window of opportunity of finding an accused guilty of mass atrocities at the ICC even narrower than might have been suggested by critics of the Court. The empirical analysis of ICC cases reveals that, to end up in a conviction, cases have need to both obtain the political support of states *and* meet the high standards of imposing criminal responsibility, that have been promoted by some members of the ICL epistemic community within and outside the ICC.

This finding problematizes both the critical and the liberal ICL scholarship. It demonstrates the limitations of state-centred critical accounts, which illuminate some power relations affecting specific aspects of ICL, such as the jurisdictional reach of the Court, the handling of self-referrals and the selection of individual suspects. The critical analysis of these aspects reveals the power imbalance between the Global North and the Global South that continues to dominate international trials. But the critical literature fails to examine the power struggles taking place within the legal field – the struggle over competing visions of justice, founded on competing visions of international order As Chapters 7 to 9 demonstrated, *that* power struggle is crucial for understanding the outcomes of ICC trials and it provides insights into the future development of the discipline.

Indeed, a critic might object by saying that the internal political struggles of the legal field are not really 'political' in the sense that the ICL community shares an overall political belief in Western legalism. But internal debates within the ICL field still display a variety of political ideas, in this case, between a minimalist contractualist idea of the international society and a more communitarian vision that seeks to establish strong moral bonds between members of the international community of mankind.

Furthermore, the analysis problematizes the common perception within the liberal-legalist literature that the ICL field juxtaposes self-interested states who seek to limit the reach of the law against idealistic lawyers who aim to expand its scope. Neither do states have monolithic interests with respect to the scope of the law, as demonstrated by their utilization of 'self-referrals' and voluntary cooperation with the ICC in cases involving opposition leaders, nor do lawyers, NGOs, and academics hold a unanimous understanding on those issues. The next section examines the question whether the understanding shared by many within and outside the ICC of the importance of high-quality process is sustainable in the long-term in the ICL field and whether we can draw lessons from the analysis of the assessment of criminal responsibility in order to better understand the internal ideological battles taking place with respect to other aspects of ICL.

10.2 Insights for Future Analysis

It is possible that the cautiousness of many ICC judges, displayed at the *Bemba* AC Majority and the *Gbagbo and Blé Goudé* TC Majority, not to over-stretch the notion of personal culpability could create a backlash within the ICL epistemic community in favour of a more balanced approach of the assessment of criminal responsibility. The cold rational language of those ICC judgments stood in stark contrast with the emotionally charged discourse that generally surrounds international trials. For decades that discourse has publicly defined international tribunals. From the UN Security Council being 'shamed' into taking action to address the atrocities in the former Yugoslavia and in Rwanda, to the advocacy of human rights advocates and NGOs for the establishment of the ICC, the institutionalization of ICL has been accompanied with references to the plight of the victims and the moral consciousness of humankind.

In fact, this backlash may already be observable. While many members of the ICL epistemic community became increasingly concerned that the practices of the UN tribunals came dangerously close to the attribution of guilt by association, the restrained approach of the ICC judges has begun to trigger the opposite reaction. NGOs criticized the ICC judges for 'overly strictly' applying the culpability principle.[3] Similarly, some scholars who had been advocating for greater compliance with criminal responsibility principles in ICL[4] became concerned that the ICC had 'over-corrected' the practices of the UN tribunals.[5] Notably, some ICC judges, who shared a humanitarian concern for expanding the protection of civilians during conflict, departed from the approach to criminal responsibility taken by the majority of their colleagues, as illustrated by the dissenting opinion of Judge Herrera-Carbuccia at the *Gbagbo and Blé Goudé* TC. The humanitarian perspective may still constitute the minority position at the ICC, but if the backlash intensifies, that could change.

Nevertheless, two factors need to be considered that may halt, or at least slow down this shift back towards substantive justice. Firstly, because of the intersubjective nature of international legal norms, any change in the dominant set of shared understandings at an institution takes time and, in fact, it may prove particularly challenging at the ICC. The practices of the UN tribunals regarding the assessment of criminal responsibility did change over time, but a radical departure from those practices only took place with the transition to ICC. The dispassionate approach to delivering international judgments may prove unsustainable in the long run, but at the moment it holds a firm grip on the ICC.

Secondly, the ICC prosecutor may adjust to the strict criminal responsibility requirements enforced by the majority of the ICC judges, and present at the Court only those cases that are supported by solid evidence, thus increasing the chances of conviction and avoiding more embarrassing acquittals. In fact, most cases in which the charges were confirmed in the past few years, including *Al-Mahdi*, *Al-Hassan*, *Yekatom*, *Abd-Al-Rahman*, and *Said*, have involved allegations of the accused's direct participation in the criminal conduct, which renders the link between the accused and crimes easier to establish. As demonstrated by the reactions to the *Ntaganda* and *Ongwen* judgments, those cases that involve abundant evidence of the accused's personal role in the crimes strike a balance between the different visions of legalism – the one driven by the moral impulse to punish the perpetrators of mass atrocities and the one emphasizing high-quality process. While the accused in all the aforementioned cases constitute mid-level insurgent commanders, this could change in

[3] Women's Initiatives for Gender Justice, 'Gender Report Card 2018', 147.
[4] See Robinson, 'Identity Crisis'.
[5] See Robinson, 'International Criminal Law'.

the future if the prosecutor manages to collect abundant and high-quality evidence against a leadership figure. The prosecutor has already taken steps in that regard by proposing in the OTP's official strategy to target mid-level perpetrators as a means to eventually link their commanders to the crimes.[6] Given the slow pace of ICC proceedings, inevitably slowed even further by the challenges of international investigations, it might take years before a senior official is convicted at the court.[7] Therefore, it is up to future research to examine whether the prosecutor's apparent strategy has been successful.

The observations of this book point to the conclusion that the politics *of the legal field*, i.e. the promotion and contestation of different understandings of the law by various actors, has rendered the restrained approach to criminal responsibility highly influential at the ICC, with discernible consequences for trial outcomes. The critical scholarship and the liberal-legalist theories have provided insightful but limited accounts of the dynamics taking place within the ICL field, resulting from their focus on the interests of states and politically powerful classes. This book presented a new dimension of the dynamics of the ICL field that enables a more comprehensive analysis of the outcomes of ICC proceedings. Unlike rationalistic international relations theories of judicial independence that seek generalizable results over a large set of samples, the aim of this book is to contribute to the gradual process of building a body of interdisciplinary literature that examines in detail a variety of aspects of ICL practice. This 'bottom-up' approach presents a long-needed transformation of the study of the ICC and enables better integration between political science and international law for the purpose of enabling truly interdisciplinary research on international criminal justice and bridging the liberal-legalist scholarship and the critical scholarship.

This book has examined the ICL filed from the outside, avoiding normative assessments of the different approaches to criminal responsibility employed in ICL. The aim of this book is to facilitate dialogue inside the ICL field by elucidating the major debates on criminal responsibility rather than taking a side in those debates. But if this book is allowed one normative reflection in conclusion, it is that, 20 years after the ICC began operation, it is time to move beyond the claims that ICL is above politics and to engage in a more open discussion of the internal politics that govern even the most apparently technical debates within the ICL field and their implications for the construction of international criminal justice.

6 ICC, Office of the Prosecutor, *Strategic Plan June 2012–2015*, 11 October 2013, 14.

7 Interview with Kevin Heller, 11 August 2020.

BIBLIOGRAPHY

Books, Articles, Statements, and NGO Reports

Abbott, K. 1989. 'Modern International Relations Theory: A Prospectus for International Lawyers', 14(2) *The Yale Journal of International Law* 335–411.

Abbott, K. and D. Snidal. 2000. 'Hard and Soft Law in International Governance', 54(3) *International Organization* 421.

Abbott, K., Keohane, R., Moravcsik, A., Slaughter, A.-M., and D. Snidal. 2000. 'The Concept of Legalization', 54(3) *International Organization* 401.

Abbott, K. and D. Snidal. 2013. 'Law, Legalization and Politics: An Agenda for the Next Generation of IR Scholars', in J. Dunoff and M. Pollack (eds.), *Interdisciplinary Perspectives on International Law and International Relations: The State of the Art* (Cambridge: Cambridge University Press).

Aboa, A. 2019. 'Ivorian President Does Not Rule Out Running for Third Term in 2020', *Reuters* (26 January), www.reuters.com/article/us-ivorycoast-politics/ivorian-president-does-not-rule-out-running-for-third-term-in-2020-idUSKCN1PK0J8.

Adler, E. and V. Pouliot. 2011. 'International Practices: Introduction and Framework', in E. Adler, and V. Pouliot (eds.), *International Practices* (Cambridge: Cambridge University Press).

Ainley, K. 2011. 'Excesses of Responsibility: The Limits of Law and the Possibilities of Politics', 25(4) *Ethics & International Affairs* 407.

Akhavan, P. 2001. 'Beyond Impunity: Can International Criminal Justice Prevent Future Atrocities?', 95(1) *The American Journal of International Law* 1.

Akhavan, P. 2009. 'Are International Criminal Tribunals a Disincentive to Peace?: Reconciling Judicial Romanticism with Political Realism', 31(3) *Human Rights Quarterly* 624.

Aksenova, M. 2015. 'The Modes of Liability at the ICC: The Labels That Don't Always Stick', 15(4) *International Criminal Law Review* 629–644.

Aksenova, M. 2019. 'Solidarity as a Moral and Legal Basis for Crimes against Humanity: A Durkheimian Perspective', in M. Aksenova, E. van Sliedregt, and S. Parmentier (eds.), *Breaking the Cycle of Mass Atrocities: Criminological and Socio-Legal Approaches in International Criminal Law* (Oxford: Hart Publishing).

Alexander, L., Ferzan, K. K., and S. Morse. 2009. *Crime and Culpability: A Theory of Criminal Law* (Cambridge: Cambridge University Press).

Allen, T. and M. Schomerus. 2006. 'A Hard Homecoming: Lessons Learned from the Reception Center Process in Northern Uganda: An Independent Study', 2006, http://eprints.lse.ac.uk/28888/1/__lse.ac.uk_storage_LIBRARY_Secondary_libfile_shared_repository_Content_Schomerus,%20M_Hard%20homecoming_Schomerus_Hard%20homecoming_2014.pdf.

Alter, K. 2006. 'Delegation to International Courts and the Limits of Re-contracting Political Power', in D. Hawkins, D. Lake, D. Nielson, and M. Tierney (eds.), *Delegation and Agency in International Organizations* (Cambridge: Cambridge University Press).

Alter, K. 2008. 'Agents or Trustees? International Courts in Their Political Context', 14(1) *European Journal of International Relations* 33.

Alter, K. 2014. *The New Terrain of International Law: Courts, Politics, Rights* (Princeton and Oxford: Princeton University Press).

Alter, K. and L. Helfer. 2010. 'Nature or Nurture? Judicial Lawmaking in the European Court of Justice and the Andean Tribunal of Justice', 64(4) *International Organization* 563.

Alter, K., Helfer, L., and M. Madsen. 2018a. 'International Court Authority in a Complex World', in K. Alter, L. Helfer, and M. Madsen (eds.), *International Court Authority* (Oxford: Oxford University Press).

Alter, K., Helfer, L., and M. Madsen. 2018b. 'How Context Shapes the Authority of International Courts', in K. Alter, L. Helfer, and M. Madsen (eds.), *International Court Authority* (Oxford: Oxford University Press).

Altwicker, T. and O. Diggelmann. 2014. 'How Is Progress Constructed in International Legal Scholarship?', 25(2) *European Journal of International Law* 425.

Amann, D. M. 2003. 'Assessing International Criminal Adjudication of Human Rights Atrocities', 16 *Third World Legal Studies* 169.

Amann, D. M. 2013. International Decisions: Prosecutor v. Lubanga, University of Georgie School of Law Research Paper Series, *Paper No. 2013–23*, 106 *American Journal of International Law* (2012) 809–817.

Amann, D. M. 2018. 'In Bemba and Beyond, Crimes Adjudged to Commit Themselves', EJIL: *Talk*, (13 June), www.ejiltalk.org/in-bemba-and-beyond-crimes-adjudged-to-commit-themselves/.

Ambos, K. 1996. 'Establishing an International Criminal Court and an International Criminal Code: Observations from an International Criminal Law Viewpoint', 7(4) *European Journal of International Law* 519.

Ambos, K. 2002. 'Superior Responsibility', in A. Cassese, P. Gaeta, and J. R. W. D. Jones (eds.), *The Rome Statute of the International Criminal Court* Vol. II (Oxford: Oxford University Press).

Ambos, K. 2003. 'Current Issues in International Criminal Law', 14(3) *Criminal Law Forum* 225.

Ambos, K. 2006. 'Remarks on the General Part of International Criminal Law', 4(4) *Journal of International Criminal Justice* 660.

Ambos, K. 2007. 'Joint Criminal Enterprise and Command Responsibility', 5(1) *Journal of International Criminal Justice* 159.

Ambos, K. 2009a. 'Command Responsibility and *Organisationsherrschaft*: Ways of Attributing International Crimes to the "Most Responsible"', in A. Nollkaemper and H. van der Wilt (eds.), *System Criminality in International Law* (Cambridge: Cambridge University Press).

Ambos, K. 2009b. 'Critical Issues in the *Bemba* Confirmation Decision', 22(4) *Leiden Journal of International Law* 715.

Ambos, K. 2012a. 'Expanding the Focus of the "African Criminal Court"', in W. Schabas, Y. McDermott, and N. Hayes (eds.), *Ashgate Research Companion to International Criminal Law: Critical Perspectives* (Farnham: Ashgate).

Ambos, K. 2012b. 'The First Judgment of the International Criminal Court (Prosecutor v. Lubanga): A Comprehensive Analysis of the Legal Issues', 12(2) *International Criminal Law Review* 115.

Ambos, K. 2013. *Treatise on International Criminal Law. Volume 1, Foundations and General Part* (Oxford: Oxford University Press).

Ambos, K. 2015a. 'The Overall Function of International Criminal Law: Striking the Right Balance between the Rechtsgut and the Harm Principles', 9(2) *Criminal Law and Philosophy* 301.

Ambos, K. 2015b. 'The ICC and Common Purpose—What Contribution Is Required under Article 25(3)(d)?', in C. Stahn (ed.), *The Law and Practice of the International Criminal Court* (Oxford: Oxford University Press).

Ambos, K. 2016. 'Article 25: Individual Criminal Responsibility', in K. Ambos and O. Triffterer (eds.), *Rome Statute of the International Criminal Court: A Commentary*, 3rd ed. (London: Bloomsbury T&T Clark).

Amnesty International. 1994a. 'A Call for UN Human Rights Action on Rwanda and Burundi', (30 April), www.amnesty.org/download/Documents/184000/ior410021994en.pdf.

Amnesty International. 1994b. 'Rwanda: Mass Murder by Government Supporters and Troops in April and May 1994', (23 May 1994b), www.amnesty.org/download/Documents/184000/afr470111994en.pdf.

Amnesty International. 2016. 'Kenya: Ruto and Sang Decision Must Not Derail Efforts to Ensure Justice for Victims', (5 April), www.amnesty.org/en/latest/news/2016/04/kenya-ruto-and-sang-decision-must-not-derail-efforts-to-ensure-justice-for-victims/.

Amnesty International. 2018a. 'Bemba Judgment Warrants Better Investigations and Fair Trials – Not Efforts to Discredit the Decision', 19 June 2018, https://hrij.amnesty.nl/bemba-verdict-warrants-better-investigations-and-fair-trials/.

Amnesty International. 2018b. 'The ICC Must Become a Champion of Justice over Abuse of Power', (23 February), www.amnesty.org/en/latest/news/2018/02/the-icc-must-become-a-champion-of-justice-over-abuse-of-power/.

Amnesty International. 2019a. 'Cote d'Ivoire: Acquittal of Gbagbo and Blé Goudé a Crushing Disappointment to Victims of Post-election Violence',

(15 January), www.amnesty.org/en/latest/news/2019/01/cote-acquittal-of-gbagbo-a-crushing-disappointment-to-victims/.

Amnesty International. 2019b. 'DRC: ICC Conviction of Ntaganda Provides Long Awaited Justice for Victims of Grotesque Crimes', (8 July), www.amnesty.org/en/latest/news/2019/07/drc-icc-conviction-of-ntaganda-provides-long-awaited-justice-for-victims-of-grotesque-crimes/.

Amnesty International. 2021. 'Central African Republic: Dozens Suspected of Criminal Responsibility for War Crimes and Crimes against Humanity Remain at Large', (8 December), www.amnesty.org/en/latest/news/2021/12/central-african-republic-dozens-suspected-of-criminal-responsibility-for-war-crimes-and-crimes-against-humanity-remain-at-large/.

Anderson, J. H. 2018. 'Ocampo's Shadow Still Hangs over the ICC', *International Justice Tribune*, 18 June 2018, www.justicetribune.com/blog/ocampos-shadow-still-hangs-over-icc.

Anderson, K. 2009. 'The Rise of International Criminal Law: Intended and Unintended Consequences', 20(2) *European Journal of International Law* 331.

Anderson, K. 2021. 'Dominic Ongwen: It Is Very Difficult to Balance All That', *Justice in Conflict*, 2 February 2021, https://justiceinconflict.org/2021/02/02/dominic-ongwen-it-is-very-difficult-to-balance-all-that/.

Arendt, H. 1964. *Eichmann in Jerusalem: A Report on the Banality of Evil* (New York: Viking Press).

Arenella, P. 1990. 'Character, Choice and Moral Agency: The Relevance of Character to Our Moral Culpability Judgments', 7(1) *Social Philosophy & Policy* 59.

Aukerman, M. J. 2002. 'Extraordinary Evil, Ordinary Crime: A Framework for Understanding Transitional Justice', 15 *Harvard Human Rights Journal* 39.

Baaz, M. 2015. 'Dissident Voices in International Criminal Law', 28(3) *Leiden Journal of International Law* 673.

Badar, M. E. 2006. '"Just Convict Everyone!" – Joint Perpetration: From *Tadić* to *Stakić* and Back Again,' 6(2) *International Criminal Law Review* 293.

Badar, M. E. 2008. 'The Mental Element in the Rome Statute of the International Criminal Court: A Commentary from a Comparative Criminal Law Perspective', 19(3) *Criminal Law Forum* 473.

Badar, M. E. 2009. 'Dolus Eventualis and the Rome Statute Without It?', 12(3) *New Criminal Law Review: An International and Interdisciplinary Journal* 433.

Bantekas, I. 2006. 'Reflections on Some Sources and Methods of International Criminal and Humanitarian Law', 6(1) *International Criminal Law Review* 121.

Barnett, M. and L. Coleman. 2005. 'Designing Police: Interpol and the Study of Change in International Organizations', 49(4) *International Studies Quarterly* 593.

Barnett, M. and M. Finnemore. 1999. 'The Politics, Power, and Pathologies of International Organizations', 53(4) *International Organization* 699.

Barnett, M. and M. Finnemore. 2004. *Rules for the World: International Organizations in Global Politics* (Ithaca, New York: Cornell University Press).

Bass, G. 2000. *Stay the Hand of Vengeance: The Politics of War Crimes Tribunals* (Princeton and Oxford: Princeton University Press).

Bassiouni, M. 2005a. *The Legislative History of the International Criminal Court: Introduction, Analysis, and Integrated Text of the Statute, Elements of Crimes and Rules of Procedure and Evidence*, Vol. 1 (Ardsley, New York: Transnational Publishers, Inc.).

Bassiouni, M. 2005b. *The Legislative History of the International Criminal Court: An Article by Article Evolution of the Statute from 1994–1998*, Vol. 2 (Ardsley, New York: Transnational Publishers, Inc.).

Bassiouni, M. 2006. 'International Recognition of Victims' Rights', 6(2) *Human Rights Law Review* 203.

Bassiouni, M. and B. Ferencz. 2008. 'The Crime against Peace and Aggression: From Its Origins to the ICC', in M. C. Bassiouni (ed.), *International Criminal Law*, Vol. I, 3rd ed. (Leiden: Martinus Nijhoff Publishers).

Bassiouni C. and D. Hansen. 2016. 'The Inevitable Practice of the Office of the Prosecutor', in R. Steinberg (ed.), *Contemporary Issues Facing the International Criminal Court* (Leiden: Brill Nijhoff).

Batros, B. 2019. 'The ICC Acquittal of Gbagbo: What Next for Crimes against Humanity', *Just Security*, (18 January), www.justsecurity.org/62295/icc-acquittal-gbagbo-crimes-humanity/

Bayles, M. 1982. 'Character, Purpose, and Criminal Responsibility', 1(1) *Law and Philosophy* 5.

BBC. 2012. 'DR Congo Warlord Thomas Lubanga sentenced to 14 years', (10 July), www.bbc.com/news/world-africa-18779726

Bellelli, R. 2016. 'The Establishment of the System of International Criminal Justice' in R. Bellelli (ed.), *International Criminal Justice: Law and Practice from the Rome Statute to Its Review* (London and New York: Routledge).

Berman, N. 1999. 'In the Wake of Empire', 14(6) *American University of International Law Review* 1521.

Bensouda, F. 2012. 'Keynote speech, OpenForum 2012: Money, Power and Sex: The Paradox of Unequal Growth', (23 May), www.icc-cpi.int/NR/rdonlyres/A73A2D85-37C4-40C0-8CB2-0577D90436B7/284578/23052012DPSpeechOpenForumPowerDay.pdf.

Bensouda, F. 2013. 'Address to the Assembly of State Parties, 12th Session of the Assembly of State Parties', (20 November), https://asp.icc-cpi.int/iccdocs/asp_docs/ASP12/ASP12-OP-Statement-PROS-ENG-FRA.pdf.

Bergsmo M. and W. Wiley. 2008. 'Human Rights Professionals and the Criminal Investigation and Prosecution of Core International Crimes', in I. Hurley and H. Mark (eds.), *Manual on Human Rights Monitoring: An Introduction for Human Rights Field Officers* (Oslo: Norwegian Centre for Human Rights), www.jus.uio.no/smr/english/about/programmes/nordem/publications/manual/current/kap10.pdf

Bertodano, S. 2002. 'Judicial Independence in the International Criminal Court', 15(2) *Leiden Journal of International Law* 409.

Bibas, S. and W. Burke-White. 2010. 'International Idealism Meets Domestic-Criminal-Procedure Realism', 59(4) *Duke Law Journal* 637.

Bikundo, E. 2012. 'The International Criminal Court and Africa: Exemplary Justice', 23(1) *Law and Critique* 21.

Black, J. 2008. 'Constructing and Contesting Legitimacy and Accountability in Polycentric Regulatory Regimes', 2(1) *Regulation & Governance* 137.

Boas, G. 2010. 'Omission Liability at the International Criminal Tribunals – A Case for Reform', in S. Darcy and J. Powderly (eds.), *Judicial Creativity at the International Criminal Tribunals* (Oxford: Oxford University Press).

Boas, G., Bischoff, J. L., and N. L. Reid. 2008. *International Criminal Law Practitioner Library, Vol. I. Forms of Responsibility in International Criminal Law* (Cambridge: Cambridge University Press).

Bohlander, M. 2011. 'Radbruch Redux: The Need for Revisiting the Conversation between Common and Civil Law at Root Level at the Example of International Criminal Justice', 24(2) *Leiden Journal of International Law* 393.

Boister, N. 2010. 'The Application of Collective and Comprehensive Criminal Responsibility for Aggression at the Tokyo International Military Tribunal', 8(2) *Journal of International Criminal Justice* 425.

Bonafe, B. 2007. 'Finding a Proper Role for Command Responsibility', 5(3) *Journal of International Criminal Justice* 599.

Borgwardt, E. 2007. *A New Deal for the World* (Cumberland, USA: Harvard University Press).

Bosco, D. 2014. *Rough Justice: The International Criminal Court in a World of Power Politics* (New York: Oxford University Press).

Bourdieu, P. 1987. 'The Force of Law: Toward a Sociology of the Juridical Field', translated by R. Terdiman, 38(5) *Hastings Law Journal* 805.

Boyle, A. and C. Chinkin. 2007. *The Making of International Law* (New York: Oxford University Press).

Bradfield, P. 2021. 'The Moral and Legal Correctness of Dominic Ongwen's Conviction', *Justice in Conflict*, (10 February), https://justiceinconflict.org/2021/02/10/the-moral-and-legal-correctness-of-dominic-ongwens-conviction/.

Branch, A. 2007. 'Uganda's Civil War and the Politics of ICC Intervention', 21(2) *Ethics & International Affairs* 179.

Branch A. 2010. 'What the ICC Review Conference Can't Fix', in *Oxford Transitional Justice Research: Debating International Justice in Africa* (The Foundation for Law, Justice and Society; The Centre for Socio-Legal Studies, University of Oxford).

Branch, A. 2011. *Displacing Human Rights: War and Intervention in Northern Uganda* (New York: Oxford University Press).

Branch, A. 2017. 'Dominic Ongwen on Trial: The ICC's African Dilemmas', 11(1) *International Journal of Transitional Justice* 30.

Brannigan, A. 2011. 'Is the Sun Setting on Cosmopolitan Justice?', 48(5) *Society* 420.

Broomhall, B. 2004. *International Justice and the International Criminal Court: Between Sovereignty and the Rule of Law* (Oxford: Oxford University Press).

Broomhall, B. 2016. 'Article 22: *Nullum Crimen Sine Lege*', in K. Ambos and O. Triffterer (eds.), *Rome Statute of the International Criminal Court: A Commentary*, 3rd ed. (London: Bloomsbury T&T Clark).

Brunnée J. and S. Toope. 2010. *Legitimacy and Legality in International Law: An Interactional Account* (Cambridge: Cambridge University Press).

Brunnée J. and S. Toope. 2011. 'Interactional International Law and the Practice of Legality', in E. Adler and V. Pouliot (eds.), *International Practices* (Cambridge: Cambridge University Press).

Brunnée J. and S. Toope. 2013. 'Constructivism and International Law', in J. Dunoff and M. Pollack (eds.), *Interdisciplinary Perspectives on International Law and International Relations: The State of the Art* (Cambridge: Cambridge University Press).

Bueno, O. 2015. 'Between Hope and Skepticism: Congolese Await the Trial of Ntaganda', *International Justice Monitor*, (2 September), www.ijmonitor.org/2015/09/between-hope-and-skepticism-congolese-await-the-trial-of-ntaganda/.

Cakaj, L. 2010. 'The Lord's Resistance Army of Today', Enough Project, (November 2010), www.enoughproject.org/files/publications/lra_today.pdf.

Carayannis, T. 2016. 'Making Justice Work: The Bemba Case and the ICC's Future', *Foreign Affairs*, (5 April), www.foreignaffairs.com/articles/central-african-republic/2016-04-05/making-justice-work.

Carlson, K. 2019. 'Why the Ntaganda Judgment Shows that the ICC Has Found Its Footing', *The Conversation*, (16 July), https://theconversation.com/why-the-ntaganda-judgment-shows-that-the-icc-has-found-its-footing-120433.

Cassese, A. 2002. 'From Nuremberg to Rome: International Military Tribunals to the International Criminal Court', in A. Cassese, P. Gaeta, and J. R. W. D. Jones (eds.), *The Rome Statute of the International Criminal Court*, Vol. I (Oxford: Oxford University Press).

Cassese, A. 2006. 'Is the ICC Still Having Teething Problems?', 4(3) *Journal of International Criminal Justice* 434.

Cassese, A. 2008a. 'The Statute of the International Criminal Court: Some Preliminary Reflections', in A. Cassese, P. Gaeta, and S. Zappalà (eds.), *The Human Dimension of International Law: Selected Papers of Antonio Cassese* (Oxford: Oxford University Press).

Cassese, A. 2008b. *International Criminal Law*, 2nd ed. (Oxford: Oxford University Press).

Cassese, A. 2011. 'Reflections on International Criminal Justice', 9(1) *Journal of International Criminal Justice* 271.

Cassese, A. et al. 2009. 'Amicus Curiae Brief of Professor Antonio Cassese and Members of the Journal of International Criminal Justice on Joint Criminal Enterprise Doctrine,' 20(2–3) *Criminal Law Forum* 289.

Chapman, T. and S. Chaudoin. 2013. 'Ratification Patterns and the International Criminal Court', 57(2) *International Studies Quarterly* 400.

Chappell, L. 2014. 'Conflicting Institutions and the Search for Gender and Justice at the International Criminal Court', 67(1) *Political Research Quarterly* 183–196.

Charbonneau, B. 2012. 'War and Peace in Côte d'Ivoire: Violence, Agency, and the Local/International Line', 19(4) *International Peacekeeping* 508.

Charney, J. 1999. 'Progress in International Criminal Law?', 93(2) *American Journal of International Law* 452.

Chayes, A. and A. Chayes. 1995. *The New Sovereignty: Compliance with International Regulatory Agreements* (Cambridge: Harvard University Press).

Chimni, B. 2017. *International Law and World Order: A Critique of Contemporary Approaches*, 2nd ed. (Cambridge: Cambridge University Press).

Christensen, M. 2017. 'Preaching, Practicing and Publishing International Criminal Justice: Academic Expertise and the Development of an International Field of Law', 17(2) *International Criminal Law Review* 239.

Clark, P. 2008. 'Law, Politics and Pragmatism: The ICC and Case Selection in the Democratic Republic of Congo and Uganda', in N. Waddell and P. Clark (eds.), *Courting Conflict? Justice, Peace at the ICC in Africa* (London, SOAS: Royal African Society).

Clark, P. 2018. *Distant Justice: The Impact of the International Criminal Court on African Politics* (Cambridge: Cambridge University Press).

Clark, R. 2001. 'The Mental Element in International Criminal Law: The Rome Statute of the International Criminal Court and the Elements of Offences', 12(3) *Criminal Law Forum* 291.

Clark, R. 2008. 'Drafting a General Part to a Penal Code: Some Thoughts Inspired by the Negotiations on the Rome Statute of the International Criminal Court and by the Court's First Substantive Law Discussion in the *Lubanga Dyilo* Confirmation Proceedings', 19(3–4) *Criminal Law Forum* 519.

Clarke, K. 2009. *Fictions of Justice: The International Criminal Court and the Challenge of Legal Pluralism in Sub-Saharan Africa* (New York: Cambridge University Press).

Clarke, K. 2011. 'The Rule of Law through Its Economies of Appearances: The Making of the African Warlord', 18(1) *Indiana Journal of Global Legal Studies* 7.

Clarke, K. 2015. 'Refiguring the Perpetrator: Culpability, History and International Criminal Law's Impunity Gap', 19(5) *International Journal of Human Rights* 592.

Coalition for the ICC. 2019. 'Côte d'Ivoire: Laurent Gbagbo and Charles Blé Goudé Acquitted by ICC and Released on Conditions', (16 January), http://www.coalitionfortheicc.org/news/20190116/cote-divoire-laurent-gbagbo-and-charles-ble-goude-acquitted-icc.

Coalition for the ICC. 2021. 'Trial Chamber IX Found Mr Dominic Ongwen Guilty of 61 Counts of Crimes against Humanity and War Crimes', (4 February), www.coalitionfortheicc.org/news/20210204/Ongwen-verdict.

Cohen, D. and Y. Totani. 2018. *The Tokyo War Crimes Tribunal: Law, History, and Jurisprudence* (Cambridge: Cambridge University Press).

Cohen, J. 2013. 'Critical Social Theory and Feminist Critiques', in J. Meehan (ed.), *Feminists Read Habermas* (London: Taylor and Francis).

Cole, R. 2013. 'Africa's Relationship with the International Criminal Court: More Political than Legal', 14(2) *Melbourne Journal of International Law* 670.

Combs, N. 2010. *Fact-Finding without Facts: The Uncertain Evidentiary Foundations of International Criminal Convictions* (Cambridge: Cambridge University Press).

Combs, N. 2017. 'Grave Crimes and Weak Evidence: A Fact-finding Evolution in International Criminal Law', 58(1) *Harvard International Law Journal* 47.

Corrias, D. and G. Gordon. 2015. 'Judging in the Name of Humanity International Criminal Tribunals and the Representation of a Global Public', 13(1) *Journal of International Criminal Justice* 97.

Cryer, R. 2009a. 'Royalism and the King: Article 21 of the Rome Statute and the Politics of Sources', 12(3) *New Criminal Law Review: An International and Interdisciplinary Journal* 390.

Cryer, R. 2009b. 'The Definitions of International Crimes in the *Al Bashir* Arrest Warrant Decision', 7(2) *Journal of International Criminal Justice* 283.

Cryer, R. 2010. 'The *Ad Hoc* Tribunals and the Law of Command Responsibility: A Quiet Earthquake', in S. Darcy and J. Powderly (eds.), *Judicial Creativity at the International Criminal Tribunals* (Oxford: Oxford University Press).

Cryer, R. 2015. 'Then and Now: Command Responsibility, the Tokyo Tribunal and Modern International Criminal Law', in K. Sellars (ed.), *Trials for International Crimes in Asia* (Cambridge: Cambridge University Press).

Cryer, R., Friman, H., Robinson, D., and E. Wilmhurst. 2014. *An Introduction to International Criminal Law and Procedure*, 3rd ed. (Cambridge: Cambridge University Press).

Cupido, M. 2014. 'Pluralism in Theories of Liability: Joint Criminal Enterprise versus Joint Perpetration', in E. van Sliedregt and S. Vasiliev (eds.), *Pluralism in International Criminal Law* (Oxford: Oxford University Press).

Dale, P. 2019. 'Bosco Ntaganda – the Congolese "Terminator"', BBC, (8 July), www.bbc.com/news/world-africa-17689131.

Damaška, M. 2001. 'The Shadow Side of Command Responsibility', 49(3) *The American Journal of Comparative Law* 455.

Damaška, M. 2008. 'What Is the Point of International Criminal Justice', 83(1) *Chicago-Kent Law Review* 329.

Danilenko, G. 2000. 'The Statute of the International Criminal Court and Third States', 21(3) *Michigan Journal of International Law* 454.

Danner, A. 2003. 'Enhancing the Legitimacy and Accountability of Prosecutorial Discretion at the International Criminal Court', 97(3) *American Journal of International Law* 510.

Danner, A. 2006. 'When Courts Make Law: How the International Criminal Tribunals Recast the Laws of War', 59(1) *Vanderbilt Law Review* 1.

Danner A. and J. Martinez. 2005. 'Guilty Associations: Joint Criminal Enterprise, Command Responsibility, and the Development of International Criminal Law', 93(1) *California Law Review* 75.

Darcy, S. 2007. 'Imputed Criminal Liability and the Goals of International Justice', 20(2)*Leiden Journal of International Law* 377–404.

Darcy, S. 2010. 'Bridging the Gaps in the Laws of Armed Conflict? International Criminal Tribunals and the Development of Humanitarian Law', in N. Quenivet and S. Shah-Davis (eds.), *International Law and Armed Conflict: Challenges in the 21st Century* (The Hague: T.M.C. Asser Press).

De Vlaming, F. 2012. 'Selection of Defendants', in L. Reydams, J. Wouters, and C. Ryngaert (eds.), *International Prosecutors* (Oxford: Oxford University Press).

De Vos, C. 2011. 'Prosecutor v. Lubanga – Someone Who Comes between One Person and Another: Lubanga, Local Cooperation and the Right to a Fair Trial', 12(1) *Melbourne Journal of International Law* 217.

De Vos, C. 2013. 'Investigating from Afar: The ICC's Evidence Problem', 26(4) *Leiden Journal of International Law* 1009.

De Vos, C. 2020. *Complementarity, Catalysts, Compliance: The International Criminal Court in Uganda, Kenya, and the Democratic Republic of Congo* (Cambridge: Cambridge University Press).

DeFalco, R. 2013. 'Contextualizing Actus Reus under Article 25(3)(d) of the ICC Statute: Thresholds of Contribution', 11(4) *Journal of International Criminal Justice* 715.

DeGuzman, M. 2016a. 'Is the ICC Targeting Africa Inappropriately? A Moral, Legal, and Sociological Assessment', in R. Steinberg (ed.), *Contemporary Issues Facing the International Criminal Court* (Leiden: Brill Nijhoff).

DeGuzman, M. 2016b. 'Applicable Law', in K. Ambos and O. Triffterer (eds.) *Rome Statute of the International Criminal Court: A Commentary*, 3rd ed. (London: Bloomsbury T&T Clark).

Deitelhoff, N. 2009. 'The Discursive Process of Legalization: Charting Islands of Persuasion in the ICC Case,' 63(1) *International Organization* 33.

Dixon, P., and C. Tenove. 2013. 'International Criminal Justice as a Transnational Field: Rules, Authority and Victims', 7(3) *International Journal of Transitional Justice* 393.

Drumbl, M. 2007. *Atrocity, Punishment, and International Law* (Cambridge: Cambridge University Press).

Drumbl, M. 2016. 'Victims Who Victimise', 4(2) *London Review of International Law* 217.

Drumbl, M. 2021. '"Getting" an Unforgettable Gettable: The Trial of Dominic Ongwen', *Justice in Conflict*, 5 February 2021, https://justiceinconflict.org/2021/02/05/getting-an-unforgettable-gettable-the-trial-of-dominic-ongwen/.

Drumbl M. and K. Gallant. 2001. 'Appeals in the Ad Hoc International Criminal Tribunals: Structure, Procedure, and Recent Cases', 3(2) *Journal of Appellate Practice and Process* 589.

Dubber, M. 2006. 'Comparative Criminal Law', in M. Reimann and R. Zimmermann (eds.), *The Oxford Handbook of Comparative Law*, 1st ed. (Oxford: Oxford University Press).

Dubber, M. 2011. 'Common Civility: The Culture of Alegality in International Criminal Law', 24(4) *Leiden Journal of International Law* 923.

Dubois, A. and L. Gadde. 2002. 'Systematic Combining: An Abductive Approach to Case Research', 55(7) *Journal of Business Research* 553.

Duff, R. A. 1993. 'Choice, Character, and Criminal Liability', 12(4) *Law and Philosophy* 345–383.

Duff, R. A. 2008. 'Responsibility and Liability in Criminal Law,' in M. H. Kramer, C. Grant, B. Colburn, and A. Hatzistavrou (eds.), *The Legacy of H. L. A. Hart: Legal, Political, and Moral Philosophy* (Oxford: Oxford University Press).

Dunoff, J. and M. Pollack. 2013. 'International Law and International Relations: Introducing an Interdisciplinary Dialogue', in J. Dunoff and M. Pollack (eds.), *Interdisciplinary Perspectives on International Law and International Relations: The State of the Art* (Cambridge: Cambridge University Press).

Eldar, S. 2013. 'Exploring International Criminal Law's Reluctance to Resort to Modalities of Group Responsibility', 11(2) *Journal of International Criminal Justice* 331.

Ellis, M. 2019. 'The Latest Crisis of the ICC: The Acquittal of Laurent Gbagbo', *OpinioJuris*, (28 March), http://opiniojuris.org/2019/03/28/the-latest-crisis-of-the-icc-the-acquittal-of-laurent-gbagbo/.

Engle, K. 2016. 'A Genealogy of the Criminal Turn in Human Rights', in K. Engle, Z. Miller, and D. Davis (eds.), *Anti-Impunity and the Human Rights Agenda* (Cambridge: Cambridge University Press).

Engle, K., Miller, Z., and D. Davis. 2016. *Anti-Impunity and the Human Rights Agenda* (Cambridge: Cambridge University Press).

Eser, A. 1993. 'The Need for a General Part', 11(1) *Nouvelles Études Pénales* 43.

Eser, A. 2001. 'Towards an International Criminal Court: Genesis and Main Features of the Rome Statute', 20(1) *University of Tasmania Law Review* 1.

Eser, A. 2002a. 'Mental Elements – Mistake of Fact and Mistake of Law', in A. Cassese, P. Gaeta, and J. Jones (eds.), *The Rome Statute of the International Criminal Court*, Vol. 1 (Oxford: Oxford University Press).

Eser, A. 2002b. 'Individual Criminal Responsibility', in A. Cassese, P. Gaeta, and J. Jones (eds.), *The Rome Statute of the International Criminal Court*, Vol. 1 (Oxford: Oxford University Press).

Evenson, E. and J. O'Donohue. 2016. 'States Shouldn't Use ICC Budget to Interfere with Its Work', Amnesty International, (23 November), www.amnesty.org/en/latest/news/2016/11/states-shouldnt-use-icc-budget-to-interfere-with-its-work/

Farhang, C. 2010. 'Point of No Return: Joint Criminal Enterprise in Brđanin', 23(1) *Leiden Journal of International Law* 137.

Fenrick, W. 1998. 'The Development of the Law of Armed Conflict through the Jurisprudence of the International Criminal Tribunal for the Former Yugoslavia', 3(2) *Journal of Armed Conflict Law* 197.

Ferencz, B. 1998. 'International Criminal Courts: The Legacy of Nuremberg', 10(1) *Pace International Law Review* 203.

FIDH, 2018. 'Acquittal of Jean Pierre Bemba on Appeal: An Affront to Thousands of Victims', (8 June), www.fidh.org/en/region/Africa/central-african-republic/acquittal-of-jean-pierre-bemba-on-appeal-an-affront-to-thousands-of

Finegan, E. 2010. 'Legal Writing: Attitude and Emphasis', in M. Coulthard and A. Johnston (eds.), *The Routledge Handbook of Forensic Linguistics* (London: Routledge).

Finnemore, M. 2000. 'Are Legal Norms Distinctive?', 32(3) *New York University Journal of International Law & Politics* 699.

Finnin, S. 2012. 'Mental Elements under Article 30 of the Rome Statute of the International Criminal Court: A Comparative Analysis', 61(2) *International and Comparative Law Quarterly* 325.

Fish, S. 1980. *Is There a Text in This Class?: The Authority of Interpretive Communities* (Cambridge, Mass.: Harvard University Press).

Fletcher, G. P. 1978. *Rethinking Criminal Law* (Boston: Little, Brown).

Fletcher, G. 1998. 'Truth in Codification', 31(3) *U.C. Davis Law Review* 745.

Fletcher, G. 2002. 'The Storrs Lectures: Liberals and Romantics at War: The Problem of Collective Guilt', 111(7) *The Yale Law Journal* 1499.

Fletcher, G. 2011. 'New Court, Old Dogmatik', 9(1) *Journal of International Criminal Justice* 179.

Fletcher, G. and J. D. Ohlin. 2005. 'Reclaiming Fundamental Principles of Criminal Law in the Darfur Case', 3(3) *Journal of International Criminal Justice* 539.

Fletcher, L. 2005. 'From Indifference to Engagement: Bystanders and International Criminal Justice', 26(4) *Michigan Journal of International Law* 1013.

Fletcher, L. and H. Weinstein. 2002. 'Violence and Social Repair: Rethinking the Contribution of Justice to Reconciliation', 24(3) *Human Rights Quarterly* 573.

Foreign & Commonwealth Office. 2018. 'UK Statement to ICC Assembly of States Parties 17th session', (5 December), www.gov.uk/government/speeches/uk-statement-to-icc-assembly-of-states-parties-17th-session

Franck, T. M. 1990. *Power of Legitimacy among Nations* (Cary: Oxford University Press).

Franck, T. M. 1998. *Fairness in International Law and Institutions* (Oxford: Oxford University Press).

Fraser, N. 1985. 'What's Critical about Critical Theory? The Case of Habermas and Gender', 35(1) *New German Critique* 97.

Freedman, J. 2017. *A Conviction in Question: The First Trial at the International Criminal Court* (Toronto: University of Toronto Press).

Fuller, L. L. 1958. 'Positivism and Fidelity to Law: A Reply to Professor Hart', 71(4) *Harvard Law Review* 630.

Fuller, L. 2004[1963]. *The Morality of Law*, Revised ed. (Delhi: Universal Law Publishing).

Gaeta, P. 2016. 'The History and the Evolution of the Notion of International Crimes', in R. Bellelli (ed.), *International Criminal Justice: Law and Practice from the Rome Statute to Its Review* (London and New York: Routledge).

Galand, A. 2019. 'The Systemic Effect of International Human Rights Law on International Criminal Law', in M. Scheinin (ed.), *Human Rights Norms in 'Other' International Courts* (Cambridge: Cambridge University Press).

Gallant, K. S. 2008. *The Principle of Legality in International and Comparative Criminal Law* (Cambridge: Cambridge University Press).

Gardner, J. 1994. 'Criminal Law and the Uses of Theory: A Reply to Laing', 14(2) *Oxford Journal of Legal Studies* 217.

Gattini, A. 2009. 'A Historical Perspective: From Collective to Individual Responsibility and Back', in A. Nollkaemper and H. van der Wilt (eds.), *System Criminality in International Law* (Cambridge: Cambridge University Press).

Gee J. P. and M. Handford. 2012. 'Introduction', in J. P. Gee and M. Handford (eds.), *The Routledge Handbook of Discourse Analysis* (London: Routledge).

Giddens, A. 1984. *The Constitution of Society: Outline of the Theory of Structuration* (Cambridge: Polity Press).

Gil, A. 2014. 'Mens Rea in Co-perpetration and Indirect Perpetration According to Article 30 of the Rome Statute. Arguments against Punishment for Excesses Committed by the Agent or the Co-perpetrator', 14(1) *International Criminal Law Review* 82.

Gil, A. G. and E. Maculan. 2015. 'Current Trends in the Definition of "Perpetrator" by the International Criminal Court: From the Decision on the Confirmation of Charges in the *Lubanga* Case to the *Katanga* Judgment', 28(2) *Leiden Journal of International Law* 349.

Ginsburg, T. 2013. 'Political Constraints on International Courts', in C. Romano, K. Alter, and Y. Shany (eds.), *The Oxford Handbook of International Adjudication*, 1st ed. (Oxford: Oxford University Press).

Glasius, M. 2006. *The International Criminal Court: A Global Civil Society Achievement* (London: Routledge).

Glasius, M. 2009. 'What Is Global Justice and Who Decides?: Civil Society and Victim Responses to the International Criminal Court's First Investigations', 31(2), *Human Rights Quarterly* 496–520.

Goldsmith, J. and E. Posner 2006. *The Limits of International Law* (Cary: Oxford University Press).

Goldstein, J., Kahler, M., Keohane, R., and A.-M. Slaughter. 2000. 'Introduction: Legalization and World Politics', 54(3) *International Organization* 385.

Goldston, J. 2010. 'More Candour about Criteria: The Exercise of Discretion by the Prosecutor of the International Criminal Court', 8(2) *Journal of International Criminal Justice* 383.

Goy, B. 2012. 'Individual Criminal Responsibility before the International Criminal Court: A Comparison with the *Ad Hoc* Tribunals', 12(1) *International Criminal Law Review* 1.

Granik, M. 2015. 'Indirect Perpetration Theory: A Defence', 28(4) *Leiden Journal of International Law* 977.

Grant R. and R. Keohane. 2005. 'Accountability and Abuses of Power in World Politics', 99(1) *American Political Science Review* 29.

Greenawalt, A. K. A. 2011. 'The Pluralism of International Criminal Law', 86(3) *Indiana Law Journal* 1063.

Grey, R. 2019. 'Gender-based Crimes: A Monumental Day for the ICC', *IntLawGrrls*, (8 July), https://ilg2.org/2019/07/08/gender-based-crimes-a-monumental-day-for-the-icc/

Grey, R. 2021. 'Gender-based Persecution against Men: the ICC's Abd-al-Rahman Case', *OpinioJuris*, (35 May), http://opiniojuris.org/2021/05/30/gender-based-persecution-against-men-the-iccs-abd-al-rahman-case/

Grover, L. 2010. 'A Call to Arms: Fundamental Dilemmas Confronting the Interpretation of Crimes in the Rome Statute of the International Criminal Court', 21(3) *European Journal of International Law* 543.

Guilfoyle, D. 2011. 'Responsibility for Collective Atrocities: Fair Labelling and Approaches to Commission in International Criminal Law', 64(1) *Current Legal Problems* 255.

Guilfoyle, D. 2019a. 'This Is Not Fine: The International Criminal Court in Trouble Part II', (22 March), www.ejiltalk.org/part-ii-this-is-not-fine-the-international-criminal-court-in-trouble/

Guilfoyle, D. 2019b. 'A Tale of Two Cases: Lessons for the Prosecutor of the International Criminal Court? (Part I)', *EJIL: Talk!*, (28 August), www.ejiltalk.org/a-tale-of-two-cases-lessons-for-the-prosecutor-of-the-international-criminal-court/

Guilfoyle, D. 2019c. 'Lacking Conviction: Is the International Criminal Court Broken? An Organisational Failure Analysis'. *Melbourne Journal of International Law*, 20(2), 1–52.

Gustafson, K. 2007. 'The Requirement of an Express Agreement for Joint Criminal Enterprise Liability', 5(1) *Journal of International Criminal Justice* 134.

Guzman, A. 2008. *How International Law Works: A Rational Choice Theory* (New York: Oxford University Press).

Haan, V. 2005. 'The Development of the Concept of Joint Criminal Enterprise at the International Criminal Tribunal for the Former Yugoslavia', 5(2) *International Criminal Law Review* 167.

Habermas, J. 1996. *Between Facts and Norms: Contributions to a Discourse Theory of Law and Democracy* (Cambridge: Polity Press).

Hagan, J. 2003. *Justice in the Balkans: Prosecuting War Crimes in the Hague Tribunal* (Chicago: University of Chicago Press).

Hagan, J. and R. Levi. 2005. 'Crimes of War and the Force of Law', 83(4) *Social Forces* 1499.

Hall, C. 2004. 'The Powers and Role of the Prosecutor of the International Criminal Court in the Global Fight against Impunity', 17(1) *Leiden Journal of International Law* 121.

Happold, M. 2007. 'The International Criminal Court and the Lord's Resistance Army', 8(1) *Melbourne Journal of International Law* 159–184.

Harrington, J. 2010. 'An End to War Through a Court of Law? Perhaps-and in Time', *EJIL: Talk!*, (14 June), www.ejiltalk.org/an-end-to-war-through-a-court-of-law-perhaps-and-in-time/

Hart, H. L. A. 1958. 'Positivism and the Separation of Law and Morals', 71(4) *Harvard Law Review* 593.

Hart, H. L. A. 1983. 'Problems of the Philosophy of Law', in H. L. A. Hart (ed.), *Essays in Jurisprudence and Philosophy* (Oxford: Oxford University Press).

Hart, H. L. A. 2008. *Punishment and Responsibility: Essays in the Philosophy of Law*, 2nd ed. (Oxford: Oxford University Press).

Hayes, N. 2016. 'The Bemba Trial Judgement – A Memorable Day for the Prosecution of Sexual Violence by the ICC', PhD Students in Human Rights, 21 March 2016, http://humanrightsdoctorate.blogspot.com/2016/03/hayes-bemba-trial-judgement-memorable.html

Hazan, P. 2004. *Justice in a Time of War* (College Station: Texas A&M University Press).

Heath, J. 2012. 'Human Dignity at Trial: Hard Cases and Broad Concepts in International Criminal Law', 44(2) *George Washington International Law Review* 317.

Hedinger, D. 2016. 'A Global Conspiracy? The Berlin – Tokyo – Rome Axis on Trial and Its Impact on the Historiography of the Second World War', 14(4) *Journal of Modern European History* 500.

Heinze, A. 2018. 'Some Reflections on the Bemba Appeals Chamber Judgment', *OpinioJuris*, 18 June 2018, http://opiniojuris.org/2018/06/18/some-reflections-on-the-bemba-appeals-chamber-judgment/

Helfer, L. and A. Slaughter. 2005. 'Why States Create International Tribunals: A Response to Professors Posner and Yoo', 93(3) *California Law Review* 899.

Heller, K. J. 2010. 'The Rome Statute of the International Criminal Court', in K. J. Heller and M. Dubber (eds.), *The Handbook of Comparative Criminal Law* (Stanford: Stanford University Press).

Heller, K. J. 2011. *The Nuremberg Military Tribunals and the Origins of International Criminal Law* (Oxford: Oxford University Press).

Heller, K. J. 2012. 'Lubanga Decision Roundtable: More on Co-Perpetration', *OpinioJuris*, (16 March), http://opiniojuris.org/2012/03/16/lubanga-decision-roundtable-more-on-co-perpetration/

Heller, K. J. 2016a. 'Radical Complementarity', 14(3) *Journal of International Criminal Justice* 637.

Heller, K. J. 2016b. 'Why Bemba's Conviction Was Not a "Very Good Day" for the OTP (Updated)', *OpinioJuris* (22 March), http://opiniojuris.org/2016/03/22/a-few-thoughts-on-bembas-conviction/

Heller, K. J. 2019. 'Bim, Bam, Bem-Boom!', *OpinionJuris*, 12 March 2019, http://opiniojuris.org/2019/03/12/bim-bam-bemb-oom/

Henquet, T. 2002. 'Convictions for Command Responsibility Under Articles 7(1) and 7(3) of the Statute of the International Criminal Tribunal for the Former Yugoslavia', 15(4) *Leiden Journal of International Law* 805.

Higgins, R. 1995. *Problems and Process: International Law and How We Use It* (Oxford: Clarendon Press).

Hillebrecht, C. and S. Straus. 2017. 'Who Pursues the Perpetrators?: State Cooperation with the ICC', 39(1) *Human Rights Quarterly* 162.

Holmes, O. W. 1997 [1897]. 'The Path of Law', 110(5) *Harvard Law Review* 991.

Huigens, K. 1995. 'Virtue and Inculpation', 108(7) *Harvard Law Review* 1423.

Human Rights Watch. 2005. 'Uprooted and Forgotten: Impunity and Human Rights Abuses in Northern Uganda', 24–35 (2005), www.hrw.org/sites/default/files/reports/uganda0905.pdf

Human Rights Watch. 2009. 'Justice for Liberia: The Truth and Reconciliation Commission's Recommendation for an Internationalized Domestic War Crimes Court', (10 December), www.hrw.org/news/2009/12/10/justice-liberia#_Definitions

Human Rights Watch. 2011a. '"They Killed Them Like It Was Nothing" The Need for Justice for Côte d'Ivoire's Post-Election Crimes', www.hrw.org/sites/default/files/reports/cdi1011webwcover_0.pdf

Human Rights Watch. 2011b. 'Côte d'Ivoire: Ouattara Forces Kill, Rape Civilians during Offensive', www.hrw.org/news/2011/04/09/cote-divoire-ouattara-forces-kill-rape-civilians-during-offensive.

Human Rights Watch. 2012. 'ICC: Pursue Case against Rwandan Rebel Leader', 1 June 2012, www.hrw.org/news/2012/06/01/icc-pursue-case-against-rwandan-rebel-leader

Human Rights Watch, 2019. 'ICC: Congo Warlord Guilty of Crimes against Humanity', (8 July), www.hrw.org/news/2019/07/08/icc-congo-warlord-guilty-crimes-against-humanity

Hunt, C. T. 2016. 'Côte d'Ivoire', in A. J. Bellamy and T. Dunne (eds.), *The Oxford Handbook of the Responsibility to Protect* (Oxford: Oxford University Press).

Hunt, D. 2004. 'The International Criminal Court', 2(1) *Journal of International Criminal Justice* 56.

Husak, D. 2010. *The Philosophy of Criminal Law: Selected Essays* (Oxford and New York: Oxford University Press).

ICC. 2007. 'Background: Situation in the Central African Republic', (22 May), www.icc-cpi.int/NR/rdonlyres/B64950CF-8370-4438-AD7C-0905079D747A/144037/ICCOTPBN20070522220_A_EN.pdf.

ICC. 2018a. 'Situation in Central African Republic II: Alfred Yekatom Surrendered to the ICC for Crimes against Humanity and War Crimes', (17 November), www.icc-cpi.int/Pages/item.aspx?name=pr1418

ICC. 2018b. 'Situation in Central African Republic II: Patrice-Edouard Ngaïssona Arrested for Crimes against Humanity and War Crimes', (12 December), www.icc-cpi.int/Pages/item.aspx?name=PR1425

ICC, Office of the Prosecutor. 2006. *Report on the Activities Performed during the First Three Years (June 2003–June 2006),* (12 September), www.icc-cpi.int/NR/rdonlyres/D76A5D89-FB64-47A9-9821-725747378AB2/143680/OTP_3yearreport20060914_English.pdf.

ICC, Office of the Prosecutor. 2012. 'Statement ICC Prosecutor on New Applications for Warrants of Arrest DRC Situation', www.icc-cpi.int/Pages/item.aspx?name=otpstatement14052012

ICC, Office of the Prosecutor. 2013. *Strategic Plan June 2012–2015,* (11 October), www.icc-cpi.int/iccdocs/otp/OTP-Strategic-Plan-2013.pdf.

ICC ASP. 2012a. Intervention de la France de S. E. Monsieur l'Ambassadeur Perre Ménat, Chef de Délégation, (15 November), https://asp.icc-cpi.int/iccdocs/asp_docs/ASP11/GenDeba/ICC-ASP11-GenDeba-FRA-FRA.pdf.

ICC ASP. 2012b. Kingdom of Belgium, Eleventh session of the Assembly of States Parties to the Rome Statute of the International Criminal Court, The Hague, (14 November), https://asp.icc-cpi.int/iccdocs/asp_docs/ASP11/GenDeba/ICC-ASP11-GenDeba-BEL-ENG.pdf.

ICC ASP. 2012c. Statement by Denmark, 11th Session of the Assembly of States Parties to the Rome Statute of the International Criminal Court, The Hague, (15 November), https://asp.icc-cpi.int/iccdocs/asp_docs/ASP11/GenDeba/ICC-ASP11-GenDeba-DEN-ENG.pdf.

ICC ASP. 2012d. Statement by H. E. Dr. Bogdan Aurescu, State Secretary for Strategic Affairs, Ministry of Foreign Affairs Romania, The Hague, (15 November), https://asp.icc-cpi.int/iccdocs/asp_docs/ASP11/GenDeba/ICC-ASP11-GenDeba-ROM-ENG.pdf.

ICC ASP. 2012e. Statement by H. E. Mr. Yasumasa Nagamine Ambassador of Japan to the Netherlands, The Hague, (15 November), https://asp.icc-cpi.int/iccdocs/asp_docs/ASP11/GenDeba/ICC-ASP11-GenDeba-JPN-ENG.pdf.

ICC ASP. 2012f. Statement on Behalf of the European Union and Its Member States delivered by H. E. Mr. Andreas D. Mavroyiannis, Deputy Minister for European Affairs to the President of the Republic of Cyprus at the Eleventh Session of the Assembly of State Parties of the International Criminal Court, The Hague, https://asp.icc-cpi.int/iccdocs/asp_docs/ASP11/GenDeba/ICC-ASP11-GenDeba-CYP-ENG.pdf.

ICC ASP. 2012g. Statement on Behalf of the Republic of Estonia by H. E. Mr. Urmas Paet Minister of Foreign Affairs of the Republic of Estonia, The Hague, (15 November), https://asp.icc-cpi.int/iccdocs/asp_docs/ASP11/GenDeba/ICC-ASP11-GenDeba-EST-ENG.pdf.

ICC ASP. 2018. 'Report to the Assembly of States Parties on the Projects and the Activities of the Board of Directors of the Trust Fund for Victims for the Period 1 July 2017 to 30 June 2018', ICC-ASP/17/14, (23 July), www.trustfundforvictims.org/sites/default/files/reports/ICC-ASP-17-14-ENG.pdf.

Ignatieff, M. 2000. 'Human Rights as Politics. Human Rights as Idolatry', in *The Tanner Lectures on Human Values*, Princeton University, (April 4–7), https://tannerlectures.utah.edu/_documents/a-to-z/i/Ignatieff_01.pdf.

Ignatieff, M. 2015. 'International Justice Possible Only When in the Interest of Powerful States', *International Center for Transitional Justice*, (9 February), www.ictj.org/debate/article/justice-interests-of-powerful-states.

Jackson, M. 2015. *Complicity in International Law* (Oxford: Oxford University Press).

Jackson, M. 2016. 'The Attribution of Responsibility and Modes of Liability in International Criminal Law', 29(3) *Leiden Journal of International Law* 879.

Jackson, M. 2018a. 'Commander's Motivations in Bemba', *EJIL: Talk!*, (15 June), www.ejiltalk.org/commanders-motivations-in-bemba/.

Jackson, M. 2018b. 'Geographical Remoteness in Bemba', *EJIL: Talk!*, (30 July), www.ejiltalk.org/geographical-remoteness-in-bemba/.

Jain, N. 2011. 'The Control Theory of Perpetration in International Criminal Law', 12(1) *Chicago Journal of International Law* 159.

Jain, N. 2014. *Perpetrators and Accessories in International Criminal Law: Individual Modes of Responsibility for Collective Crimes* (London: Hart Publishing).

Jescheck, H. 2004. 'The General Principles of International Criminal Law Set Out in Nuremberg, as Mirrored in the ICC Statute', 2(1) *Journal of International Criminal Justice* 38.

Jessberger, F. and J. Geneuss. 2008. 'On the Application of a Theory of Indirect Perpetration in Al Bashir', 6(5) *Journal of International Criminal Justice* 853.

Jessberger, F. and J. Geneuss. 2012. 'The Many Faces of the International Criminal Court. *Journal of International Criminal Justice*', 10(5) *Journal of International Criminal Justice* 1081.

Jia, B. B. 1998. 'The Doctrine of Command Responsibility in International Law: With Emphasis on Liability for Failure to Punish', 45(3) *Netherlands International Law Review* 325.

Jia, B. B. 2000. 'The Doctrine of Command Responsibility: Current Problems', 3 *Yearbook of International Humanitarian Law* 131.

Johnstone, I. 2011. *The Power of Deliberation: International Law, Politics and Organizations* (New York: Oxford University Press).

Johnstone, I. 2013. 'Law-Making by International Organizations: Perspectives from IL/IR Theory', in J. Dunoff and M. Pollack (eds.), *Interdisciplinary Perspectives on International Law and International Relations: The State of the Art* (Cambridge: Cambridge University Press).

Kadish, S. 1985. 'Complicity, Cause and Blame: A Study in the Interpretation of Doctrine', 73(2) *California Law Review* 323.

Kadish, S. 1997. 'Reckless Complicity', 87(2) *Criminal Law & Criminology* 369.

Kahan, D. 1994. 'Lenity and Federal Common Law Crimes,' 1994 *Supreme Court Review* 345.

Kahan, D. 1997. 'Ignorance of Law Is an Excuse: But Only for the Virtuous', 96(1) *Michigan Law Review* 127.

Kaufman, Z. 2010. 'The Nuremberg Tribunal v. the Tokyo Tribunal: Designs, Staffs, and Operations', 43(3) *John Marshall Law Review* 753.

Kaul, H.-P. 2012. 'Ten Years International Criminal Court', (2 October), www.icc-cpi.int/NR/rdonlyres/FB16B529-3A60-441D-8DBE-5D6A768CA6FF/284995/02102012_Berlin_DGAP_THEICCatTen_Final.pdf

Kaoutzanis, C. 2013. 'A Turbulent Adolescence Ahead: The ICC's Insistence on Disclosure in the Lubanga Trial,' 12(2) *Washington University Global Studies Law Review* 263.

Kasande, S. K. and J. Mugero. 2021. 'The Ongwen Verdict: A Step Closer to Acknowledgment and Justice for Victims in Northern Uganda', International Center for Transitional Justice, (2 August), www.ictj.org/news/ongwen-verdict-step-closer-acknowledgment-and-justice-victims-northern-uganda

Kelman, H. 2009. 'The Policy Context of International Crimes', in A. Nollkaemper and H. van der Wilt (eds.), *System Criminality in International Law* (Cambridge: Cambridge University Press).

Kelsen, H. 1947. 'Will the Judgment in the Nuremberg Trial Constitute a Precedent in International Law?', 1(2) *The International Law Quarterly* 153.

Keohane, R. 1997. 'International Relations and International Law: Two Optics', 38(2) *Harvard International Law Journal* 502.

Keppler, E. 2018. 'No Redress for Central African Victims', Human Rights Watch, (11 June), www.hrw.org/news/2018/06/11/no-redress-central-african-victims

Keppler, E. 2021. 'Litany of Horrors by LRA Leader: Ongwen Was No "Puppet on A String"', *Justice in Conflict*, (8 February), https://justiceinconflict.org/2021/02/08/litany-of-horrors-by-lra-leader-ongwen-was-no-puppet-on-a-string/.

Kersten, M. 2016. *Justice in Conflict: The Effects of the International Criminal Court's Interventions on Ending Wars and Building Peace* (Oxford: Oxford University Press).

Kersten, M. 2019. 'Whither the Aspirational ICC, Welcome the 'Practical' Court?', *EJIL: Talk!* (22 May), www.ejiltalk.org/whither-the-aspirational-icc-welcome-the-practical-court/

Khomami, N. 2017. '"It Was as If I Had Peered into Hell": The Man Who Brought the Nazi Death Squads to Justice', *Guardian* (7 February), www.theguardian.com/law/2017/feb/07/nazi-death-squads-nuremberg-trials-benjamin-ferencz

Kirabira, T. 2021. 'Ongwen at the International Criminal Court', (19 May), American Society of International Law, www.asil.org/insights/volume/25/issue/7

Kirchheimer, O. 2015[1961]. *Political Justice: The Use of Legal Procedure for Political Ends* (Princeton: Princeton University Press).

Kiyani, A. 2017. 'Legitimacy, Legality, and the Possibility of a Pluralist International Criminal Law', in N. Hayashi and C. Bailliet (eds.), *The Legitimacy of International Criminal Tribunals* (Cambridge: Cambridge University Press).

Knox, R. 2016. 'Marxist Approaches to International Law', in A. Orford and F. Hoffmann (eds.), *The Oxford Handbook of the Theory of International Law* (Oxford: Oxford University Press).

Knoops, G.-J. A. 2016. 'Introductory Note', in G. Z. Capaldo (ed.), *The Global Community of International Law and Jurisprudence 2015* (New York: Oxford University Press).

Kopelman, E. 1991. 'Ideology and International Law: The Dissent of the Indian Justice at the Tokyo War Crimes Trial', 23(2) *N.Y.U. Journal of International Law and Politics* 373.

Kortfält, L. 2015. 'Sexual Violence and the Relevance of the Doctrine of Superior Responsibility in the Light of the *Katanga* Judgment at the International Criminal Court', 84(4) *Nordic Journal of International Law* 533.

Koskenniemi, M. 2002. 'Between Impunity and Show Trials', 6(1) *Max Planck Yearbook of United Nations Law* 1.

Koskenniemi, M. 2006. *From Apology to Utopia: The Structure of International Legal Argument* (Cambridge: Cambridge University Press).

Koskenniemi, M. 2009. 'The Politics of International Law – 20 Years Later', 20(1) *European Journal of International Law* 7.

Kratochwil F. 1989. *Rules, Norms, and Decisions: On the Conditions of Practical and Legal Reasoning in International Relations and Domestic Affairs* (Cambridge: Cambridge University Press).

Kratochwil, F. 2001. 'How Do Norms Matter?' in Byers, M. (ed.), *The Role of Law in International Politics* (Oxford: Oxford University Press).

Kratochwil, F. 2011. 'Making Sense of "International Practices"', in E. Adler, and V. Pouliot (eds.), *International Practices* (Cambridge: Cambridge University Press).

Krebs, B. 2010. 'Joint Criminal Enterprise', 73(4) *Modern Law Review* 578.

Krever, T. 2013. 'International Criminal Law: An Ideology Critique', 26(3) *Leiden Journal of International Law* 701.

Krever, T. 2014. 'Dispensing Global Justice', 85(1) *New Left Review* 67.

Lamb, S. 2002. 'Nullum Crimen, Nulla Poena Sine Lege in International Criminal Law', in A. Cassese, P. Gaeta, and J. R. W. D. Jones (eds.), *The Rome Statute of the International Criminal Court* Vol. I (Oxford: Oxford University Press).

Lange, M. 2013. *Comparative-Historical Methods* (London: Sage Publications).

Lattanzi, F. 2016. 'Concurrent Jurisdictions between Primacy and Complementarity', in R. Bellelli (ed.), *International Criminal Justice: Law and Practice from the Rome Statute to Its Review* (London and New York: Routledge).

Lechner, S. and M. Frost. 2018. *Practice Theory and International Relations* (Cambridge: Cambridge University Press).

Lee, R. (ed.) 1999. *The International Criminal Court: The Making of the Rome Statute – Issues, Negotiations, Results* (The Hague: Kluwer Law International).

Levine, E. 2005. 'Command Responsibility: The *Mens Rea* Requirement', *Global Policy Forum*, www.globalpolicy.org/component/content/article/163/28306.html

Levine, J. D. 2007. 'The Doctrine of Command Responsibility and Its Application to Superior Civilian Leadership: Does the International Criminal Court Have the Correct Standard?', 193 *Military Law Review* 52.

Lippman, M. 2001. 'Humanitarian Law: The Uncertain Contours of Command Responsibility', 8(2) *Tulsa Journal of Comparative & International Law* 1.

Liu, D. 2015. 'Contribution of the United Nations Ad Hoc Tribunals to the Development of International Criminal Law', in M. Bergsmo, C. W. Ling, S. Tianying, and Y. Ping (eds.), *Historical Origins of International Criminal Law: Volume 4* (Brussels: Torkel Opsahl Academic EPublisher).

Lohne, K. 2017. 'Global Civil Society, the ICC, and Legitimacy in International Criminal Justice', in N. Hayashi and C. Bailliet (eds.), *The Legitimacy of International Criminal Tribunals* (Cambridge: Cambridge University Press).

Lowe, V. 2001. 'The Politics of Law-Making: Are the Method and Character of Norm Creation Changing?', in Byers, M. (ed.), *The Role of Law in International Politics* (Oxford: Oxford University Press).

Luban, D. 2010. 'Fairness to Rightness: Jurisdiction, Legality, and the Legitimacy of International Criminal Law', in S. Besson and J. Tasioulas (eds.), *The Philosophy of International Law* (Oxford: Oxford University Press).

Luban, D. 2013. 'After the Honeymoon: Reflections on the Current State of International Criminal Justice', 11(3) *Journal of International Criminal Justice* 505.

Luban, D. 2018. 'The Enemy of All Humanity', 47(1) *Netherlands Journal of Legal Philosophy* 112.

Lugano, G. 2017. 'Counter-Shaming the International Criminal Court's Intervention as Neocolonial: Lessons from Kenya', 11(1) *International Journal of Transitional Justice* 9–29.

Lutz, E. and K. Sikkink. 2001. 'The Justice Cascade: The Evolution and Impact of Foreign Human Rights Trials in Latin America', 2(1) *Chicago Journal of International Law* 1.

MacGovern, M. 2011. *Making War in Côte d'Ivoire* (London: Hurst).

Mackenzie, R. and P. Sands. 2003. 'International Courts and Tribunals and the Independence of the International Judge', 44(1) *Harvard International Law Journal* 271.

Mahoney, P. 2008. 'The International Judiciary – Independence and Accountability', 7(3) *Law & Practice of International Courts and Tribunals* 313.

Majone, G. 2001. 'Two Logics of Delegation: Agency and Fiduciary Relations in EU Governance', 2(1) *European Union Politics* 103.

Mamdani, M. 2009. 'The New Humanitarian Order', 36(122) *Review of African Political Economy* 621.

Manacorda, S. and C. Meloni. 2011. 'Indirect Perpetration versus Joint Criminal Enterprise: Concurring Approaches in the Practice of International Criminal Law', 9(1) *Journal of International Criminal Justice* 159.

Mantovani, F. 2003. 'The General Principles of International Criminal Law: The Viewpoint of a National Criminal Lawyer', 1(1) *Journal of International Criminal Justice* 26.

Marchesi, D. 2021. 'Intercepted Communications in the *Ongwen* Case: Lessons to Learn on Documentary Evidence at the ICC', *International Criminal Law Review* 1–21, DOI: 10.1163/15718123-bja10104.

Marks, S. 2011. 'Human Rights and Root Causes', 74(1) *The Modern Law Review* 57.

Mattioli-Zeltner, G. 2016. 'Dispatches: High-Profile ICC Warning to Commanders on Rape', Human Rights Watch, (21 March), www.hrw.org/news/2016/03/21/dispatches-high-profile-icc-warning-commanders-rape.

May, L. 2004. *Crimes against Humanity* (Cambridge: Cambridge University Press).

May, L. 2008. *Aggression and Crimes against Peace* (New York: Cambridge University Press).

May, L. and S. Fyfe. 2017. *International Criminal Tribunals: A Normative Defense* (Cambridge: Cambridge University Press).

McDermott, Y. 2017a. 'Strengthening the Evaluation of Evidence in International Criminal Trials', 17(4) *International Criminal Law Review* 682.

McGoldrick, D. 2004. 'The Legal and Political Significance of a Permanent International Criminal Court', in D. McGoldrick, P.J. Rowe, and E. Donnelly (eds.), *The Permanent International Criminal Court: Legal and Policy Issues* (Oxford and Portland Oregon: Hart Publishing).

McGovern, M. 2009. 'Proleptic Justice: The Threat of Investigation as a Deterrent to Human Rights Abuses in Côte d'Ivoire', in K. M. Clarke and M. Goodale (eds.), *Mirrors of Justice: Law and Power in the Post-Cold War Era* (New York: Cambridge University Press).

McManus, P. 2017. 'Enemy of Mankind or Just No Powerful Friends Left? Insights from International Relations about the Efficacy of the ICC', 17(2) *International Criminal Law Review* 302.

Mearsheimer, J. J. 1994. 'The False Promise of International Institutions', 19(3)*International Security* 5.

Meron, T. 1987. 'The Geneva Conventions as Customary Law,' 81(2) *American Journal of International Law* 348.

Meron, T. 1995. 'From Nuremberg to the Hague', 149(1) *Military Law Review* 107.

Meron, T. 2005. 'Revival of Customary Humanitarian Law', 99(4) *American Journal of International Law* 817.

Merope, S. 2011. 'Recharacterizing the Lubanga Case: Regulation 55 and the Consequences for Gender Justice at the ICC', 22(3) *Criminal Law Forum* 311.

Mettraux, G. 2006. *International Crimes and the Ad Hoc Tribunals* (Oxford: Oxford University Press).

Mégret, F. 2012. 'Where Does the Critique of International Human Rights Stand? An Exploration in 18 Vignettes', in J. M. Beneyto, D. Kennedy, J. C. Varela, and J. Haskell (eds.), *New Approaches to International Law: The European and the American Experiences* (The Hague: Springer).

Mégret, F. 2014. 'International Criminal Justice: A Critical Research Agenda', in C. Schwöbel (ed.), *Critical Approaches to International Criminal Law: An Introduction* (Abingdon and New York: Routledge).

Mégret, F. 2015. 'What Sort of Global Justice Is 'International Criminal Justice'?', 13(1) *Journal of International Criminal Justice* 77.

Mégret, F. 2019. 'International Criminal Justice History Writing as Anachronism: The Past That Did Not Lead to the Present', in I. Tallgren and T. Skouteris (eds.), *The New Histories of International Criminal Law* (Oxford: Oxford University Press).

Miéville, C. 2006. *Between Equal Rights: A Marxist Theory of International Law* (London: Pluto).

Minow, M. 1998. *Between Vengeance and Forgiveness: Facing History after Genocide and Mass Violence* (Boston: Beacon Press).

Militello, V. 2007. 'The Personal Nature of Individual Criminal Responsibility and the ICC Statute', 5(4) *Journal of International Criminal Justice* 941.

Mills, K. 2012. '"Bashir Is Dividing Us": Africa and the International Criminal Court', 34(2) *Human Rights Quarterly* 404.

Ministère de l'Europe et des Affaires Étrangères. 2020. 'International Criminal Court – Surrender of Ali Muhammad Ali Abd-Al-Rahman (Ali Kushayb) to the International Criminal Court (09 June 2020)', www.diplomatie.gouv.fr/en/french-foreign-policy/international-justice/news/article/international-criminal-court-surrender-of-ali-muhammad-ali-abd-al-rahman-ali.

Minkova, L. G. 2021. 'Expressing What? The Stigmatization of the Defendant and the ICC's Institutional Interests in the Ongwen Case', 34(1) *Leiden Journal of International Law* 223–245.

Minkova, L. G. 2022. 'Control over the Theory: Reforming the ICC's Approach to Establishing Commission Liability?', *International Criminal Law Review* 1–29, DOI: 10.1163/15718123-bja10129.

Mistry, H. 2017. 'The Significance of Institutional Culture in Enhancing the Validity of International Criminal Tribunals', 17(4) *International Criminal Law Review* 703.

Moffett, L. 2015. 'Meaningful and Effective? Considering Victims' Interests through Participation at the International Criminal Court', 26(2) *Criminal Law Forum* 255.

Moffett, L. 2019. 'Why Gbagbo Acquittal Is a Bigger Blow for the ICC than the Bemba Decision', *The Conversation*, (15 January), https://theconversation.com/why-gbagbo-acquittal-is-a-bigger-blow-for-the-icc-than-the-bemba-decision-109913.

Montmarquet, J. 1999. 'Zimmerman on Culpable Ignorance', 109(4) *Ethics* 842.

Moore M. 1990. 'Choice, Character, and Excuse', 7(1) *Social Philosophy & Policy* 29.

Moore, M. 2009. 'A Tale of Two Theories', 28(1) *Criminal Justice Ethics* 27.

Moore, M. 2010 [1993]. *Act and Crime: The Philosophy of Action and Its Implications for Criminal Law* (Oxford: Oxford University Press).

Morgenthau, H. 1948. *Politics among Nations: The Struggle for Power and Peace* (New York: Knopf).

Moyn, S. 2016. 'Anti-Impunity as Deflection of Argument', in K. Engle, Z. Miller, and D. Davis (eds.), *Anti-Impunity and the Human Rights Agenda* (Cambridge: Cambridge University Press).

Mutua, M. 2001a. 'Savages, Victims and Saviors: The Metaphor of Human Rights', 42(1) *Harvard International Law Journal* 201.

Mutua, M. 2001b. 'Politics and Human Rights: An Essential Symbiosis', in M. Byers (ed.), *The Role of Law in International Politics* (Oxford: Oxford University Press).

Mutua, M. 2016. 'Closing the "Impunity Gap" and the Role of State Support in the ICC', in R. Steinberg (ed.), *Contemporary Issues Facing the International Criminal Court* (Leiden: Brill Nijhoff).

Nanda, V. 1998. 'The Establishment of a Permanent International Criminal Court: Challenges Ahead', 20(2) *Human Rights Quarterly* 413.

Nerlich, V. 2007. 'Superior Responsibility under Article 28 ICC Statute: For What Exactly Is the Superior Held Responsible?', 5(3) *Journal of International Criminal Justice* 665.

Nersessian, D. 2006. 'Whoops, I Committed Genocide – The Anomaly of Constructive Liability for Serious International Crimes', 30(1) *The Fletcher Forum of World Affairs* 81.

Nesiah, V. 2016. 'Doing History with Impunity', in K. Engle, Z. Miller and D. Davis (eds.), *Anti-Impunity and the Human Rights Agenda* (Cambridge: Cambridge University Press).

Nilsson, J. 2018. 'Prosecutor v. Bemba et al. Case No. ICC-01/05-01/13', 112(3), *American Journal of International Law*, 473–479.

Nino, C. S. 1996. *Radical Evil on Trial* (New Heaven, CT: Yale University Press).

Noferi, M. 2006. 'Towards Attenuation: A New Due Process Limit on Pinkerton Conspiracy Liability,' 33(2) *American Journal of Criminal Law* 91.

Nollkaemper, A. 2009. 'Introduction', in A. Nollkaemper and H. van der Wilt (eds.), *System Criminality in International Law* (Cambridge: Cambridge University Press).

Nouwen, S. 2013. *Complementarity in the Line of Fire* (Cambridge: Cambridge University Press).

Nouwen, S. 2016. 'International Criminal Law: Theory All Over the Place', in A. Orford and F. Hoffmann (eds.), *The Oxford Handbook of the Theory of International Law* (Oxford: Oxford University Press).

Nouwen S. and W. Werner. 2011. 'Doing Justice to the Political: The International Criminal Court in Uganda and Sudan', 21(4) *European Journal of International Law* 941.

Novosseloff, A. 2015. 'United Nations Operation in Côte d'Ivoire (UNOCI)', in J. A. Koops, T. Tardy, N. MacQueen, and P. D. Williams (eds.), *The Oxford Handbook of United Nations Peacekeeping Operations* (Oxford: Oxford University Press).

Olásolo, H. 2009a. 'Joint Criminal Enterprise and Its Extended Form: A Theory of Co-Perpetration Giving Rise to Principal Liability, a Notion of Accessorial Liability, or a Form of Partnership In Crime?', 20(2) *Criminal Law Forum* 263.

Olásolo, H. 2009b. *The Criminal Responsibility of Senior Political and Military Leaders as Principals to International Crimes* (Oxford; Portland, Or.: Hart).

Olásolo, H. and R. Carnero. 2015. 'Forms of Accessorial Liability under Article 25(3) (b) and (c)', in C. Stahn (ed.), *The Law and Practice of the International Criminal Court* (Oxford: Oxford University Press).

Ohlin, J. D. 2007. 'Three Conceptual Problems with the Doctrine of Joint Criminal Enterprise,' 5(1) *Journal of International Criminal Justice*, 69–90.

Ohlin, J. D. 2011. 'Joint Intentions to Commit International Crimes', 11(2) *Chicago Journal of International Law* 693.

Ohlin, J. D. 2014. 'Organizational Criminality', in E. van Sliedregt and S. Vasiliev (eds.), *Pluralism in International Criminal Law* (Oxford: Oxford University Press).

Ohlin, J. D. 2015. 'Co-Perpetration: German Dogmatik or German Invasion?', in C. Stahn (ed.), *The Law and Practice of the International Criminal Court* (Oxford: Oxford University Press).

Osiel, M. 1999. 'Making Public Memory, Publicly', in C. Hesse and R. Post (eds.), *Human Rights in Political Transitions: Gettysburg to Bosnia* (New York: Zone Books).

Osiel, M. 2005. 'Modes of Participation in Mass Atrocity', 38(3) *Cornell International Law Journal* 793.

Osiel, M. 2009. *Making Sense of Mass Atrocity* (New York: Cambridge University Press).

O'Sullivan, J. 2015. 'The Relationship between the Office of the Prosecutor and the Judicial Organ', in M. Minow, C. True-Frost, and A. Whiting (eds.), *The First Global Prosecutor: Promise and Constraints* (Ann Arbor: University of Michigan Press).

Pauwelyn, J. and M. Elsig. 2013. 'The Politics of Treaty Interpretation: Variations and Explanations across International Tribunals', in J. Dunoff and M. Pollack (eds.), *Interdisciplinary Perspectives on International Law and International Relations: The State of the Art* (Cambridge: Cambridge University Press).

Pearson, Z. 2006. 'Non-Governmental Organizations and the International Criminal Court: Changing Landscapes of International Law', 39(2) *Cornell International Law Journal* 243.

Pella, V. 1950. 'Towards an International Criminal Court', 44(1) *The American Journal of International Law* 37.

Pellet, A. 2002. 'Applicable Law', in A. Cassese, P. Gaeta, and J. R. W. D. Jones (eds.), *The Rome Statute of the International Criminal Court*, Vol. II (Oxford: Oxford University Press).

Peniguet, M. 2018. 'CPI: Jean-Pierre Bemba, chronique d'un acquittement surprise', *Dalloz: Actualité,* (22 June), www.dalloz-actualite.fr/flash/cpi-jean-pierre-bemba-chronique-d-un-acquittement-surprise#.XVJpfC2Q0zU.

Perrin, B. 2008. 'Searching for Law While Seeking Justice: The Difficulties of Enforcing International Humanitarian Law in International Criminal Trials', 39(2) *Ottawa Law Review* 367.

Peskin, V. 2008. *International Justice in Rwanda and the Balkans* (Cambridge: Cambridge University Press).

Peskin, V. 2017. 'Things Fall Apart: Battles of Legitimation and the Politics of Noncompliance and African Sovereignty from the Rwanda Tribunal to the ICC', in N. Hayashi and C. Bailliet (eds.), *The Legitimacy of International Criminal Tribunals* (Cambridge: Cambridge University Press).

Pérez, A. 2017. 'From Judicial Independence to Interdependence in the International Sphere', 24(4) *Maastricht Journal of European and Comparative Law* 462.

Pieters, N. E. and T. Kirabira. 2021. 'The Ongwen Judgement at the ICC: A Missed Opportunity for Former Child Soldiers?', *International Law Blog,* (22 June), https://internationallaw.blog/2021/06/22/the-ongwen-judgement-at-the-icc-a-missed-opportunity-for-former-child-soldiers/.

Pigaroff, D. and D. Robinson., 2016. 'Article 30: Mental Element', in K. Ambos and O. Triffterer (eds.), *Rome Statute of the International Criminal Court: A Commentary*, 3rd ed. (London: Bloomsbury T&T Clark).

Pollack, M. 2013. 'Political Science and International Adjudication', in C. Romano, K. Alter, and Y. Shany (eds.), *The Oxford Handbook of International Adjudication*, 1st ed. (Oxford: Oxford University Press).

Popovski, V. 2000. 'International Criminal Court: A Necessary Step towards Global Justice', 31(4) *Security Dialogue* 405.

Posner, E. and A. Sykes. 2013. *Economic Foundations of International Law* (Cumberland: Harvard University Press).

Posner E. and J. Yoo. 2004. 'A Theory of International Adjudication', University of Chicago Law & Economics, Olin Working Paper No. 206; UC Berkeley Public Law Research Paper No. 146. Available at: https://ssrn.com/abstract=507003.

Powderly, J. 2010. 'Judicial Interpretation at the Ad Hoc Tribunals: Method from Chaos?', in S. Darcy and J. Powderly (eds.), *Judicial Creativity at the International Criminal Tribunals* (Oxford: Oxford University Press).

Powderly, J. 2018. 'Introductory Note to Prosecutor v. Jean-Pierre Bemba Gombo: Judgment on the Appeal of Mr. Jean-Pierre Bemba Gombo against Trial Chamber III's "Judgment Pursuant to Article 74 of the Statute" (Int'l Crim. Ct.)', 57(6) *American Journal of International Law* 1031–1079.

Powles, S. 2004. 'Joint Criminal Enterprise – Criminal Liability by Prosecutorial Ingenuity and Judicial Creativity', 2(2) *Journal of International Criminal Justice* 606.

Radbruch, G. 2006[1946]. 'Statutory Lawlessness and Supra-Statutory Law (1946), translated by Bonnie Litschewski Paulson, & Stanley L. Paulson', 26(1) *Oxford Journal of Legal Studies* 1.

Raimondo, F. 2010. 'General Principles of Law, Judicial Creativity, and the Development of International Criminal Law', in S. Darcy and J. Powderly (eds.), *Judicial Creativity at the International Criminal Tribunals* (Oxford: Oxford University Press).

Ratner, S. 2003. 'The International Criminal Court and the Limits of Global Judicialization', 38(3) *Texas International Law Journal* 445.

REDRESS, 2018. 'Efforts to Afford Justice for Sexual Crimes in CAR Must Not Stop with Bemba's acquittal', (8 June), https://redress.org/news/efforts-to-afford-justice-for-sexual-crimes-in-car-must-not-stop-with-bembas-acquittal/.

Ricard, M. 2017. 'Historicity of Extraversion in Côte d'Ivoire and the 'Post-conflict', 35(4) *Journal of Contemporary African Studies* 506.

Rieff, D. 2018. 'The End of Human Rights?', *Foreign Policy* (9 April), foreignpolicy.com/2018/04/09/the-end-of-human-rights-genocide-united-nations-r2p-terrorism/.

Robertson, G. 2006. 'General Editor's Introduction to Essays on Fairness and Evidence in War Crimes Trials', 4(1) *International Commentary on Evidence* 1.

Robinson, D. 2008 'The Identity Crisis of International Criminal Law', 21(4) *Leiden Journal of International Law* 925.

Robinson, D. 2009. 'Legality and Our Contradictory Commitments', in S. Sivakumaran, B. Van Schaack, D. Robinson, T. Meron, and B. Roth, *The Principle of Legality in International Criminal Law*, Proceedings of the Annual Meeting, American Society of International Law, Vol. 103. Washington: Cambridge, University Press.

Robinson, D. 2013a. International Criminal Law as Justice', 11(3) *Journal of International Criminal Justice* 699.

Robinson, D. 2013b. 'A Cosmopolitan Liberal Account of International Criminal Law', 26(1) *Leiden Journal of International Law* 127.

Robinson, D. 2017. 'A Justification of Command Responsibility', 28(4) *Criminal Law Forum* 633.

Robinson, D. 2019. 'The Other Poisoned Chalice: Unprecedented Evidentiary Standards in the Gbagbo Case? (Part 1)', *EJIL: Talk!* (5 November), www.ejiltalk.org/the-other-poisoned-chalice-unprecedented-evidentiary-standards-in-the-gbagbo-case-part-1/.

Robinson, D. 2020. *Justice in Extreme Cases: Criminal Law Theory Meets International Criminal Law* (Cambridge: Cambridge University Press).

Rock, P. 1974. 'The Sociology of Deviancy and Conceptions of Moral Order', 14(2) *British Journal of Criminology* 139.

Rodman, K. and P. Booth. 2013. 'Manipulated Commitments: The International Criminal Court in Uganda', 35(2) *Human Rights Quarterly* 271.

Roht-Arriaza, N. 1996. 'Combating Impunity: Some Thoughts on the Way Forward', 59(4) *Law and Contemporary Problems* 93.

Roht-Arriaza, N. 2013. 'Just a Bubble? Perspectives on the Enforcement of International Criminal Law by National Courts', 11(3) *Journal of International Criminal Justice* 537.

Rosenberg, S. 2017. 'The International Criminal Court in Côte d'Ivoire: Impartiality at Stake?', 15(3) *Journal of International Criminal Justice* 471.

Roth, B. 2009. 'Moral Disagreement, Sovereign Authority, and the Limits to Extraterritorial Prosecution of Human Rights Violators', in S. Sivakumaran, B. Van Schaack, D. Robinson. T. Meron, and B. Roth (eds.) *The Principle of Legality in International Criminal Law*. American Society of International Law. Washington: Cambridge, University Press.

Roth, B. 2010. 'Coming to Terms with Ruthlessness: Sovereign Equality, Global Pluralism, and the Limits of International Criminal Justice', 8(1) *Santa Clara Journal of International Law* 231.

Roth N. and S. Sundby. 1985. 'The Felony-Murder Rule a Doctrine at Constitutional Crossroads,' 70(3) *Cornell Law Review* 446.

Roxin, C. 2011[1963]. *Täterschaft und Tatherrschaft*, 1st ed., (Hamburg: Cram, de Gruyter & Co.).

Sadat, L. N. 2018a. 'Prosecutor v. Jean-Pierre Bemba Gombo. Case No. ICC-01/05-01/08. Appeals Judgment', 113(2) *American Journal of International Law* 353.

Sadat, L. N. 2018b. 'Fiddling While Rome Burns? The Appeals Chamber's Curious Decision in Prosecutor v. Jean-Pierre Bemba Gombo', EJIL: *Talk*, (12 June), www.ejiltalk.org/fiddling-while-rome-burns-the-appeals-chambers-curious-decision-in-prosecutor-v-jean-pierre-bemba-gombo/.

Sadat, L. and J. Jolly. 2014. 'Seven Canons of ICC Treaty Interpretation: Making Sense of Article 25's Rorschach Blot', 27(3) *Leiden Journal of International Law* 755.

Safferling, C. 2004. 'Can Criminal Prosecution Be the Answer to Massive Human Rights Violations', 5(12) *German Law Journal* 1469.

Safferling, C. 2012. *International Criminal Procedure* (Oxford: Oxford University Press).

Saland, P. 1999. 'International Criminal Law Principles', in R. Lee (ed.), *The International Criminal Court: The Making of the Rome Statute – Issues, Negotiations, Results* (The Hague: Kluwer Law International).

Sander, B. 2010. 'Unravelling the Confusion Concerning Successor Superior Responsibility in the ICTY Jurisprudence', 23(1) *Leiden Journal of International Law* 105.

Sander, B. 2015. 'International Criminal Justice as Progress: From Faith to Critique', in M. Bergsmo, C. Wui Ling, S. Tianying, and Y. Ping (eds.), *Historical Origins of International Criminal Law: Volume 4* (Brussels: Torkel Opsahl Academic EPublisher).

Sander, B. 2016. 'We Need to Talk about Ongwen: The Plight of Victim-Perpetrators at the ICC', *Justice in Conflict*, (19 April), https://justiceinconflict.org/2016/04/19/we-need-to-talk-about-ongwen-the-plight-of-victim-perpetrators-at-the-icc/.

Sander, B. 2019. 'The Expressive Turn of International Criminal Justice: A Field in Search of Meaning', 32(4) *Leiden Journal of International Law* 851.

Sassòli M. and L. Olson. 2000. 'The Judgment of the ICTY Appeals Chamber on the Merits in the Tadic Case', 82(839) *International Review of the Red Cross* 733.

Satō, H. 2012. 'International Criminal Responsibility Concerning "Control over an Organization" and Command Responsibility Lato Sensu', 12(2) *International Criminal Law Review* 293.

Satzger, H. 2002. 'German Criminal Law and the Rome Statute – A Critical Analysis of the New German Code of Crimes against International Law', 2(3) *International Criminal Law Review* 261.

Schabas, W. 2000. 'Canadian Implementing Legislation for the Rome Statute', 3 *Yearbook of International Humanitarian Law* 337.

Schabas, W. 2001. 'Editorial: International Criminal Court: The Secret of Its Success', 12(4) *Criminal Law Forum* 415.

Schabas, W. 2003a. 'Mens Rea and the International Criminal Tribunal for the Former Yugoslavia', 37(4) *New England Law Review* 1036.

Schabas, W. 2003b. 'Interpreting the Statutes of the Ad Hoc Tribunals', in L. C. Vohrah et al. (eds.) *Man's Inhumanity to Man: Essays on International Law in Honour of Antonio Cassese* (The Hague: Kluwer Law International).

Schabas, W. 2006. *The UN International Criminal Tribunals* (Cambridge: Cambridge University Press).

Schabas, W. 2007. *An Introduction to the International Criminal Court*, 3rd ed. (Cambridge: Cambridge University Press).

Schabas, W. 2008a. 'Complementarity in Practice': Some Uncomplimentary Thoughts', 19(1) *Criminal Law Forum* 5.

Schabas W. 2008b. 'Prosecutorial Discretion v. Judicial Activism at the International Criminal Court', 6(4) *Journal of International Criminal Justice* 731.

Schabas, W. 2012. *Unimaginable Atrocities: Justice, Politics, and Rights at the War Crimes Tribunals* (Oxford: Oxford University Press).

Schabas, W. and C. Stahn. 2008. 'Introductory Note: Legal Aspects of the Lubanga Case'. 19(3) *Criminal Law Forum* 431.

Schachter, O. 1977–1978. 'The Invisible College of International Lawyers', 72(2) *Northwestern University Law Review* 217.

Scheffer, D. 2002. 'The Future of Atrocity Law', 25(3) *Suffolk Transnational Law Review* 389.

Scheffer, D. 2010. 'The International Criminal Court', in W. Schabas and N. Bernaz (eds.), *Routledge Handbook of International Criminal Law* (London: Routledge).

Schiff, B. 2008. *Building the International Criminal Court* (New York: Cambridge University Press).

Schwöbel-Patel, C. 2016. 'Spectacle in International Criminal Law: The Fundraising Image of Victimhood', 4(2) *London Review of International Law* 247.

Seay L. and M. Broache. 2016. 'A Congolese Warlord Was Just Convicted. So Why Isn't Everyone Thrilled about It?', *The Washington Post*, (24 March), www.washingtonpost.com/news/monkey-cage/wp/2016/03/24/a-congolese-warlord-was-just-convicted-so-why-isnt-everyone-thrilled-about-it/.

Segun M. and D. Traoré. 2019. 'A Shrinking Window for Justice in Côte d'Ivoire', Human Rights Watch, (30 January), www.hrw.org/news/2019/01/30/shrinking-window-justice-cote-divoire.

Sellars, K. 2010. 'Imperfect Justice at Nuremberg and Tokyo', 21(4) *European Journal of International Law* 1085.

Semien, E.-A. 2017. 'Simone Gbagbo Acquitted by the Abidjan Assize Court: Between the Independence of the Judiciary and a Political Twist to Save the Day', *International Justice Monitor*, (5 May), www.ijmonitor.org/2017/05/simone-gbagbo-acquitted-by-the-abidjan-assize-court-between-the-independence-of-the-judiciary-and-a-political-twist-to-save-the-day/.

Sepinwall, A. 2009. 'Failures to Punish: Command Responsibility in Domestic and International Law', 30(2) *Michigan Journal of International Law* 251.

Shahabuddeen, M. 2004. 'Does the Principle of Legality Stand in the Way of Progressive Development of Law', 2(4) *Journal of International Criminal Justice* 1007–1017.

Shahabuddeen, M. 2010. 'Judicial Creativity and Joint Criminal Enterprise', in S. Darcy and J. Powderly (eds.), *Judicial Creativity at the International Criminal Tribunals* (Oxford: Oxford University Press).

Shaw, M. 2003. *International Law*, 5th ed. (Cambridge: Cambridge University Press).

Shklar, J. 1964. *Legalism* (Cambridge, Mass. and London, England: Harvard University Press).

Sikkink, K. 2011. *The Justice Cascade: How Human Rights Prosecutions Are Changing World Politics* (New York and London: W. W. Norton & Company).

Simester, A. and S. Shute. 2002. 'On the General Part in Criminal Law', in A. Simester and S. Shute (eds.), *Criminal Law Theory: Doctrines of the General Part* (Oxford: Oxford University Press).

Simmons, B. and A. Danner. 2010. 'Credible Commitments and the International Criminal Court', 64(2) *International Organization* 225.

Simons, K. 1992. 'Rethinking Mental States', 72(3) *Boston University Law Review* 463.

Simons, M. 2010. 'For International Criminal Court, Frustration and Missteps in Its First Trial', *The New York Times*, (21 November), www.nytimes.com/2010/11/22/world/europe/22court.html.

Simpson, G. 2007. *Law, War and Crime: War Crime Trials and the Reinvention of International Law* (Cambridge: Polity Press).

Sinclair, A. 2010. *International Relations Theory and International Law: A Critical Approach* (Cambridge: Cambridge University Press).

Slaughter Burley, A.-M. 1993. 'International Law and International Relations Theory: A Dual Agenda', 87(2) *The American Journal of International Law* 205.

Sluiter, G. 2016. '*Ad hoc* International Criminal Tribunals (Yugoslavia, Rwanda, Sierra Leone)', in W. Schabas (ed.), *The Cambridge Companion to International Criminal Law* (Cambridge: Cambridge University Press).

Smeulers, A. 2019. 'Historical Overview of Perpetrator Studies', in A. Smeulers, M. Weerdesteijn, and B. Holá (eds.), *Perpetrators of International Crimes: Theories, Methods, and Evidence* (Oxford: Oxford University Press).

Spiga, V. 2011. 'Non-retroactivity of Criminal Law', 9(1) *Journal of International Criminal Justice* 5.

Spiro, P. 2013. 'Nongovernmental Organizations in International Relations (Theory)', in J. Dunoff and M. Pollack (eds.), *Interdisciplinary Perspectives on International Law and International Relations: The State of the Art* (Cambridge: Cambridge University Press).

Stahn, C. 2012. 'Between "Faith" and "Facts": By What Standards Should We Assess International Criminal Justice?', 25(2) *Leiden Journal of International Law* 251.

Stahn, C. 2014. 'Justice Delivered or Justice Denied?', 12(4) *Journal of International Criminal Justice* 809.

Steer, C. 2014. 'Legal Transplants or Legal Patchworking? The Creation of International Criminal Law as a Pluralistic Body of Law', in E. van Sliedregt and S. Vasiliev (eds.), *Pluralism in International Criminal Law* (Oxford: Oxford University Press).

Steinberg, R. 2004. 'Judicial Lawmaking at the WTO: Discursive, Constitutional, and Political Constraints', 98(2) *American Journal of International Law* 247.

Stephen, C. 2012. 'International Criminal Law: Wielding the Sword of Universal Criminal Justice?', 61(1) *International and Comparative Law Quarterly* 55.

Sterio, M. 2017. 'Individual Criminal Responsibility for the Destruction of Religious and Historic Buildings: The *Al Mahdi* Case', 49(1–2) *Case Western Reserve Journal of International Law* 63.

Sterio, M. 2020. 'The International Criminal Court: Current Challenges and Prospect of Future Success', Cleveland State University: Law Faculty Articles and Essays. 1136, 467–478.

Stewart, J. 2012. 'The End of 'Modes of Liability' for International Crimes', 25(1) *Leiden Journal of International Law* 165.

Straus, S. 2011. '"It's Sheer Horror Here": Patterns of Violence during the First Four Months of Côte d'Ivoire's Post-Electoral Crisis', 110(440) *African Affairs* 481.

Swart, M. 2010. 'Is There a Text in This Court? The Purposive Method of Interpretation and the ad hoc Tribunals', 70 *ZaöRV* 767.

Swigart L. and D. Terris. 2013. 'Who Are International Judges?' in C. Romano, K. Alter, and Y. Shany (eds.), *The Oxford Handbook of International Adjudication*, 1st ed. (Oxford: Oxford University Press).

Tallgren, I. 2002. 'The Sensibility and Sense of International Criminal Law', 13(3) *European Journal of International Law* 561.

Tallgren, I. 2015. 'The Voice of the International: Who Is Speaking?', 13(1) *Journal of International Criminal Justice* 135.

Tambay, E. 2021. 'ICC Should Pursue Higher-Level Seleka from Central African Republic', Human Rights Watch, (11 October), www.hrw.org/news/2021/10/11/icc-should-pursue-higher-level-seleka-central-african-republic.

Tampa, V. 2019. 'A Brutal Warlord Has Been Convicted – So Why Doesn't It Feel Like a Triumph?', *The Guardian*, (8 July), www.theguardian.com/commentisfree/2019/jul/08/warlord-bosco-ntaganda-democratic-republic-of-the-congo-congolese.

Teitel, R. G. 2014. *Globalizing Transitional Justice* (New York: Oxford University Press).

The Guardian. 2019. 'US to Deny Visas for ICC Members Investigating Alleged War Crimes', (15 March), www.theguardian.com/us-news/2019/mar/15/mike-pompeo-us-war-crimes-investigation-international-criminal-court.

The New Humanitarian. 2012. 'Lubanga Verdict "A First Step"', (14 March), http://www.thenewhumanitarian.org/report/95073/drc-lubanga-verdict-"-first-step".

Tomuschat, C. 2006. 'The Legacy of Nuremberg', 4(4) *Journal of International Criminal Justice* 830.

Tosa, H. 2018. 'Global Constitutional Order and the Deviant Other: Reflections on the Dualistic Nature of the ICC Process', 18(1) *International Relations of the Asia-Pacific* 45.

Totani, Y. 2011. 'The Case against the Accused', in Y. Tanaka, T. McCormack, and G. Simpson (eds.), *Beyond Victor's Justice? The Tokyo War Crimes Trial Revisited* (Leiden, Boston: Martinus Nijhoff).

Trahan, J. 2018. 'Bemba Acquittal Rests on Erroneous Application of Appellate Review Standard', *OpinioJuris*, (25 June), http://opiniojuris.org/2018/06/25/bemba-acquittal-rests-on-erroneous-application-of-appellate-review-standard/.

Trahan, J. 2020. 'The Significance of the ICC Appeals Chamber's Ruling in the Afghanistan Situation', *OpinioJuris,* (10 March), http://opiniojuris.org/2020/03/10/the-significance-of-the-icc-appeals-chambers-ruling-in-the-afghanistan-situation/.

Trechsel, S. 2009. 'Command Responsibility as a Separate Offense', 3(1) *Berkley Journal of International Law Publicist* 26.

Triffterer, O. 2002. 'Causality, a Separate Element of the Doctrine of Superior Responsibility as Expressed in Article 28 Rome Statute?', 15(1) *Leiden Journal of International Law* 179.

Trondal, J., Marcussen, M., Larsson, T., and F. Veggeland. 2010. *Unpacking International Organizations: The Dynamics of Compound Bureaucracies* (Manchester: Manchester University Press).

U.S. Department of State. 2021. 'Welcoming the Verdict in the Case against Dominic Ongwen for War Crimes and Crimes against Humanity', Press Statement, (4 February), www.state.gov/welcoming-the-verdict-in-the-case-against-dominic-ongwen-for-war-crimes-and-crimes-against-humanity/.

Van Schaack, B. 2008. 'Crimen Sine Lege: Judicial Lawmaking at the Intersection of Law and Morals', 97(1) *Georgetown Law Journal* 119.

Van Schaack, B. 2009. 'Legality & International Criminal Law', in S. Sivakumaran, B. Van Schaack, D. Robinson. T. Meron and B. Roth, *The Principle of Legality in International Criminal Law,* Proceedings of the Annual MeetingAmerican Society of International Law. Washington: Cambridge University Press.

Van den Ber S. and C. Sengenya, 2019. 'Ntaganda's Conviction, a Sweeping Win for the ICC Prosecutor', *Justiceinfo,* (9 July), www.justiceinfo.net/en/tribunals/icc/41897-ntaganda-s-conviction-a-sweeping-win-for-the-icc-prosecutor.html.

Van der Vyver, J. 2005. 'The International Criminal Court and the Concept of Mens Rea in International Criminal Law', 12(1) *University of Miami International and Comparative Law Review* 57.

Van der Vyver, J. 2010. 'Prosecutor v. Jean-Pierre Bemba Gombo', 104(2) *American Journal of International Law* 241–247.

Van der Wilt, H. 2007. 'Joint Criminal Enterprise – Possibilities and Limitations', 5(1) *Journal of International Criminal Justice* 91–108.

Van der Wilt, H. 2009. 'The Continuous Quest for Proper Modes of Criminal Responsibility', 7(2) *Journal of International Criminal Justice* 307.

Van Dijk, T. 2001. 'Critical Discourse Analysis', in D. Schiffrin, D. Tannen, and H. E. Hamilton (eds.), *The Handbook of Discourse Analysis,* 1st ed. (Malden, Mass: Blackwell Publishers Ltd).

Van Sliedregt, E. 2007. 'Joint Criminal Enterprise as a Pathway to Convicting Individuals for Genocide', 5(1) *Journal of International Criminal Justice* 184.

Van Sliedregt, E. 2011. 'Command Responsibility at the ICTY—Three Generations of Case-Law and Still Ambiguity', in B. Swart, A. Zahar, and G. Sluiter (eds.), *The Legacy of the International Criminal Tribunal for the Former Yugoslavia* (Oxford: Oxford University Press).

Van Sliedregt, E. 2012a. *Individual Criminal Responsibility in International Law* (Oxford: Oxford University Press).

Van Sliedregt, E. 2012b. 'Pluralism in International Criminal Law', 25(4) *Leiden Journal of International Law* 847.

Van Sliedregt, E. 2014. 'International Criminal Law', in M. D. Dubber and T. Hörnle (eds.), *The Oxford Handbook of Criminal Law* (Oxford: Oxford University Press).

Van Sliedregt, E. 2021. 'The ICC Ntaganda Appeals Judgment: The End of Indirect Co-perpetration?', *Just Security,* (14 May), www.justsecurity.org/76136/the-icc-ntaganda-appeals-judgment-the-end-of-indirect-co-perpetration/.

Van Sliedregt, E., Ohlin, J. D., and T. Weigend. 2013. 'Assessing the Control Theory', 26(3) *Leiden Journal of International law* 725.

Vanacore. G. 2015. 'Legal Culpability and Dogmatik: A Dialogue between the EctHR, Comparative and International Criminal Law', 15(5) *International Criminal Law Review* 823.

Vasiliev, S. 2015. 'On Trajectories and Destinations of International Criminal Law Scholarship', 28(4) *Leiden Journal of International Law* 701.

Vasiliev, S. 2017. 'Between International Criminal Justice and Injustice: Theorising Legitimacy', in N. Hayashi and C. Bailliet (eds.), *The Legitimacy of International Criminal Tribunals* (Cambridge: Cambridge University Press).

Vetter, G. 2000. 'Command Responsibility of Non-Military Superiors in the International Criminal Court', 25(1) *The Yale Journal of International Law* 89.

Viebig P. 2016. *Illicitly Obtained Evidence at the International Criminal Court* (The Hague: T. M. C. Asser Press).

Vinjamuri, L. 2018. 'The International Criminal Court and the Paradox of Its Authority', in K. Alter, L. Helfer, and M. Madsen (eds.), *International Court Authority* (Oxford: Oxford University Press).

Voeten, E. 2007. 'The Politics of International Judicial Appointments: Evidence from the European Court of Human Rights', 61(4) *International Organization* 669.

Voeten, E. 2013a. 'International Judicial Independence', in J. Dunoff and M. Pollack (eds.), *Interdisciplinary Perspectives on International Law and International Relations: The State of the Art* (Cambridge: Cambridge University Press).

Voeten, E. 2013b. 'International Judicial Behaviour', in C. Romano, K. Alter, and Y. Shany (eds.), *The Oxford Handbook of International Adjudication*, 1st ed. (Oxford: Oxford University Press).

Voigt, S. 2017. 'The Independence of International Courts – Making Reputation Work?', 24(4) *Maastricht Journal of European and Comparative Law* 511.

Von Bogdandy A. and J. Habermas. 2013. 'Discourse Theory and International Law: An Interview with Jürgen Habermas', *Verfassungsblog,* (12 May), https://verfassungsblog.de/discourse-theory-and-international-law-an-interview-with-jurgen-habermas/.

Wagner, N. 2003. 'The Development of the Grave Breaches Regime and of Individual Criminal Responsibility by the International Criminal Tribunal for the former Yugoslavia', 85(850) *International Review of the Red Cross* 351.

Wakabi, W. 2016. 'Reactions to Bemba's Conviction', *International Justice Monitor*, (31 March), www.ijmonitor.org/2016/03/reactions-to-bembas-conviction/.

Wakabi, W. 2020a. 'Judges Confirm Charges against Two Former Central African Militiamen', *International Justice Monitor*, (2 January), www.ijmonitor.org/2020/01/judges-confirm-charges-against-two-former-central-african-militiamen/.

Wakabi, W. 2020b. 'Government Says Gbagbo's Return Would Destabilize the Ivory Coast', *International Justice Monitor*, (31 January), www.ijmonitor.org/2020/01/government-says-gbagbos-return-would-destabilize-the-ivory-coast/.

Weigend, T. 2008. 'Intent, Mistake of Law, and Co-perpetration in the *Lubanga* Decision on Confirmation of Charges', 6(3) *Journal of International Criminal Justice* 471.

Weigend, T. 2011. 'Perpetration through an Organization: The Unexpected Career of a German Legal Concept', 9(1) *Journal of International Criminal Justice* 91.

Weigend, T. 2014. 'Subjective Elements of Criminal Liability', in M. Dubber and T. Hörnle (eds.), *The Oxford Handbook of Criminal Law* (Oxford: Oxford University Press).

Weigend, T. 2015. 'Indirect Perpetration', in C. Stahn, (ed.), *The Law and Practice of the International Criminal Court* (Oxford: Oxford University Press).

Weiner, A. S. 2013. 'Prudent Politics: The International Criminal Court, International Relations, and Prosecutorial Independence', 12(3) *Washington University Global Studies Law Review* 545.

Welch, C. and A. Watkins. 2011. 'Extending Enforcement: The Coalition for the International Criminal Court', 33(4) *Human Rights Quarterly* 927.

Werle, G. 2005. *Principles of International Criminal Law* (The Hague: TMC Asser Press).

Werle, G. 2007. 'Individual Criminal Responsibility in Article 25 ICC Statute', 5(4) *Journal of International Criminal Justice* 953.

Werle, G. 2012. 'Do Crimes against Humanity Require the Participation of a State or a "State-Like" Organization?' 10(5) *Journal of International Criminal Justice* 1158.

Werle, G. and B. Burghardt. 2011. 'Indirect Perpetration: A Perfect Fit for International Prosecution of Armchair Killers?' 9(1) *Journal of International Criminal Justice* 85.

Werle G. and B. Burghardt. 2014. 'Establishing Degrees of Responsibility: Modes of Participation in Article 25 of the ICC Statute', in E. van Sliedregt and S. Vasiliev (eds.), *Pluralism in International Criminal Law* (Oxford: Oxford University Press).

Werle G. and F. Jessberger. 2005. 'Unless Otherwise Provided: Article 30 of the ICC Statute and the Mental Element of Crimes under International Criminal Law', 3(1) *Journal of International Criminal Justice* 35.

Wessel, J. 2006. 'Judicial Policy-Making at the International Criminal Court: An Institutional Guide to Analyzing International Adjudication', 44(1) *Columbia Journal of Transnational Law* 377.

Whiting, A. 2018. 'Appeals Judges Turn the ICC on Its Head with Bemba Decision', *Just Security*, (14 June), www.justsecurity.org/57760/appeals-judges-turn-icc-head-bemba-decision/.

Williams, G. 1964. *Criminal Law: The General Part*, 2nd ed. (London: Stevens & Sons Ltd).

Williams, G. 1983. 'Convictions and Fair Labelling', 42(1) *Cambridge Law Journal* 85.

Wirth, S. 2012. 'Co-perpetration in the Lubanga Trial Judgment', 10(4) *Journal of International Criminal Justice* 971.

Women's Initiatives for Gender Justice. 2011. *Gender Report Card on the International Criminal Court 2011*, https://4genderjustice.org/ftp-files/publications/Gender-Report-Card-on-the-International-Criminal-Court-2011.pdf.

Women's Initiatives for Gender Justice. 2012. 'Legal Eye on the ICC – March 2012', https://4genderjustice.org/home/publications/eletters/legal-eye-on-the-icc-march-2012/.

Women's Initiatives for Gender Justice. 2014a. 'Partial Conviction of Katanga by ICC: Acquittals for Sexual Violence and Use of Child Soldiers', (7 March), http://www.iccwomen.org/images/Katanga-Judgement-Statement-corr.pdf.

Women's Initiatives for Gender Justice. 2014b. 'Legal Eye on the ICC – September 2014 – Special Issue — Ntaganda Confirmation of Charges', https://4genderjustice.org/home/publications/eletters/legal-eye-on-the-icc-september-2014-special-issue-ntaganda-confirmation-of-charges/.

Women's Initiatives for Gender Justice. 2018. *Gender Report Card on the International Criminal Court 2018*, https://4genderjustice.org/ftp-files/publications/Gender-Report_design-full-WEB.pdf.

Women's Initiatives for Gender Justice. 2019. 'Statement on the Sentencing of Bosco Ntaganda', (7 November), https://4genderjustice.org/statement-on-the-sentencing-of-bosco-ntaganda/.

Women's Initiatives for Gender Justice. 2021. 'Trailblazing ICC Judgment on SGBC – Ongwen Verdict Advances International Accountability for Forced Marriage and Forced Pregnancy', (4 February), https://4genderjustice.org/trailblazing-icc-judgment-on-sgbc-ongwen-verdict/.

Woolaver, H. and E. Palmer. 2017. 'Challenges to the Independence of the International Criminal Court from the Assembly of States Parties', 15(4) *Journal of International Criminal Justice* 641.

Wrigth Q. 1949. 'International Law and Guilt by Association', 43(4) *American Journal of International Law* 746.

Yanev, L. 2015. 'A Janus-Faced Concept: Nuremberg's Law on Conspiracy vis-à-vis the Notion of Joint Criminal Enterprise', 26(3) *Criminal Law Forum* 419.

Yanev L. and T. Kooijmans. 2013. 'Divided Minds in the Lubanga Trial Judgment: A Case against the Joint Control Theory', 13(4) *International Criminal Law Review* 789–828.

Zacklin, R. 2004. 'The Failings of Ad Hoc International Tribunals', 2(2) *Journal of International Criminal Justice* 541.

Zahar, A. 2014. 'Pluralism and the Rights of the Accused in International Criminal Proceedings', in E. van Sliedregt and S. Vasiliev (eds.), *Pluralism in International Criminal Law* (Oxford: Oxford University Press).

Zehfuss, M. 2002. *Constructivism in International Relations: The Politics of Reality* (Cambridge: Cambridge University Press).

Zolo, D. 2009. *Victors' Justice: From Nuremberg to Baghdad*, translated by M. W. Weir (London, New York: Verso).

International Treaties, Statutes, Drafts, and Reports

Annual Report on the ICTY

United Nations. 1994. 'Annual Report of the International Tribunal for the Prosecution of Persons Responsible for Serious Violations of International Humanitarian Law Committed in the Territory of the Former Yugoslavia since 1991,' A/49/342 (29 August), http://www.icty.org/x/file/About/Reports and Publications/AnnualReports/annual_report_1994_en.pdf.

Draft Statute for an International Criminal Court 1994

International Law Commission, Draft Statute for an International Criminal Court with Commentaries, 1994 [2005], *Yearbook of the International Law Commission, 1994*, vol. II, Part Two, http://legal.un.org/ilc/texts/instruments/english/commentaries/7_4_1994.pdf.

Draft Statute – France

Draft Statute of the International Criminal Court: Working Paper Submitted by France, A/AC.249/L.3, 6 August 1996, www.legal-tools.org/doc/4d28ee/pdf/.

Fourth Hague Convention

Fourth Hague Convention, Laws and Customs of War on Land. 1907. (The Hague), www.loc.gov/law/help/us-treaties/bevans/m-ust000001-0631.pdf.

ICC Rules of Procedure and Evidence

ICC, Rules of Procedure and Evidence, 2013[2005], The Hague, www.icc-cpi.int/iccdocs/pids/legal-texts/rulesprocedureevidenceeng.pdf.

ICTR Statute

Statute of the International Criminal Tribunal for the Prosecution of Persons Responsible for Genocide and Other Serious Violations of International

Humanitarian Law Committed in the Territory of Rwanda and Rwandan Citizens Responsible for Genocide and Other Such Violations Committed in the Territory of Neighbouring States, between 1 January 1994 and 31 December 1994, www.ohchr.org/EN/ProfessionalInterest/Pages/StatuteInternationalCriminalTribunalForRwanda.aspx.

ICTY Statute

Updated Statute of the International Criminal Tribunal for the Former Yugoslavia, Adopted 25 May 1993 by Resolution 827, as Amended 7 July 2009 by Resolution 1877, www.icty.org/x/file/Legal%20Library/Statute/statute_sept09_en.pdf.

IMT Principles of International Law

United Nations, Principles of International Law Recognized in the Charter of the Nürnberg Tribunal and in the Judgment of the Tribunal. 2005[1950]. http://legal.un.org/ilc/texts/instruments/english/draft_articles/7_1_1950.pdf.

Informal Group 1996 Proposal

Informal Group on General Principles of Criminal Law, Proposed New Part [III bis] for the Statute of an International Criminal Court: General Principles of Criminal Law, A/AC.249/CRP.13, 26 August 1996, www.legal-tools.org/doc/30f74a/pdf/.

International Convention for the Suppression of Terrorist Bombings

International Convention for the Suppression of Terrorist Bombings. 1997. https://treaties.un.org/doc/Treaties/1997/12/19971215%2007-07%20AM/ch_XVIII_9p.pdf.

Joint State Proposal on Criminal Responsibility

Working Paper Submitted by Canada, Germany, Netherlands and the United Kingdom. Paper on Criminal Responsibility Submitted by Informal Group Representing Various Legal Systems: Individual Responsibility, A/AC.249/1997/WG.2/DP.1, 14 February 1997, www.legal-tools.org/doc/1ca763/pdf/.

Nuremberg Charter

United Nations. 1945. 'Charter of the International Military Tribunal – Annex to the Agreement for the Prosecution and Punishment of the Major War Criminals of the European Axis ("London Agreement")'. (8 August). www.refworld.org/docid/3ae6b39614.html.

PrepCom 1998 Draft

Report of the Preparatory Committee on the Establishment of an International Criminal Court, United Nations Diplomatic Conference of Plenipotentiaries on the Establishment of an International Criminal Court, A/CONF.183/2/Add.1, 14 April 1998, https://documents-dds-ny.un.org/doc/UNDOC/GEN/N98/101/05/PDF/N9810105.pdf?OpenElement.

PrepCom Summary

UN General Assembly, Summary of the Proceedings of the Preparatory Committee during the Period 25 March–12 April 1996, A/AC.249/1, 7 May 1996, www.legal-tools.org/doc/d7aad5/pdf/.

PrepCom Report 1996, Vol. I

Report of the Preparatory Committee on the Establishment of an International Criminal Court (Vol. I), UN General Assembly Official Records (GAOR), 51st Sess., Supp. No. 22, U.N. Doc. A/51/22 (1996) www.legal-tools.org/doc/e75432/pdf/.

PrepCom Report 1996, Vol. II

Report of the Preparatory Committee on the Establishment of an International Criminal Court (Vol. II), UN General Assembly Official Records (GAOR), 51st Sess., Supp. No. 22A, U.N. Doc. A/51/22 (1996) www.legal-tools.org/doc/03b284/pdf/.

Rome Conference Official Records, Vol. II

United Nations Diplomatic Conference of Plenipotentiaries on the Establishment of an International Criminal Court Rome, 15 June–17 July 1998, Vol. II: Summary Records of the Plenary Meetings and of the Meetings of the Committee of the Whole, https://legal.un.org/icc/rome/proceedings/E/Rome%20Proceedings_v2_e.pdf.

Rome Statute

Rome Statute of the International Criminal Court, 17 July 1998, Rome, https://legal.un.org/icc/statute/99_corr/cstatute.htm.

Siracusa Draft

Draft Statute for an International Criminal Court: Alternative to the ILC-Draft (Siracusa-Draft), July 1995, Siracusa/Freiburg, www.legal-tools.org/doc/39a534/pdf/

Statute of the International Court of Justice

Statute of the International Court of Justice, www.icj-cij.org/en/statute.

State Proposals 1996

State Proposals on General Principles of Criminal Law: Articles A, B, C, D, E, F, G, H, I, J, K, L, M, N, O, P, Q, R, S and T, UD/A/AC-249/1996/WG-2/IP, 13 August 1996, www.legal-tools.org/en/doc/39c14c/.

Vienna Convention on the Law of Treaties

Vienna Convention on the Law of Treaties (with annex). 1969. (Vienna, 23 May). https://treaties.un.org/doc/Publication/UNTS/Volume%201155/volume-1155-I-18232-English.pdf.

UN Security Council Resolution 827

United Nations Security Council, S/RES/827, 25 May 1993, www.refworld.org/docid/3b00f21b1c.html.

UN Security Council Resolution 955

United Nations Security Council, S/RES/955, 8 November 1994, www.refworld.org/docid/3b00f2742c.html

Working Group 1997 proposal

Chairman's Text, Article B b., c. and d.: Individual Criminal Responsibility, A/AC.249/1997/WG.2/CRP.2/Add.2, 19 February 1997, www.legal-tools.org/doc/ff3055/pdf/.

Zupten Draft

Report of the Inter-sessional Meeting from 19 to 30 January 1998 in Zupten, The Netherlands, www.legal-tools.org/doc/7ba9a4/pdf.

CASES

IMT, IMTFE, and the US Military Court at Nuremberg

IMT Nuremberg Judgment

Trial of the Major War Criminals before the International Military Tribunal, Nuremberg, 14 November 1945 – 1 October 1946, Vol. 22, www.loc.gov/rr/frd/Military_Law/pdf/NT_Vol-XXII.pdf.

IMTFE Indictment

Indictment from the International Military Tribunal for the Far East. Bontecou Papers, World War II File. Japanese War Crimes Trials – general. Harry S. Truman Presidential Museum & Library, www.trumanlibrary.org/whistlestop/study_collections/nuremberg/documents/index.php?documentid=18-2&pagenumber=1.

IMTFE, Judge Bernard's Opinion

International Military Tribunal for the Far East, 'Dissenting Judgment of the Member from France of the International Military Tribunal for the Far East, 1948, www.legal-tools.org/doc/d1ac54/pdf.

IMTFE, Judge Pal's Dissent

International Military Tribunal for the Far East, 'Judgment of the Hon'ble Mr. Justice Pal's Dissent', 1984, Part 1 (pp. 1–374), www.legal-tools.org/doc/712ef9/pdf/.

IMTFE Judgment

International Military Tribunal for the Far East Judgment of 4 November 1948, www.legal-tools.org/doc/8bef6f/pdf.

'The Justice Case' Judgment

Trials of War Criminals before the Nuremberg Military Tribunals under Control Council Law No. 10, Vol. III, 'The Justice Case', October 1946–April 1949, www.legal-tools.org/doc/a7608a/pdf/.

ICTY and ICTR

Prosecutor v. *Bagilishema*

Bagilishema Appeals Judgment

Bagilishema, Judgment, ICTR-95-1A-A, Appeals Chamber, 3 July 2002, http://unictr.irmct.org/sites/unictr.org/files/case-documents/ictr-95-1a/appeals-chamber-judgements/en/020703.pdf.

Prosecutor v. *Blaškić*

Blaškić Appeals Judgment

Blaškić, Judgment, IT-95-14-A, Appeals Chamber, 23 July 2004, http://www.icty.org/x/cases/blaskic/acjug/en/bla-aj040729e.pdf.

Prosecutor v. *Brđanin*

Brđanin Appeals Judgment

Brđanin, Judgment, IT-99-36-A, Appeals Chamber, 3 April 2007, http://www.icty.org/x/cases/brdanin/acjug/en/brd-aj070403-e.pdf.

Prosecutor v. *Furundžija*

Furundžija Trial Judgment

Furundžija, Judgment, IT-95-17/1-T, Trial Chamber, 10 December 1998, http://www.icty.org/x/cases/furundzija/tjug/en/fur-tj981210e.pdf.

Prosecutor v. *Gacumbitsi*

Gacumbitsi, Opinion of Judge Schomburg

Gacumbitsi, Separate Opinion of Judge Schomburg on the Criminal Responsibility of the Appellant for Committing Genocide, ICTR-2001-64-A, 7 July 2006, Appeals Chamber, http://hrlibrary.umn.edu/instree/ICTR/GACUMBITSI_ICTR-01-64/GACUMBITSI_ICTR-2001-64-A_appeals.pdf.

Prosecutor v. *Hadžihasanović, Alagic and Kubura*

Hadžihasanović et al. Majority Decision

Hadžihasanović, Alagic and Kubura, Decision on Interlocutory Appeal Challenging Jurisdiction in Relation to Command Responsibility, IT-01-47-AR72, 16 July 2003, Appeals Chamber, http://www.icty.org/x/cases/hadzihasanovic_kubura/acdec/en/030716.htm#5.

Hadžihasanović et al. Dissent of Judge Shahabuddeen

Hadžihasanović, Alagic and Kubura, Partial Dissenting Opinion of Judge Shahabuddeen, IT-01-47-AR72, 16 July 2003, Appeals Chamber, www.legal-tools.org/uploads/tx_ltpdb/HADZIH3_01.HTM.

Hadžihasanović et al. Dissent of Judge Hunt

Hadžihasanović, Alagic and Kubura, Partial Dissenting Opinion of Judge Hunt, IT-01-47-AR72, 16 July 2003, Appeals Chamber, http://www.icty.org/x/cases/hadzihasanovic/acdec/en/030716so.htm.

Prosecutor v. *Karemera, Ngirumpatse, Nzirorera, and Rwamakuba*

Karemera et al. Judgment

Karemera, Ngirumpatse, Nzirorera, and Rwamakuba, Judgment, ICTR-98-44-T, Trial Chamber, 11 May 2004, http://www.worldcourts.com/ictr/eng/decisions/2004.05.11_Prosecutor_v_Karemera.pdf.

Prosecutor v. *Kayishema and Ruzindana*

Kayishema and Ruzindana Trial Judgment

Kayishema and Ruzindana, Judgment, ICTR-95-1-T, Trial Chamber, 21 May 1999, http://unictr.irmct.org/sites/unictr.org/files/case-documents/ictr-95-1/trial-judgements/en/990521.pdf.

Prosecutor v. *Milutinović, Šainović and Ojdanić*

Milutinović et al., Ojdanić's Motion Decision

Milutinović, Šainović and Ojdanić, Decision on Dragoljub Ojdanić's Motion Challenging Jurisdiction – Joint Criminal Enterprise IT_99-37-AR72, Appeals Chamber, 21 May 2003, AC, www.legal-tools.org/doc/d51c63/pdf/.

Prosecutor v. *Nikolić*

Momir Nikolić Judgment

Nikolić, Sentencing Judgment, IT-02-60/1-S, Trial Chamber, 2 December 2003, www.icty.org/x/cases/nikolic/tjug/en/mnik-sj031202-e.pdf.

Prosecutor v. *Simić, Tadić and Zarić*

Simić et al., Dissenting Opinion of Judge Lindholm

Simić, Tadić and Zarić, Judgment, Separate and Partly Dissenting Opinion of Judge Per-Johan Lindholm, IT-95-9-T, Trial Chamber, 17 October 2003, http://www.icty.org/x/cases/simic/tjug/en/sim-tj031017e.pdf.

Prosecutor v. *Stakić*

Stakić Trial Judgment

Stakić, Judgment, IT-97-24-T, 31 July 2003, Trial Chamber, http://www.icty.org/x/cases/stakic/tjug/en/stak-tj030731e.pdf.

Stakić Appeals Judgment

Stakić, Judgment, IT-97-24-A, 22 March 2006, Appeals Chamber, http://www.icty.org/x/cases/stakic/acjug/en/sta-aj060322e.pdf.

Prosecutor v. *Tadić*

Tadić Jurisdiction Decision

Tadić, Decision on the Defence Motion for Interlocutory Appeal on Jurisdiction, IT-94-1, 2 October 1995, Appeals Chamber, http://www.icty.org/x/cases/tadic/acdec/en/51002.htm.

Tadić Trial Judgment

Tadić Opinion and Judgment, IT-94-1-T, 7 May 1997, Trial Chamber, http://www.icty.org/x/cases/tadic/tjug/en/tad-tsj70507JT2-e.pdf.

Tadić Appeals Judgment

Tadić, Judgment, IT-94-1-A, Appeals Chamber, 15 July 1999, www.icty.org/x/cases/tadic/acjug/en/tad-aj990715e.pdf.

The 'Čelebići' Case (Prosecutor v. *Delalić, Mucić, Delić and Landžo)*

Čelebići Trial Judgment

Delalić, Mucić, Delić and Landžo, Judgment, IT-96-21-T, Trial Chamber, 16 November 1998, http://www.icty.org/x/cases/mucic/tjug/en/981116_judg_en.pdf.

Čelebići Appeals Judgment

Delalić, Mucić, Delić and Landžo, IT-96-21-A, Judgment, Appeals Chamber, 20 February 2001, http://www.icty.org/x/cases/mucic/acjug/en/cel-aj010220.pdf.

The 'Media' Case (Prosecutor v. *Nahimana, Barayagwiza and Ngeze)*

The 'Media Case' Judgment

Nahimana, Barayagwiza and Ngeze, Judgment and Sentence, ICTR-99-52-T, Trial Chamber, 3 December 2003, https://unictr.irmct.org/sites/unictr.org/files/case-documents/ictr-99-52/trial-judgements/en/031203.pdf.

International Criminal Court

Prosecutor v. *Abd-Al-Rahman*

Abd-Al-Rahman Confirmation Decision

Abd-Al-Rahman, Corrected Version of 'Decision on the Confirmation of Charges against Ali Muhammad Ali Abd-Al-Rahman ('Ali Kushayb')', 9 July

2021, ICC-02/05- 01/20-433, ICC-02/05-01/20-433-Corr, Pre-Trial Chamber II, 23 November 2021, www.icc-cpi.int/CourtRecords/CR2021_10734.PDF.

Abd-Al-Rahman Summary

Abd-Al-Rahman, Annex A13-Corr: Summary of Charged Crimes and Modes of Liability, ICC-02/05-01/20-346-AnxA13-Corr, Pre-Trial Chamber II, 21 May 2021, www.icc-cpi.int/RelatedRecords/CR2021_04670.PDF.

Prosecutor v. *Abu Garda*

Abu Garda Confirmation Decision

Abu Garda, Public Redacted Version – Decision on the Confirmation of Charges, ICC-02/05-02/09-243-Red, Pre-Trial Chamber I, 8 February 2010, www.icc-cpi.int/CourtRecords/CR2010_00753.PDF.

Abu Garda DCC

Abu Garda, Public Redacted Version of Prosecution's 'Document Containing the Charges Submitted Pursuant to Article 61(3) of the Statute' filed on 10 September 2009, ICC-02/05-02/09-91-Red, Pre-trial Chamber I, 24 September 2009, www.icc-cpi.int/CourtRecords/CR2009_06989.PDF.

Prosecutor v. *Al-Bashir*

Al-Bashir Arrest Warrant Decision 2009

Al Bashir, Decision on the Prosecution's Application for a Warrant of Arrest against Omar Hassan Ahmad Al Bashir, ICC-02/05-01/09-3, Pre-Trial Chamber I, 4 March 2009, www.icc-cpi.int/CourtRecords/CR2009_01517.PDF.

Prosecutor v. *Al-Mahdi*

Al-Mahdi, Judgment and Sentence

Al-Mahdi, Judgment and Sentence, ICC-01/12-01/15-171, Trial Chamber VII, 27 September 2016, www.icc-cpi.int/CourtRecords/CR2016_07244.PDF.

Prosecutor v. *Al-Hassan*

Al-Hassan Confirmation Decision

Al-Hassan, 'Rectificatif à la Décision relative à la confirmation des charges portées contre Al Hassan Ag Abdoul Aziz Ag Mohamed Ag Mahmoud', ICC-01/12-01/18-461-Corr-Red, Pre-Trial Chamber I, 13 November 2019, www.icc-cpi.int/CourtRecords/CR2019_06927.PDF.

Prosecutor v. *Banda and Jerbo*

Banda and Jerbo Confirmation Decision

Banda and Jerbo, Corrigendum of the 'Decision on the Confirmation of Charges' ICC-02/05-03/09-121-Corr-Red, Pre-Trial Chamber I, 13 March 2011, www.icc-cpi.int/CourtRecords/CR2011_02580.PDF.

Banda and Jerbo Summons to Appear

Banda and Jerbo, Second Decision on the Prosecutor's Application under Article 58, ICC-02/05-03/09-1-RSC, Pre-Trial Chamber I, 27 August 2009, www.icc-cpi.int/CourtRecords/CR2012_09541.PDF.

Prosecutor v. *Bemba*

Bemba Arrest Warrant Decision

Bemba, Decision on the Prosecutor's Application for a Warrant of Arrest against Jean-Pierre Bemba Gombo, ICC-01/05-01/08-14-tENG, Pre-Trial Chamber III, 10 June 2008, www.icc-cpi.int/CourtRecords/CR2008_04180.PDF.

Bemba Amended DCC

Bemba, 'Public Redacted Version of the Amended Document Containing the Charges Filed on 30 March 2009, ICC-01/05-01/08-395-Anx3, Pre-Trial Chamber III, 30 March 2009, www.icc-cpi.int/RelatedRecords/CR2009_02181.PDF.

Bemba Amicus Curiae

Bemba, 'Amicus Curiae Observations on Superior Responsibility Submitted Pursuant to Rule 103 of the Rules of Procedure and Evidence', ICC-01/05-01/08-406, Pre-Trial Chamber II, 20 April 2009, www.icc-cpi.int/CourtRecords/CR2009_02766.PDF.

Bemba, Decision Adjourning the Hearing

Bemba, Decision Adjourning the Hearing Pursuant to Article 61(7)(c)(ii) of the Rome Statute, ICC-01/05-01/08-388, Pre-Trial Chamber III, 3 March 2009, www.icc-cpi.int/CourtRecords/CR2009_01500.PDF.

Bemba, Prosecution's Submission

Bemba, Prosecution's Submission of Amended Document Containing the Charges, Amended List of Evidence and Amended In-Depth Analysis Chart of Incriminatory Evidence with Under Seal, *Ex Parte* Prosecution Only Annexes 1A, 1B, 1C, 1D, 1E, and Confidential, Prosecution and Defence Only

Annexes 2A, 2B, 2C, 2D, 2E and Public Annexes 3, 4 and 5, ICC-01/05-01/08-395, Pre-Trial Chamber III, 30 March 2009, www.icc-cpi.int/CourtRecords/CR2009_02170.PDF.

Bemba Confirmation Decision

Bemba, Decision Pursuant to Article 61(7)(a) and (b) of the Rome Statute on the Charges of the Prosecutor against Jean-Pierre Bemba Gombo, ICC-01/05-01/08-424, Pre-Trial Chamber II, 15 June 2009, www.icc-cpi.int/CourtRecords/CR2009_04528.PDF.

Bemba Trial Judgment

Bemba, Judgment Pursuant to Article 74 of the Statute, ICC-01/05-01/08-3343, Trial Chamber III, 21 March 2016, www.icc-cpi.int/CourtRecords/CR2016_02238.PDF.

Bemba Defence Notice

Bemba, 'Defence Notice of Appeal against the Judgment Pursuant to Article 74 of the Statute, ICC-01/05-01/08-3343', ICC-01/05-01/08-3348, Appeals Chamber, 4 April 2016, www.legal-tools.org/doc/90b102/pdf/.

Bemba Appeals Judgment

Bemba, Judgment on the Appeal of Mr Jean-Pierre Bemba Gombo against Trial Chamber III's 'Judgment pursuant to Article 74 of the Statute', ICC-01/05-01/08-3636-Red, Appeals Chamber, 8 June 2018, www.icc-cpi.int/CourtRecords/CR2018_02984.PDF.

Bemba Appeals Judgment Dissenting Opinion

Bemba, Dissenting Opinion of Judge Sanji Mmasenono Monageng and Judge Piotr Hofmański ICC-01/05-01/08-3636-Anx1-Red, Appeals Chamber, 8 June 2018, www.icc-cpi.int/RelatedRecords/CR2018_02987.PDF.

Bemba Appeals Judgment, Judges Van den Wyngaert and Morrison Opinion

Bemba, Separate opinion Judge Christine Van den Wyngaert and Judge Howard Morrison, ICC-01/05-01/08-3636-Anx2, Appeals Chamber, 8 June 2018, www.icc-cpi.int/RelatedRecords/CR2018_02989.PDF.

Bemba Appeals Judgment, Judge Eboe-Osuji Opinion

Bemba, Concurring Separate Opinion of Judge Eboe-Osuji, ICC-01/05-01/08-3636-Anx3, 14 June 2018, Appeals Chamber, www.icc-cpi.int/RelatedRecords/CR2018_03077.PDF.

Prosecutor v. *Bemba et al.*

Bemba et al. DCC

Bemba et al., 'Public Redacted Version of "Document Containing the Charges", 30 June 2014, ICC- 01/05-01/13-526-Conf-Anx B1', ICC-01/05-01/13-526-AxnB1-Red, Pre-Trial Chamber II, 3 July 2014, www.legal-tools.org/doc/cdbe96/pdf/.

Bemba et al. Trial Judgment

Bemba et al., Judgment Pursuant to Article 74 of the Statute, ICC-01/05-01/13-1989-Red, Trial Chamber VII, 19 October 2016, www.icc-cpi.int/CourtRecords/CR2016_18527.PDF.

Bemba et al. Appeals Judgment

Bemba et al., 'Judgment on the Appeals of Mr Jean-Pierre Bemba Gombo, Mr Aimé Kilolo Musamba, Mr Jean-Jacques Mangenda Kabongo, Mr Fidèle Babala Wandu and Mr Narcisse Arido against the Decision of Trial Chamber VII Entitled "Judgment Pursuant to Article 74 of the Statute"', ICC-01/05-01/13-2275-Red, Appeals Chamber, 8 March 2018, www.icc-cpi.int/CourtRecords/CR2018_01638.PDF.

Bemba et al., Prosecution Detailed Notice

Bemba et al., 'Prosecution Detailed Notice of Additional Sentencing Submissions', ICC-01/05-01/13-2296, Trial Chamber VII, 2 July 2018, www.icc-cpi.int/CourtRecords/CR2018_03430.PDF.

Bemba et al., Decision Re-sentencing

Bemba et al., 'Decision Re-sentencing Mr Jean-Pierre Bemba Gombo, Mr Aimé Kilolo Musamba and Mr Jean-Jacques Mangenda Kabongo', Trial Chamber VII, 17 September 2018, www.icc-cpi.int/CourtRecords/CR2018_04355.PDF.

Prosecutor v. *Gbagbo and Blé Goudé*

Blé Goudé Arrest Warrant

Blé Goudé, Warrant of Arrest for Charles Blé Goudé, ICC-02/11-02/11-1, Pre-Trial Chamber III, 25 December 2011, www.icc-cpi.int/CourtRecords/CR2015_05632.PDF.

Blé Goudé Arrest Warrant Decision

Blé Goudé, Decision on the Prosecutor's Application Pursuant to Article 58 for a Warrant of Arrest against Charles Blé Goudé, ICC-02/11-02/11-3, Pre-Trial Chamber III, 06 January 2012, www.icc-cpi.int/CourtRecords/CR2015_05630.PDF.

Blé Goudé Confirmation Decision

Blé Goudé, Decision on the Confirmation of Charges against Charles Blé Goudé, ICC-02/11-02/11-186, Pre-trial Chamber I, 11 December 2014, www.icc-cpi.int/CourtRecords/CR2015_05444.PDF.

Blé Goudé Confirmation Decision, Partly Dissenting Opinion

Blé Goudé, Confirmation of Charges Decision, Partly Dissenting Opinion of Judge Christine Van den Wyngaert, ICC-02/11-02/11-186-Anx, PTC I, 11 December 2014, www.icc-cpi.int/RelatedRecords/CR2015_05443.PDF

Blé Goudé DCC

Blé Goudé, 'Annexe 1 Publique Version corrigée de ICC-02/11-02/11-124-Anx1 Document de notification des charges', ICC-02/11-02/11-124-Anx1-Corr, Pre-Trial Chamber I, 27 August 2014, www.icc-cpi.int/RelatedRecords/CR2015_05522.PDF.

Gbagbo Amended DCC

Laurent Gbagbo, 'Annexe 1 Publique Document amendé de notification des charges', ICC-02/11-01/11-592-Anx1, Pre-Trial Chamber I, 13 January 2014, www.icc-cpi.int/RelatedRecords/CR2015_04780.PDF.

Gbagbo Arrest Warrant

Gbagbo, Warrant of Arrest for Laurent Koudou Gbagbo, ICC-02/11-01/11-1, Pre-trial Chamber III, 23 November 2011, www.icc-cpi.int/CourtRecords/CR2015_05372.PDF.

Gbagbo Arrest Warrant Decision

Gbagbo, Public Redacted Version of 'Decision on the Prosecutor's Application Pursuant to Article 58 for a Warrant of Arrest against Laurent Koudou Gbagbo', ICC-02/11-01/11-9-Red, Pre-Trial Chamber III, 30 November 2011, www.icc-cpi.int/CourtRecords/CR2015_05368.PDF.

Gbagbo PTC Hearing (Transcript 17)

Gbagbo, Confirmation of Charges Hearing, Transcript 17, ICC-02/11-01/11-T-17-Red-ENG, 22 February 2013, Pre-Trial Chamber I, www.icc-cpi.int/Transcripts/CR2013_02637.PDF.

Gbagbo Confirmation Decision

Gbagbo, Decision on the Confirmation of Charges against Laurent Gbagbo, ICC-02/11-01/11-656-Red, Pre-Trial Chamber I, 12 June 2014, www.icc-cpi.int/CourtRecords/CR2015_04777.PDF.

Gbagbo Confirmation Decision, Dissenting Opinion

Gbagbo, Decision on the Confirmation of Charges against Laurent Gbagbo, Dissenting Opinion of Judge Christine Van den Wyngaert, ICC-02/11-01/11-656-Anx, Pre-Trial Chamber I, 12 June 2014, www.icc-cpi.int/RelatedRecords/CR2015_04555.PDF.

Gbagbo, Decision Adjourning the Hearing

Gbagbo, Decision Adjourning the Hearing on the Confirmation of Charges Pursuant to Article 61(7)(c)(i) of the Rome Statute, ICC-02/11-01/11-432, Pre-Trial Chamber I, 3 June 2013, www.icc-cpi.int/CourtRecords/CR2015_04878.PDF.

Gbagbo and Blé Goudé, Decision to Join the Cases

Gbagbo and Blé Goudé, Decision on Prosecution Requests to Join the Cases of *The Prosecutor* v. *Laurent Gbagbo* and *The Prosecutor* v. *Charles Blé Goudé* and Related Matters, ICC-02/11-01/15-1, Trial Chamber I, 11 March 2015, www.icc-cpi.int/CourtRecords/CR2015_02801.PDF.

Gbagbo and Blé Goudé, Blé Goudé Defence Motion

Gbagbo and Blé Goudé, 'Public Redacted Version of "Corrigendum to the 'Blé Goudé Defence No Case to Answer Motion' (ICC-02/11-01/15-1198-Conf), 23 July 2018," 3 August 2018, ICC- 02/11-01/15-1198-Conf-Corr', ICC-02/11-01/15-1198-Corr-Red, Trial Chamber I, 28 September 2018, www.icc-cpi.int/CourtRecords/CR2018_04638.PDF.

Gbagbo and Blé Goudé, Gbagbo Defence Motion

Gbagbo and Blé Goudé, 'Version corrigée de la « Requête de la Défense de Laurent Gbagbo afin qu'un jugement d'acquittement portant sur toutes les charges soit prononcé en faveur de Laurent Gbagbo et que sa mise en liberté immédiate soit ordonnée ».', ICC-02/11-01/15-1199-Corr, Trial Chamber I, 25 September 2018, www.icc-cpi.int/CourtRecords/CR2018_04515.PDF.

Gbagbo and Blé Goudé, Judge Herrera-Carbuccia Dissenting Opinion

Gbagbo and Blé Goudé, 'Dissenting Opinion Judge Herrera Carbuccia (Public Redacted Version)', ICC-02/11-01/15-1263-AnxC-Red, Trial Chamber I, 16 July 2019, www.icc-cpi.int/RelatedRecords/CR2019_03856.PDF.

Gbagbo and Blé Goudé, Opinion of Judge Tarfusser

Gbagbo and Blé Goudé 'Opinion of Judge Cuno Tarfusser', ICC-02/11-01/15-1263-AnxA Trial Chamber I, 16 July 2019, www.icc-cpi.int/RelatedRecords/CR2019_03854.PDF.

Gbagbo and Blé Goudé, Prosecutor's Response

Gbagbo and Blé Goudé, 'Public: With Confidential Annex 1 and Confidential Annexes A and B Prosecution's Response to Defence No Case to Answer Motions', ICC-02/11-01/15-1207, Trial Chamber I, 10 September 2018, www.icc-cpi.int/CourtRecords/CR2018_04248.PDF.

Gbagbo and Blé Goudé, Reasons for Oral Decision on 15 January 2019

Gbagbo and Blé Goudé, 'Reasons for oral decision of 15 January 2019 on the Requête de la Défense de Laurent Gbagbo afin qu'un jugement d'acquittement portant sur toutes les charges soit prononcé en faveur de Laurent Gbagbo et que sa mise en liberté immédiate soit ordonnée, and on the Blé Goudé Defence no case to answer motion', ICC-02/11-01/15-1263, Trial Chamber I, 16 July 2019, www.icc-cpi.int/CourtRecords/CR2019_03853.PDF.

Gbagbo and Blé Goudé, Reasons of Judge Henderson

Gbagbo and Blé Goudé, 'Reasons of Judge Geoffrey Henderson', ICC-02/11-01/15-1263-AnxB-Red, Trial Chamber I, 16 July 2019, www.icc-cpi.int/RelatedRecords/CR2019_07450.PDF.

Gbagbo and Blé Goudé, Trial Decision

Gbagbo and Blé Goudé, Delivery of Decision, ICC-02/11-01/15-T-232-ENG ET WT, Trial Chamber I, 15 January 2019, www.icc-cpi.int/Transcripts/CR2019_00115.PDF.

Gbagbo and Blé Goudé, Trial Hearing (Transcript 9)

Gbagbo and Blé Goudé, Trial Hearing, Transcript ICC-02/11-01/15-T-9-ENG, Trial Chamber I, 28 January 2016, www.icc-cpi.int/Transcripts/0CR2016_00664.PDF.

Gbagbo and Blé Goudé, Trial Hearing (Transcript 10)

Gbagbo and Blé Goudé, Trial Hearing, Transcript ICC-02/11-01/15-T-10-ENG, Trial Chamber I, 29 January 2016, www.icc-cpi.int/Transcripts/0CR2016_00728.PDF.

Prosecutor v. *Katanga and Ngudjolo*

Katanga and Ngudjolo Confirmation Decision

Katanga and Ngudjolo, Decision on the Confirmation of Charges, ICC-01/04-01/07-717, Pre-Trial Chamber I, 14 October 2008, www.icc-cpi.int/CourtRecords/CR2008_05172.PDF.

Katanga and Ngudjolo Defence Observations

Katanga and Ngudjolo Chui, Defence Written Observations Addressing Matters That Were Discussed at the Confirmation Hearing, ICC-01/04-01/07-698, Pre-Trial Chamber I, 28 July 2008, www.icc-cpi.int/CourtRecords/CR2008_04315.PDF.

Ngudjolo Judgment

Ngudjolo, Judgment Pursuant to Article 74 of the Statute, ICC-01/04-02/12-3-tENG, Trial Chamber II, 18 December 2012, www.icc-cpi.int/CourtRecords/CR2013_02993.PDF.

Ngudjolo Judgment, Judge Van den Wyngaert Opinion

Ngudjolo, Judgment Pursuant to Article 74 of the Statute, Concurring Opinion of Judge Christine Van den Wyngaert, ICC-01/04-02/12-4, Trial Chamber II, 18 December 2012, www.icc-cpi.int/CourtRecords/CR2012_10250.PDF.

Katanga Trial Judgment

Katanga, Judgment Pursuant to Article 74 of the Statute, ICC-01/04-01/07-3436-tENG, Trial Chamber II, 7 March 2014, www.icc-cpi.int/CourtRecords/CR2015_04025.PDF.

Katanga Judgment, Judge Van den Wyngaert Opinion

Katanga, Minority Opinion of Judge Christine Van den Wyngaert, ICC-01/04-01/07-3436-AnxI, Trial Chamber II, 7 March 2014, www.icc-cpi.int/RelatedRecords/CR2014_02619.PDF.

Prosecutor v. *Kenyatta, Muthaura and Ali*

Muthaura and Kenyatta, Withdrawal of Charges against Kenyatta

Kenyatta, Notice of Withdrawal of the Charges against Uhuru Muigai Kenyatta, ICC-01/09-02/11-983, Trial Chamber V(B), 5 December 2014, www.icc-cpi.int/CourtRecords/CR2014_09939.PDF.

Muthaura and Kenyatta Additional Prosecution Observations

Muthaura and Kenyatta, Public Redacted Version of the Additional Prosecution Observations on the Defence's Article 64 Applications, Filed in Accordance with Order Number ICC-01/09-02-11-673, ICC-01/09-02/11-683-Red, Trial Chamber V, 8 March 2013, www.icc-cpi.int/Pages/record.aspx?docNo=ICC-01/09-02/11-683-Red.

Muthaura and Kenyatta, Withdrawal of Charges against Muthaura

Muthaura and Kenyatta, Prosecution Notification of Withdrawal of the Charges against Francis Kirimi Muthaura, ICC-01/09-02/11-687, Trial Chamber V, 11 March 2013, www.icc-cpi.int/CourtRecords/CR2013_01871.PDF.

Kenyatta, Muthaura and Ali, DCC

Kenyatta, Muthaura and Ali, Document Containing the Charges, ICC-01/09-02/11-280-AnxA, Pre-Trial Chamber I, 2 September 2011, www.icc-cpi.int/RelatedRecords/CR2011_15006.PDF.

Kenyatta, Muthaura and Ali Confirmation Decision

Kenyatta, Muthaura and Ali, Decision on the Confirmation of Charges Pursuant to Article 61(7)(a) and (b) of the Rome Statute, ICC-01/09-02/11-382-Red, Pre-Trial Chamber II, 29 January 2012, www.icc-cpi.int/CourtRecords/CR2012_01006.PDF.

Prosecutor v. *Lubanga*

Lubanga Arrest Warrant

Lubanga, Warrant of Arrest, ICC-01/04-01/06-2-tEN, Pre-Trial Chamber I, 10 February 2006, www.icc-cpi.int/CourtRecords/CR2006_02234.PDF.

Lubanga 2006 DCC

Lubanga, Public Redacted Version Document Containing the Charges, Article 61(3)(a), ICC-01/04-01/06-356-Anx2, Pre-Trial Chamber I, 28 August 2006, www.icc-cpi.int/CourtRecords/CR2006_02827.PDF.

Lubanga Confirmation Decision

Lubanga, Decision on the Confirmation of Charges, ICC-01/04-01/06-803-tEN, Pre-Trial Chamber I, 19 January 2007, www.icc-cpi.int/CourtRecords/CR2007_02360.PDF.

Lubanga, Prosecutor's Reply

Lubanga, 'Prosecution's Reply to the « Conclusions finales de la Défense »,' ICC-01/04-01/06-2778-Red, Trial Chamber I, 1 August 2011, www.icc-cpi.int/CourtRecords/CR2011_12284.PDF.

Lubanga, First Decision to Stay Proceedings

Lubanga, 'Decision on the Consequences of Non-disclosure of Exculpatory Materials Covered by Article 54(3)(e) Agreements and the Application to Stay the Prosecution of the Accused, Together with Certain Other Issues Raised at the Status Conference on 10 June 2008', ICC-01/04-01/06-1401, Trial Chamber I, 15 June 2020, www.icc-cpi.int/CourtRecords/CR2008_03428.PDF.

Lubanga, Second Decision to Stay Proceedings

Lubanga, 'Redacted Decision on the Prosecution's Urgent Request for Variation of the Time Limit to Disclose the Identity of Intermediary 143 or Alternatively to Stay Proceedings Pending Further Consultations with the VWU', ICC-01/04-01/06-2517-Red, Trial Chamber I, 8 July 2010, www.icc-cpi.int/CourtRecords/CR2010_04749.PDF.

Lubanga, Appeals Judgment against the Stay of Proceedings

Lubanga, 'Judgment on the Appeal of the Prosecutor against the Decision of Trial Chamber I of 8 July 2010 Entitled "Decision on the Prosecution's Urgent Request for Variation of the Time-Limit to Disclose the Identity of Intermediary 143 or Alternatively to Stay Proceedings Pending Further Consultations with the VWU"', ICC-01/04-01/06-2582, Appeals Chamber, 8 October 2010, www.icc-cpi.int/CourtRecords/CR2010_07188.PDF.

Lubanga Trial Judgment

Lubanga, Judgment Pursuant to Article 74 of the Statute, ICC-01/04-01/06-2842, Trial Chamber I, 14 March 2012, www.icc-cpi.int/CourtRecords/CR2012_03942.PDF.

Lubanga Trial Judgment, Judge Fulford Opinion

Lubanga, Judgment Pursuant to Article 74 of the Statute, Separate Opinion of Judge Adrian Fulford, ICC-01/04-01/06-2842, Trial Chamber I, 14 March 2012, www.icc-cpi.int/CourtRecords/CR2012_03942.PDF.

Lubanga Appeals Judgment

Lubanga, Public Redacted Judgment on the Appeal of Mr Thomas Lubanga Dyilo against His Conviction, ICC-01/04-01/06-3121-Red, Appeals Chamber, 1 December 2014, www.icc-cpi.int/CourtRecords/CR2014_09844.PDF.

Prosecutor v. *Mbarushimana*

Mbarushimana Appeals Judgment, Judge Fernández de Gurmendi Opinion

Mbarushimana, 'Judgment on the Appeal of the Prosecutor against the Decision of Pre-Trial Chamber I of 16 December 2011 Entitled "Decision on the Confirmation of Charges"', Separate Opinion of Judge Silvia Fernández de Gurmendi, ICC-01/04-01/10-514, Appeals Chamber, 30 May 2012, www.icc-cpi.int/CourtRecords/CR2012_06457.PDF.

Mbarushimana Arrest Warrant Decision

Mbarushimana, Decision on the Prosecutor's Application for a Warrant of Arrest against Callixte Mbarushimana, ICC-01/04-01/10- 1, Pre-Trial Chamber I, 29 September 2010, www.icc-cpi.int/CourtRecords/CR2010_06674.PDF.

Mbarushimana Confirmation Decision

Mbarushimana, 'Public Redacted Version: Decision on the Confirmation of Charges', ICC-01/04-01/10-465-Red, PTC I, 16 December 2011, www.legal-tools.org/doc/63028f/pdf/.

Mbarushimana Prosecution's Written Submissions

Mbarushimana, 'Prosecution's Written Submissions on the Confirmation of Charges', ICC-01/04-01/10-448-Red, Pre-Trial Chamber I, 6 October 2011, www.icc-cpi.int/CourtRecords/CR2011_17005.PDF.

Mbarushimana PTC Hearing

Mbarushimana, Transcript ICC-01/04-01/10-T-8-Red2-ENG, Pre-Trial Chamber I, 20 September 2011, www.icc-cpi.int/Transcripts/CR2011_16984.PDF.

Prosecutor v. *Mudacumura*

Mudacumura Arrest Warrant Decision

Mudacumura, 'Public Redacted Version: Decision on the Prosecutor's Application under Article 58', ICC-01/04-01/12-1-Red, Pre-Trial Chamber II, 13 July 2012, www.icc-cpi.int/CourtRecords/CR2012_07502.PDF.

Prosecutor v. *Ntaganda*

Ntaganda 2007 Arrest Warrant Decision

Ntaganda, Decision on the Prosecution Application for a Warrant of Arrest, ICC-01/04-02/06-1-Red-tENG, Pre-Trial Chamber I, 6 March 2007, www.icc-cpi.int/CourtRecords/CR2008_00874.PDF.

Ntaganda Case Information Sheet

Ntaganda, Case Information Sheet ICC-01/04-02/06, ICC-PIDS-CIS-DRC-02-016/19_Eng Updated: February 2020, www.icc-cpi.int/CaseInformationSheets/NtagandaEng.pdf.

Ntaganda Confirmation Decision

Ntaganda, Decision Pursuant to Article 61(7)(a) and (b) of the Rome Statute on the Charges of the Prosecutor against Bosco Ntaganda, ICC-01/04-02/06-309, Pre-Trial Chamber II, 14 June 2014, www.icc-cpi.int/CourtRecords/CR2014_04750.PDF.

Ntaganda DCC

Ntaganda, Public Document Containing the Charges, ICC-01/04-02/06-203-AnxA, 10 January, 2014, www.icc-cpi.int/RelatedRecords/CR2014_00587.PDF.

Ntaganda, Second Arrest Warrant Application

Ntaganda, Second Corrigendum of the Public Redacted Version of the Prosecutor's Application under Article 58 Filed on 14 May 2012, ICC-01/04-611-Red-Corr2,16 May 2012, www.icc-cpi.int/CourtRecords/CR2012_06097.PDF.

Ntaganda, Trial Hearing (Transcript 23)

Ntaganda, Trial Hearing Transcript, ICC-01/04-02/06-T-23-ENG, Trial Chamber VI, 2 September 2015, www.icc-cpi.int/Transcripts/CR2015_15501.PDF.

Ntaganda, Trial Hearing (Transcript 24)

Ntaganda, Trial Hearing Transcript, ICC-01/04-02/06-T-24-ENG, Trial Chamber VI, 3 September 2015, www.icc-cpi.int/Transcripts/CR2015_15528.PDF.

Ntaganda Trial Judgment

Ntaganda, Public with Public Annexes A, B, and C Judgment, ICC-01/04-02/06-2359, Trial Chamber IV, 8 July 2019, www.icc-cpi.int/CourtRecords/CR2019_03568.PDF.

Ntaganda Appeals Judgment

Ntaganda, 'Judgment on the Appeals of Mr Bosco Ntaganda and the Prosecutor against the Decision of Trial Chamber VI of 8 July 2019 entitled "Judgment"', ICC-01/04-02/06-2666-Red, 30 March 2021, Appeals Chamber, www.icc-cpi.int/CourtRecords/CR2021_03027.PDF.

Ntaganda Appeals Judgment, Opinion of Judge Morrison

Ntaganda, Annex 2: Separate Opinion of Judge Howard Morrison on Mr Ntaganda's Appeal, ICC-01/04-02/06-2666-Anx2, Appeals Chamber, 30 March 2021, www.icc-cpi.int/RelatedRecords/CR2021_03021.PDF.

Ntaganda Appeals Judgment, Opinion of Judge Eboe-Osuji

Ntaganda, Annex 5: Partly Concurring Opinion of Judge Chile Eboe-Osuji, ICC-01/04-02/06-2666-Anx5, Appeals Chamber, 30 March 2021, www.icc-cpi.int/RelatedRecords/CR2021_03022.PDF.

Prosecutor v. *Ongwen*

Ongwen Arrest Warrant

Ongwen, Warrant of Arrest for Dominic Ongwen, ICC-02/04-01/05-10-US-Exp, Pre-Trial Chamber II, 8 July 2005, www.icc-cpi.int/CourtRecords/CR2006_01020.PDF.

Ongwen Arrest Warrant Decision

Ongwen, Decision on the Prosecutor's Application for Warrants of Arrest, ICC-02/04-01/05-1-US-Exp, Pre-Trial Chamber II, 8 July 2005, www.icc-cpi.int/CourtRecords/CR2015_01132.PDF.

Ongwen DCC

Ongwen, Document Containing the Charges, ICC-02/04-01/15-375-AnxA-Red, Pre-Trial Chamber II, 22 December 2015, www.icc-cpi.int/RelatedRecords/CR2015_25222.PDF.

Ongwen Confirmation Decision

Ongwen, Decision on the Confirmation of Charges against Dominic Ongwen, ICC-02/04-01/15-422-Red, Pre-Trial Chamber II, 26 March 2016, www.icc-cpi.int/pages/record.aspx?uri=2228214.

Ongwen Trial Hearing (Transcript 26)

Ongwen, Trial Hearing Transcript ICC-02/04-01/15-T-26-ENG, Trial Chamber IX, 6 December 2016, www.icc-cpi.int/Transcripts/CR2016_25802.PDF.

Ongwen Trial Hearing (Transcript 27)

Ongwen, Trial Hearing Transcript ICC-02/04-01/15-T-27-ENG, Trial Chamber IX, 7 December 2016, www.icc-cpi.int/Transcripts/CR2016_25803.PDF.

Ongwen Trial Judgment

Ongwen, Trial Judgment, ICC-02/04-01/15-1762-Red, Trial Chamber IX, 4 February 2021, www.icc-cpi.int/CourtRecords/CR2021_01026.PDF.

Prosecutor v. *Ruto, Kosgey and Sang*

Ruto and Sang Trial Decision

Ruto and Sang, 'Decision on Defence Applications for Judgments of Acquittal', ICC-01/09-01/11-2027-Red-Corr, Trial Chamber V(A), 5 April 2016, www.icc-cpi.int/CourtRecords/CR2016_04384.PDF.

Ruto, Kosgey and Sang Amended DCC

Ruto, Kosgey and Sang, Public Document Containing the Charges, ICC-01/09-01/11-261-AnxA, Pre-Trial Chamber II, 15 August 2011, www.icc-cpi.int/RelatedRecords/CR2011_12219.PDF.

Ruto, Kosgey and Sang Confirmation Decision

Ruto, Kosgey and Sang, Decision on the Confirmation of Charges Pursuant to Article 61(7)(a) and (b) of the Rome Statute, ICC-01/09-01/11-373, Pre-Trial Chamber II, 4 February 2012, www.icc-cpi.int/CourtRecords/CR2012_01004.PDF.

Prosecutor v. *Said*

Said Confirmation Decision

Said, Decision on the Confirmation of Charges against Mahamat Said Abdel Kani, ICC-01/14-01/21-218-Red, Pre-Trial Chamber II, 9 December 2021, www.icc-cpi.int/CourtRecords/CR2021_11432.PDF.

Said DCC

Said, Corrected Version of 'Public Redacted Version of "Document Containing the Charges, ICC-01/14-01/21-144-Conf", dated 16 August 2021', ICC-01/14-01/21-144-Red, dated 17 October 2021, ICC-01/14-01/21-144-Corr2, Pre-Trial Chamber II, 27 October 2021, www.icc-cpi.int/CourtRecords/CR2021_09494.PDF.

Prosecutor v. *Simone Gbagbo*

Simone Gbagbo Arrest Warrant

Simone Gbagbo, Warrant of Arrest for Simone Gbagbo, ICC-02/11-01/12-1, Pre-Trial Chamber III, 29 February 2012, www.icc-cpi.int/Pages/record.aspx?docNo=ICC-02/11-01/12-1.

Simone Gbagbo Arrest Warrant Decision

Simone Gbagbo, Decision on the Prosecutor's Application Pursuant to Article 58, ICC-02/11-01/12-2-Red, Pre-Trial Chamber III, 2 March 2012, www.icc-cpi.int/CourtRecords/CR2012_10200.PDF.

Prosecutor v. *Yekatom and Ngaïssona*

Yekatom Appeals Decision

Yekatom and Ngaïssona, Judgment on the Appeal of Mr Alfred Yekatom against the Decision of Trial Chamber V of 29 October 2020 Entitled 'Decision on Motions on the Scope of the Charges and the Scope of Evidence at Trial', ICC-01/14-01/18-874, Appeals Chamber, 5 February 2021, www.icc-cpi.int/CourtRecords/CR2021_01142.PDF.

Yekatom and Ngaïssona, Confirmation Decision

Yekatom and Ngaïssona, Corrected Version of Public Redacted Version of 'Decision on the Confirmation of Charges against Alfred Yekatom and Patrice-Edouard Ngaïssona', ICC-01/14-01/18-403-Red-Corr, Pre-Trial Chamber II, 14 May 2020, www.icc-cpi.int/CourtRecords/CR2020_01948.PDF.

Situation in Afghanistan

Decision on the Authorisation of an Investigation in Afghanistan

Situation in the Islamic Republic of Afghanistan, Decision Pursuant to Article 15 of the Rome Statute on the Authorisation of an Investigation into the Situation in the Islamic Republic of Afghanistan, ICC-02/17-33, Pre-Trial Chamber II, 12 April 2019, www.icc-cpi.int/CourtRecords/CR2019_02068.PDF.

Situation in Côte d'Ivoire

Côte d'Ivoire, Decision to Open Investigation

Situation in Côte d'Ivoire, Corrigendum to 'Decision Pursuant to Article 15 of the Rome Statute on the Authorisation of an Investigation into the Situation in the Republic of Côte d'Ivoire', ICC-02/11-14-Corr, Pre-Trial Chamber III, 15 November 2011, www.icc-cpi.int/CourtRecords/CR2011_18794.PDF.

Côte d'Ivoire, Further Information

Situation in Côte d'Ivoire, Prosecution's Provision of Further Information Regarding Potentially Relevant Crimes Committed between 2002 and 2010, ICC-02/11-25, Pre-Trial Chamber III, 3 November 2011, www.icc-cpi.int/CourtRecords/CR2011_18008.PDF.

Côte d'Ivoire, Investigation Request

Situation in Côte d'Ivoire, Request for Authorisation of an Investigation Pursuant to Article 15, 23 June 2011, ICC-02/11-3, Pre-Trial Chamber III, 23 June 2011, www.icc-cpi.int/CourtRecords/CR2011_07959.PDF.

Situation in the Democratic Republic of the Congo

DRC, First Arrest Warrants Decision

Situation in the Democratic Republic of Congo, Decision on the Prosecutor's Application for Warrants of Arrest, Article 58, ICC-01/04-02/06-20-Anx2, Pre-Trial Chamber I, 10 February 2006, www.icc-cpi.int/RelatedRecords/CR2008_04250.PDF.

Situation in Uganda

Kony Arrest Warrant

Situation in Uganda, Warrant of Arrest for Joseph Kony Issued on 8 July 2005 as Amended on 27 September 2005, ICC-02/04-01/05-53, 13 October 2005, www.icc-cpi.int/CourtRecords/CR2006_01096.PDF.

INDEX

For EU product safety concerns, contact us at Calle de José Abascal, 56–1°,
28003 Madrid, Spain or eugpsr@cambridge.org.

www.ingramcontent.com/pod-product-compliance
Lightning Source LLC
LaVergne TN
LVHW011703200926
848484LV00004B/1052
* 9 7 8 1 0 0 9 3 2 0 1 7 7 *